The
Enterprising
Admiral

The Enterprising Admiral

The Personal Fortune of Admiral Sir Peter Warren

by Julian Gwyn

McGill-Queen's University Press   Montreal and London   1974

© McGILL-QUEEN'S UNIVERSITY PRESS 1974
ISBN 0 7735 0170 3
LIBRARY OF CONGRESS CATALOG NUMBER 74-75970
LEGAL DEPOSIT THIRD QUARTER 1974
BIBLIOTHÈQUE NATIONALE DU QUÉBEC
DESIGN BY RICHARD HENDEL
PRINTED IN CANADA BY JOHN DEYELL

This book has been published with the help of a grant from the
Social Science Research Council of Canada using funds provided
by the Canada Council.

To Bill and Eileen

Contents

Part I: Introduction

Part II: America

Part III: England and Ireland

Illustrations

Tables

Abbreviations

BERO	Bank of England Record Office
BM	British Museum
IOR	India Office Records
MHS	Massachusetts Historical Society
NYHS	New-York Historical Society
PRO	Public Record Office, London
WLCL	William L. Clements Library
£	Sterling
NY£	New York Currency
I£	Irish Currency
M£	Massachussetts Currency
SC£	South Carolina Currency

Currency Exchange Rates

In 1737 the value of the guinea was established at 21s. (English) and 22s. 9d. (Irish), thus making 12 English units worth 13 Irish. Until 1797 Irish currency was considered at par with sterling when the premium on sterling was at $8\frac{1}{3}$ per cent.

New York currency depreciated during the last thirty-five years of colonial rule, ranging from a low of NY£160 for £100 in the 1740s to a high of NY£195 for £100 in the 1760s.

Massachusetts currency suffered severe depreciation in the first half of the eighteenth century, ranging from a low of M£133 for £100 in 1702 to a high of M£1,100 for £100 in 1749-50.

South Carolina currency experienced sharp depreciation until 1731, when the rate of exchange became rather stable at SC£700 for £100.

Acknowledgements

This study has been made possible through the generosity of both the Canada Council and the Social Science Research Council of Canada. They first put funds at my disposal between 1966 and 1972 not only to carry out research but also to finance the typing of successive drafts of the manuscript. The second, by way of subsidy, has helped substantially with the costs of publication.

I wish also to express my appreciation for help from Dr. P.G.M. Dickson, D.Phil., Fellow and Tutor of St. Catherine's College, Oxford, who read early drafts of the manuscript, and whose profound understanding of eighteenth-century finance enabled me to solve many problems.

In addition I wish to acknowledge the assistance I have received from the staffs of the various archives listed in the Bibliography, in particular Arthur Breton, formerly of the New-York Historical Society, William Ewing of the William L. Clements Library, Judith Brent of the East Sussex Record Office, and K.W. Dickens, Esq. of the Sussex Archaeological Society.

Earlier versions of chapters 5 and 6 appeared in *New York History* and the *New England Quarterly*, and are reproduced with the permission of these periodicals.

Grateful thanks for permissions to reproduce illustrations are due to the Trustees of the National Library of Ireland, the Trustees of the National Maritime Museum, the Dean and Chapter of Westminister Abbey, the Trustees of the British Museum, the Trustees of the William L. Clements Library, the Trustees of the New-York Historical Society, the Trustees of the New York Public Library, as well as Mrs. Edith M. Fox, Viscount Gage, and Jack Leonard, Esq. The maps and graphs were prepared by David Farnsworth of the University of Ottawa.

Many others at different stages of my work have been most generous with their help. I wish to mention especially David H. LeRoy-Lewis, Esq. and Mrs. Mary Wilson for information about Westbury House, Commander and Mrs. Sherrard Manners, who kindly showed me the grounds at Westbury, Jack Leonard, Esq., who acted as my guide over the estates once owned by Warren in county Meath, Dr. Peter Willis of the University of Nottingham for information about Charles Bridgeman, Major General and the Hon. Mrs. E.M. Sale of Heveningham House, Halesworth, Suffolk for allowing me to photograph their portraits of Warren, his daughter and son-in-law, the Hon. Charles Fitzroy, and to Professor William A. Kearns for having first introduced me to the history of colonial New York.

Finally I acknowledge my considerable debt to my wife, whose encouragement sustained me throughout my study, and to my children whose impatience to see completed "The 'ventures of Peter Warren" was exceeded only by my own.

JULIAN GWYN

Part I

Introduction

Chapter 1

Introduction

The financial impact of war in the eighteenth century upon the corps of naval officers has not been systematically studied. Nor have the opportunities of a naval career to exploit such sidelines as trade, money-lending, and land purchases in the colonies, where officers spent much of their time, been looked at carefully. The present study analyses in detail the fortune of a single naval officer, Admiral Sir Peter Warren, whose principal wealth came from prize money: the capture of enemy vessels in wartime. He emerges as a new type of entrepreneur, with his feet well planted on both sides of the Atlantic, equally at home in the financial circles of New York, Boston, Charleston, Dublin, and London. Owing to the mobility of his naval career he became familiar with the economic prospects in these scattered places, while he possessed the necessary imagination to take advantage of their commercial opportunities. Mobility also enabled him to select personally the agents who served his varied interests. Neither his widow nor his heirs had the same advantages, nor did they possess the same degree of business sense, with the result that his fortune, invested internationally, was eventually repatriated to England.

The study falls into two principal divisions, the first dealing with America, the second with England and Ireland. It spans the growth of Warren's investments from their inception until their dispersal among his heirs following the death of Lady Warren in 1771. It describes the important role played by the DeLancey and Johnson families in managing the Warren affairs both in America and Ireland, and shows how their connection with Warren helped secure their own financial status. In America the study describes the failure of Warren's one serious attempt at colonization on the Mohawk river frontier in New York, a failure as much attributable to the uncertainties of frontier life (in turn due to Anglo-French warfare) as to the carelessness of his agents there. In Ireland the study focuses on Warren's successful attempt to repurchase the alienated part of his ancestral estate, and his additons to it.

In England, an estate in Hampshire, conveniently close to Portsmouth, was acquired, though the bulk of Warren's capital was kept in government and allied stock and in money lending. Warren's private money lending was extensive, and spans his entire life from his earliest days as a post captain until the last few weeks before his death. It proved to be as stable and enduring an investment as land. His stock market dealings were rather more hectic, but were nonetheless profitable. Such investments made at a discount during wartime were partly sold between 1749 and 1752 at great profit, the proceeds being reinvested in land and money lending in England and Ireland. His sudden death in 1752, while in Ireland on business, caused his widow to call in all outstanding loans and to reinvest the capital in government stock. Only in her native New York was she prepared to encourage new money lending, though on a reduced scale. Warren's assets at his death were in excess of £159,000. Through the rise in land values in New York and Ireland, and by living moderately in England, Lady Warren benefited after 1752 from a substantial advance in her husband's fortune, so that by the time of her death in 1771 it amounted to almost £205,000. Repatriation of this fortune was hastened by the outcome of the American War of Independence, for though the Warren interests suffered no confiscation, the heirs sold their property, despite its long-term favourable economic prospects. In 1798 revolt in Ireland had the same psychological impact on the heirs, and most of their property was sold in the first decade of the nineteenth century. Here, as in America earlier, the sale of land realized a substantial capital gain on the original investment.

A number of general conclusions emerge from this study. In the first place, a naval career clearly offered many more opportunities for economic advancement than historians have hitherto noted. In Warren's case the change was one from obscure mediocrity in Catholic Ireland to great wealth resting upon international investments. Secondly, American investments, which formed such an important part of Warren's concerns, suffered but little from the American War of Independence, despite his very close connection with the DeLanceys and Johnsons, two prominent Loyalist families. In Ireland, Warren's case shows that too much has been made by historians of the significance of "Protestant" and "Catholic" landownership, while the evidence supports the view that Ireland in the second half of the eighteenth century had a generally flourishing economy. Moreover, in contrast to property in England, the Warren land in Ireland was very profitable in terms of rising income and of capital appreciation. Furthermore, the private lending market in Ireland proved just as secure as the English market, despite the reluctance of English creditors to lend on Irish land. Warren's land purchases in Hampshire conform to the pattern suggested by Habakkuk and other scholars of the amalgamation of land in fewer hands and larger units. The pattern of Warren's investments also makes clear that there was no real incentive for an investor of his type in this period to sink capital into industry, whether in America (where he expressly declined to become involved in iron), England, or Ireland. Lastly, the conservative approach to finance adopted by his wife and heirs, which led to a serious misreading of long-term movement in the London stock market and to the repatriation of capital to England, emphasized the impermanence of such a fortune as Warren's, established through a mixture of aggressiveness and good luck, and invested with imagination and wisdom, but lacking a corporate structure, the one characteristic which might have ensured a growth commensurate with the economic opportunities which opened at the beginning of the nineteenth century.

Admiral Warren has left few tangible traces, and none of them are well known. The site of his grave is lost in the tangle of a ruined Irish graveyard. There is a large, unlovely monument of him and his wife in the east transept of Westminster Abbey, carved by François Roubilliac. There are streets named after him in Louisbourg, New York, Charleston, and London, which also unwittingly affixed his name to an underground station. Two undistinguished portraits of him have survived: one by John Smybert in the Athanaeum at Portsmouth, New Hampshire painted in 1746, and three copies of another by Henry Hudson, all completed in 1752, of which one is in the National Maritime Museum at Greenwich, another in Heveningham House, Halesworth, Suffolk, and the third sold by Christie's in London in 1967 and bought by Dr. D.M. McDonald.

To these must be added the mass of naval papers in the Public Record Office, London, the British Museum, and the National Maritime Museum, which long ago could have enabled historians to write an account of his career at sea. As the interest of naval historians has largely focused upon the heroes of great sea battles and voyages of exploration and piracy, Warren did not catch their attention.

An impressive body of Warren's private papers has also survived. Though they contain much of interest to a naval biographer, they point unmistakably to an assessment of his personal fortune. The papers came principally through his grand-daughter, Susanna Maria Skinner, and after her marriage in 1789 to Henry Gage, through the Gage family of Firle Place, Sussex. Part of the collection was sold before 1930 and ultimately became part of the William L. Clements Library at Ann Arbor, Michigan. The rest was deposited by the present Viscount Gage, between 1957 and 1965, in the Sussex Archaeological Society at Lewes.[1] Moreover several archives in the United States, notably the New-York Historical Society in New York City and the Massachusetts Historical Society in Boston, have acquired additional Warren manuscripts, particularly relating to his American interests.

The nature of this material indicated that a study of the Warren fortune ought to be attempted not only as a contribution to eighteenth century economic history, but also as a unique opportunity of studying a fortune made largely from prize money. Far too little is yet known of the extent to which naval officers enriched themselves while carrying out the Admiralty's orders, or of the way they invested the fortunes some were lucky enough to make. Part of the trouble is that too few of the necessary private papers have survived. What family keeps forever the bill- and cheque-books, the bank- and letter-books, the invoices and receipts, the records of stock transfers, credit advances, leases, and property deals upon which alone such studies can be based? The almost inevitable disappearance of such crucial documents means that perhaps at best only a few detailed accounts of private fortunes in the eighteenth century will ever be written. The fortunes, for instance, of none of the prominent naval officers of the eighteenth century, except that of Rodney,[2] has received more than brief mention. Thus the analysis of Warren's fortune becomes a matter of more than passing interest. His wealth casts light on the acquisitive enterprise of the entire naval profession. What merits attention is thus not so much the manner of Warren's accumulating wealth, for that was not exceptional. It is the mere fact that, like William Braund in England or the Pinney family in Nevis, Warren's fortune can be studied, while those of so many of his contemporaries cannot.[3]

Chapter 2

Peter Warren

and the Origin

of His Fortune

Peter Warren was born in 1703 or early 1704 at Warrenstown in the parish of Knockmark, county Meath.[1] He was the third son and youngest child of a family of five. His parents were descendant from English families long established in Ireland, and they still adhered to the Catholic faith.[2] His father, Michael, served as an officer in the army of James II, and was freed and received back his estate under the terms of the Capitulation of Limerick. His mother, Catherine, was the only daughter of another of King James's adherents, Sir Christopher Aylmer, first baronet of Balrath, and of the widow of Sir Nicholas Plunkett.[3]

His father's death in 1712 left him with few prospects. As a Catholic, he was destined to the steadily declining economic condition of his class. Even to be converted to Protestantism, as some of the Warrens, Aylmers, and Plunketts had done, was no guarantee that life would be easier, for the Warrens were in reduced financial circumstances. The one asset, the 700–acre farm of Warrenstown, was heavily mortgaged;[4] and in any case, Peter, as third son, had little hope of inheriting it. That his father's will left him nothing and his mother's later only three pounds Irish for a mourning ring is testimony enough of the limited prospects of his early years.[5]

Sometime after his father's death it was decided that Peter should be raised Protestant and make a career in the navy, thereby following the path his eldest brother, Oliver, had already taken. Here his mother's Protestant relations proved of great value. Her brother,

Matthew Aylmer, had become a Protestant in 1674 and had made a successful career in the navy.[6] When Peter Warren joined the navy Aylmer was Admiral of the Fleet and Governor of the Royal Hospital at Greenwich. In 1718 he crowned his career by accepting an Irish peerage, Baron Aylmer of Balrath in county Meath. Aylmer's patronage was reinforced by that of Admiral Sir John Norris, who in 1699 had married Aylmer's daughter, Elizabeth, Peter Warren's first cousin.[7] Though virtually penniless, with such connections Peter Warren obviously had distinct and well-recognized advantages.

He entered the navy at Dublin in April 1716 as an ordinary seaman on board the *Rye* (30 guns), on which his brother served as midshipman.[8] Thus began a naval career that was to last thirty-two years at sea and four in retirement. Until 1739, England was largely at peace, although there were times of considerable international anxiety and some years of war. The fear of Jacobite invasion lingered after 1715 for many years, keeping successive British governments in varying states of alarm.[9] To the Jacobite problem were added the ambitions of George I to play a role in northern Europe, unprecedented for England, with the result that fleets were several times sent into the Baltic, the last in 1727. Yet Britain's principal active rival at sea was Spain. Hardly a year went by between 1713 and 1739 that did not witness some sharp dispute with Spain, and twice (in 1718-21 and in 1726-28) diplomatic relations were severed and hostilities ensued. Most of the action took place in the West Indies, where Spanish *guarda-costas* attempted to check British and American commercial invasion of her colonies. From 1739 until 1748 England was involved in war first with Spain and then with France and this provided Warren with the opportunities of glory and enrichment for which he had been waiting during two decades of more or less routine peacetime service.

Serving first in Irish waters, Warren spent most of these early years either on the coast of West Africa or in the West Indies, hunting pirates and searching for *guarda-costas.* He rose steadily in his profession, in 1723 reaching lieutenant's rank off the Liberian coast, when the natives killed one of his brother officers.[10] Death again intervened to advance his career. In March 1726 his captain died at sea, and Warren, as senior lieutenant of the *Falkland* (50 guns), assumed command until she was paid off.[11] He took post a year later as captain of the *Grafton* (70 guns), the largest ship he was to command for twenty years. This promotion was made at Copenhagen by Admiral Norris, who was then commanding the Baltic fleet.[12] This advantageous connection had facilitated his entry into the navy, and in 1727 it brought him a crucial advancement at an early age.

Norris's patronage also kept him regularly employed, sometimes as part of a large squadron, as in the Baltic, but usually in independent command. From the Baltic under Norris he was transferred to Gibraltar under Sir Charles Wager in the winter of 1727-28. He again served under Wager in command of the *Leopard* (50 guns) at Spithead in 1729. He had a second tour of duty in the same ship in 1734 and 1735, serving part of the time under Norris at Lisbon. But for the most part he was on his own. In 1728 in the *Solebay* (20 guns) he carried to Jamaica and Vera Cruz news of the peace preliminaries between England and Spain, calling at South Carolina on his homeward passage. In 1730 he again commanded the *Solebay* on the New York and South Carolina stations, not returning home until 1732. He next received a North American appointment in 1736, when ordered to Boston in command of the station ship, the *Squirrel* (20 guns); and did not return to England until 1741.[13]

As Warren gained experience of the sea and the command of men, he was also introduced to the possibilities of gain. Like all captains, he was specifically enjoined by his instructions to refrain from trading on his own behalf, yet he had seen how such orders were ignored. Both his captains in the West Indies, on board the *Rose* and the *Falkland,* were accused by colonial governors of carrying on trade and creating grievances among the merchants.[14] The incident off the African coast, which involved the death of a naval officer and some seamen, had developed when his then captain had transformed an expedition to get fresh water and firewood into a trade fair. That Warren traded on a small scale in wines and spirits, slaves, and other commodities, is apparent from his private papers, though this never came to the notice of his superiors nor caused dismay among the merchants of the ports he served.[15] He also had learned that there were other ways to earn handsome profits in peacetime. In 1726 the *Falkland,* which he brought into Spithead from the West Indies, carried bullion belonging to the South Sea Company; and he was probably paid 1 per cent or 1½ per cent of its value by way of freight money.[16] Indeed, in 1728 when he negotiated the release of several South Sea Company ships at Vera Cruz on the orders of the government, he certainly earned the praise of the London merchant community, and may well have been rewarded by the company for his trouble.

All this was a prelude to the great improvement in his fortune experienced in 1730-31. In March 1730 he acquired that part of his father's Irish farm which had not been sold by his eldest brother, Oliver, to pay off family debts. Oliver Warren had died in 1724, and the next brother, Christopher, sold Peter Warren his share of the property for £500 in 1730.[17] These unexpected developments gave Warren an annual income of £150 beyond his naval wages.

His independent income and the social status of an Irish landowner enabled him to conclude an attractive marriage alliance the following year in New York. In July 1731 he married Susannah DeLancey, the elder daughter of Stephen DeLancey and Ann Van Cortlandt of New York. DeLancey, a Huguenot refugee from Caen, had come to New York in 1686, where he established himself in the fur trade.[18] DeLancey's marriage into the Van Cortlandt family, with its connections throughout the Dutch element in the colony, enabled him not only to expand his business, but also to lay the foundation of a successful political career.[19] His wealth and position allowed him to send his eldest son, James, to Cambridge University and to secure for him the hand of Anne Heathcote, whose father was the wealthy mayor of New York and who had important political connections in England.[20] The Warrens' marriage contract created two funds: a "marriage portion" of NY£3,000, which was paid Warren at once, and a jointure of NY£6,000, held in trust by James DeLancey, to be invested in New York securities, principally in the form of bonds and mortgages.[21] During their joint lives, the Warrens were to have full use of the interest from these securities, the principal passing to whichever partner survived the other. For his part Warren agreed to make over to his wife all his Irish property, and a small farm on Manhattan Island with a water meadow on the New Jersey shore of the Hudson which he had bought a few weeks before. The properties could be disposed of only with Susannah's consent.

The importance to Warren of the DeLancey connection only began with this marriage contract. The financial and business contacts that were at once open to him, as well as the business acumen and experience thereby placed at his disposal and for his direct benefit were obviously of enormous value although they could not be measured in terms of hard cash. In addition Susannah Warren was to be a beneficiary of both her father's and mother's wills in 1742 and 1743, and of the will of her brother, Stephen, who died in 1745. The property settlement brought the Warrens a share in Cortlandt Manor in Westchester County, Minisink patent on the New Jersey border, a small house on Broadway in New York City, a share in Rumbout's patent on Wappinger's Creek above Cortlandt Manor, and a share in the cash assets as well as a number of bonds, that both Stephen DeLancey and his son had taken as security for debts owed them. A rough estimate at the time these assets passed into the Warrens' hands places their value at not less than NY£8,500.[22]

Warren has left a few impressions of what this wealth meant to him. In August 1742 he wrote to Admiral George Clinton, the Governor designate for New York, and spoke of his "little fortune, Indeed equal to most of the degree I desire to be of there."[23] In 1745 he wrote to Admiral George Anson, acknowledging that he had received "what in that Country is esteem'd a tolerable fortune, and indeed I think she has had a dear Bargain of me, since so little of my time has been at her disposal."[24] Though his fortune perhaps was nothing to boast of among Englishmen, among the colonists at least it was considered respectable, and he had transformed his standard of living from nearly total dependence on wages and perquisites of naval service to that of modest affluence. The DeLancey wealth was not merely used to improve his standard of living, but was invested in land in various parts of New York province. Part also was used to lend money in Ireland and South Carolina, where Warren also received almost 2,000 acres in land grants, which he began to develop in the 1730s by employing indentured white servants.[25]

The outbreak of war with Spain in 1739 put an end to his quiet life in New York and Boston as the commander of a station ship which was only rarely out of port. The war proved a marvellous opportunity for him. At the outset he was just one of many undistinguished officers. By 1748 he, Anson, and Admiral Edward Hawke were the most successful, most honoured, and richest naval figures to emerge from the long war. For Warren the war fell into two phases: from 1739 to 1745, when he developed his fighting skills and advanced his fortune by good luck as a prize hunter; and from 1745 to 1748, when he achieved recognition by the Admiralty, was given high command, and acquired great wealth.

At first he was involved in the inglorious siege of St. Augustine in Florida in 1740. Yet he emerged with the only two prizes taken by the small British squadron sent to help the colonial expeditionary force. He also escaped the criticism that was voiced both against the senior naval officer, Vincent Pearce, and the general, James Oglethorpe, who commanded the operation, the one for his inflexibility and reluctance to take risks, the other for his woeful shortcomings as a military leader.[26] On the contrary he was thought, at least by the colonials, to have done all in his power to have made the attack a success. His own view was that it was "Ill concerted and worse conducted," adding "I hope I shall never have any Part in Such an Expedition again."[27] From Florida he went to Jamaica to serve under Vernon, who thought him an "active good officer"[28] for his success in taking Spanish prizes, and for the despatch with which he carried out his orders. Official recognition came more slowly. In August 1742 the Admiralty adopted a suggestion he had earlier made to them to employ some of the station ships on the North American coast in the West Indies in the winter months.[29] The Admiralty now ordered him to New York for the summer months, and each winter to command a small squadron in the Leeward Islands and at Barbados.

This order established the pattern of his movements until the spring of 1745. His Leeward Islands' squadron distinguished itself only as a prize hunter, its biggest coup taking place at the outbreak of war with France on 18 March 1744, news of which reached Warren only in mid-May. Evidence of a diplomatic break had been gathering for weeks beforehand, and Warren had taken the precaution of ordering his squadron to bring in all French shipping they met. The result for Warren was a large increase in his fortune, a spot of publicity at home, appropriate expressions of pleasure from the Admiralty, and the temporary discomfiture of the enemy.[30]

Warren's great opportunity came in 1745 as a result of a decision of the Massachusetts General Court, led by the governor, William Shirley, to launch an attack against the great French fortress of Louisbourg.[31] In February Warren learned of the plan from Shirley and the need for naval assistance. Warren only felt free to leave Antigua with part of his squadron when orders came from England appointing him commander in chief of a new North American squadron. Warren had already told the Admiralty twice, once in 1743 and again in 1744, that "nothing cou'd be a greater acquisition to Great Brittain, and its Dominions, then the dispossessing the French of Cape Bretton, and Quebeck, by which the whole Furr, and Fish Trade, wou'd be in our hands, a Source of immense Treasure."[32] Yet as soon as the opportunity came and the call to duty was clear, he had grave doubts about the ability of the New Englanders to succeed.[33]

The fall of Louisbourg, quite unexpected and the only successful combined naval–military operation of the war, owed as much to the audacity of the New Englanders as to the effective blockade of the harbour by Warren's squadron. The squadron, which included some fine New England vessels, succeeded in taking several prizes during the siege, chief among which was the *Vigilant* (64 guns) sent from France to relieve the garrison. The defenders of the fortress sued for terms only after a massive pounding from the New England gunners, and in the face of large-scale preparations for a general assault by land and by sea. Generous terms were granted; and the French garrison and most of the population of the town were shipped back to France. News of the victory was greeted with much excitement both in the colonies and at home. Warren was roundly praised and a grateful government made him an admiral, and there was talk of a baronetcy. He was also made Governor of Cape Breton, and the military commander, William Pepperrell, was given powers to raise a regiment in America.[34]

Of greater value to Warren was the fortune in prize money that came to him at Louisbourg. Not only had he his share of the prizes taken during the siege, but in the weeks that followed several enormously rich French merchant ships, homeward bound and fully laden from the East Indies and South Seas, fell into the hands of his squadron, without difficulty or loss of life.

Warren enthusiastically pressed the government to broaden its war policy in North America.[35] He hoped to see an attack on Canada as the next step, with Cape Breton ultimately becoming a colony on its own. For the attack on Canada he proposed a joint colonial–British expedition supported by a powerful squadron. These proposals, which were backed by Shirley and Pepperrell, were adopted by the ministry, but so late in 1746 that there was no hope of implementing them. Warren, having resigned the governorship of Cape Breton on grounds of ill health, was asked to coordinate the colonial preparations for the expedition. The scheme was abortive, frustrated by the failure of the British squadron at Spithead to put to sea and because a French fleet, bent upon the recapture of Louisbourg, had stolen across the Atlantic.[36] The appearance of the French fleet on the Nova Scotia coast gave Warren anxious days, until he learned that so great was the sickness raging among the French crews, that the fleet was powerless to attempt anything. In October 1746 it limped back to France, having escaped a British squadron awaiting its return.[37]

Warren thereupon sailed home from Boston, and was immediately summoned before the Privy Council and questioned closely about the policy to be adopted against the French in North America.[38] He was less sanguine then than he had been a year before about the possibilities of conquering Canada, and was more concerned with the protection of Cape Breton and the development of Nova Scotia. Early in March 1747 he was ordered to command a squadron to be sent to North America, but by the end of the month the plans were abruptly changed.[39] Intelligence had reached the Admiralty of a French fleet preparing to put to sea, and Vice Admiral Anson was now ordered to assume command of the "Western" squadron with Warren as his rear admiral.[40] This cruise was highly successful, for on 3 May 1747 Anson and Warren overpowered the French off Cape Ortegal in the first significant naval battle of the war. Anson was given a peerage, and Warren made a knight of the Bath, while their share of the prize money amounted to almost £95,000.[41]

With Anson back at his place on the Admiralty Board, Warren took command of the squadron, in high hopes of repeating his success. No decisive action resulted, but the Western squadron captured a fleet of about fifty French merchant ships homeward bound from the West Indies, and his prize fortune yet again increased. Illness prevented him from taking the squadron out again that year. It was left to his successor, Edward Hawke, whom Warren had strongly recommended, to achieve the second victory that had eluded him, this one even more crushing than the first.[42]

As a result of the successes achieved by Anson, Warren, and Hawke in 1747, neither France nor Spain could mount an effective counterstroke in 1748. With Warren once again in command of the Western squadron, aided by a Dutch force, Britain's sea power had never been more obvious since the war began. Yet no decisive battle was fought in 1748. The French made no attempt to put to sea, while the one Spanish squadron that ventured forth escaped with the loss of part of its convoy. Instead the French concentrated upon the war in the Austrian Netherlands and invested the key fortress of Maestricht, far earlier in the campaigning season than Britain and her allies had anticipated, and with a much larger army than the allies could gather. The result was an early agreement in April over the peace preliminaries first with France and later with Spain. Warren was ordered home with his squadron from the Spanish coast, striking his flag at Spithead on 4 August 1748 for the last time.[43] The Peace of Aix la Chapelle, concluded in October, which involved the return to France of Ile Royale and Louisbourg, amounted to the restoration of the *status quo ante bellum.* Britain could have hoped for no more. The humiliation her armies had suffered in Flanders from 1745 onwards had fortunately been avenged by her navy's success at sea. Yet such success had not been decisive. In the end it had served only to protect England against direct invasion.

The war had made Warren a man rich in his own right. For this he had to thank principally the Admiralty, not only for giving ample opportunity to take prizes, but also for the nature of the prize law. Warren was one of that group of naval officers who first profited from the amended prize law of 1708, by which both the Crown and the Treasurer of the Navy abdicated their rights to share prize money.[44] The new law greatly favoured the fortunate captain of a warship who took an enemy vessel, for he received three-eighths of the value of the prize. If he took the prize single-handedly, the share was his alone. If he took it in company with other warships or privateers, his share was divided with his fellow captains. If he was serving under a commodore or admiral, he lost one of his eighths. In wartime a captain in an active theatre of operations had to be very unlucky not to share in a few prizes, though he had to be exceptionally lucky to make a great fortune. For an admiral actively engaged at sea the making of a modest fortune was almost a certainty from the war of 1739-48 onwards.

Warren, like so many of his fellow officers, had discovered that war was to a large extent a not unhappy blending of duty and personal gain. His instructions from the Admiralty invariably emphasized the protection of trade by convoying and cruising. But such instructions could be interpreted in both an offensive and defensive sense. Warren believed that to protect English trade was essentially the same as to attack and capture an enemy warship. For him the war against France and Spain was very obviously commercial in nature as well as a power struggle. He believed, for instance, that the French colonies of Canada and Cape Breton should be seized, thereby giving the British exclusive control of the fisheries and the wealth of the continental interior.[45] Defensively, by contrast, to lose but a single member of a convoy, a privateer, or a warship was a very serious matter.[46] To suspect that some merchants willingly allowed their ships to fall into the enemy's hands for the profit from insurance struck him as shameful.[47] That

England's friends and allies openly supplied the enemy with provisions in wartime he found exasperating.[48] He felt obliged, such was his sense of duty and profit, to apologize for failing to overtake enemy warships protecting a convoy, even though many of the merchantmen fell into his hands.[49] The prospect of doing the enemy some harm, while enriching himself, made him impatient with the weather, deserting seamen, leaky ships, and officers less energetic than himself. It also led him to take risks, and to plague the Admiralty at times with his pressing demands for better ships and adequate supplies of naval stores. In the West Indies, for instance, his chief and constant demand was for fast, small vessels to aid him in his search for enemy privateers and merchantmen.[50] When he found the Admiralty slow to react to these requests, he, on his own initiative, commissioned the best of his prizes and asked the Navy Board to foot the bill. This they invariably did though not without complaint.

On one occasion Warren was accused of being more interested in prizes and personal profit than in the safety of His Majesty's subjects. In the summer of 1744, Governor Shirley asked his help in defending Nova Scotia against invasion from the French at Louisbourg, by sending his warship, then at New York, at Annapolis Royal.[51] Warren could not act because his ship, the *Launceston* (44 guns), was undergoing repairs at the Turtle Bay careening wharf; she was not ready for sea until late September. Yet it so happened that when at length the *Launceston* put to sea, news reached Warren that a small squadron of French warships was on its way from France to Louisbourg to convoy home a number of East Indiamen, fur ships from Quebec, and fishing vessels as well as a rich merchantman from Vera Cruz. The British had no equivalent force concentrated anywhere along the American coast; and an officer less ambitious than Warren would have been content to avoid the enemy's attention. Yet Warren decided to attack the enemy with whatever force he could gather. He even asked Shirley for assistance, much to the governor's irritation, for Shirley had sent his only vessel to protect Annapolis Royal, when Warren's earlier unhelpful reply had been received at Boston. To Shirley, Warren had acted frivolously in the face of a serious enemy threat, while Warren viewed his actions quite differently as seen from the letter he sent to the Admiralty after hopes of collecting a naval force to attack the Louisbourg convoy had faded: "You will see by my publick letter what a glorious Opportunity of Serving my Country and making my fortune I am like to loose for want of a proper force. Sure this wou'd be almost equal if it could be Effected to y^t. good fortune of my worthy friend M^r. Anson."[52]

The precise extent of Warren's prize fortune cannot be known. He kept no separate prize account book, and though there are numerous references to prize income throughout those of his general account books that have survived, the picture is incomplete, and can only partially be reconstructed by using High Court of Admiralty or Navy Board papers. The value of his prizes is not usually mentioned by the court, while the Navy Board mentions specific amounts only when the prize was commissioned, limiting its concern to the vessel itself and useful naval stores. Other materials were sold by auction and no record of such transactions survives except in the private papers of merchants and the individuals concerned. Information is also lacking about the amount paid by way of fee to the court, *maitres vendeurs,* attorneys, and prize agents; so it is rarely possible to know exactly how much prize money actually reached the captors. Admiral Vernon, for instance, complained for years that no prize distribution ever took place for the Spanish warships taken and destroyed at Cartagena in 1741, even though it was the most important blow struck against the Spanish navy during the entire war.

A further difficulty arises from the shortage of information about Warren's special private arrangements concluded from time to time with his fellow naval officers for the sharing of prize money. For instance Warren agreed with Captain William Laws to share all prize money during the siege of St. Augustine.[53] Later, when Warren commanded the Leeward Islands' squadron he shared part of his prize money with Captain Knowles, who remained at Antigua to supervise the building of fortifications and dock facilities at English Harbour.[54]

Warren also made arrangements for sharing prize money when in 1747 and 1748 he served with the Western Squadron. From the end of March 1747, when he became Anson's second-in-command, until 20 July 1747, when he himself assumed command of the Western Squadron, Warren's share was one-third of the flag's prize money, while Anson took the balance. In 1748 when Warren was again in command of this squadron, the flag's eighth share in prize money was divided not only with his second-in-command, Edward Hawke, but also Vice Admiral Schryver, who commanded a Dutch squadron attached to the Western squadron. The details of the arrangement concluded between Warren and the Dutch admiral are not known; but from Warren's accounts it appears that Schryver took one-quarter of the flag's share, while Warren kept two-thirds of the balance, the remainder going to Hawke.[55]

Though there are too many unknown factors to allow for a full statement of Warren's prize income, nevertheless much of his earnings can be itemized. His first two prizes were taken off St. Augustine in September 1739 and April 1740. One was valued at only £180, the other, the *San Felipe,* which was carrying some pieces of eight, at £1,715.[56] Warren's share of both came to about £460.

Warren next moved to the West Indies, where he served under Admiral Vernon; between October 1740 and February 1741 he took seven prizes. As Warren was invariably employed by Vernon on missions independent of the rest of the Jamaica squadron, his prize money had only to be shared with the admiral and his own crew, but not his fellow captains. Nothing is known of the specific value of any of these prizes, as both Warren's papers and the records of the Vice Admiralty Court at Jamaica are of little use.[57] Some idea, however, of Warren's net profit can be gathered from a study of his correspondence and accounts with Messrs. Baker, his London agents. By March 1741 he had remitted more than £1,500 from Jamaica to London.[58] In addition, upon his return to England from Jamaica late in 1741 he put a further £900 into the Baker's hands.[59] Shortly afterwards he also conveyed to the Bakers bills of exchange from the West Indies merchants Edward Lascelles and James Woodcock, amounting to £1,105.[60] Thus £3,505 can be assumed to have been the principal part of the Jamaica prize money.

Warren's next prizes were taken in the Bay of Biscay off San Sebastian in April–May 1742. In command of the newly-built *Launceston,* in company with the *Port Mahon* sloop, Warren took the Spanish privateer *Peregrina* and several English vessels which the Spanish had taken and converted into privateers. When payment was eventually made in September 1743, the prizes brought Warren a further £1,550.[61]

Before final payment was received Warren had taken three more prizes in March 1743 on his passage from Antigua to New York. One, the *San José,* brought Warren almost £600.[62] Another came to £1,054; and about the value of the third nothing is known.[63] Warren's net receipts were then in excess of £1,654.

His next successes came with the outbreak of war with France in the spring of 1744, when as commander of all ships stationed in the Leeward Islands and at Barbadoes, he took with the help of his squadron some fifteen prizes. All were condemned by the Vice Admiralty Court at Antigua; and although there is much information about their cargoes, armament, and size of crew, nothing is known of their gross value as prizes. A study of Warren's accounts with the Bakers shows that not less than £3,800 was credited him by February 1745 from sources in Antigua.[64]

When Warren left Antigua in May 1744, another prize fell into his hands, the *Saint François Xavier*. She was condemned at New York in July 1744 and was valued at NY£9,264. Warren's share was not less than NY£3,125 or £1,850.[65]

From New York in the autumn of 1744 Warren once again returned to the West Indies to resume command of the squadron based at Antigua. Further prizes were taken, although payment in some cases was delayed until 1750. The net value to Warren was £7,084.[66] Thus by the spring of 1745, Warren had earned not less than £20,083 from prizes taken since November 1739!

Warren left the West Indies for the last time in March 1745, and sailed for Cape Breton. There, during and after the siege of Louisbourg his squadron took numerous French prizes, some quite valuable. Two of these prizes were commissioned by the Admiralty, which instructed the Navy Board as well to purchase all their stores and provisions. One ship, renamed the *Louisbourg Fireship,* sold for £800, with provisions worth £2,616. When captured, she had also carried 100,000 pieces of eight.[67] Warren's eighth share of this came to some £5,740. The other ship, the *Vigilant,* a new 64–gun warship, carried stores and provisions valued by Warren at £2,296, even though the Board of Ordnance would pay only £500 "for all Guns, Carriages, Shott, and Gunners stores."[68]

The value to Warren of the *Vigilant* and of other rich prizes is not exactly known. When three other principal prizes, *La Charmante, Le Héron,* and *La Notre Dame de la Délivrance,* were taken, Warren gave a rough estimate of their value. To John Wickman, then serving at Newfoundland, he wrote: "Since you Sail'd from hence some of the squadron under my Command have brought in two East India Ships, and a South Seaman, the two former being valu'd at near Two hundred thousand Pound Sterling each, and the latter at about Four hundred thousand St. £. Three hundred and Thirty thousand pounds in Cash."[69] Warren's estimate was undoubtedly high and his proportions between the three prizes definitely wrong. Had he been right his share alone would have come to £100,000. Later Governor Shirley visited Louisbourg, and privately estimated that Warren was "near Seventy thousand Pound Sterling" richer from the Louisbourg adventure.[70] Both estimates seem high, but an exact reckoning is impossible. What is known is that Warren used some of the captured coin to finance the garrison and squadron, and hoped to be repaid by the several government departments upon which he drew bills of exchange. By mid-January 1746, when the final entry of the surviving portion of his accounts with Messrs. Baker was made, bills identifiable as deriving from Louisbourg had been paid into his account to the amount of £33,477.[71] In June 1746 Warren believed that "my being kept at Louisbourg last winter is near Twenty thousand pounds out of my pocket."[72] This was his rough estimate of the funds already dispensed by him at Louisbourg on behalf of the government, but for which he had yet to be given credit. Thus it can be estimated that at least £53,500 came to Warren from Louisbourg prizes, whose gross value was eight times this amount, or £428,000.

Warren added nothing more to his prize fortune until April 1747, when he joined Anson in the Western squadron. The flag's share of the prizes taken from the French off Cape Ortegal on 3 May came to £94,487, from a total net amount of £755,896. Anson received £62,991 and Warren £31,496.[73] During Warren's next cruise, the squadron took more than fifty French merchant ships, whose net value was £386,866, the flag's share being £48,358.[74] Though in London at the Board of Admiralty, Anson took two-thirds and Warren one-third: £32,241 and £16,117 respectively. In addition the two admirals shared the proceeds of nine other privateers taken between the beginning of April and the end of June 1747. The amount this time was a mere £1,159,[75] but it brought their total share for 1747 to £144,104: Anson's share being £96,005 and Warren's £48,099.

This marked the end of Warren's great prize hauls, for the advent of peace in October 1748 made the campaigning season that year quite short. Nevertheless prize money continued to trickle into his accounts from the 1748 campaign until the end of 1751. Warren's accounts provide only a partial story of his 1748 successes, but they take note of receipts from prizes amounting to a further £5,723.[76]

Thus from the evidence reviewed here, Warren clearly earned at least £127,405 from prizes between 1739 and 1748; the bulk of it in 1745 and 1747. This figure can be considered as accurate as the serious gaps in his accounts, especially for the Louisbourg prizes, will allow. Warren's prize fortune was probably the largest, next to Anson's, accumulated by a naval officer before the Seven Years' War.

The coming of peace enabled Warren, then forty-five years old, to devote a good deal of time to politics. As early as 1742 he had expressed the ambition of becoming governor of New York, but eventually had to be satisfied with a place on the New York Council.[77] Three years later he offered to purchase the governorship from Admiral George Clinton, and spoke to Anson of the proposal as the "Pinnacle of my ambition and happyness" and "more agreeable to me . . . then being Lord High Admiral."[78] Despite his success at Louisbourg shortly afterwards and the great wealth it brought him, his views did not change, and he entered into negotiations with Clinton to purchase the governorship. By August 1746 Clinton had accepted his offer of an annuity of "one third of the Income of that government during y^r. and M^{rs}. Clintons Life and my holding it."[79] Yet the bargain was not struck.

The explanation is doubtless to be found in the curious turn New York politics had taken in 1746, which greatly affected Warren.[80] His brother-in-law, Chief Justice James DeLancey, having firmly supported Governor Clinton for the first three years of his administration, suddenly, for reasons that are by no means clear, went into opposition, hoping to force Clinton's resignation by making life unbearable for him. Warren had no desire to pick a quarrel with Clinton, for their views were akin, nor did he see any reason to upset Clinton's powerful allies at home, the Duke of Newcastle and Henry Pelham, whose sister had married Clinton's brother. At least until the end of 1747, Warren hoped that DeLancey and Clinton would settle their differences amicably.[81] He wrote two rather naive letters of accommodation to Clinton in October and December 1747, which Clinton took as certain proof that Warren was a subtle intriguer, who "stiks at nothing for ye sake of his own Interest and Friends, however prejudicial to mine."[82] Warren had no desire to choose between James DeLancey and Clinton, and his attempts at compromise earned the distrust of Clinton, and at times the disappointment of the "faction," as the DeLanceys and their allies were called. His value to the faction was limited to helping secure a commission for DeLancey as Lieutenant Governor, and securing the appointment of his secretary, Robert Charles, as agent of the New York Assembly in London; the one he accomplished in 1747, the other early in 1748.[83] As the faction failed to bring about Clinton's downfall until after Warren's death, Warren received no political benefit for being identified with the DeLanceys. Indeed, Clinton's determination to fight his detractors cost Warren his ambition of becoming a colonial governor.

Warren did not confine his political ambitions to New York. In 1746 he expressed a half-serious intention "to get into Parliament and perhaps venture to open my mouth there with more temper tho less Eloquence than our friend M[r]. Vernon."[84] When in 1747 the king dissolved Parliament with a year of its term still to run, his opportunity came. Warren was at sea at the time, and it was agreed between Anson and Bedford that he should stand as one of the candidates for the borough of Westminster. With its 12,000 voters, and a franchise that excluded only the "lowest and poorest," it was by far the largest urban constituency "and invariably returned men of the highest social standing."[85] As Warren then owned no land in England the necessary parliamentary qualification was supplied by Bedford selling him for £4,800 an annuity of £300 a year "during his life to be issuing out of Lands and not determinable on a Term of years. . . ."[86] Polling day saw Warren still at sea, which did not prevent him and his stable mate, Viscount Trentham, the twenty-six year old son of Lord Gower, and Bedford's brother-in-law, from achieving an easy victory.[87] Warren's share of the election costs was £2,200 which together with his annuity meant an outlay of £7,000 to get into Parliament.[88]

A seat in Parliament did not satisfy him, and when peace left him with much leisure time, he sought office under the Pelhams. His chance came in December 1748, when the Hon. James Stanhope, Member of Parliament for Derby, brother to the Earl of Chesterfield, and recent appointee to the Admiralty Board, suddenly died. Warren at once solicited Anson's help: "I rely Intirely on your Lordships Interest and Friendship to get me appointed in his Room."[89] There were many applications to the Pelhams of a similar kind; and at length Henry Pelham brought two names to the king, Warren and the Hon. Thomas Villiers.[90] Villiers, who was member for Tamworth and son of the Earl of Jersey, and had hitherto made his career as a diplomat, was selected, despite Warren's obvious qualifications.[91] Another vacancy in the Admiralty Board occurred six months later when Lord Vere Beauclerk resigned, but Warren then did not even bother to apply, and the position went to his youthful, inexperienced, but exceedingly well-connected colleague for the borough of Westminster, Viscount Trentham.[92]

That Warren was not considered again for preferment is explained by the stand he had taken in Parliament since the spring of 1749. He played a leading role in opposition to one part of a bill relating to the navy which was Anson's brainchild.[93] The bill, introduced into the Commons early in February, sought to reduce all acts of Parliament relating to the navy into one act, a reform of great importance.[94] But there was one significant new item, the thirty-fourth article, by which officers on half pay were made subject to court martial, on grounds identical to those affecting serving officers. The Admiralty argued that all officers, serving or not, ought to be subject to the same discipline. Those who objected, and Warren was one of their principal spokesmen, claimed it was a fearful attack on their liberty, for it gave the board an unprecedented power over the officers. Political and professional rivals could be subdued, it was argued, by ordering them to disagreeable posts, which, from their position of rank and seniority, they would be forced to decline, and thereby leave themselves open to court martial, and possible loss of half-pay. They argued that half-pay was a reward for past service, not a retainer for the future. Pamphlets were written, though not apparently by Warren.[95] Naval officers, through advertisements in the newspapers, were summoned to meetings, at which Warren and Admiral Norris presided.[96] In February 1749 a petition, signed by thirty-one officers, was read to the Admiralty Board, a most unusual circumstance.[97] The next day a great crowd of naval officers of different shades of opinion met the board; and young Captain Augustus Hervey reported in his journal, "Sir Peter Warren, Admiral Lee, Admiral Smith, Mr. Rowley, and Mr. West spoke against the article, and only Mr. Mostyn for it."[98] Sandwich, the board's spokesman, convinced some of the sense of the article, and ninety-seven officers signed a counter-petition in favour of the bill. Warren's name was not amongst them.[99] Warren and his supporters won a complete victory, a rare example in that parliament of the government conceding a material point in one of its bills.[100]

The cost to Warren was his alliance with Bedford and the Earl of Sandwich, which he had fostered since 1745. Politically he was estranged from Anson, though they apparently still remained friends. As late as October 1750 Warren wrote to Anson about the incident: "I hope your Lordship will do me the Justice to believe, that however I might have to My own prejudice Differ'd in oppinion with my friends on a former occasion, y[t]. no other Motive but Principles of honour and self Conviction . . . Coud have Induc[d] mee to take a part so Inconsistent with my own ease and Private Interests."[101]

Instinctively Warren was ill at ease in opposition to the ministry. Like many rebuffed politicians he gravitated toward Leicester House, and was even listed by the Earl of Egmont as one of the commissioners of the Admiralty in the administration to be formed on the accession of the Prince of Wales.[102] Yet this did not prevent him from playing an active role in the Commons in support of ministry bills. He was named to sixty committees in his brief parliamentary career, serving several as chairman, bringing in bills and twice carrying them to the Lords.[103] He was very interested in anything that touched upon his own constituency, and gave active support, for instance, to the scheme to establish a fish market in Westminster.[104] He was one of the best informed members on affairs concerning America, being active in matters touching colonial trade, currency problems, the rebate to the colonies for their Louisbourg expenses, the New York–New Jersey boundary dispute, and the fisheries. In foreign affairs he was deeply suspicious of the ambitions of the court of France. He advocated a strong navy, in the face of the ministry's policy of economic austerity. He supported an active policy of alliances between Britain and friendly European states who shared Britain's fear of the power of France.[105]

Like so many men of his time Warren was something of a philanthropist.[106] His philanthropy was distinguished more by its variety than its extent. In England he was particularly interested in hospitals. For several years he was both a vice-president of the Middlesex hospital and steward of the London hospital. He also subscribed funds to St. Bartholomew's, the Westminster infirmary, the Lock hospital, and the county hospital at Winchester.[107] In Ireland he was from 1742 particularly concerned with the Incorporated Society for Promoting Protestant Working Schools, to which he was a regular subscriber.[108] In America he contributed to building funds of churches both in New York City and Boston.[109] His most enduring act of philanthropy was in New England. In 1749 he was given a commission of £900 by the Massachusetts government for helping secure reimbursement of £182,649 for its expenses at Louisbourg in 1745 and 1746.[110] Warren wanted to put his commission to some "Publick Use in the Province," and first intended to help the building fund for a new townhall at Cambridge.[111] In the end he used £150 to buy and ship to Boston two stallions for the improvement of the breed in New England.[112] The remaining £750 he used for the education of Indian children, a project perfectly blending his religious and political attitudes. All his letters on the subject emphasize the advantage of bringing the Indians to "the

Knowledge of and Subjection to the Glorious Redeemer of the World" and the importance of attaching them to the "British Interest."[113]

The coming of peace in 1748 also afforded Warren his first chance since 1739 of again living a more or less settled family life. In May 1747 he had summoned his wife and children from New York to settle in England. Though they made their home in England, they never quite gave up the idea of returning to New York. In all they had six children, two born in Boston probably in 1738 and 1739, two more in New York, one in 1744 and another sometime after 1740, and two in London. Two of the children, including his only son, died in an epidemic in New York in 1744.[114] The family was established in a house in Cavendish Square, where they spent the winter and spring months, and in a country house in Hampshire, where the rest of the year was passed.[115]

After 1748 Warren travelled little. In 1751 he took his family to Scarborough for the benefit of the waters, as his health, which had been first impaired during the winter of 1745-46 at Louisbourg, was again the cause of some concern. His only visit to Ireland since 1733 proved fatal, for he died after a four-day battle with an infection on 29 July 1752.[116]

His sudden death at the age of forty-eight was a cruel blow to his young family, though his fortune allowed his wife a dignified widowhood and his daughters handsome dowries which enabled them to make advantageous matches. Lady Warren survived him by almost twenty years, dying in London in November 1771.[117] His eldest daughter, Ann, only thirteen in 1752, six years later married the Hon. Charles Fitzroy, later Baron Southampton, who was the younger brother of the third Duke of Grafton.[118] Susanna, who was eight in 1752, in 1767 married her cousin, William Skinner, whose father was the first rector of St. Peter's in Perth Amboy, New Jersey.[119] She died in 1772, leaving an infant daughter, Susanna Maria, who in 1789 married Henry, later third Viscount Gage.[120] Charlotte, Warren's third surviving daughter, who was three when he died, in 1768 married the fourth Earl of Abingdon.[121] Warren's youngest daughter, Catherine, an infant of four months at the time of his death, died at the age of three or four.[122]

His death cut down a man whose active talent seems only to have begun to emerge. It ended a naval career which, however distinguished, had achieved nothing memorable, though it had held much promise in the last years of war. By dying during the brief interval of peace before the onset of the Seven Years' War he not only missed the chance of playing a leading role at sea, but of also making a second great prize fortune. His death closed a brief political career which must only have disappointed him and his friends. Born into an Irish Catholic family of the declining gentry, he was raised a Protestant, which enabled him to break from the confines imposed by law on Irish Catholics, and to make a career. Then partly through skill, but chiefly by good luck, he became a man of wealth. His rapid prosperity and popular naval sucesses brought him to the outer fringes of power. His lack of strong political patrons and his own independent spirit, buoyed up doubtlessly by the very size of his fortune, ultimately isolated him from the centre of political power.

Part II

America

Chapter 3

American Estates I:

Manhattan Island,

Fort Edward, and

Cortlandt Manor

1731-1787

Warren's 1731 marriage into the DeLancey family was a crucial event in his life for it provided him with capital and gave him a new focus for his activity. Thereafter his connection with New York gave him every incentive, so long as he was active in the navy, to serve in American waters. Had he chosen at any time to leave the service, his prospects in New York would have afforded him an attractive alternative to living the life of a small Irish landowner, which otherwise would have been his lot.

His marriage caused him to buy land in New York, at first merely to provide himself and his bride with a home. The dowry she brought was at once invested in the New York money market, partly in mortgage loans. When some of these defaulted the choice necessarily arose whether to recoup his principal from the proceeds of the sale of the mortgaged property or to keep the property himself as an investment. His decision to keep the land stimulated his interest in this sort of investment. Simultaneously a fortuitous meeting with the widow of William Cosby, a former New York governor, added a new dimension to his speculation in land. For a nominal sum he found himself in 1736 possessed of a large tract of virgin land on the Mohawk river frontier of the province. Unlike so many land speculators in New York Warren decided not to neglect the tract; instead, as will be seen in the next chapter, he made it his principal land investment in America. To oversee the development of what he hoped would become a prosperous settlement, he brought out from Ireland two of his nephews. One of them, William Johnson, a man of rare business talents, laid the foundations of one of the most successful enterprises in colonial New York.

Besides his large Mohawk valley property Warren acquired many parcels of land on Manhattan Island. The most important were at Greenwich, at Turtle Bay on the East River, and in New York City proper, especially along Broadway and Cortlandt Street. Furthermore, through his wife's inheritance and by his own direct purchase, Warren had a large stake in Cortlandt Manor in Westchester County. Further afield he speculated in land on the east side of the upper Hudson in the neighbourhood of Fort Edward. His interest in land was not confined to New York. He was given two land grants by the government of South Carolina and bought land on a small scale on the New Jersey shore of the Hudson opposite his Greenwich estate. Moreover his estate ultimately included property in Massachusetts, for he had held the mortgage on this property through loans made to New Englanders.

Doubtless his principal motive in buying land was that it constituted an excellent investment. The social position which land ownership accompanied must have been equally important to him, as it was to his contemporaries. Instead of satisfying land hunger, the availability of land in New York colony as elsewhere in the mainland colonies merely intensified the desire to accumulate larger holdings. It is also clear that land speculation, like other forms of New World investment — farming, trade, and money lending — was not confined to the monied class of which Warren was an example. Land speculation attracted men from every occupational and social group, appealing to townsmen as well as to rural folk, to those with little capital and those with much. The great incentive to speculate in land was the steady and at times rapid growth of population which led investors to expect land values to rise. Nowhere was this more obvious than in the towns, the farmland immediately adjacent to towns, and the farmland in the fertile valleys elsewhere.

Until the outbreak of war in 1739 Warren was limited in the amount of capital at his disposal, being dependent on the terms of his marriage agreement, his income from his Irish farm, and what he could save from the navy. However, as has been discussed, as the war gathered momentum, a vast new source of capital flowed into his hands in the form of prize money. Initially much of this was invested in New York land and in money lending. In 1746 a large amount was put out to interest in New England. Thereafter most of the prize money was invested not in America, but in England and Ireland, in land and money lending, but principally in government securities.

Warren's New York investments, both in land and money lending, were not only lucrative, but provided him with a suitable social position should he have decided to settle in the province. For some time after his departure from America in 1746 he still entertained the idea of returning to America in a private capacity. Thus at the time of his death in 1752 he still had a large stake both in New York and New England.

Surprisingly, his widow decided not to return to New York, where all her family resided. However, she agreed to leave undisturbed most of her husband's New York investments. She was anxious to call in all outstanding loans both in New England and New York, yet she was fully prepared to reinvest part of the principal (though only in New York). The terms of Warren's will prevented her from disposing of his real estate in New York, for she had use of only one-third of the income arising from it, the rest being assigned to her three surviving daughters as they married and came of age. The daughters in their turn decided to retain the land, though they encouraged no new money-lending ventures. The orderly development and growth of their New York land investments was severely interrupted by the War of Independence. Yet the Warren heirs suffered no form of confiscation, and in the two decades following the War, they set about disposing of the last of their American assets. This chapter and the next discuss the history of Warren's American estates in detail and show both the opportunities and the difficulties which purchases of American land by a non-resident involved.

Warren's association with New York began in 1730 when he was ordered to command the *Solebay*, appointed station ship for the province. He was then twenty-seven and had already served almost a dozen years in the West Indies. On one earlier occasion, in 1718, when a volunteer on the *Rose,* he had spent three months in New York, while his ship was refitting. As captain of the *Solebay* he spent eighteen months in the city before being sent to Charleston, South Carolina. Though this marked the only time when he was long resident in New York, he managed to return often: for a month in 1732 and in 1736, for two months in 1737, 1740, and 1741. In 1742 he was again appointed commander of the New York station ship, though he was only on that station during the summer months of 1742, 1743, and 1744, the rest of the time commanding a squadron based at Antigua. He left New York for the last time in September 1744, and the American coast altogether two years later.

As he was so often absent from the city after December 1731, his affairs there, which multiplied with the years, were largely left to the care of his relations. By his marriage agreement with the DeLancey family of New York, Warren accepted his brother-in-law, James DeLancey, as the trustee for the NY £6,000 jointure established for him and his bride.[1] At first James DeLancey also played an important role in Warren's land purchases. In this he was aided by Richard Nicholls, a New York attorney and one of DeLancey's political supporters.[2] At length, however, both were superseded by James DeLancey's youngest brother, Oliver, as Warren's principal agent in New York. As early as 1745 Oliver had acted for Warren by going first to Louisbourg and thence to London before returning to New York.[3] In August 1750 Warren wrote to Oliver DeLancey saying: "I . . . rely greatly on you and Mr. [John] Watts for making the most of my Litle fortune under your Care, and I shoud be glad you and he woud be my acting attourneys to receive and pay, and that nothing relative to My affairs be Transacted but with your Joint oppinions and the aprobation of the Chief Justice."[4]

Upon Warren's death two years later, Oliver DeLancey went at once to England to put the Admiral's affairs in order, and did not return to New York for almost a year. His sister, Lady Warren, had placed her full confidence in him and entrusted him as well with the management of all her affairs in America. This responsibility he undertook with an enthusiasm and devotion which flagged only moderately after her death in 1771. Her three sons-in-law, Major General the Hon. Charles Fitzroy, William Skinner, and the Earl of Abingdon, while acknowledging DeLancey's devotion to the Warren family interests, wanted to replace him by his son, Stephen, and his partner, John Watts Jr. They first mentioned it to John Watts Jr., who happened to be in London on business, and who immediately asked his father's advice and was told to decline: "The Proposals made to you of undertaking the Management of S^r. Peter Warrens Estate here in so friendly a Manner lays you under The highest Obligations, as it shows a confidence in your Conduct, but the Mode of doing it is treading on Fonder Ground, you must have no Agency in it, your Uncle woud never forgive you, and woud suspect me certainly as an accessory, of which God knows my heart is perfectly Guiltless."[5]

To Oliver DeLancey the Warren heirs suggested only that the two young men be jointly concerned in the Power of Attorney they intended sending to New York, which would authorize their acting in any matter touching the Warren interests there. They sugared the suggestion somewhat by pointing out that the experience would be of great use to the two young men, as it would "induce many people in this Country who have property there, to employ them also. . . . We can have nothing more at heart, than to see a prospect of the DeLancey family, being continually in connection with us . . . by this means we shall secure to ourselves the friendship of the descendants of Lady Warrens Brother, and Sister, and continue a family connection that must be useful to us all."[6]

Oliver, in replying, agreed only that if he found the management of their interest "too much for me and they come to be in a Settled Way with Judgment and Industry"[7] he would soon step down. In fact he continued as agent, though employing his son and nephew from time to time, until his exile from America in 1783. Thereafter John Watts Jr., a moderate Whig, became agent and supervised the liquidation of the Warren assets in America.

During his years as his sister's agent, Oliver DeLancey charged her no commission. In return, between 1761 and 1775 he lived rent-free in one of the Warren houses in Greenwich Village, the equivalent of at least eighty pounds a year. However he was greatly disappointed by Lady Warren's will, which left him only a small quantity of silverware, so that he felt obliged at least to charge the estate part of the costs of his 1752-53 trip to England, some NY£554.[8] From 1774 onwards he charged the estate a 5 per cent commission for receiving and 2½ per cent for paying accounts. John Watts Jr. also made similar charges.

The decades during which the Warrens were associated with America witnessed a rapid expansion of population. The increase was due principally to the natural growth rate, which appears to have been between 26 per cent and 30 per cent per decade, or somewhat below the estimate of Malthus who thought the population doubled every twenty-five years.[9] Even this was impressive for it meant a rate of natural growth "considerably higher than that to be found in England at any time in the eighteenth and nineteenth centuries."[10] There was a general contemporary view, unsupported by statistical evidence, that the rapid growth was due to early marriage. Moreover, statistics are too fragmentary to calculate the birth rate, but available figures (for New Jersey) suggest an astonishingly low infant mortality rate compared with England's. This factor and the generally high productivity of American agriculture provide the necessary explanation for this rapid growth. Immigration, though not unimportant, has been exaggerated as a factor. Of America's 3,170,000 population at the first census in 1790 only a few were foreign-born; and not many more than 350,000 whites and 250,000 blacks had come to the mainland colonies since 1700"[11]

The province of New York, where the Warrens' principal interests were concentrated, shared in this remarkable increase, though many New York historians have taken a different view. If it is assumed after studying the available manuscripts that about 60,000 immigrants came to New York between 1700 and 1790, then the rate of population growth in New York was higher than the American average and "very close to the Malthusian 32 per cent."[12] New York's increase was part of the general rise to prominence of the Middle Colonies in the eighteenth century.

At the beginning of the century the population of the Middle Colonies was about half that of New England, yet by 1775 the two were almost equal. This outstanding demographic and economic feature of the period has largely been played down by New York historians in their desire to criticize the land system of New York. They allege that since land was held in large blocs by a few landowners, comparatively few settlers were attracted to New York, when other neighbouring colonies offered greater prospects for small-holders owning land. New York's landlords have been described as exploitative and repressive.[13] This traditional view has now been challenged and substantially rejected.[14] In its place the great landlords of New York are convincingly depicted as the active and successful "promoters of settlement, not its obstructors."[15] The settlers, with the support of their landlords, were able to establish their leaseholds "with a minimum of the deprivation and hardship which would otherwise have been their lot,"[16] and in time prospered sufficiently to purchase the land they had improved. That New York grew somewhat less rapidly than Pennsylvania can be explained only if due attention is given to the insecurity of the New York frontier, while Pennsylvania was protected by mountain ranges.[17] The Mohawk frontier and the upper Hudson valley remained but very sparsely settled until the removal of the French threat after 1763, when settlements were at last established on a permanent basis. With some 80,000 souls in 1750, New York had doubled its population by 1770, while the first federal census in 1790 credited her with 314,000, fourth after Virginia, Pennsylvania, and Massachusetts.[18]

This rapid growth was felt particularly in New York City itself, where the Warrens had their most valuable properties. A census of 1730 estimated its population at 8,226.[19] By 1747, when Lady Warren left the city for the last time, the population had probably passed 11,000; and by 1775 it had doubled to between 22,000 and 25,000, becoming second only to Philadelphia among the cities of America. This growth put a premium both on urban land and the land lying to the north of the city, particularly in the direction of Greenwich. This congestion allowed many of the larger properties both in the city and suburbs to be profitably subdivided before 1776; and Manhattan began to lose its rural character.

Though New York City in Warren's day had been established for more than a century, its rapid growth in the eighteenth century gave it the appearance of a new town. The houses, at first dominated by the older Dutch style with their stepped gable ends toward the streets, gave the city an appearance quite different from other American seaports. Later the English interpretation of the classical style of architecture became established. Trees were planted along the streets, which made Pehr Kalm, the Swedish naturalist who visited New York in 1748, think it "quite like a garden."[20] The first public park, called Bowling Green, was established only in 1733 at the southern tip of the island near Fort George. Many of the city's churches, the principal buildings at the time, were erected or enlarged in Warren's day. The most impressive, Trinity Church, on the west side of Broadway, was opened in 1698 and greatly added to in 1737, but destroyed in the great fire that swept New York in 1776. A second Anglican church, St. George's Chapel, was completed in 1752. In 1729 a second Dutch church was built on Nassau Street; and the same year the Jews of the city built their synagogue on Mill Street. The other communities (for New York was the most cosmopolitan centre in America), the Huguenots, Presbyterians, Quakers, Baptists, Lutherans, and Moravians all established new places of worship in Warren's day.

In New York as elsewhere in the colonies the taverns, markets, shops, and coffee houses were the centres of business activity and social life. New York's scores of public houses helped to give the city its contemporary reputation as the liveliest place in America. Its six markets were more than either Boston or Philadelphia boasted. New shops began to establish themselves in great numbers particularly after 1730, the most substantial clustered about Hanover Square, which became Manhattan's first shopping centre. Of the several coffee houses established in the early eighteenth century, the "Exchange," opened in 1729, quickly became the principal scene of real estate transactions.

Three of the four principal land purchases made by Warren in New York form the scope of this chapter: Manhattan Island, Fort Edward on the upper Hudson River, and Cortlandt Manor on the Croton River in Westchester County. The fourth, Warren's settlement in the Mohawk valley, is discussed separately in the next chapter. The Manhattan properties included three farms at Greenwich village, a careening wharf and storehouse used by naval vessels at Turtle Bay on the East River, and numerous small lots in the city of New York proper.

By purchasing three farms at Greenwich village on the Hudson north of New York City Warren created a 300–acre estate. It is doubtful that he had this ambition when he made his first purchase in 1731 on the eve of his marriage to Susannah DeLancey, his purpose then being only to provide for his wife. The property, a seventeen-acre farm with twelve acres of watermeadow on the New Jersey side of the river, was sold to him by Anthony Duane, a native of county Galway who before settling in New York in 1717 had been a purser in the navy.[21] The farmhouse, built in 1700 by Duane's father-in-law, Captain Johannes Densen, stood on high ground above the river and had a magnificent view of the surrounding land. The property, called Greenwich Old Farm, had access to the city by means of Greenwich Lane which ended at the farm having followed the Hudson shoreline. In 1737 and 1741, Warren made two additions to the property, amounting to a further 170 acres, from Cornelius Webber.[22] The purchase also included eighteen more acres on the New Jersey side of the Hudson. In 1744 Warren again added to his Greenwich estate by purchasing 121 acres from the widow of Dr. James Henderson.[23] The farmhouse, built about 1727, was the finest of all the houses owned by Warren in New York and commanded the highest rents. Although even as late as 1750 Warren was anxious to add still further to this estate, and thereby make it "most Comodious,"[24] the only addition after the Henderson purchase was an eleven-acre grant from the city of New York in 1745: "In Consideration of the Singular and Immenent Services . . . performed by him not Only for the Kingdom of Great Britain in Generall but for this City and Colony in particular, and also to Testify the Grateful Acknowledgements of the Corporation of this City to the Said Cap[t]. Peter Warren and the Great Esteem and Affection they have for his person."[25]

This fine estate, which had cost him only NY£1,930, formed a compact holding with its western limits running along the Hudson shore.[26] Its eastern boundary was formed by a turbulent brook called Mannett's Creek, which also formed part of the southern limits as it made its way toward the Hudson. The rest of the southern boundary was formed by a road, which in 1773 was called Skinner, while the northern boundary, roughly the present site of 21st Street West, ran along the Bloomingdale road.

The only other property bought by Warren on Manhattan Island on the outskirts of New York City was at Turtle Bay, a small inlet where Mill Creek flowed into East River.[27] The property, which consisted of a small farm of some sixty acres, included a careening wharf and naval storehouse. Warren bought it from Admiral Robert Long, who had commanded the New York station ship in 1728-30 and 1732-35, and who before leaving America for the last time had promised to leave the property to a Miss Mary Ashfield of New York City. Thus when in 1750 Warren and Long agreed to the sale, Oliver DeLancey had as well to secure the consent of Miss Ashfield.[28] Though Long had only paid £280 for the property, Warren agreed to pay him an annuity of £25. Long was then about sixty, and it must have seemed a fair bargain; but in fact he far outlived Warren's expectations, dying only in 1771. The cost then amounted to £525 (about NY£885), a most expensive purchase.

In 1750 Warren had also hoped to buy land adjoining this property, which formed part of the original 1639 land grant. He instructed Oliver DeLancey to manage the arrangements "very privately," but nothing came of his negotiations.[29]

Although New York historians in general correctly identify Warren's holdings both at Greenwich and Turtle Bay, they have been in ignorance of his land within the urban part of Manhattan Island. They credit him quite erroneously with having built a remarkably fine house at No. 1 Broadway, even though as long ago as 1877 the correct account of the ownership of that property had been written.[30] Warren owned land on Broadway, but the only structure he is known to have built was a school house at Greenwich. In 1731 Warren probably bought a lot on the west side of Broadway from Jeremiah Van Rensselaer for NY£190, with a stable and coach house on it.[31] A few years later he also purchased the land immediately between this lot and the shore of the Hudson River for NY£150 from his father-in-law, his sister-in-law, Mary Miln, and his wife's cousin, Philip Van Cortlandt.[32] Warren also acquired property on the east side of Broadway at Little Queen Street. Part of this was acquired from Oliver DeLancey and John Watts for NY£83 in 1744;[33] but most was bought in public auction in 1736 for NY£798. Warren had first held the mortgage on this property, then owned by Joseph Royden Jamaine, and bought the land rather than receive the proceeds of the sale by way of compensation.[34]

There were two other properties of Jamaine's which Warren acquired in the same 1736 auction, and on which he held part of the mortgage. These were near the custom house in another part of the city. They were two houses, standing on either end of a small lot, one facing north into Bridge Street, the other south into Great Dock Street.[35] To them Warren added an adjoining property formerly belonging to John Barbarie, a New York merchant friend of Stephen DeLancey's. Neither the cost nor the date of sale are known, though by 1759 Oliver DeLancey valued all three properties at NY£1,300.[36]

Warren owned one other lot in this the oldest part of New York City, on Pearl Street, near the governor's residence in Fort George, and on it stood a house and stable. Warren bought it in 1737; and in 1751 to improve his title to the property, paid the original owner, Captain Richard Riggs who had retired to Dorset, an additional £155 sterling, part of this sum being made up by means of a hogshead of madeira and three dozen hogsheads of rum.[37] Oliver DeLancey later said the property had cost in all NY£400, "a Great Price at that time."[38]

The last group of New York City properties owned by Warren were along Cortlandt Street, between Broadway and the Hudson. In 1741, for NY£385 he bought from Andrew Braested and John Hunt almost all the lots on the north side of the street.[39] In 1750 he applied to the Corporation of New York City for a grant of water lots adjoining the property, a petition which was approved only when Oliver revived the request in 1755.[40]

Warren's principal land venture in New York Province, other than the Mohawk valley tract to be considered in the next chapter, was in Cortlandt Manor. The manor, amounting to 83,000 acres, had been granted to Susannah Warren's grandfather, Stephanus Van Cortlandt, by Governor Fletcher in 1697.[41] The great estate had been divided between 1732 and 1734 more or less equally among Van Cortlandt's heirs, one of whom was Warren's mother-in-law. Her share amounted to 8,289 acres, then valued at NY£1,289.[42]

More than half this amount came into the Warrens' hands. The first portion came by way of inheritance, when in October 1743 a partial division of Mrs. DeLancey's estate took place among her six surviving children.[43] The Warrens' share was 3,100 acres, half of South Lot Five, the other half going to her sister Mrs. John Watts. The Watts's share was purchased by Warren less than a year later for NY£1,250.[44] That same year Warren bought Oliver DeLancey's share of his inheritance, known as Front Lot Six, and amounting to 1,250 acres. The cost was NY£1,000.[45] The last addition made by the Warrens to their Cortlandt Manor property occurred in 1747. For NY£900 they acquired 986 acres on the south side of Croton River, known as Lot Nine. It had belonged to Stephen DeLancey Jr., who died during the 1745 smallpox epidemic in New York City, and whose real and personal property was disposed of in February 1747.[46] As Warren was then in England, the arrangements were seen to by his wife, who joined him a few months later. In this way the Warrens acquired 5,336 acres of good farm land within easy reach of New York City both by road and river. A summary of the details of all these purchases can be found in table 1.

Part of Susannah Warren's inheritance from her parents was a share in two iron works in Cortlandt Manor. New York's numerous iron deposits were well known but were slow to develop as many were too distant from the main waterways and needed more capital to exploit than New York landowners were at first prepared to advance. In 1738 Lieutenant Governor Clarke told the Board of Trade: "It is universally agreed that this Province abounds in Iron Oar, and in lands proper for raising Hemp and yet both lye useless; Iron Works require considerable sums of money to bring them to perfection, or at least more than private persons who own those mines can command . . . the Assembly had these things under their consideration the last Session, intending

TABLE 1 *New York Property: Cost*

Property	Date Acquired	Cost		
Manhattan Island		at least NY£3,820	17s.	2d.
Greenwich				
Duane's farm	1731	500		
Webber's farm	1737-41	529	10s.	
Henderson's farm	1744	900		
Turtle Bay	1750-71	885		
Broadway				
Van Rensselear	1731 (?)	190		
Oliver DeLancey	1744	41	8s.	7d.
John Watts	1744	41	8s.	7d.
Jamaine	1736	798		
Bridge Street				
Jamaine	1736	(as above)		
Barbarie	1730s (?)	(?)		
Lombard Street				
Mary Miln	1736	50		
Stephen DeLancey Sr.	1737 (?)	50	(?)	
Philip Van Cortlandt	1738	50		
Pearl Street	1737-51	400	(?)	
Cortlandt Street	1741	384	10s.	
Elsewhere in New York		3,553	12s.	9d.
Cortlandt Manor				
Mrs. John Watts	1744	1,250		
Oliver DeLancey	1744	1,000		
Stephen DeLancey Jr.	1747	900		
Fort Edward	1737-68	403	12s.	9d.
	Total	NY£7,374	9s.	11d.

Source: Detailed references found in notes.

if they could to enable the proprietors to build furnaces and forges for pig and barr iron."[47]

    There was then only one small iron works in operation at Ancram Creek, established by the Livingstons in 1734. In 1750 Parliament passed an act to encourage export of American bar and pig iron to Britain, but forbade the erection of mills for slitting or rolling iron, for making steel, or forges employing tilt hammers.[48] These restrictive clauses were "almost entirely disregarded by the colonies,"[49] and New York at length contributed to an upswing in the iron industry from 1750 onwards. She exported no iron to England before 1743, and her average exports between 1743 and 1749 amounted to only 25 tons. Yet between 1750 and 1755 this average rose to 136 tons,[50] and for the remainder of the colonial era she followed Pennsylvania, Maryland, and Virginia in colonial iron exports to England. To this the Cortlandt Manor works made no contribution before 1765, when capital came from a group of English investors who created the American Iron Company, "the most remarkable of all the early industrial enterprises in the colonies."[51] The Warren family played no part in this adventure for, typical of many New York landowners before 1750, they chose not to operate the iron works in which they had a share. In 1743 and 1744 they sold for NY£1,571 their shares to other members of the family,[52] and put the capital immediately into land.

Warren twice attempted to secure land grants in New York outside New York City, the most common way in which lands passed from the Indians to the settlers. The first attempt in which he was concerned, along with his ship's doctor, Alexander Ramsay, and his purser, William Tattum, was made in May 1737.[53] They asked for 6,000 acres in Albany county, no patentee being entitled to more than 2,000 acres. In New York, land grants were the prerogative of the governor-in-council, who insisted that first of all a warrant to purchase the land concerned had to be obtained from the Indians. A survey then had to be officially authorized; and finally the patent itself had to be granted. The usual procedure was for several individuals to band together, but once their patent was granted several of them would sell their shares either to one or two of the principals concerned in the deal, or to others for whom they had in fact formed a trust. In the case of the Warren-Ramsay-Tattum request, it is most likely that both the doctor and purser intended to sell their shares to Warren once the patent had been received. Their petition was submitted to a five-man committee of the New York Council, which shelved the matter without bringing in a verdict.

A second attempt in 1737 in which Warren was concerned was successful. In December 1737 Warren joined a consortium of New York merchants and land speculators in a request for 12,000 acres on the east shore of the upper Hudson River near where Fort Edward was built in 1755.[54] His partners included Philip Livingston, John Cuyler Jr., William Kettle, and Peter Bayard. They jointly entered a second agreement with six other New York merchants — John Schuyler Jr., Philip Schuyler, James Stevensen, John Livingston, Stephen Bayard, and Samuel Bayard Jr., by which they gave the merchants NY£500 to undertake the petition procedure. If the grant proved a success, the New York merchants undertook to reconvey to the original six speculators, including Warren, 7,500 acres within ten days. The grant was made and Warren's share was "about two thousand acres,"[55] but no attempt was made during Warren's lifetime to settle the land.

Warren was interested at least in two other large estates, which are worth mentioning as examples of his continued interest in American land. In 1746 he began negotiations to purchase the Lloyd's Neck property on Long Island belonging to Henry Lloyd Sr. His brother-in-law, James DeLancey, had first brought him notice early in the year, when Warren was Governor of Cape Breton. That June, Warren went to Boston to coordinate efforts for the planned assault on Canada, and this gave him the opportunity to carry on negotiations with Henry Lloyd Jr., a merchant in the city. With him he agreed to pay £8,000, but eventually learned that the father was resolved "not to sell even for twenty shillings short of £10,000."[56] Robert Temple, Henry Lloyd Sr.'s agent, reported Warren's reactions: "He Immediately told me, that had it not been for the Interposition of your Son, he wou'd e're this time have Viewed your place by himself, or some friend, and If it was worth the £10,000 wou'd have taken the purchase uppon which I called Coz Henry to him face to face, who readily acknowledged the fact, but told the Admiral he wou'd never Interfeir any More; And I presume you will now have new overtures about your Estate."[57]

Though Warren hesitated and returned to England in November 1746 without having made a formal offer for the property, his interest was still alive in 1750 when he asked Oliver DeLancey: "Is there no More Talk of Lloyds Neck to be sold."[58] In fact the Lloyd family had decided in the intervening years to retain their estate.

A year later in 1751, Warren, still interested in buying land in America, looked beyond New York for an investment. He began negotiating with George Thomas, former lieutenant governor of Pennsylvania and then in retirement in Sussex, for the purchase of his American estate. The proposal was for a property in Pennsylvania, for which Thomas wanted £2,500. In a June 1751 letter Warren expressed interest but insisted first that the property be inspected by his brother-in-law, Oliver DeLancey. The idea of a conditional sale did not appeal to Thomas, who felt that it would prevent him from accepting other offers. He assured Warren that he had refused an offer of more than £3,000 for it, adding: "I then had thoughts of the Government of Pennsa. so I refused it. However, as it is not now probable that either I or my Son shall ever see that Country again, I will take Two thousand Five hundred Pounds Sterling for it, to be paid absolutely and without any further conditions."[59]

What reply Warren made to this letter is uncertain; but as he was on the point of leaving London for a three months' visit to Scarborough to take the waters, he probably asked for further time to consider the offer. It is certain only that Warren never bought land in Pennsylvania.

Though Warren received some revenue from his New York properties before his death in 1752, it was only later that his heirs reaped a substantial return from his landed investments. His rent roll in 1752 amounted to NY£307. By 1759 it had risen to NY£590, by 1772 to NY£1,152, and in 1787 when the Warren heirs made plans to sell their American estates, the rent roll stood at NY£1,185. The details are found in table 2.

TABLE 2 *New York Property: Rents Receivable*

	1752	1759	1772	1787
Greenwich	NY£83 15s.	NY£150	NY£236	NY£746 1s. 7d.
Turtle Bay	—	68 11s. 6d.	102 17s.	30
New York City	129	277	356	409
Cortlandt Manor	94	94	399 10s. 10d.	—
Fort Edward	—	—	57 12s.	—
Total	NY£306 15s.	NY£589 11s. 6d.	NY£1,151 19s. 10d.	NY£1,185 1s. 7d.

Source: Warren Papers and Gage Papers.

The Greenwich estate was one of Warren's most lucrative New York properties. The estate was sometimes let as a whole, and sometimes in part to several tenants. Initially the Warrens cultivated much of it themselves, letting only the houses bought from Webber and Henderson. They kept horses, a small herd of cows, and some sheep. They developed a large garden and orchard, planting crops of clover, buckwheat, wheat, peas, maize, and potatoes.[60] The labour was supplied by slaves, eight in all by the time Lady Warren left New York for England in 1747.[61] Old Greenwich Farm, the initial purchase made by Warren and used as the family home, was untenanted even after 1747, for he still had hopes of returning to New York either as governor of the province or even in a private capacity. The house was used by John Watts and his family. "Tis always at their service till they get a better place of their own or We Want it ourselves," Warren assured Oliver DeLancey in 1750.[62] Webber's farm house, much older than Greenwich Old Farm, was in poor repair and never brought more than NY£10 a year. By 1762, Oliver DeLancey reported it near collapse, but declined repairing it, the rent in time dropping to NY£7 per annum.[63] By contrast, Henderson's house was the finest of Warren's Greenwich houses and commanded very high rents. Its first tenant was Governor George Clinton, who paid £50 a year until his return to England in 1753.[64]

With Warren's death in 1752 and his widow's decision not to return to her people in New York, the entire Greenwich estate was looked upon as an important source of income. Oliver DeLancey was instructed to sell all the livestock and implements as well as all the furniture in the Duane house, and let the estate either to one tenant or in parcels.[65] By the time he returned to New York in September 1753, his brother, James DeLancey, the Chief Justice, and John Watts had agreed to let the Duane house and the three farms to Richard Nicholls, the Postmaster, for NY£80 a year. Nicholls also bought most of the livestock and all the implements, and finding the farm "in very bad order, hardly a pannell of good Fence about it," carried out the necessary repairs at his own expense.[66] Nicholls was also allowed to carry out NY£125 in repairs to the house, which was found to be in "bad Condition," and to charge the amount against his rent.[67] Oliver DeLancey was induced to accept this in view of the seven years' lease Nicholls signed. He was therefore very annoyed when Nicholls gave up the lease after only four years, as he explained to his sister: "Mr. Nicholl after all the Expence he has Layed out at Greenwich on Your Acct. has Most Dirtyly left on My Hands and gives me no Other Reason than that His Business wont let Him Live in the Country and to Make as Much of it as possible before he goes off as he has Sold the Dung to Your Old Gardiner William which the Chief Justice Says I must Sue Him for and I am Determined to do."[68]

Within a few months DeLancey had found a new tenant in Christopher Kilby, one of the contractors for victualling His Majesty's forces in North America. Kilby wanted only part of the estate for NY£50 a year; but at his own expense "made Many additional buildings So that the House is at least NY£250 better for His being there."[69] Two years later DeLancey admitted that he had yet to ask Kilby for any payment as the tenant had "laid out above £1,000 on buildings and Improvements and very Much bettered the Estate."[70]

When Kilby retired from business in 1761 he gave up his lease, and Oliver DeLancey moved in himself and for the next fifteen years the Duane house became his home. He also cultivated much of the estate himself. He even offered to purchase the Duane house and farm from the Warren heirs. He offered NY£2,000. If Lady Warren chose not to sell it then he was prepared to rent it at NY£100 a year. He also offered substantially to rebuild the house and in the end put about NY£700 into it.[71] He also applied to New York City in 1762 to build a new road linking the farm to Greenwich Lane. When the permission was granted, he explained to his sister that the new road "Makes Your House quite private and the Old Road is Enclosed as part of Your Little Farm and Makes it Much better."[72] Lady Warren would not sell nor would she demand rent.

Meanwhile those parts of Webber's farm which neither Christopher Kilby nor Oliver DeLancey made use of were let for NY£36 a year.[73] Henderson's house and land, after Governor Clinton returned to England in 1753, was also tenanted. It was let to William Kempe, the New York Attorney General, newly arrived from England, at NY£60 a year for five years from 1 May 1754.[74] Kempe died in July 1759 leaving NY£152 10s. in unpaid rent and his son, John Tabor Kempe, refused to honour his father's debt. Apparently the Warren estate never received it, although young Kempe became a man of wealth. From 1759 Brigadier Robert Moncton took a six years' lease. Though Moncton spent very little time in New York as long as the war lasted with France, and though he left New York for the last time in 1763, he continued as tenant until April 1765.[75] From 1765 to 1772 Henderson's farm and house were let to David Johnson at NY£90 a year.[76] The Warren estate also collected a further NY£30 a year rent from William McAdam, a New York merchant, who rented 25 unused acres from September 1765 on a twenty-one year lease.[77] Thus by the time of Lady Warren's death in 1771, the rental income of the Greenwich estate amounted to NY£163 a year, though had she accepted her brother's offer of NY£100 for his part based on the Duane farm, it would have amounted to NY£263.

Lady Warren's death meant that the entire Warren fortune passed equally to her three daughters; and DeLancey henceforth took his orders from the sons-in-law, Charles Fitzroy, William Skinner, and the Earl of Abingdon. They, having no personal attachment to or experience of New York, tended to look upon their American affairs from a narrow business viewpoint. They were determined not to sell the land, but to let it at the highest possible rate, with the burden of maintaining the properties in good repair to fall upon the future tenants.[78] DeLancey readily admitted that "the Rents of Greenwich certainly are Small Compared to the Value of the Estate which from Costing a Trifle has in a few Years Grown very Much S^r. Peter Gave D^r. Henderson for his Estate £900 it would now sell for almost as Many Thousands."[79] He recommended that the Greenwich estate be subdivided into small lots and let on long leases to encourage building.[80] Only in 1774 was this advice accepted by the Warren heirs, and the subdivision began.[81] Unfortunately, he was told by the heirs that their marriage contracts precluded them giving leases longer than twenty-one years. It was fifteen months before they realized that this information was incorrect, thus causing DeLancey great trouble.[82] It had been his intention to grant thirty-one year leases and he had actually concluded a number of arrangements on such terms before having to cancel them. He complained to the heirs that by granting leases at only twenty-one years they were competing unfavourably with their neighbours, Bayard, Rutgers, Hening, and the Church, who were all busily subdividing their adjoining estates on longer leases and at higher rents. Nevertheless the return promised to grow prodigiously as a result of the subdivision; and by January 1776 with less than half the lots let, gross income amounted to NY£484.

The timber on the Greenwich estate was especially valuable. In 1750 Warren had noted that there were "a great many fine young Cedar Trees" on Henderson's farm, and ordered them to be preserved.[83] He instructed Oliver DeLancey: "I am very fond of Trees and if not too Expensive I should like to have some Clumps of Trees Planted about the Land Especially on the sand Hills and most Barren, and fenced in with Post and rails to keep the Catle from them." When Oliver DeLancey became tenant at Greenwich he greatly added to the plantation, using the timber to fence the farm and to erect wharves on the Warren property at Turtle Bay on the East River and at the foot of Cortlandt

Street in New York City. Much of the wood was pillaged in the 1770s; Oliver DeLancey spoke of his increasing difficulties "to preserve the Wood at Greenwich which by its nearness to the Town is very Lyable to be Plundered of the Most Valuable Wood as they Come in the Night with Saws and Cutt it down to prevent being discovered by the Noise which axes would Make."[84] He complained also that young fruit trees were dug up and carried off. The outbreak of war in New York in 1776 caused severe damage to the Greenwich woods, from which it never recovered. DeLancey's last surviving letter to the Warren heirs refers to the loss: "I have now only to tell you that The Woods at Greenwich Which I ever took Such Pains to preserve is Ruined and Cutt Down for Military uses and out of My Power to Prevent by any Interference."[85] The destruction had been occasioned by the arrival in New York early in 1776 of the American General Charles Lee, who, having anticipated Henry Clinton's descent from Boston, hurriedly attempted to put New York City in a state of defence and used the abundant woods for fascines and batteries.

Turtle Bay, the next of Warren's Manhattan estates to be considered, was a property unique in New York. Its particular importance was as a careening place for naval vessels stationed at New York. It was the only one in the province, the nearest being at Boston. The income from Turtle Bay depended in large measure upon the Navy Board's willingness to make use of its facilities. New York was normally not an important naval base with usually only one frigate appointed to the station. However, between 1756 and 1760, when it became the chief port for the supply of the British army in America, and again between 1776 and 1783 when the British made it their principal armed camp in the war with the Americans, it acquired vital though temporary strategic importance. In 1751 when Captain Henry Cosby, commander of the *Centaur,* was appointed to the New York station, Warren made an agreement with him whereby he let Turtle Bay facilities for £60 a year as long as Cosby remained on the station.[86] The idea was that Cosby in turn would ask compensation for his expenses from the Navy Board. Cosby died in October 1753, and the settlement of his affairs dragged on for many years; it is not known when the Warren heirs were credited with the £120 owing them from Cosby.

Oliver DeLancey as early as 1754 wanted the affairs of Turtle Bay put on a firm footing, but it remained untenanted until 1758. In 1754 he broached the idea by suggesting to his sister that a long-term contract be concluded with the Navy Board to let the facilities at a fixed rate. He suggested that she "gett some friend to lett them know that there is no other Place in this Country where Men of War Can Careen and unless they will give £60 a year for the use of it You Must Convert it to Some other Employment."[87] DeLancey felt certain that if the Admiralty compared this amount to the annual cost that had been incurred over the years by naval captains serving at New York, they would conclude that such a contract would afford them a great saving. Lady Warren apparently did nothing except to leave her brother free to open negotiations with the Admiralty if he wished. In December, 1755, DeLancey again remarked: "Turtle Bay is left untenanted and unless the Navy Board will allow a Yearly Rent it will be a Poor Estate and very Expensive as it requires More Repairs by being unused 2 or 3 Years than a ship's being there a Year will pay for."[88] He suggested £40 a year as a suitable rent, with the Navy Board free to erect whatever buildings were needed but also to bear the cost of all repairs. Even as late as October 1757 he complained again to his sister that he occasionally received "a little Money for Ships lying at Turtle Bay but Scarcely So Much as will pay Capt. Long's annuity."[89]

It was not until 1758 that the Admiralty at last agreed to the sort of contract DeLancey had earlier suggested. At first Turtle Bay was let for £68 11s. 6d. a year, but from the 1760s the rent rose to £102 17s.[90] Payment was regularly received until the end of British occupation of New York in 1783. Throughout the war Turtle Bay was let to the Board of Ordnance and was occupied by both their officers and those of the artillery. It was even briefly subjected to attack by the Americans. The end of hostilities greatly altered the fortune of Turtle Bay. It was rented for £93 to John Jarvis until he became insolvent, and thereafter fetched only £30 a year until it was sold by the Warren heirs in 1791.[91]

Though income from Warren's lots in New York City proper eventually became considerable, ranking first in 1759 and second only to Cortlandt Manor in 1772, it actually amounted to little in his own lifetime. His first purchase, the coach house and stable on Broadway was let for NY£10.[92] Oliver DeLancey, who played such an important role in expanding the Warren interests in New York, later divided the lot into two and by the 1760s received rents of NY£35.[93] The great fire of 1776 destroyed both the coach house and the stable, and neither was rebuilt before being sold in the 1790s.[94]

On the Lombard Street lots, owned by Warren, immediately to the rear of his Broadway property, houses were eventually erected at the expense of the tenants, two on the east side and four on the west side. Each was rented at NY£12 a year though the length of the leases is not known.[95] The tenants were among the poorest on the Warren rent roll; and DeLancey often had difficulty in getting rent from them. In 1776 when war came to New York, all the tenants were driven from their homes when the American General Lee decided to site a battery there to range across the Hudson. Those houses not destroyed for the battery were burned down by the September 1776 fire.[96] No compensation was ever paid nor is there evidence that the properties were covered by fire insurance.

The Warren lots on the east side of Broadway at Little Queen Street became important only in 1738 when the inhabitants of the West Ward of New York City petitioned the Common Council for the erection of a market on Broadway. Until then all the city's markets were on the other side of town near the East River water-front. The petition was successful and in 1739 a market house, called Oswego Market, was built in the middle of Broadway almost opposite the Warren lots, which until then had no shops built on them.[97] Oswego market enjoyed a prosperous existence on that spot for some thirty years; but as Broadway acquired commercial importance and as new streets were laid down to the north the street became very congested and the presence of the market a great obstacle to traffic. In 1771 it was moved to Cortlandt Street, where Warren also owned property; and there Oswego market flourished, subsequently expanding greatly and being renamed Washington Market, the most important in the city.

Despite the establishment of Oswego market in 1739, Warren's lots on the east side of Broadway were developed only in 1750. Warren divided them into five properties, offering twenty-five-year leases at NY£8 a year.[98] In the post-war years, before they were sold by the Warren heirs, the rent had risen from NY£40 to NY£62 10s.[99]

The development of Warren's property on Cortlandt Street took place only after his death, and was due entirely to Oliver DeLancey's initiative. In 1755 DeLancey had revived a petition, originally made in 1750 by Warren, for a grant by New York City of the water lots on the Hudson at the foot of Cortlandt Street.[100] The petition was successful; and the grant was made in 1755 on the eve of war. Within two years troops in large numbers were landing with all their equipment in New York to begin their passage to the Mohawk–Hudson frontier to do battle with the French. New York dock facilities were soon inadequate so DeLancey asked the city's permission to build a wharf at the foot of Cortlandt Street, making use of the water lots granted him in 1755. Permission to erect the wharf was granted in the spring of 1758, and it was built hurriedly by John DePeyster.[101] It was an immediate success, and helped considerably to ease the congestion on the wharves of New York. On 5 June 1758, Christopher Kilby, one of the contractors for victualling his majesty's forces in America, rented fourteen of the twenty-three lots available from the Warrens near Warren's Wharf, at NY£6 per lot.[102] The rest of the lots were soon taken up and produced in all a gross rent of NY£132, offset only by occasional repairs to the wharf.[103] Warren's Wharf thus became the principal quay over which most of the supplies of the British forces under Abercrombie and Amherst passed. The navy thought it so important that they erected a storehouse there which they occupied until 1783.

Warren's other New York City properties stood in the oldest part of the city between Bridge and Great Dock streets and on Pearl Street near Fort George. All were old and occasioned constant repairs which ate into the rental income which amounted to NY£46 in the 1750s, NY£56 8s. by 1772, and NY£60 1s. in 1787.[104] The Pearl Street property, which consisted of a house and stable, was originally let together at NY£25, later separately for NY£35, no tenant remaining more than a few years.[105]

Something of a dispute as to the Warren heirs' title to the Pearl Street lot arose in 1774, when the Governor Sir William Tryon decided to demolish the stable bordering on his garden, which he wished to enlarge. DeLancey was contacted and informed the Warren heirs that Tryon was prepared to pay a reasonable price for it.[106] When in 1774 Tryon returned briefly to England to consult the administration of Lord North about the worsening relations between the colonies and England, he made his proposals to Col. William Skinner. Skinner reported at once to DeLancey: "He is willing to pay the Value of it provided we can make out a Title, he says that when Rigs sold the Lott to S^r. Peter Warren . . . he included the piece of Ground on which the Stable stands, which stable he built by leave of Govr. Hunter, and had no right to the Ground, which circumstance is well known to Govr Colden, if this can be proved it must be given up, however we would have you ask Councell on the Affair, and if it appears that it was M^r. Riggs Property, we are in that case ready to accomodate Tryon with it, he paying the full value which can be easily ascertained by the appointing 3 Gent^n. and you three, to be decided by their Opinion."[107]

DeLancey was reluctant to seek counsel, and replied to the heirs by saying that he would merely ask Tryon what he was prepared to pay. He had valued it at NY£500 in 1772, which he thought still a fair price.[108] The deal must have been concluded for by 1787 when the heirs set about dividing Warren's American assets, the property was not mentioned.[109]

The collection of rents due on Warren property outside New York City and its environs was invariably less certain than the collection of rents in the city itself. Oliver DeLancey rarely went out of town on Warren business; instead he made use of under-agents both at Cortlandt Manor and Fort Edward. There was no great urgency as far as the latter was concerned, as will be seen shortly, for settlement there was not possible until after 1763. Cortlandt Manor, however, was a different matter. Ultimately the property was divided into twenty-two farms, yet even as early as 1748 twenty of these had tenants. Theoretically this produced an annual rental income of NY£94.[110] As little of this was paid, Warren complained to DeLancey in 1750: "I wrote to you several times about the Rents of the Lands in the Mannor of Courtlandt, which by the Tennants own Concent so long ago as when I was at N York amounted to near £100 pr. annum. Surely something ought to be done or Else they will think the Lands their own in time."[111] The problem of rent collection was not resolved in Warren's lifetime or for some years after his death. In 1755 DeLancey excused his lack of success by promise of future action: "I have Excessive Trouble with you[r] Tennants in Cortlands Mannor being hardly able ever to gett rent from them but by means of the Law and I am Determined to turn most of them off and put on New Ones."[112] A couple of years later, when a total of NY£45 2s. 6d.[113] had been received since 1753, he lamented, "half the Tennants in Courtlands Mannor Pay their Rent and near th Other half so Poor they Cant."[114] The situation improved only when DeLancey appointed his cousin, Pierre Van Cortlandt, who lived on the spot, as collector of rents for the Warren estate at Cortlandt Manor. Tenants who failed to pay their rents were turned off, and new ones put on the vacated farms, the improvements for which they had to pay in addition to their normal rents. At the same time rents were raised as table 3 shows. Income began to be received regularly and rose from NY£139 4s. 10d. in 1758 to NY£259 7s. in 1771.[115] This still represented a 26 per cent shortfall in income; and the situation improved substantially in 1773-74 when NY£346 14s. and NY£329 13s. were respectively collected. This was still 15.4 per cent short of the 1774 rent roll.[116] DeLancey was still not satisfied, and, even in the late autumn of 1775 after a visit to the Manor, he complained he still "Could gett no Money from six or seven Tennants that are in arrear for rents."[117] Despite this difficulty for more than fifteen years he had managed to make the property a regular source of income for the Warren heirs.

Some general observations can be made about the property. Most tenants were given leases which specified only the amount of rent to be paid and not the length of tenure.[118] In 1769, the year for which the most detailed rent roll exists, only four of twenty-one tenants had leases which mentioned a definite term: in each case eleven years. At first rents were very low, ranging from NY£3 5s. to NY£12, and can be considered merely nominal as the farms were slowly established. Thereafter, during the two decades before 1776 there was a rapid rise in rents, so that an average of NY£19 1s. was achieved. There was surprisingly little turnover among tenants, after the appointment of Pierre Van Cortlandt. In the twenty-year interval before 1776[119] eight farms kept the same one tenant, and three of these had been tenants since 1748 or earlier. Nine further farms had but two tenants over the same period, and in two of these cases the new tenant was a member of the same family as the one replaced.[120] This relative stability among the tenantry indicated that the rents, however much they rose, were on the whole economical. It also indicated that tenants-at-will experienced as great security under the Warrens as those with leases. Rapid turnover of tenants occurred only among a minority of the poorest, who, it was found, could readily be replaced, especially in the years after the war with the French.

The general relationship between tenants and landlords on Cortlandt Manor has recently been studied in detail, and has resulted in an altered historical view of the role of the landlord.[121] Historians have focused much attention on rioting among tenants which marked the year 1766.[122] Called by some, the "tenant rebellion," the drama has now been placed in proper prospective. No rebellion, it was "an extremely limited and short-lived disturbance . . . which resulted from difficulties between one landlord, John Van Cortlandt, and a handful of his tenants."[123] Later, during the War of Independence, most manor tenants sided with their landlords, not against them. The manor was a scene of great destruction owing to the bitter hatreds that di-

TABLE 3 *Cortlandt Manor: Rents Receivable*

Acres		1748 ca.	1769	1774
South Lot Five				
Lot 1	211	NY£3 5s.	NY£15 6s. 6d.	NY£15 6s. 6d.
2	196	4 10s.	14 14s.	17 6s. 6d.
3	227	4 10s.	15 16s. 6d.	15 6d.*
4	198	3 10s.	19 16s.	19 16s.
5	210	4	12 11s.	12 11s.
6	174½	4 10s.	14 10s. 1½d.†	22 10s.†
7	203½	3 10s.	15 5s. 3d.	15 5s. 3d.
8	180¼	3 10s.	13 10s. 4½d.	23
9	180¼	4 10s.	13 10s. 4½d.	13 10s. 4½ d.
10	203	4 10s.	15 5s 3d.	15 5s. 3d.
11	160½	3	12 2d.	23
12	119¼	3	—	—
13	105	3 15s.	7 15s. 6d.	7 17s. 6d.
14	390½	3 10s.	29 6s. 6d.	29 5s. 6d.
15	341	3 10s.	25 11s. 6d.	23 1s.*
Front Lot Six				
Lots 1 & 2	279½	7	25	32
3 & 4	242½	—	12 2s. 6d.	15
Lot Nine				
Lot 1	136	12	13 19s.	20
2 & 6	220	6	8	8
3	233	6	17 9s. 6d.	21
4	234	6	17 10s.	17 10s.
5	112¾	—	8 5s.	33 6s.
Total		NY£94	NY£327 4s. 3d.	NY£399 10s.10½d.

Source: Sleepy Hollow Restorations, MS. V 1689; Warren Papers 55, NYHS; Gage Papers, G/Am/79a, G/Am/82, G/Am/158, G/Am/170.

*In South Lot Five, both lots 3 and 15 experienced a slight decrease in rents.

†From mid-1750s, lots 6 and 12 were let together.

vided both tenants and small freeholders, some siding with the American cause and others with the Loyalist.[124]

Most of the Warren tenants appear to have identified themselves with the American cause. Only one, James Cock, a cooper, who was tenant of farm five on South Lot Five, emigrated from the manor, settling in Nova Scotia during the war.[125] The remainder were not the downtrodden tenants that some historians have described them. David Montross, a Warren tenant from at least 1748, leased four farms in Cortlandt Manor by 1773. His 1806 will left NY£3,000 in personal property, part of it in land. He had been a captain of militia before 1776.[126] Joseph Sherwood was a Justice of the Peace in the 1760s, and in 1765 was appointed by the New York Assembly to be one of the Commissioners of Highways at Cortlandt Manor. He not only leased a farm from Warren, but owned another elsewhere in the manor. Several of the Warren tenants either owned a farm as well or leased more than one from other Cortlandt Manor landholders. John Veal, for instance, paid NY£818 for a farm bought from the Skinner family. Abraham Wright bought farms from both Peter Kemble and John Watts. John Pinkey owned for a short time, from 1765 to 1771, a 123–acre farm bought from the Skinners. Joseph Osborne in 1769 bought 482 acres from Peter DeLancey. Nathan Whitney owned estates worth NY£5,000 before 1776, while Gilbert Totten, besides being a Warren tenant, owned a 233–acre tract in Rye, and by his 1766 will left two slaves and NY£200 in cash. Several of the Warren tenants were sufficiently well placed after 1783 to speculate in land in Vermont. John Veal and Walter Ward speculated in land in Mansfield while Peter Montross, brother of Captain David Montross, speculated in Stowe. The conclusion emerges that the Cortlandt Manor tenants were for the most part successful farmers, several owning land amounting to hundreds of acres, and several with sufficient capital to speculate in the development of the Vermont frontier with Canada. That there were poor tenants of Cortlandt Manor is undeniable, but they were in the minority, and having leases in many cases dependent on the will of the landowner, could be dismissed and replaced with those possessing the necessary abilities to reap a profit from the rich farmland of the Croton river valley.

Though many farms had been destroyed during the War of Independence, most tenants, if they left the land, returned by 1783 and resumed payment of their rents to John Watts Jr., on behalf of the Warren heirs. For them the war in America had effected a temporary serious dislocation, but had altered nothing essential. They remained tenants with obligations to landlords, who though members of the British aristocracy, had not suffered confiscation. Rents were collected by Watts as late as 1794, when the last of the farms were sold, in many cases to the tenants themselves.[127]

The Warren share in the upper Hudson speculation near where Fort Edward was built in 1755 was the last to develop into a revenue-producing asset. Fort Edward was built to prevent a French and Canadian attack on the Albany neighbourhood, similar to the disastrous one of 1745. Some settlement took place clandestinely under the supervision of Colonel John Henry Lydius, the son of the Dutch Reformed minister of Albany, who possessed no patent to the land but had bought directly from the Indians.[128] Only in 1759 after the French threat from Canada had vanished did the government of New York feel sufficiently confident about its ability to protect this northern frontier for the Lieutenant Governor, James DeLancey, to issue a proclamation declaring the lands between Fort Edward and Lake George open for settlement. Potential settlers were encouraged by the information that there were at least two dozen cleared lots, then vacant, which had huts built upon them, and which had been used by the British troops and New York levies in 1757 and 1758. The huts were to be made available to those families who wished to settle the land. Upon DeLancey's death in 1760, his successor as Lieutenant Governor, Cadwallader Colden, rescinded this proclamation and declared that settlement near Fort Edward would have to await a settled peace.

As far as the patented lands in which Warren had a part were concerned nothing was done until 1765, when the patent holders ordered a survey to be made at a cost of NY£589 4s.[129] Warren's share came to 1,924 acres. There were twenty-four lots in the principal division, of which half fronted on the east bank of the Hudson and the rest were immediately to the rear.[130] In 1768, Margaret Sherriff, the daughter of Peter Bayard, who had been one of Warren's original partners in the land grant, sold her share of the patent to the other partners. The cost to the Warren heirs was NY£302 12s. 9d.[131] This represented the only occasion that DeLancey ever added to the land holdings of the Warrens.

Of the original patentees to the Fort Edward tract, the Warrens were the last to organize settlement on their portion. DeLancey used as his agent Patrick Smyth, the local Justice of the Peace at Fort Edward, who already acted on behalf of several of the patentees and who had informed DeLancey that several of Lydius's tenants were cutting down much timber on the Warren tract.[132] DeLancey, when appointing Smyth in May 1768, instructed him not to: "suffer any Person to Settle on or Committ any Trespass or Cutt Timber but as soon as possible

Turn off every Person that Pretends to Hold under Lydius and Put such people on as are like to be good Tennants and will immediately take Leases and You meet with any Difficulty apply to M^r. Peter Silvester that they may be lawfully ejected."[133] Silvester was an attorney in Schenectady, whom DeLancey employed on his own behalf and on behalf of the Warren estate on matters relating to their tracts on the Mohawk.[134]

There then remained the matter of finding suitable tenants, giving them leases, and hoping that their improvements would be such that they would in time be able to pay their rents. Even before the 1765 survey was undertaken one of Colonel Lydius's settlers, Daniel Dunham, had attempted without success to contact DeLancey to ask him for a lease. In May 1767 Dunham, fearing that he would be turned off the land he had improved, wrote to DeLancey begging for a lease. He pointed out that he and his son-in-law, Ezekiel Spicer, had settled about 160 or 170 acres, and since their arrival four years earlier they had fenced about sixty and cleared about half of this.[135] An accommodation was worked out, by which Dunham and Spicer received a lease for ninety-seven acres. The rest of the farm was let to John Reid, on a twenty-one years' lease. Like all other leases it was rent free for the first five years, and thereafter he had to pay NY£4 6s. a year and 3s. 1d. quit rent. Almost two-thirds of the Warren tract was filled by tenants on the eve of the War of Independence, by which time the Warren estate could expect an annual rental income of NY£57 12s.[136] In fact, no such sums were ever forthcoming, the war, which witnessed much fighting in the neighbourhood, having entirely frustrated DeLancey's plans. Even by 1787, when the Warren interest in New York began to be divided, there was not a tenant on the tract.[137]

What mattered of course was not the gross income but the net, and this depended as much upon the tenant's ability and willingness to pay his rent as upon the fluctuating rate of exchange on sterling bills, by which Oliver DeLancey transferred funds to the Warrens and their heirs. Unfortunately it is impossible to state the exact net income from the Warrens' New York land investments. Warren certainly received very little by way of rent from his American properties in his own lifetime. The only income came from that part of his Greenwich estate let to Governor Clinton, from his houses and stables, and his few tenants on Cortlandt Manor. No accounts have survived to provide a detailed picture, but it is improbable that his income exceeded £150 in any one year from 1745 to 1752. After his death neither his widow nor his children ever received income equal to the stated rents, despite the vigilance of DeLancey in New York City and of Pierre Van Cortlandt at the manor. The refusal of John Tabor Kempe to honour his father's debts to the Warren estate was a dramatic example of where rental income, although apparently perfectly secure, failed to be paid. The reluctance of the executors of Captain Henry Cosby to claim from the Navy Board the rental income due to the Warren estate for the facilities at Turtle Bay affords a similar example. However, the usual difficulty was the poverty of the tenant. There were always a few such families both at Cortlandt Manor and in New York, particularly on Lombard Street. Some of these cases were turned out of their homes and off their farms and replaced by more reliable tenants. Nevertheless it is clear from DeLancey's accounts that he managed to collect usually as much as eighty per cent of the rent due to the estate as a whole. This was impressive in view of the difficult circumstances owing to the scattered nature of the Warren properties. Nevertheless these figures compared unfavourably with those on the Warren estates in Ireland and Hampshire, where there is no evidence to show that rents ever went uncollected.[138]

The War of Independence disturbed this pattern considerably, for all the Warren properties except those on Manhattan Island remained in American hands for most of the war years. This loss of income was partly offset by the inflationary rents that prevailed in New York City during this period. The return of peace led to the resumption of rent payments, though on a much reduced scale, until the New York properties were disposed of after 1787. The decline in the income from Turtle Bay was dramatic, while there were many vacant tenancies at Oswego Market on Cortlandt Street even in the late 1780s. Fort Edward tract was without tenants, and Cortlandt Manor, at least temporarily, had few tenants willing to pay rent.

The effect of war, however important, was but temporary; of more lasting influence was the effect of inflation upon rental income. Since the principal part of rents collected were remitted to England,[139] what is important here in calculating the effect of inflation is not a study of New York prices,[140] but a consideration of the movement of prices in England and the fluctuation in the rate of exchange between New York currency and sterling. Estimates based on English consumers' goods show that the Price Index moved from 93 in 1752 (1701 = 100), to

100 in 1759, then to 117 in 1772, where it also stood unchanged in 1787.[141] If the figures for rents receivable on the Warren New York estates are adjusted to take into account this modest rate of inflation, by using the formula rent roll/price index × 100, then the real gross rents receivable were rather different from the nominal rents, as table 4 explains.

TABLE 4 *New York: Adjusted Rents Receivable*

Date	Rent Roll	Price Index	Adjusted Rent Roll
1752	NY£306 15s.	93	NY£320 3s. 3d.
1759	589 11s. 6d.	100	589 11s. 6d.
1772	1151 19s. 10d.	117	984 12s.
1787	1185 1s. 7d.	117	1011 19s.

Base: 1701 = 100

Source: Miscellaneous Warren Papers and Gage Papers.

In addition to the slight impact of inflation, the Warrens' position was marginally affected by fluctuations in the exchange rate between New York currency and sterling. Their absentee status after 1747 meant that remissions of rent were made to England. The depreciation of New York's currency from the 1740s to the 1790s was not great, though it was subject to much fluctuation, which sometimes caused the Warren interests losses. The range was between NY£160 to NY£195 for £100.[142] Heavy wartime borrowing in 1746-47 and the generally unfavourable impact of war on trade brought about a sharp rise in the exchange rate, so that by 1748 NY£190 was needed for a £100 bill. Peace in 1748 brought an immediate decline to around NY£175; and in the years following the exchange rate did not reach wartime levels.

With the onset of a new war, of particular importance to New York after 1756 when the province became the principal base of British operations against the French in America, many good sterling bills were available at remarkably cheap rates, often as low as NY£170. However from 1760 the situation deteriorated moderately bringing about a rise in the exchange rate. The tapering off of military expenditure in New York and the economic dislocation caused by the general peace in 1763 were the initial causes. Thereafter until the Revolution the effect of Britain's serious intervention in the commercial life of the colonies and the consequent hostile reaction of the American merchant community caused the rate to rise and fluctuate between NY£180 and NY£185 From the viewpoint of Warren, his widow, and heirs it was irritating never to be certain in advance what their New York properties would produce, but in fact their losses resulting both from the eroding effects of inflation and fluctuating exchange rates must have been no more than 1 per cent per annum.

Another inroad on income from New York land, of more consequence than these, was the cost of maintaining the properties themselves. In most years at least 5 per cent of the gross rental income was absorbed by the cost of repairs to Manhattan Island property alone. The older houses at Greenwich and in New York City proper, as well as the wharf at Turtle Bay and Warren's Wharf at the foot of Cortlandt Street, were the chief culprits.[143]

Taxes were an equally heavy burden. New York's first property tax law had been passed in 1683.[144] In the first half of the eighteenth century such taxes became more frequent to meet the cost of provincial borrowing.[145] Thus of a NY£48,350 loan floated in 1737 NY£8,350 was to be secured by land tax income, based on an assessment to be carried out throughout the colony. In 1746 the entire new loan of NY£53,000 was secured by tax on real estate and personal estate assessments. A further NY£28,000 was added in 1747, NY£125,000 in 1755-56, NY£350,000 in 1758-59, NY£60,000 in 1760, and finally NY£120,000 in 1770, all of which loans were secured more or less on the same basis of projected land and personal income tax. As land was by far the chief item of wealth in colonial New York, it bore the principal burden of this direct taxation. In addition property owners were assessed the tithe for the support of the established Church, and rates for the support of the poor of the parish. Finally some property, usually land granted by the crown or city, paid quit rent annually. All such charges were familiar enough to English landowners. There was one significant difference between the situation in New York and in England, for, whereas in England the level of assessment was borne unevenly from county to county, and had become fixed, in New York assessments were brought up to date with the changing value of property, while the tax was borne by the counties best able to pay.[146]

In the matter of quit rents the whole of Cortlandt Manor, according to the terms of the original 1697 grant, paid a token forty shillings currency per annum. None of this small amount was payable by the Warren estate. On the other hand the property at Fort Edward paid the usual 4s. per 100 acres; but DeLancey had succeeded in making such payment part of the tenants' leases; so it was in theory no loss to the estate. In 1773 DeLancey asked the Receiver General of New York, Andrew Elliott, the amount then owing on the Warrens' share of the Fort Edward grant, and in June 1774 paid NY£108 19s. 3d.[147] Much of this of course was never received from the Fort Edward tenants because of the onset of war, and because the tract was only partially tenanted by 1776. Quit rent was also due to New York for the ten acres granted Warren in 1745 adjoining his Greenwich estate. This amounted to NY£4 a year at the rate of 8s. an acre. Furthermore, a quit rent was charged on Warren's Wharf for the 1758 grant of the water lots on which it was erected; and this amounted to almost NY£2 a year.

As far as the land tax, the tithe, and poor rate were concerned both Cortlandt Manor and Fort Edward were free of assessment, payment being restricted to Warren's Manhattan properties. In his accounts, DeLancey did not make a distinction between the poor rate and the tithe which, for instance, in the period 1772-74 amounted to NY£39 (see table 5).

TABLE 5 *New York: Poor Rates And Tithes*

	1772	1773	1774
Greenwich estate	NY£ 3 17s. 3d.	NY£ 4 19s. 2d.	NY£ 7 14s. 2d.
Turtle Bay	3	2 16s. 8d.	3 1s. 8d.
New York City	5 5s.	5 7s. 8d.	4 19s. 2d.
Total:	NY£11 2s. 3d.	NY£12 3s. 6d.	NY£15 15s.

Source: Gage Papers, G/Am/142, G/Am/158, G/Am/170.

In the matter of the land tax the 1768 assessment serves as an example. The tax was ten per cent of the assessed value, with Greenwich being assessed at NY£100, Turtle Bay at NY£30, and the New York City properties at NY£70 for a total of NY£200 and a total tax payment of NY£20.[148]

Finally, from the gross income of the estate the agents' fees had to be paid. In lieu of a commission, Oliver DeLancey lived rent-free at Greenwich Old Farm from 1761 to 1775. In 1772 he charged the Warren estate part of the costs he had himself borne when in 1752-53 he went to England to put Admiral Warren's affairs in order. In 1774 he demanded a commission for handling the affairs of the Warren heirs, the only occasion when such a demand was made by him. His successor in 1783 as agent for the Warren interests in America, John Watts Jr., invariably charged a commission both for paying and receiving money, as well as for effecting sales of land.[149] In addition Pierre Van Cortlandt, the collector of rents at Cortlandt Manor, also was paid a commission, for instance, NY£4 4s. 9d. in 1768 and NY£6 10s. in 1772.[150] In general the accounts are too fragmentary to form a complete picture of this cost to the estate, and all the others mentioned earlier. Table 6 attempts a recapitulation of the evidence already

TABLE 6 *Summary of Outgoings: New York Property*

Uncollected rent	20% of gross per annum
Inflation and depreciation	1
Commissions	10
Repairs	5
Taxes, tithes, quit rent, and poor rate	5
Miscellaneous (surveys, etc.)	4
Total Up to	45

Source: Miscellaneous Warren Papers and Gage Papers.

presented. Even though little income was received during Admiral Warren's lifetime, the gross rents receivable were in excess of NY£195. A trickle came from Cortlandt Manor, none from Fort Edward, very small amounts from New York City, none from Turtle Bay, while only Greenwich produced substantial income. The income from Greenwich probably more or less paid the expenses arising from the entire estate for maintenance, taxes, quit rents, tithes, poor rate, and depreciation of the currency. Only when Oliver DeLancey took charge of the Warren estates in 1753 was there regular income, though a reasonable estimate must place the net amount at no more than 55 per cent of the gross rents receivable on average from 1753 to 1775. After 1783 the estate would have been lucky to have received as much as 10 per cent of its anticipated rents, and undoubtedly was carried on at a loss.[151]

The situation would have been intolerable long before 1776 had not the New York properties experienced the great rise in rents already described.[152] This general rise was reflected in a steady growth in the estimated value of the estate as a whole. The details are outlined in table 7.

TABLE 7 *New York Property: Estimated Value*

	Cost	1759	1772	1787
Greenwich	NY£1,930	NY£ 4,600	NY£ 4,610	NY£12,560
Turtle Bay	885	1,000	2,000	1,500
New York City	2,005	6,900	11,000	11,450
Cortlandt Manor	3,150	9,800	13,500	13,145
Fort Edward	404	—	2,500	2,100
Total	NY£8,374	NY£22,300	NY£43,610	NY£40,755

Source: Gage Papers, G/Am/69, G/Am/141, Warren Papers 68, NYHS.

In the cost has been included not only the purchase price, but also such capital costs as surveys, road building, and the erection of wharves. For lack of evidence, the total does not include the cost of some New York City properties. Otherwise instead of NY£8,374, the actual cost would probably have been over NY£8,500. This relatively small investment grew prodigiously before the outbreak of war in 1776; but the capital gain was not realized since neither the Warrens nor their heirs were inclined to sell the New York property. Their confidence in the soundness of the investment, both for the income it produced and the capital gain it promised, remained unshaken throughout the colonial era. The value of the property was of course somewhat inflated owing to the general rise in prices after 1752; and

TABLE 8 *New York Property: Adjusted Valuation*

Date	Nominal Value	Price Index	Adjusted Value
to 1752	NY£ 8,500	93	NY£ 9,140
1759	22,300	100	22,300
1772	43,610	117	37,265
1787	40,755	117	34,786

Base: 1701 = 100

Source: Schumpeter, "English Prices and Public Finances," p. 35.

table 8 adjusts the stated valuation in relation to the rise in prices of English consumers' goods.

The confident estimate by the Warrens and their heirs of New York as a province growing in wealth was doubtlessly based principally upon the increased value of their landed property there. Advised by Oliver DeLancey, whose principal wealth was also in land and whose career was as much that of land speculator as merchant and contractor to the British army in America, they were conscious of the advantages of holding on to their estates. Part of the rise, as table 8 shows, was occasioned by inflation, of which they could have only been vaguely aware. Part resulted from the advantageous location of their property in areas of New York which experienced the principal population growth, namely Manhattan Island and Westchester County where the Cortlandt Manor estates were located.

The 1776-83 war severely dislocated this steady growth in income and upset the land market for some time afterwards. The settlements near Fort Edward were entirely abandoned, the tenants dispersed, and improvements curtailed. At Cortlandt Manor internal war broke out between the tenants and small farmers; many farms as a result were destroyed and some tenants forced to flee. New York City, held by the British from the arrival of Howe in 1776 until the peace in 1783, lost much of its American population in the great exodus of 1776. However, by making the city the chief military arsenal in America, the British created a boom for landowners. This inflationary situation was further artificially generated by the influx of Loyalist refugees, for whom the city was a temporary haven before exile was forced on them in 1783. Thus, the Warren properties in the city reaped a large income before 1776, and during the war income seems to have advanced substantially, despite the fact that at least seven houses had been destroyed by the 1776 fire and were not rebuilt so long as they remained part of the Warren estate.

The outcome of the war with the colonists convinced the Warren heirs that they must sell their New York properties, though the laws neither of New York State nor later of the United States made this mandatory. The Treaty of Versailles had not only ensured that those Loyalists who had suffered confiscation would receive compensation, but also that those British subjects who owned real estate in the former colonies would have a year in which to make good their titles if they were in any way disputed by American citizens. Later the Treaty of London in 1794 stipulated that "British Subjects who now hold Lands in the Territories of the United States . . . shall continue to hold them according to the Nature and Tenure of their respective Estates therein, and may grant, sell, or Devise the same to whom they please, in like manner as if they were Natives; and that neither they nor their Heirs or assigns shall, so far as may respect the said Lands, and the legal remedies incident thereto, be regarded as Aliens."[153] The same rights were accorded American citizens who owned land in His Majesty's dominions.

The exact reason influencing the decision of the Warren heirs to sell their property is not known, but undoubtedly it was connected with the desire of the Earl of Abingdon to dispose of his wife's one-third share. Already in 1774 he had sold his share in the Warrens' Irish estate to the other two Warren sons-in-law, Charles Fitzroy, and Col. William Skinner, while the year before in 1773 he and Fitzroy had sold their shares of the Warrens' Hampshire estate to Col. Skinner. In 1772 Abingdon had seriously considered selling his share of the American assets but delayed until war interrupted his plans. When the war was over he took an early opportunity to order a survey of the Warren property in New York, upon which an equitable division could be made. In March 1787, with the survey completed, an elaborate agreement was concluded between Abingdon, Fitzroy, who since 1780 had had the title of Lord Southampton, and Susanna Maria Skinner, a minor and the only daughter of Col. Skinner, who died in 1780.[154] The property, based on a new evaluation, was divided as equally as possible into three shares. The Greenwich estate, Cortlandt Manor, and the properties in New York City were divided between the three, while Turtle Bay went to Miss Skinner, the Fort Edward tract being divided between Abingdon and Southampton.

The property had been valued at NY£40,755 and was disposed of largely by John Watts. How much the property fetched or how quickly it was sold is uncertain; however, the decision to sell had been taken in the midst of a serious post-war slump in land prices, which did not recover until late in 1791. It is known that Miss Skinner received NY£13,180 which was 3.7 per cent above the 1787 estimated value of her NY£12,710 share of the division of property.[155] This increase partly stems from some of the property being sold as late as 1794, when land prices had greatly recovered. The delay in disposing of her share, which apparently proved fortuitous, was because she remained a minor until 1791, two years after her marriage to Henry Gage, the son of General Thomas Gage and Margaret Kemble, the daughter of Peter Kemble the President of the New Jersey Council. Her husband, who through his father had also inherited extensive lands in the upper Mohawk valley, appointed John Watts and Peter Kemble Jr., his uncle, to oversee the disposal of all his and Susanna Maria's New York property. In April 1791 Greenwich Old Farm, Warren's first New York purchase, was sold by them for NY£2,000 to DeWitt Clinton, the future governor of New York State.[156] Later in the same year Turtle Bay was sold for NY£1,500 to Francis Winthrop.[157] Both properties fetched exactly the 1787 estimate of their value. Several of the Gage properties were subsequently sold to tenants. The ten-acre lot given Warren in 1745 by New York City, let to Isaac Varion at NY£30 a year before the war, was sold to him for NY£600, some NY£50 above the 1787 valuation.[158] One of the Cortlandt Manor farms was sold in 1794 to a long-time tenant, Captain David Montross for NY£418 16s. or NY£2 8s. an acre, when the 1787 estimate thought it worth NY£3 an acre.[159] In all, the Cortlandt Manor farms owned by the Gages sold for NY£3,300, well below the NY£4,260 estimated value, and at an average of NY£2 6s. 8d. per acre.

In view of the great appreciation in New York land values in the eighteenth century, Warren's investments appear both wise and visionary, while the sale by his heirs by contrast appears short-sighted and unimaginative. Warren's investment was based upon extensive and intimate knowledge of the province's economy, while the subsequent sale was occasioned as much by the absentees' ignorance of New York as by the impact of the War of Independence. Warren had possessed an enthusiasm for the new world which his heirs never experienced. The heirs in fact epitomized the aristocratic hostility to the successful American revolution. Fitzroy earlier had sacrificed his own political career to aid his brother, the Duke of Grafton, whose attitude consistently opposed the radical American position. Henry Gage, later the third Viscount Gage, son of General Thomas Gage, commander-in-chief in North America from 1763 until after Bunker Hill in 1775, adopted an equally unrelenting hostility towards the American New Whigs. The Earl of Abingdon's view was rather different, for in 1778 he had published in Oxford a pamphlet[160] which soundly rebuked Burke for not following up with sufficient energy his first great speeches against the American war. The publication established his place as one of the noteworthy defenders in Parliament of the American cause. His motive in taking a stand so unpopular among his fellow peers might have been liberal, but in view of his own pressing financial difficulties, which had obliged him to liquidate his share of the Warren assets both in England and Ireland, he was perhaps trying to protect his considerable American assets in land and loans, which temporarily were to his embarrassment quite illiquid. Thus all three of Warren's heirs were debarred either psychologically or financially from retaining their large financial stake in America on behalf of a further generation. Had the Warren daughters and grand-daughters chosen as husbands other than members of the English and Irish peerage, the story could well have been different. It might in that case have resembled more the history of the family of George Clarke, who had served as New York's Secretary for more than thirty years before acting as Lieutenant Governor between 1736 and 1743, and retiring to England. Clarke's years in New York had secured him a considerable fortune, especially in land on the frontier.[161] His property had not been confiscated during the American war; and his heirs subsequently returned, laid successful claim to his estate, and settled in New York where their descendants still thrive.

Clarke's long association with the province had "bred in him little feeling for the province and no social attachment to it,"[162] while Warren had a passionate and enduring love for his adopted home. Warren's feelings, curiously, were not shared by his widow, a native New Yorker, who chose to remain in England after his death. Nor was Warren a mere absentee manipulator, like Governor William Cosby who made a modest fortune by demanding kickbacks on all lands which he granted, or like the Duke of Chandos, another large absentee landowner, who, though having no connection with New York, used his position at court to secure the royal patent to the "Oblong," that vast tract ceded by Connecticut to New York in settlement of a serious boundary dispute. Yet, unlike the Livingstons, one of the wealthiest of New York's landowning families who successfully developed iron ore on their estates, Warren clearly had no taste for industrial development. Venture capital was needed to develop the Cortlandt Manor iron works; but instead of advancing it, Warren sold his share in the enterprise. Its successful exploitation would have put his heirs in a good position to participate in the modest boom which was enjoyed by the industry between 1750 and 1775.[163]

Warren's relatively small capital investment (roughly NY£8,500) in land grew prodigiously, its nominal value rising almost four times by 1775. When after 1787 the estates were sold, land values had more or less again reached their pre-war levels as the economy of New York State gathered momentum. Subsequently the price of land, especially on Manhattan Island, made sharp advances.

In view of the rapid rise in the nominal value of the estates it was not surprising that the gross rate of return was small. If figures adjusted for inflation are used,[164] then a return of 2.3 per cent was achieved in 1752 and 2.6 per cent in 1772. If, as it has been argued, up to 45 per cent of rents receivable were not remitted to England, then the net rate of return was only 1.3 per cent in 1752 and 1.5 per cent in 1772.

The sale of land after 1787 might have come sooner had not Warren's will specifically left his property in common to his three daughters, with his wife acting as tenant until they came of age. In fact he would have had little to fear from his widow for she never expressed the least interest in selling land, even where she was absolutely free to do so. For instance, Greenwich Old Farm was reckoned to be hers by way of gift from her husband, yet she refused Oliver DeLancey's very attractive offers of purchase. Besides the share in Cortlandt Manor which she had inherited from her mother, she also inherited a small house on Broadway, a 1,413–acre spread at Clifton Park, two farms amounting to 362 acres on Wappinger's Creek (a tributary of the Hudson lying north of Cortlandt Manor), and a share in the Minisink Patent in the counties of Orange and Ulster. Oliver DeLancey at times advised her to sell these lands, but she refused, leaving them jointly to her daughters, who divided them in 1787.

Ironically her resistance to DeLancey's sales pressure arose partly from the success which had characterized his management of her interests. A skilled land speculator himself, he had for years exploited the possibilities of Warren's investments in land on her behalf. As tenant in Greenwich Old Farm he had rebuilt the house, laid out orchards, plantations of trees, ornamental gardens, and cultivated the soil fully conscious of advanced farming methods, thus adding substantially to the value of the property. Failing to induce his sister to sell the property, he suggested the subdivision of the Greenwich estate; and when this was agreed upon by the Warren heirs, he superintended the development and thereby greatly increased its value. Through DeLancey's efforts the Cortlandt Street property was subdivided at great profit to the Warren estate. It was he who suggested the erecting of Warren's Wharf, which in the wartime boom of 1758-60 and for long afterwards brought a vastly increased income to the Warrens. He scrambled to get bills of exchange for his remittances to the Warrens at the most favourable rates of exchange, as if the money were his. Finally he kept both his sister and the Warren heirs much better informed than Peter Warren had been about his affairs, when James DeLancey and Richard Nicholls handled them. If Peter Warren was the man with the capital ready to risk in the new world, DeLancey was the entrepreneur working in the best interests of the shareholders, while making only a modest amount for his skill and devotion.

This study of the Warrens' New York interests also highlights the role of the absentee landowner whose estates survived intact the era of the American Revolution. Although the role of the Loyalists, who suffered confiscation and were forced into exile, has at least received some attention from scholars,[165] the position of those British subjects who held American assets up to 1783 but who were protected by the terms of the Peace Treaty of 1783 has largely been ignored.[166] The Warrens and their heirs were one such family; but whether they were part of a large group or a very select few in New York or elsewhere in America has yet to be established. Only further research into the American affairs of British subjects in the post-war era will reveal how unsettling to their interests the war actually proved to be. Such a study would reveal, for instance, how property under American rule during the war actually escaped confiscation. Although there is no evidence that the Warren interests received special consideration from the State of New York, the Warren heirs could surely count themselves fortunate that their lands were left untouched, especially in view of their close connection with the DeLancey family, which sustained massive losses for its very active role against the Americans. Until more is known it is impossible to say if the experience of the Warren estate was typical or very rare.

Chapter 4

American Estates II:

Mohawk Valley Settlement

1736-1787

Of all his properties in America the 16,200–acre tract on the Mohawk River near Fort Hunter at the confluence of the Schoharie interested Warren the most. His vision was to transform a wilderness into a prosperous settlement. His willingness to venture a great deal of capital on the scheme in the late 1730s and early 1740s was quite unique in the Mohawk Valley until after the defeat of French power in Canada.

Long the home of the Mohawk tribe, one of the five nations of the Iroquois confederacy, the Mohawk valley had only been opened to American settlers a few decades before Warren's interest focused there. As the domain of the Indian it had seen only the occasional fur trader, some French Jesuits, and French raiding parties sent down from Montreal and Quebec. The first Dutch settlements had made their way into the valley from Fort Orange (Albany) in 1661, when Schenectady was founded seventeen miles to the northwest. The village was abandoned in 1690 when Canadians and their Indian allies destroyed the settlement killing many of the inhabitants. Only when Fort Hunter was built in 1711 still farther to the west did permanent settlements become established in the valley. Only in 1723 were the first homesteads erected west of Fort Hunter, and until the defeat of the French in 1760 it remained in every sense a frontier. Little of the land still belonged to the Indians, most of it being held by speculators like Lieutenant Governor George Clarke, whose elaborate plan for the settlement of the New York frontier from Schenectady to the Genesee

Valley never matured. The land speculator, while going to the trouble and expense of gaining title to the land, was not then prepared to put up the necessary capital for its development.

Yet all agreed that the valley had unlimited prospects. The surveyor-general of New York, Cadwallader Colden, believed that no other part of the province had such rich soil, grew such fine wheat, or offered better pasturage. In view of the excellent river systems, Albany and New York were easily accessible. Moreover only a short portage separated the Mohawk from the headwaters of the Susquehanna and the tidewater ports of Pennsylvania, Maryland, and Virginia. Alternatively, by carrying on to the northwest, across the Oneida carrying place, men could easily reach Lake Ontario, Lake Erie, and the interior of the continent.[1]

Warren's tract, called Chuctenunda and later Warrensburg, was largely part of a grant made in August 1735 to Charles Williams and seven other New Yorkers, who then conveyed most of it to Governor William Cosby. Cosby died the following March, and his widow sold it to Warren in July 1736 for £130. Warren, who had been absent from American waters since 1732, had been named captain of the New England station ship, and on his way to Boston from Spithead had put in at New York. He agreed to convey Mrs. Cosby to Boston; and during their brief passage the deal was concluded.[2] When the news of the sale reached New York it proved sufficiently noteworthy for Daniel Horsmanden, a member of the Provincial Council and supporter of Cosby's to remark to Cadwallader Colden, another Cosby advocate and fellow-councillor: "How she became so Infatuated I know not, Sure it could not be so trifling a Sum ready money that Bewitched her but so it is Which being done I suppose the Captn. will have no thoughts at present abo^t. getting any other Tract, and I understand as much from the Chief Justice the other day talking upon This Subject."[3]

Warren was able in time to add to this initial large purchase so that when the first accurate survey was taken in 1765-66, the tract measured 16,200 acres.[4] Two thousand acres were added by a purchase from the attorney general of New York, Richard Bradley, though neither the date of sale nor the cost to Warren is known. In addition, there was a choice parcel of land on the banks of the Mohawk in the very middle of Warren's tract lying across the flats formed by the confluence of Chuctenunda Creek and the Mohawk, which Warren coveted. This property was purchased by Joseph Cowley in 1736 from Captain Walter Butler, occasional commander of the garrisons both at Fort Hunter

and Oswego. To finance the purchase Cowley raised a NY£300 mortgage from Abraham Lodge. In November 1742 the mortgage and
unpaid interest, then amounting in all to NY£398 15s. was assigned to
Warren.[5] As early as 1738 Warren had had his eye on it, saying, "I
make no doubt of haveing it one time or another."[6] Cowley never
attempted to recover the property, so that by the 1750s it was considered part of the Warren estate.[7] Finally Warren also bought a 600–acre
tract on the north side of the Mohawk River, roughly opposite his
Chuctenunda land, but not on the shoreline. It was acquired before
May 1740 from the Reverend John Miln, Susannah Warren's brother-
in-law, though the actual price and date of sale are not known.[8]

The Chuctenunda tract, or Warrensburg, was an irregular quadrangle with its northeast base on the south bank of the Mohawk. Its
northwest boundary was formed by a straight line drawn from a point
two and a half miles downstream from the confluence of the Mohawk
and Schoharie Creek, to a point some three miles up the Schoharie.
The Schoharie then formed the western limits of the tract for about
five miles. The last side of the quadrangle was formed by a straight line
from the Schoharie to a point on the Mohawk roughly opposite present
day Cranesville, a distance of almost eight miles.[9] On a modern map
it forms most of the township of Florida in the county of Montgomery,
and includes the southern portion of the town of Amsterdam, which
straddles the Mohawk. This southern ward, formerly Port Jackson, was
situated at the mouth of Chuctenunda Creek, which roughly divided
the tract into two equal parts. Along the Mohawk a road linking Fort
Hunter and Schenectady had been hacked out of the primeval forest.
The land was rolling. Much of it was situated 600 feet above the river
valley. From the valley the ground rose steeply leaving little of the
desirable flats, on which the Indians for generations had raised their
corn, wheat, and peas. Nevertheless the highland had good soil, clay
covered by a layer of loam, which erosion in time carried away. The
tract was well watered with several creeks pouring into both the Schoharie and the Mohawk.

Peter Warren was quick to realize that so long as he remained at
Boston or was otherwise actively engaged at sea he could not personally see to the details of the development of the Mohawk valley tract.
It was also too much to expect his agent in New York, the chief justice
of the province, to undertake special trips up the Hudson to Albany
to grant leases and collect rents. Warren soon decided on an alternative. He invited two of his Irish nephews to come to America and

superintend the settlement. One was William Johnson,[10] the eldest son of Warren's sister Anne, and the other was Michael Tyrrell, one of the two sons of his sister Mary. Early in 1738 the two young men, together with a dozen Irish families, sailed from Dublin to Boston.[11] There, after a brief stop where they collected from their uncle all the supplies purchased for their journey, they made their way overland to Albany,[12] and thence via Schenectady to the tract.[13]

Warren had a clear idea of what he wanted from his nephews. Yet since he had never actually penetrated to the frontier, he could not have known the real difficulties of the task he had asked them to undertake. He was confident especially that Johnson's "diligence and Application [would] put him in a good way."[14] Warren planned to give both Johnson and Tyrrell considerable support for the first three years, during which time the home farm would be brought into production, as many tenants as possible settled with long leases, and trade opened both with the settlers and the Indians. Warren would supply the necessary capital, for which the two would be accountable. They were not to be required to pay interest either on these funds or on the value of the goods sent to them, and they could employ the farm's profits for their own use. Warren's return was to come in time from rental income, from trade, and especially from the capital appreciation of the land through the labour of both the co-managers and their tenants.[15]

The home farm was soon established on a 200-acre lot near the Mohawk River about a mile downstream from Chuctenunda Creek, and adjoining Cowley's land.[16] Like most pioneers in the wilderness, Johnson and Tyrrell had to hack their farm acre by acre from the grip of the forest. Even though Johnson claimed to have "laboured sorely the best of My days"[17] there, he probably spent no more than two years on the place, the bulk of the work thereafter devolving upon an overseer and his wife, whom Johnson hired. Tyrrell, for his part, took the first opportunity to leave, and in June 1740 joined the New York contingent enlisted for service against Spain in the West Indies.[18] Tyrrell's companionship may have been missed, but his labour was not essential as Warren kept Johnson well-supplied with both white and black workers. From Boston he sent a smith and several other labourers, and in May 1740 there were three black slaves on the farm and four more were sent between 1740 and 1744.[19] Johnson bought a female slave in New York in August 1740, and Warren sent him another nineteen in the summer of 1744.[20] This made Warren and Johnson among the largest slave owners in the province, at a time when New York had "the largest slave force in any English colony north of Maryland.[21] Once slavery had been introduced into New York, neither the colonial administration nor private individuals made much effort to recruit free workers or even indentured labourers.[22] Despite the rise in New York's population after 1750, men complained of a continued chronic shortage of free labour, which in the last decades of the colonial era actually increased the dependence on slaves. Of the slaves at Warrensburg three were soon sold, and three more eventually returned to New York City being employed on Warren's Greenwich estate.[23] Two others were let to a tenant at Warrensburg, a profitable practice that was widespread in the colony.[24] From this it seems clear that although Johnson at first worked alongside his slaves and paid labourers, it was on them, not him, that the main burden fell.[25]

The speed with which the clearing was made and the energy expended by Johnson and Tyrrell greatly tempted Warren to come and view the improvements in 1739. The outbreak of war, and the obligation to sail from Boston at once for the Florida coast prevented him getting there in 1739. Even when the war was in its third season he still anticipated seeing the estate. In 1741, for instance, Michael Tyrrell reported to Johnson from Jamaica that Warren hoped "to go up to Albany in Next Summer to see the Improvements."[26] Warren apparently intended building a church for his tenants and erecting a small fortification for their protection. However, when Warren returned to New York in August 1741 he had orders to convoy several New England mast ships to England, and was kept in New York City by the need to prepare his ship for its homeward passage. His great ambition remained unsatisfied.

Warren had his own notions about the appearance the farm should assume. These he expressed in an early letter to Johnson:

> I hope you will plant a large Orchard in the Spring. it wont hinder your Indian Corn nor Grass, as you will plant your trees at a great distance. I shou'd think it wou'd be worth your while to inquier strictly if y[e]. Medow you Mention is on My land, for it wou'd help you with and twoud be a good place to plant Corn in . . . as you have great help now you will Girdle Many Acres, in doing which I would be regular, and do it in Square fields, and leave Hedge rows at each Side which will keep the land warm, bee very Butiful, and no more Expence then doing it in a slovenly Iregular Manner

. . . I will send you y^e. vine and the other things you Mention in the Spring . . . get y^e. best kind of fruit trees for the Orchard if they cost something More, and a good Nursery would not be amiss.[27]

There is no reason to doubt that Johnson carried out these orders as well as he could and as the lay of the land permitted, for he fully expected his uncle to appear and inspect his work. The plan of the farm shows pastureland, meadows, arable land, and woodlots, as well as two considerable orchards, one near the house and along the edge of the road, and the other midway between the house and the river.[28] Warren also wanted the farm's surplus shipped either to Boston or to New York for sale.[29] From the evidence there is every reason to believe that Johnson created a prosperous farm in a very short time, and the profit for many years from it was a comfortable source of income to him, and its produce his family's chief sustenance, even after he had established himself in a fine stone house on the other side of the Mohawk.

Of almost as much importance in Warren's mind was the trade which he wanted Johnson to carry on with settlers and Indians alike. His idea was that he would supply Johnson with the necessary goods, which would be imported from England and Ireland and which then would either be sold or traded for furs. Johnson would then remit his takings to Warren, who would use the profits to purchase more goods. In 1738 he explained his plan to Johnson and underlined some of the difficulties:

The difficulty will be in Makeing remittance, when you receive your goods if you can get a good profit for them in any of the towns and ready Mony. I wou'd sell as Many of them as I did not Imediatly want for the Suply of my Constant Customers, and remit y^e. mony as I shall hereafter direct . . . You see you will have a pretty good Cargo, the whole produce of it Must be remitted as soon As possible, to be laid out again till you with your Increase Can have a very large Store of goods of all kinds proper for that Country, pray lett Me know what Rum and all things sells for there such as Axes and other wrought iron, then I coud send from hence, If I found y^e. profit great I wou'd soon have a thousand pounds worth of goods there, what wou'd them leather Caps sell for, and what profit had you on the linnen and any of your goods.[30]

In the same letter he complained that Johnson had so far failed to give him detailed information about prices, nor even clear indications about which goods sold best. He complained, too, that Johnson did not acknowledge in detail the contents of each invoice. Warren was never able to get Johnson to cooperate as he would have liked in this matter. Although Johnson was quite prepared to sell or trade the goods his uncle sent him, he was less willing to remit funds or give detailed accounts to his uncle for anything he received from him; and even when he submitted a detailed statement of his expenses to the Warren heirs in 1754, he attached no vouchers and never produced any. Johnson's claim to be an honest steward of his uncle's estate can hardly be accepted.

Warren was very keen to have Johnson enter the fur trade directly with the Indians, and promised to ship to London whatever furs he managed to procure "and y^e. produce of them Shall be sent you in proper goods."[31] Johnson traded both at Oswego on Lake Ontario and at Oquago on the Susquehanna River, but the only record of his having used his uncle's agency is in 1741 when he sent Warren "Sundry Curious Skins" and Indian trinkets, which Warren wanted as gifts for his friends in England.[32]

Warren, true to his word, supplied Johnson and Tyrrell with an abundance of trading goods. Probably one-third of the initial shipment of supplies in 1738 was used for trade, the balance for the farm.[33] Goods sent by Warren thereafter can also be considered for trading purposes. Altogether this amounted to NY£2,932.[34] Among the trade items were rum and molasses, which Warren was keen to sell both to the Indians and the settlers at Warrensburg.[35] Johnson himself was not adverse to the sale of rum to Indians, although he cautioned his uncle about the Reverend Barclay, the parson of Queen Anne's chapel at Fort Hunter, who was then agitating for a provincial law to prohibit the trade, an attempt which proved unsuccessful.[36]

From Warren's viewpoint Johnson proved a very disappointing trader. There is no record of Johnson having remitted to him either funds or goods, except a very limited amount of farm produce, some timber, and a few Indian trinkets, for all of which Johnson later charged Warren's heirs. By the end of 1742 Warren stopped sending goods either for the farm or for trade; and took security by obliging his nephew to admit his indebtedness, in the customary manner, by signing two bonds to cover part of the cost. For his own future use, Warren also kept detailed records of what he had sent Johnson, but not a complete record. So long as these debts were unpaid, Warren received absolutely no return on the large investment he had made. Yet the importance of this credit to Johnson was immense and undoubtedly laid the basis of his own fortune.

If trade had originally held out to Warren the prospect of quick profits to help meet the costs of the Warrensburg settlement, the planting of settlers to tame the wilderness would alone guarantee long-term appreciation in the value of the tract and make the entire venture worthwhile. The settlement certainly thrived in its early years. Eight families were found to be squatting on the tract and in October 1736 they were given leases. Seven of the families were of German stock, who had come to New York in 1710 from the Rhenish Palatinate and neighbouring principalities. They had first settled on the western banks of the Hudson at Newburgh, about fifty-five miles above New York City.[37] They also settled in Livingston Manor with the view to producing naval stores for the province. But, dissatisfied with the restrictions placed on their affairs, they moved westward to the headwaters of the Schoharie, then up the valley, reaching the area of Fort Hunter by 1723. The families on Warren's tract were each assigned 200–acre lots with leases for their own lives and the lives of their eldest sons.[38] Rent was a nominal NY 5s. 9d. a year for the first ten years and NY £3 thereafter. Warren not only gave them almost NY £200 in provisions but also loaned them NY £178 free of interest for two years, and for which he took their joint bond. Later he loaned them small sums ranging between NY £3 and NY £16 16s.[39]

Later, when Johnson and Tyrrell came to Warrensburg, Warren instructed them to encourage as many families as possible to settle on the tract. He wanted them to be particularly friendly to the Palatines, explaining, "I dont Mean you should bee at any Expence in doing it only give them Countenance, and the smaller their farms y[e]. more the land will hould, and y[e]. better the Improvements will be."[40] Within a few months this policy seemed to pay off handsomely, for Johnson reported that he was being overrun by a rush of settlers, and appealed to his uncle, "Y[r]. Comeing here is much longed for by us. Severall Other who are inclined to Come and Settle on the land, but wait y[r]. Comeing, w[h]. I wish may be soon if it Suits wth. y[u]. They are all people in Good Circumstance and would like being near me in hopes of haveing a good Neighbourhood Soon here w[h]. I hope we shall."[41] A number of these families had to be housed by Johnson temporarily, while a survey of the entire tract, undertaken late in 1739 by Edward Collins, was completed.[42] By the spring of 1740, the work done, Johnson was able to conclude twenty-six leases. Several of these new settler families, like the earlier ones in 1736, were given loans by Johnson on his uncle's account.[43] This rapid influx of families proved shortlived. The outbreak of war with France in 1744, and the threat it posed for the New York frontier with Canada, undid most of Johnson's efforts and dashed Warren's hopes.

George Clarke, the lieutenant governor, spoke for many when in 1743 he told the Board of Trade of his failure to lure settlers in large numbers to the New York frontier, and explained that "the apprehension of a rupture with France deters them."[44] With the French, Canadians, and their Indian allies on the warpath in the vicinity of Fort Frederic and Saratoga, no frontiersman could feel secure. Their raids in 1745 and 1746 frightened away many, including some of Warren's new tenants. Only a few Palatine families clung tenaciously to their farms. Even after the Peace of Aix La Chapelle in 1748 few new settlers came to the Mohawk, so uncertain was the political situation between France and Britain. These years witnessed an ambitious frontier policy inspired by the governor of Canada, La Galissonière.[45] New York politicians and frontiersmen alike were gravely concerned by what they rightly considered to be a serious threat to their survival. The outbreak of hostilities with France in 1755-56, and the consequent invasion of the New York frontier confirmed their worst fears. Oliver DeLancey had visited Schenectady in 1755 in a vain attempt to collect rent from the Warren tenants. He went away empty-handed, and gravely explained to his sister, "They Complained So Much of Poverty and the Precarious Situtation they are in by the War that I could by no Means force them to Payment."[46] He earlier had told her that the mere "Rumour of French Warr"[47] had greatly depressed the value of the Mohawk tract, and that until a "Profound Peace" was concluded it would always be so. His estimate proved to be sound; the situation improved only after the fall of Montreal in 1760 and the diminution of French power in North America by the Peace of Paris in 1763.

When peace came to frontier New York in 1763, William Johnson no longer acted as the agent for the Warren interests on the Mohawk. His value to Warren had always been very limited in view of his own burgeoning business interests and his policy of milking his uncle for as much as possible. When Johnson learned the terms of Warren's will, sometime late in 1752, his usefulness came abruptly to an end, for covert resentment was then transformed into open hostility to the Warren interests. Warren's will, while expressing "great esteem" for Johnson, excused him only one-third of the debt due the Warren estate, the other two-thirds to be divided equally between Johnson's Irish brothers and sisters.[48] The debt actually amounted to NY £7,241, although Oliver DeLancey, acting for Lady Warren in 1754, only submitted an account for NY £6,820, one third being NY £2,273.[49] In Warren's mind this must have appeared a generous settlement especially in view of the profits Johnson had already enjoyed both from the produce of the home farm and from the trade financed by Warren. It was in line with what he had granted Warren Johnson, William's brother, whose debt of £1,050 had been excused.[50]

Johnson had been expecting Warren to leave him the 200–acre home farm at Warrensburg, and failing to get it he felt himself ill-used. He immediately resolved to submit an account against the Warren estate, to prove how ungenerous Warren had been. The statement amounted to NY £7,764, and included both principal and interest on the two sterling bonds he had given Warren as security for the trade and farm goods. The account also included NY £879 in miscellaneous expenses and NY £4,520 for improvements he claimed to have carried out on the home farm. What was curious was the fact that Johnson failed to attach any vouchers to his statement to prove his expenses. The NY £4,520 in farm improvements he detailed as follows:

> To the Expence of Improving that part of *Warrensburg* whereon S[r]. Peter ordered me to settle at my first coming here for 15 years and upwards, labour'd hard upon it.
>
> To an Overseer and his wife and (myself part of the time) 15 years at [NY]£50 p[r]. annum   [NY]£   750
>
> To 8 working hands employ'd thereon 15 years at [NY]£15 p[r]. Ann   [NY]£ 1,600
>
> To Cloathing said 8 hands at [NY]£6 p[r]. Ann each said time   [NY]£   720
>
> To Maintaining the Overseer and Wife and 8 Men 4 years at [NY]£8 each   [NY]£   320
>
> To Smiths work [NY]£25 p[r]. Ann: 14 Years   [NY]£   350
>
> To Wear and tare of Waggons, Carts, Plows, Harrows, Sleds,

Horses, oxen &c.: 14 Years at [NY]£30 p^r. Ann   [NY]£ 420

To Building a House, Stables, Barracks &c.   [NY]£ 160[51]

Oliver DeLancey asked two New York businessmen, John Chambers and Richard Nicholls, each representing one of the parties, to consider the conflicting claims. Despite the fact that all Warren's expenses were fully documented, and whereas Johnson could prove none of his expenses, the two men accepted both accounts as accurate statements of the claim each had upon the other. They declared the Warren estate indebted to Johnson by NY£933.[52] This greatly embarrassed DeLancey, who had neither a desire to offend Johnson, very much a rising figure in New York, nor any wish to endanger the agency with the Warren estate. DeLancey told Lady Warren, whom the Chambers–Nicholls decision greatly annoyed, that whatever the improvements on the home farm amounted to, the farm itself could certainly not be sold for a much as NY£1,000, while NY£4,250 was out of the question.[53] Susannah Warren came directly to the heart of the matter when she wrote to DeLancey, having read the Chambers–Nicholls memorandum: "I should be glad to know what he has done with the produce of all the Labour he Charges for, as he had the profits I think he has no right to make such unreasonable Charges, and I hope it wont be in any bodys power to make me pay so unjust a demand."[54]

She asked why Chambers and Nicholls were so ready to accept Johnson's word as sufficient proof of his case, and why they should set aside Warren's, for they "were no strangers to S^r. Peter Warren and therefore they must if they consider his Character know that he would not have left such a Legacy to M^r. Johnson and his Brothers and sisters unless he had been very sure that M^r. Johnson was in his debt . . . and another thing, why should M^r. Johnson give bonds if he was not in debt—it would have been proper for his uncle to have given him bonds if he had been in his Debt."[55] Legally Johnson had put himself in a very doubtful position; yet his aunt, though one of of the executors of her husband's will, never sued him as she ought to have done on behalf of Johnson's brothers and sisters.

However annoyed Johnson might have been to see his farm fall into other hands, it was ludicrous of him to overlook his uncle's generosity to him. It was also surprising that he should ignore the great expense his uncle had been put to in establishing the settlement. If we leave aside the debts of the tenants as well as Johnson's, it can easily be shown that between 1736 and 1744, Warren had spent no less than NY£6,748 on the tract:[56]

Passage to America	NY£365	8s. 6d.
Quit rent	122	10s.
Purchase price (£130)	214	10s.
Cowley's mortgage	398	15s.
Palatine provisions	196	11s. 6d.
Collins's survey	54	9s. 3d.
Goods for farm and trade	4,517	9s. 8d.
Johnson's legitimate expenses	878	14s.

These figures do not include the cost of the 2,000 acres from Richard Bradley nor the 600 acres on the north bank of the Mohawk. Yet by the time of his death in 1752, Warren appears to have received almost nothing in return. There are no records of rents having ever been collected and sent to him. There are no records of remittances having been made for the trade carried on by Johnson. If, then, the cost of Miln's and Bradley's tracts are added to the NY£6,748, it would not be an exaggeration to claim that Warren had spent at least NY£7,000 on Warrensurg and had absolutely no return. Indeed, the only result seems to have been the enrichment of William Johnson, who by refusing to acknowledge his indebtedness to Warren's widow and children, denied them their legitimate return on the large investment, while greatly diminishing his own liabilities.[57]

Johnson's dispute with Lady Warren did not put an end to his interest in Peter Warren's properties on the Mohawk. He probably continued to use his 200-acre home farm for his own profit. When he had done with it he let it to two men, Michael Fuller and John McGuire, for no rent; and they were not turned off until March 1768, when Oliver DeLancey granted a new lease to new tenants.[58] Johnson was particularly keen to buy Miln's 600 acres on the north side of the Mohawk. This he first suggested to DeLancey early in 1757.[59] When DeLancey told him the lands could not be sold, Johnson let the matter drop, but in 1765 again broached the question. He told DeLancey that the land had cost Warren "but a Trifle" and was then worth less than NY£500.[60] Despite this he was prepared to give twice its value by buying the land in exchange for granting the Warren heirs a complete release from the £933 debt which he still claimed with great fervour was his due. Johnson was then making use of the entire tract and paying no rent, for DeLancey had told him in 1762 "any thing you do to it will Rather Improve than Hurt it So Shall leave to your Discretion what Shall be Done as I Imagine you[1]. be the Purchaser when it is sold."[61] Now in 1765, as in 1757, DeLancey declined to sell the tract, telling Johnson that none of the Warren estate could be conveyed until Peter Warren's youngest daughter, Charlotte, came of age in 1770.[62] Johnson patiently waited until 1770 to raise the matter again, but still went unsatisfied.[63] His very persistence indicated that the tract, like all land in the Mohawk valley after 1763, had become of great value. His anxiety to make the purchase was enough to induce the Warren heirs to hold onto it. In 1774 Johnson went to his grave with this small matter and his overall relations with the Warren estate still unresolved.

With the demise of French control in Canada by 1760 and the retention of Canada by the terms of the Peace of Paris in 1763, the Mohawk frontier was peaceful for the first time in almost twenty years. From the early 1760s an increasing number of new settlers began to come onto the tract, replacing those who had fled during the dangerous years. They were not given leases and they paid no rent to the Warren estate, although Johnson may have collected something from them for his own benefit.[64]

It was only in 1765 that Oliver DeLancey became involved in Warren's Mohawk affairs, although he visited the Warrensburg tenants in 1760.[65] In view of the influx of squatters DeLancey ordered a new survey of the tract to be undertaken; and in August 1765 wrote to John Ralph Bleecker of Albany to carry out the work, giving him the following instructions:

What I Desire of You is first to Survey the Whole Tract which Comprehends y[e]. attorney Generals Patent and Hoffs which both now belong to S[r]. Peters heirs as Laid Down in a Draft I now Send you Made by Ed[d]. Collins Than Lay Down the Whole in Hundred Acre Lotts and Mark y[e]. Trees having in doing this a Regard to the Old Farms for which the People have Leases and Distinguish Them by a Note as O Farms and Their Bounds Should be Setled first You[l]. Please to Lay Down the Houses and Number the Farms and do it So as to Make them Most Commodious to the Persons already Settled but so as not to Hurt the General Plan of the Lotts Make Hoffs Patent [Cowley's farm] Separate from y[e]. Great Tract in Nearly Hundred Acre Lotts You[l]. Please to Inquire of every Person How Long They have been Settled what Number of Acres they have and be very Particular in Your Journal to Note Every

Thing that Can Inform me. You are to lay out 20 acres to the Mill and in the Most Convenient Place Mark 2 Lotts for a Church and Gleeb.[66]

As Bleecker had asked DeLancey to contact William Johnson in order to inform the Indians that a survey would be taken, DeLancey wrote to him late in October, asking him to ensure that the Indians did not interfere with the work.[67] He added:

> As Several Persons live on that Tract by leases from you I shall want the Copys of Those Leases to give Directions in Laying out their Lotts and be pleased to send me an Ac[t]. of what money you have rec'd from Any of them that in Stating Their Act[s]. I may give them Credit for such sums I shall esteem it a favour you[d]. send any Intelligence about this Land as I propose settling the whole and at what Rent I should put them at for 21 years after allowing 3 years free of Rent.[68]

In reply Johnson promised to smooth over relations with the Indians should the occasion arise, and also promised to send DeLancey "the Leases and with such information as you require."[69] There is no evidence that he ever sent either the leases or the accounts or indeed any advice about the tract that would have been of use to DeLancey. It was the last occasion in which DeLancey attempted to secure the cooperation of Warren's nephew. Thereafter he employed John Glen of Schenectady to collect rents and complete leases. But it was 1767 before Glen assumed this responsibility.[70]

Bleecker completed his survey in May 1766, having employed a number of the Warrensburg tenants as chain bearers, and submitted his bill for NY£166 12s. 10d. to DeLancey.[71] He noted that Collins's survey of 1739 had gone wrong only in one place at the southwestern corner of the tract at the Schoharie, where he had failed to extend the line as far as the creek's bank. This necessitated a legal opinion and occasioned a minor dispute with the owner of the adjoining patent, Mr. Remsen of New York City.[72] Bleecker also noted that he had found it "pritty difficult to keep some Regularity amongst the Lotts on account of the people haveing Setled at some places so near one another especially near the northwest Corner of the tract where Will[m]. Snook and three others have Setled themselves so near one another that a hundred Acres of Land Includes em all four."[73] In addition, what Bleecker called a village appears to have developed on the banks of the

Mohawk at the northeast corner. Not everyone, it seemed, wanted to live on neatly separated hundred-acre farms.

With the survey completed, DeLancey and his new agent, John Glen, found themselves virtually swamped by requests for land from interested settlers. By 1769, 71 of the 156 lots were leased and ought to have produced a gross rental income of NY£358 18s. after the first three rent-free years of the twenty-one year tenure.[74] The usual rates were one shilling an acre, with much higher rents for the improved farms. Thus Johnson's home farm was rented for NY£25 a year and the tenant, Abraham Hodge, was also to pay the quit rent charge of six shillings a year. John Waters rented 200 acres at NY£12 a year, while the sons of John Kain who were also renting 200 acres paid NY£10 8s. James Ellwood's 200 acres, then rented by Henry Hare for NY£16, paid the highest rent after Johnson's farm. Most of the tenants were new; indeed, only six families appear to have maintained a continuous tenure from the earliest years of the settlement to the early 1770s. Of these, four were Palatine families. Seventeen other families, many of them German, settled on the tract between 1760 and 1765, and the rest came afterwards.

Despite this considerable increase in settlers, and despite DeLancey's instructions to Glen to sue those tenants who refused to pay their rent, the rental income fell far below what had been anticipated.[75] In the decade between October 1767 and January 1776, Glen received only NY£783 9s. 4d. from the tenants, and a significant portion of this was not for rent but was part of the repayment of the original 1736 debt incurred by six Palatine families. Peter Warren had loaned them NY£177 12s., but repayment began only in 1767, when DeLancey threatened those debtors who were still on the land with legal action. From Glen's accounts it appears that no less than NY£393 11d. of the NY£783 9s. 4d. that he collected was due for the principal and interest of the 1736 loan. Thus the actual rental income only amounted to NY£423 8s. 5d. To this figure must be added another NY£58 9s. 2d. which two tenants paid directly to DeLancey in New York.[76] The total of NY£481 17s. 7d., little more than the equivalent of one year's anticipated income, was the only rental income the Warren heirs ever received from the Chuctenunda tract before the outbreak of war in 1776. Out of this came the expenses of Bleecker's survey, and the NY£127 10s. charged by Glen for his services, thus leaving a net income of NY£187 14s. 9d. Even this figure takes no account of the quit rent due on the estate, a matter which was to cause Oliver DeLancey and the Warren heirs a great deal of trouble and expense.

As with all lands originally granted by the province of New York, Warren's tract was assessed quit rent at the customary rate of 4s. per 100 acres every year. The only payment made during Warren's lifetime was recorded in 1742, and amounted to NY£122 10s.[77] Though 4s. was the usual rate, many large land grants were required to make only nominal payments. Thus the 86,000 acres of Cortlandt Manor, for instance, paid only NY£2 a year. In 1727 the New York Assembly defeated a measure adopted by the New York Council which intended to exact regular quit rents from these large, favoured estates, the grants for which had been made mainly in the seventeenth century.[78] Yet, even on those tracts which were required to pay the normal quit rent levy, New York failed to organize an effective system of collection until 1722 when Archibald Kennedy was made receiver general. Though much more devoted to his duties than his predecessors, his success was limited for the habit of non-payment was so well established that the general laxity persisted throughout his tenure of office. Indeed it proved impossible to collect much of what was owed the crown by New York landowners throughout the colonial period. Acts were passed in 1742, 1754, 1755, 1762, and finally in 1768 in vain attempts to enforce payment, but the small returns proved the system in New York a failure.

The reluctance of many landowners to pay quit rents arose not only because of the province's administrative failure, but because many genuinely believed that "Lands on the Frontier part of the Colony, untill the Reduction of Canada, could hardly be said to be in the possession of the Crown. . . . And as there were neither Forts nor Troops kept up for the defence of the planters, the patentees could derive no Advantage from their Grants."[79] The Governor and Council of New York went so far as to plead this very case in a petition to the Board of Trade, but without satisfaction. It had no recourse but to make another attempt at collection, and in 1768 passed "An Act for the more Effectual Collecting of his Majesty's Quit Rents, in the Colony of New York, and for partition of Lands in Order thereto."[80]

As a result of the 1768 act the then receiver general, Andrew Elliott, placed advertisements in the New York City newspapers listing those properties found to be in arrears in quit rent payments. The advertisement also warned, in keeping with the act, that unless debts were cleared within twelve months enough land would be sold on each patent to meet the arrears. DeLancey took sufficient notice of this to contact Elliott and actually visit his office to see the quit rent ledgers for himself. There he was told that, as of Lady Day 1767, NY£430 was owing on the Warrensburg tract, patented to Charles Williams and others.[81] DeLancey made no effort to make payment, though he later claimed he had written to Lady Warren for permission to make such a payment. That he was perfectly aware of the amount owing the crown is clear from the rent roll which he prepared for his sister in 1769. Not only did the rent roll mention the quit rent due for each rented lot at Warrensburg, but in some of the leases the tenants were obliged to meet this expense in addition to their rent charge. DeLancey quite clearly believed that the Crown would be as lax in collecting quit rents then as it had been in the past.

He had some reason to persist in this opinion for the receiver general took no further action until November 1771, when a second advertisement appeared in the newspapers, this time under Chief Justice Daniel Horsmanden's name.[82] It instructed all patent holders still in arrears to appear at his chambers to show cause if they could why a portion of their lands should not be sold to pay the quit rent owing the crown. The interviews took place on 30 December, but DeLancey failed to represent the Warren interests, for unknown reasons. In May 1772 Horsmanden instructed the sheriff of Albany, Henry Ten Eyck, to hold a public auction to sell several properties, including Chuctenunda, for as much as was owing the crown. The sale was duly held on 4 July 1772. Those gathered at the auction were merely asked how much less than the whole tract they would offer to pay off the arrears, and a consortium of four, John Bradstreet, John Morin Scott, Philip Schuyler, and Rutgers Bleecker, answered that they would buy the whole except a nominal fifty acres. As no other offer was made, those attending the sale being convinced the four were buying for the Warren interests, the sheriff declared the sale at an end. The same morning in a matter of a few hours the same procedure was followed by the consortium for nine other estates, some much larger than Warrensburg.

DeLancey did not learn of the sale until a week later, the news coming from his son, Stephen; and this was confirmed almost at once by a private letter sent him by John Bradstreet, one of the purchasers, and an old friend of Admiral Warren's from Louisbourg days in 1745.[83] DeLancey at once sprang into action, not only because of the serious threat to the Warren interests, but also to his own, for Cosby

Manor in which he had a large interest was among the properties sold
at the Albany auction. DeLancey suspected, quite rightly, that Scott,
a leading member of the New York bar and as rapacious a land speculator as DeLancey himself, was at the bottom of the conspiracy. After
failing to get Scott to give up the supposed purchase, with the promise
of being fully reimbursed for his expenses, DeLancey went immediately to the governor to inform him of the affair, and received a very
sympathetic hearing.[84] He then tried to retain William Smith as legal
counsel but Scott had beaten him there, so he engaged James Duane,
an advocate at least the equal of Smith and Scott, and an owner of
considerable property near Schenectady.[85] With Duane's help a bill
was prepared demanding an injunction on the sale, if the purchasers
refused to give up their scheme. To the bill the governor gave his
immediate consent. When on 13 July DeLancey had heard formally
from Scott that he would not retreat, DeLancey resolved to travel to
Albany and contact the other three purchasers, Bradstreet, Bleecker,
and Schuyler, and get the full facts of the sale. Scott had told him: "I
should be lost of all Sense of Duty to my family and expose myself to
the like claims from all the late proprietors of the other Tracts that
were sold should I comply with your Request."[86]

DeLancey arrived at Albany on 17 July and the business kept him
there for three weeks. Only Bradstreet was ready at once to back down.
Schuyler, Lady Warren's cousin, who held fifty per cent of the Warrensburg purchase, agreed under pressure both from Bradstreet and
DeLancey to give up his investment, and signed a deed to that effect
that very day.[87] DeLancey had less success with Rutgers Bleecker, the
son of John Ralph Bleecker who had surveyed the tract in 1765-66.
Bleecker at first agreed to forego his investment on the condition that
he be paid a gratuity, the amount to be decided by Schuyler, to indemnify him for his expenses and trouble. To this DeLancey agreed, but
left Albany on 5 August without having perfected the business, and so
gave Schuyler the necessary instructions to conclude the agreement
and to draw on him for whatever money was needed.[88] DeLancey
found upon his return to New York that Bleecker had temporized and
would not come to an immediate agreement. The injunction was
thereupon served on the sheriff of Albany and the deeds conveying the
land to the consortium held in abeyance. DeLancey busied himself in
collecting evidence about the sale, taking affidavits from witnesses, and
attempted without success to get the sheriff to accept, in trust, funds
sufficient to pay off the quit rent arrears. He sent his son Stephen, who

had accompanied him to Albany, to Warren's tract to get as many tenants as possible to sign an instrument, by which they agreed to hold their land against any outside claim derived from the pretended sale, for which DeLancey undertook to indemnify them. By 1 August, he had persuaded most of the tenants to sign the bond.[89] With his evidence collected he returned to New York to report to the Warren heirs and supply Duane with the necessary information to prepare a lengthy opinion.

Duane based his arguments principally on the contention that the sale on 4 July 1772 and the action that preceded it contravened the 1768 Quit Rent Act in so many ways that the legality of the sale could not be sustained. The act required that the parties concerned be given regular notice of their arrears, yet nothing had been done between 1768 and 1771, when the two newspaper advertisements had appeared. The act called for the proper identification of the properties, yet the advertisements referred to Warren's tract only as Charles Williams's patent when in fact it was "a respectable and well-known settlement,"[90] which was commonly called Warrensbush, Warrensburg, or Warrensborough. Duane further pointed out that the threats contained in both the 1768 and 1771 newspaper advertisements had not been carried out, for both deadlines which they contained passed without action on the part of the crown, thus lulling the parties into a false sense of security, quite repugnant to the spirit and intention of the act. In addition Duane objected to the manner in which notice of the sale at Albany had been made, for the act called for one notice to be placed in the county court house and three others elsewhere in the county. In fact only three notices were placed, one in Tryon County and two in Albany, and one of these was put up after the six day deadline, and another was taken down after being up only an hour; the third was blown away. The notices, moreover, described the tract as lying in Albany County: in fact, the act, passed on 12 March 1772, created two new counties as well as Albany County, and clearly placed the tract in the new Tryon County. For this reason, Duane argued in detail that the sale should never have taken place in Albany, and the sheriff of Albany had no right to have held the sale. Even if this could be disproved, Duane argued, the very conduct of the sale was sufficient to disallow it:

The Sheriff had Nine processes against large and valuable Tracts of Land which were to be sold for Quit Rent and to raise a very large sum of Money — He advertised and proceeded to the Sale of all of them, at the same time, place, and moment, offering them Altogether — repeating his offer of each at the same Juncture, and within only the space of three hours, struck them off (one Excepted) to the same Bidders; and all of them at the first sum proposed, which was not raised to wit. The whole of each Tract Except fifty Acres to pay the demand. This was sporting with the property of the Subject, who could not have the least Chance, in such a Scene of Confusion, and a procedure so precipitate, of getting a Sum any thing adequate to the value. It is therefore Conceived that this is such an Abuse of power, as must in Equity, at least, annul the Sale if it was free from any other Objection.[91]

He pointed out that the bidders, Scott, Schuyler, Bradstreet, and Bleecker, had discouraged other possible buyers by asserting at least once that they were buying for the owners, and in other cases that the title was in great doubt, which Duane felt would weigh against the supposed purchasers in any court of equity.

Finally he argued that the sheriff, if he were found to have any jurisdiction, ought to have ordered a survey of the tracts before the sale, so as to determine how much uncultivated land there was, as it was usual for this land to be sold first. If this had been done, it would quickly have been seen that there was enough unsettled land at Warrensburg to have paid the quit rent arrears three times over, if the land had been validly sold at the market price. Thus the selling of the entire tract less the nominal fifty acres was so oppressive and such an abuse of the act that this alone ought to convince any court to set aside the sale.

The Warren heirs were exceedingly indignant when they learned of the sale from DeLancey in November. They considered it "the greatest disgrace that could have happend, to the family and a Strong Affront, to the Memory of Sr. Peter Warren, from a Country, where his name ought to be revered."[92] They at once retained Mr. Alexander Forrester to prepare an opinion. They described him as having been much concerned in American business "and has great weight and Credit with the Privy Counsell."[93] Forrester was sure the sale would not stand, "being manifestly Fraudulent."[94] He also found it astonishing that DeLancey had for four years neglected discharging the quit rent arrears. The heirs were determined to fight the case through every stage of the law if necessary to expose in particular the "Scoundrill Scott."[95] In the end they had to pay heavily for DeLancey's blunder, which Bleecker and Scott had exploited. In 1773 the Warren heirs were told by DeLancey that both men were hinting that some financial settlement would induce them to relinquish their hold on the property. DeLancey was allowed to offer up to NY£300. By the end of the year Bleecker had settled for NY£72 10s.[96] In July 1774 Scott asked for NY£300, while DeLancey offered only NY£127 10s. which was refused. Thereupon DeLancey, after taking advice from Duane and Watts, asked the Warren heirs permission to meet this exhorbitant demand.[98]

On this basis Scott was bought off. In addition to the NY£372 10s. paid these two, the Warren heirs paid NY£850 to cover the quit rent arrears, sheriff's fees and costs of the sale, the cost of the new survey required by the act under which the sale had been held, and the attorney general's fees. Finally Duane was paid NY£70 for his trouble.[99] As the quit rent charges amounted to NY£603 15s. 7d., DeLancey's negligence had cost the Warren estate the difference, or NY£689 10s.

The affair had dragged on for almost three years. It had sorely tried the patience of both Oliver DeLancey and the Warren heirs, and undoubtedly hastened their desire to substitute his son, Stephen, and John Watts Jr. as the legal representatives of the Warren estate in New York. Still they were utterly dependent on his initiative and judgement, and in the end DeLancey earned the grudging admiration of Skinner who admitted that he displayed a "deal more Patience than I should, was I in America."[100] DeLancey took no delight in his blunder, admitting in 1773 that "Ever since the first News I had of this Sale, it has so affected my Spirits and Health that from being perfectly well before I have become continually declining ever since by a depression of Spirits, and of Consequence the Neglect of my own affairs may impoverish my Family."[101]

Warren's Mohawk venture proved to be the most costly speculation of all his American land investments: he spent between NY£8,000 and NY£8,500 on it, almost the cost of all his properties elsewhere in New York. Of this not less than NY£7,000 had been expended during his lifetime. This figure includes the capital costs of land purchases, surveys, transportation of settlers, and monies advanced and loaned to settlers and not repaid. It includes the cost of trade goods sent to William Johnson between 1738 and 1742 from which Warren received neither return nor payment. The figure also includes capital costs met after Warren's death, particularly the new survey and the cost of recovery of the part of the tract sold by auction in 1772.

According to DeLancey's estimates the Mohawk valley property grew rapidly in value after 1760. In 1759 he estimated its value at NY£10,500, and by 1772 he felt it to be worth at least NY£17,000.[102] In 1787 John Watts Jr. estimated its value at NY£23,100.[103] If, however, the rate of inflation is again taken into account, as in the case of the other New York estates owned by the Warrens, then this gain is less impressive. The real value is shown in table 9.

TABLE 9 *Mohawk Valley Property: Adjusted Valuation*

Date	Nominal Value	Price Index	Adjusted Value
1752	NY£ 7,000	93	NY£ 7,527
1759	10,500	100	10,500
1772	17,000	117	14,530
1787	23,100	117	19,744

Base: 1701 = 100

Source: Schumpeter, "English Prices and Public Finances," p.35.

The capital appreciation was considerable only after the Seven Years' War dealt with the political problem of the French in Canada; at that time settlers from New England and abroad flooded into the Mohawk valley. Demand for land was high and the expectation of improved rental income greatly enhanced. In fact Warrensburg never produced much income. No rents appear to have been paid before 1767, while the dispute over the quit rent arrears from 1772 to 1774 made rent collecting impossible. It is known that John Glen managed to collect about the equivalent of one year's rent in the years 1767 to 1775, when the average annual gross income ought to have been about NY£359. No rent reached the Warren heirs during the war years 1776-83, when the Mohawk passed completely under the control of the American patriots, except when the British and their Indian allies raided the valley, led by Sir John Johnson from Canada. By 1787 John

Watts Jr. and John Glen calculated that the annual income ought to have been NY£499 and that NY£6,329 in rental arrears was due the Warren heirs by the tenants.[104] Both Abingdon and Southampton instructed Watts to collect what he could, but he had limited success.[105]

The Mohawk valley properties were included in the 1787 division of the Warren New York real estate. Warrensburg was divided into three parts, each amounting to more than 5,000 acres. The front third along the Mohawk was drawn by lot by Miss Skinner, the future Viscountess Gage; the rear section fronting the Schoharie was drawn by Abingdon, and the middle group of lots by Southampton.[106] Each section was roughly valued at NY£7,500. Abingdon and Southampton resolved to sell their individual lots separately, though how soon the task was completed and how much they received is not known. However a record of sales on Abingdon's part for the year 1789 has survived, and indicates that the evaluation was not far wrong. According to the account, nine lots amounting to 865 of the 5,355 acres were sold for NY£1,275, at an average price of 29s. 8d. an acre, or just below the estimated value of 30s. At least eight per cent of this went to pay Watts's commission and travelling expenses from New York City to the Mohawk, as well as the legal fees connected with the sales.[107]

Miss Skinner's trustees sold her share entirely to John Watts. This decision was based on Watts's very discouraging account of the property which he had prepared in 1789.[108] Many of the tenants, he claimed, refused to pay their rent unless they were compensated for their improvements. In addition there was again a large sum owing in quit rent arrears. Moreover, the southern boundary was in dispute. Considerable expense, trouble, and time would be needed until the title to the entire tract was once again proved and the tenants brought under control. Once this was achieved, Watts thought the land ought to sell for 30 shillings an acre, but in its existing condition, it would be lucky to fetch half that amount. Miss Skinner's trustees, and later her husband Henry Gage, decided to sell the property to Watts for £2,000 to avoid further entanglements.

In the 1787 division, John Miln's 600 acres were valued at NY£600 and went to Southampton. It was of questionable value for the title to the land was disputed by several settler families, who had moved onto the tract after 1783. Before the war Oliver DeLancey had given some hint of the trouble, when in September 1774 he explained to the Warren heirs:

I had Last Week a Visit from a Grand son of Walter Butler acquainting me that his father Col°. Butler Claims Milns Share of the Land 600 Acres as he says by Virtue of a Purchase from said John Miln before he Conveyed to S^r. Peter which is a New Claim as in 1772 I spoke to Col°. Butler to pay the quitt Rents which he then said he would do and Join me in it I went to the Receiver generals Office and found Butler had made some Payments Heretofore and I was not Allow'd to Make a Partial one untill the whole came in.[109]

Such disputes were common enough, particularly since so many of the original grants by the governor and council of the colony were made without benefit of a survey. Often it was found that parts of patents overlapped. Moreover, as it was not necessary to record every conveyance, it was not always possible either for the seller or the buyer to be absolutely certain of the dimensions of the tract being disposed of. That Butler had received a deed from Miln is certain as DeLancey discovered when he consulted Butler's attorney the following April, but it was fifteen years later than Miln's to Warren. Butler's attorney thereupon agreed that his client had no claim.[110]

In contrast to Warren's real property on Manhattan Island, his lands on the Mohawk suffered from poor management and the dangers of war. William Johnson, too much involved in his own interests, in politics, and in the military defence of the frontier, never, except in his first few years on the Mohawk, gave Warren's interests the care they needed to prosper. In addition, the threat of war with France on the frontier between 1744 and 1760 caused the dislocation of the settlement Warren had hoped to see prosper. Once the threat to the frontier had been removed, Johnson through his quarrel with Warren's widow was of little use to the Warren heirs. It was several years before Oliver DeLancey assumed some responsibility for the care of the property. Though this time the settlement prospered, little profit came to the Warren heirs, for the dispute over the sale of the tract for quit rent arrears begun in 1772 lasted until the very eve of the war with the colonists. It is ironical that the one property on which Warren lavished attention and money proved so poor an investment. Without doubt his initiative helped hasten the settlement of the Mohawk, a generation earlier than, for instance, his neighbour James Duane established Duanesburg,[111] yet for this he received no benefit and has received no credit from historians. Both profit and credit went solely to his nephew, William

Johnson, a man of great versatility, resourcefulness, and considerable intelligence, but whose relationship with Peter Warren and the family was somewhat less than candid.

Chapter 5

Money Lending

in New York

1731-1795

British investment in the American colonies in the eighteenth century principally took the form of shipments of commodities on credit.[1] Such activity can be characterized as short-term, since it was generally intended that accounts be paid within a specified period, usually from four months to a year. These "book debts" left unpaid at the end of this interval then began to attract interest, and were often secured subsequently by a bond or a mortgage on real property.[2] Thus short-term investments, initially interest-free, became inadvertently, as a result of American importers' or planters' inability or unwillingness to make payments, a long-term extension of credit. Except in periods of prolonged liquidity crises the rate of interest did not fluctuate in the domestic credit markets on both sides of the Atlantic, but was generally fixed after 1714 at five per cent.[3] Planned long-term investment in the colonies by non-Americans was rare.[4] The only important example, the so-called American Iron Company, a consortium of English investors, sunk £54,000 from 1764 in iron works in New York and New Jersey, under the direction of Peter Hasenclever.[5]

The role of the Warren family in New York between 1731 and 1795 can be considered another example of such long-term investment from abroad. The size and extent of their money-lending portfolio probably made them the largest suppliers of credit, independent of trade, in the

province at mid-century. This is of general importance not only because, in the absence of proper banks and other corporate credit
institutions in colonial America, any new investigation of domestic
credit is of interest, but also because detailed research about New
York's "merchant bankers" before 1776, so vital to an understanding
of the economic fabric of the colony, is virtually impossible owing to
the disappearance of the necessary documents.[6]

The principal reason for keeping large-scale investments in America
was the promise of a good and regular return. New York was particularly attractive. Not only was there an insatiable demand for credit in
the colonies, but the legal ceiling at which credit could be advanced
in New York was substantially higher than in either England or Ireland.
In New York between 1718 and 1737 the maximum rate of interest
allowed by law was 8 per cent. In December 1737, a new provincial act
reduced the ceiling to 7 per cent, where it remained throughout the
remaining decades of the colonial era.[7]

Warren's role as a source of credit in New York began with his marriage to Susannah DeLancey in July 1731. The Warren–DeLancey
marriage contract, among other things, established a NY£6,000 trust
fund to be "putt out to Interest"[8] in New York. In fact, the full amount
of the jointure was not made available by Warren's father-in-law until
1741. Then, as a result of various bequests left to Susannah in the
1740s, and of Warren's practice of ploughing back interest received
into the capital fund, and of adding to it some of the prize money he
garnered after 1739, the Warrens' holdings in the New York money
market had more than doubled by the time of his death as table 10
illustrates.

The great majority of Warren's loans were to New York business
partnerships, some specializing in overseas trade, others concerned
more with the New York domestic market.[9] Some of his debtors were
his own tenants. Most of his loans were secured only by means of a
bond, by which the debtor simply declared himself responsible for the
sum mentioned, and added a promise to repay the debt within a fixed
interval, usually a year. Such bonds, as was the custom, prescribed a
penalty of twice the principal if unpaid when due. In fact very few of
the bonds taken by Warren were recovered within the specified interval, and at no time did Warren or his agents attempt to recover the
penal sum. Indeed, as the following graph indicates, most bond loans

TABLE 10 *New York Loans 1731-1755*

Year	Principal Added	Loans Paid Off	Balance
1731	NY£3,861	NY£ —	NY£ 3,861
1732	180	95	3,946
1733	752	775	3,923
1734	1,117	548	4,492
1735	220	400	4,312
1736	1,192	1,969	3,535
1737	1,283	100	4,718
1738	651	420	4,949
1739	296	945	4,300
1740	1,914	706	5,508
1741	3,898	681	8,725
1742	5,338	930	13,133
1743	1,700	804	14,029
1744-45	550	4,367}	12,692}
1746-47	2,480		
1748-49	3,265	5,727	10,230
1750-51	2,966	2,041	11,155
1752-53	3,777	545	14,387
1754-55	2,736	5,748	11,375

Source: Warren Papers,NYHS; Gage Papers.

were allowed to continue for many years, the bulk being repaid between eight and thirteen years after they were originally made. Many were permitted to remain unpaid for very much longer periods, one for as long as forty-five years. From the debtors' viewpoint the advantages were obvious: it gave them over a long interval the use of capital, for which they were not required to provide the best possible security then known, namely a mortgage on landed property.

Owing to the merely marginal impact of currency exchange rates and of inflation, as was seen earlier,[10] the creditors' position was not adversely affected. Probably for this reason the Warrens and their agents did not pressure debtors to convert bond security to mortgages.

NEW YORK BOND LOANS: Interval between borrowing and repayment

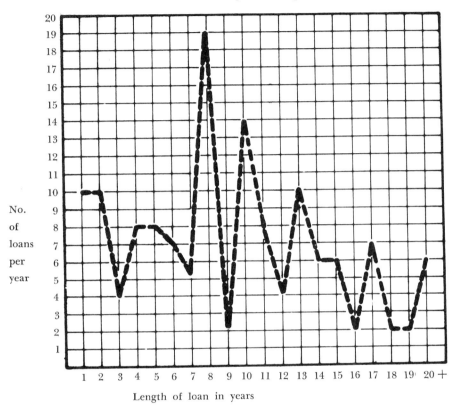

No. of loans per year

Length of loan in years

Traceable bonds and mortgages, in the Warrens' case, numbered 175, besides which there were several notes of hand.[11] Bonds and mortgages ranged in value from NY£10 to NY£2,120, the average amounting to NY£254 (NY£234 for the 157 bonds and NY£435 for the eighteen mortgages).

Many of the debts owing the Warrens originated in loans they themselves had not initiated. They were so-called assigned bonds acquired by inheritance, purchase, or as part payment for earlier debts. Most originated with Stephen DeLancey, either as part of the original NY£6,000 jointure or as the Warrens' share in the division of the estate following Stephen DeLancey's death in 1741. As DeLancey was a leading merchant of New York City, it is probable that many of the assets, thus transferred to the Warrens, originated as book debts, and thus involved no cash exchange. The earliest of these assigned bonds was a debt of NY£54 due from Thomas and John Smith dating from 1725.[12] Other examples included a NY£200 bond originally given to Mordacai Gomes by Messrs. Jeremiah and Joseph Fowler and Gill Willet and transferred to Warren in October 1731, a NY£119 bond from John Corbett, another from Messrs. Jacques Denys and Jacques Castelyan in 1734, and three bonds in 1741 originally given Captain Timothy Bagley by James Doughty amounting to NY£325, first assigned to Stephen DeLancey before being transferred to Warren. Among the Warrens' share of the division of Stephen DeLancey's estate were included bonds amounting to NY£2,400. These included a NY£1,000 bond from Messrs. Couvenhoven and Williams dating from 1737, a NY£300 bond from Henry Beekman in 1732, a NY£400 bond taken from Colonel Nathaniel Gilbert, Samuel and Stephen Bayard in 1733, a NY£300 bond from James Henderson and a NY£600 bond from Messrs. Richard Annelly and Abraham Huisman, the last two dating from 1739. In addition the Warrens also inherited a number of similar securities upon the death of Stephen DeLancey Jr. in 1745. There were an additional six bonds valued at NY£1,240, three of which had been Stephen's share in his father's estate. One of the debtors was Joseph Forman of Freehold, New Jersey, who had given a bond for NY£600 in 1738. Over the years the Warrens collected neither principal nor interest from Forman, who by the 1770s was declared a bankrupt, with his affairs vested in a trustee by an act of the New York Assembly.[13] It was one of the few failures suffered by the Warren interests in New York.

Few of the loans made on behalf of the Warrens in New York were secured by mortgages. This may have been a customary colonial business practice; but it was surely lax to allow loans to remain outstanding for great intervals merely on the security of bonds. To improve security, debtors could probably have been obliged to mortgage part of their real property, as was the custom in England. A list of these mortgages, illustrating the variety of the Warrens' portfolio, is found in table 11.

Of all these only two, Cowley's and Jamaine's debts, went unpaid. The property thus secured then passed into Warren's hands. Warren apparently never really expected Cowley's mortgage to be recovered, and was not in the least displeased by the transaction. Cowley had

TABLE 11 *New York Mortgages, 1731–1766*

18 June 1731	John Barberie, mortgage on houses in New York City, NY£700 @ 8%
24 Sept. 1731	Thomas and Nicholas Van Taerling, on New York City property, NY£200 @ 8%
13 Oct. 1731	John Royden Jamaine, on two houses in New York City, NY£500 @ 8%
4 Jan. 1733/34	Peter Brewer, on a house in Maiden Lane, New York City, NY£50 @ 8%
27 Feb. 1736/37	Daniel Bennet, NY£200 @ 8%
27 Feb. 1741/42	Jonathan Fowler, on a 119-acre farm in Eastchester, NY£150 @ 7%
3 Nov. 1742	Joseph Cowley, on a 600-acre farm on the Mohawk near Fort Hunter, NY£398 15s. @ 7%
[1743]	George Harrison, NY£300 @ 7%
20 April 1747	Walter and Thomas Dongan, NY£700 @ 6%
5 March 1747/48	William Nicholson, Gysbert Gerretson, and Gideon Castaign, on a house and lot in Cortlandt Street, New York City, NY£150 @ 7%
13 May 1748	James Denton, on a property at Newburgh, £250 @ 7%
19 Aug. 1749	Henry and Lydia George, on two houses on Broadway, New York City, NY£200 @ 7%
[1749]	Oliver DeLancey, a mortgage on unspecified New York property, £850 (or NY£1,615 @ £190 exchange) @ 5%
18 June 1750	Nathanial Johnson, on a Philadelphia property, NY£300 @ 7%
20 Oct. 1753	Dr. William Mercer, NY£300 @ 7%
Dec. 1753	Hendrick Vroom, of Middlesex, New Jersey, NY£1,316 11s. 7d. @ 7%
12 July 1759	Francis Dudley, on New York City property, NY£300 @ 6%
25 July 1766	Barent Duytchen, on property in New York, NY£195 18s. @ 7%

Source: Miscellaneous Warren Papers and Delancey Papers

originally purchased the farm in question in 1736 from Captain Walter Butler, one time commander at Fort Hunter.[14] By the time Warren became interested in the property, the principal and unpaid interest amounted to almost NY£400. The property lay in the very heart of an estate Warren had purchased on the Mohawk. The mortgage was really a cash payment to purchase the Cowley farm, though it was not legally recognized as his for some years. As far as the Jamaine mortgage was concerned, here too Warren appeared eager to purchase the land. When Jamaine's New York City houses were auctioned in 1736, Warren could have accepted his share of the proceeds of the sale by right of the mortgage he held. Instead he bid for and purchased the property himself.[15]

Among the Warren debtors in New York were a number of important kinsmen. Small amounts of credit were extended to Susannah Warren's cousin, Jeremiah Van Rensselear, and her brother, Peter DeLancey, in 1731.[16] In 1733 James DeLancey was loaned NY£200.[17] The next year another of Mrs. Warren's relations, a cousin by marriage, the Rev. William Skinner, rector of St. Peter's Church, Perth Amboy, was loaned NY£250 on his bond.[18] In 1749, as has already been noted, Oliver DeLancey borrowed £850 on the security of a mortgage on his New York property, the loan being repaid within a very few months early in 1750.[19] Again in 1752 Warren acted as DeLancey's banker by accepting a bill of exchange for NY£200 to Beverley Robinson of New York. This was repaid in 1753 while Oliver DeLancey was in England settling Admiral Warren's affairs.[20] Not all the relations were so prompt in repaying their debts. Stephen Van Cortlandt, another of Susannah Warren's cousins, was loaned NY£250 on his bond in 1745. By July 1752 no interest had been paid, so James DeLancey insisted that he complete an additional bond to cover the unpaid interest.[21] This also Van Cortlandt ignored, and the debt remained a charge against his estate at the time of his death. In 1758 when Van Cortlandt's estate was settled, Oliver DeLancey felt obliged to purchase some of his land on behalf of the Warren heirs, as he explained to Lady Warren: "to secure NY£500 he owed you & about NY£400 he Owed Me as his Estate was much Envolved and I saw no such ready way of doing it as taking the Land which I hope Soon to Sell for More Money and shall then Credit Your Account accordingly but let what will happen I will take Care You Don't Loose any thing by it."[22]

Warren also acted as banker for his brother-in-law, Chief Justice James DeLancey, by paying his son's expenses at Cambridge University between 1749 and 1752. The young James DeLancey had all his college bills sent to Warren, and then spent his vacations with Warren's family either in London or at their country seat north of Portsmouth, or, as in the summer of 1751, at Scarborough in Yorkshire. By June 1752, the young man's bills amounted to £752, and this debt went unpaid until May 1761, by which time it had risen to £1,288, interest included.[23] That the Warrens treated even their closest relatives in the same manner as outsiders of good credit standing is perhaps typical of the age. It is then not surprising that the relations were as reluctant to repay their loans as other debtors.

By far the most interesting loan made by Warren to his kinsmen in New York was to his nephew, William Johnson. The loan was made on a basis quite different from all others in New York. As has already been seen, Warren induced Johnson to leave Ireland and superintend the establishment of a settlement south of the Mohawk River in 1738. Warren did not confine himself to capital expenses on his own behalf, but liberally encouraged his nephew to extend his activities with the use of Warren's own capital. On three occasions between 1740 and 1742 he obliged Johnson to acknowledge his indebtedness by completing bonds: in August 1740 for £600 free of interest for four years, in July 1741 for £300 free of interest for twelve years, and for NY £200 in November 1742 to bear interest immediately.[24] By the time of his death Warren had advanced Johnson no less than NY £7,240, though only NY £6,820 was claimed by Oliver DeLancey, who acted for the Warren heirs. Of this, fully one-third was forgiven by Warren's last will, while the balance was assigned to Johnson's brothers and sisters in Ireland. This debt Johnson never acknowledged; and despite the protests of Lady Warren no one in New York ever seriously tried to force his compliance.

Peter Warren's death in 1752 caused no dramatic change in the level of investment in New York. Lady Warren, who had left New York for England in 1747, decided not to return to America. Her brother, Oliver DeLancey, thereupon travelled to England to help put the admiral's affairs in order. Upon his return to New York almost a year later in October 1753, he assumed responsibility for the management of all his sister's affairs in America. He convinced her to leave her New York investments intact, with the reassuring words, "As I Can Make them pay the Interest I will put it out again or remitt to you for the Childrens use as you shall direct though I think I Can make it produce more Here as I am determined to Make people indebted to Your Estate more punctual than they have been heretofore."[25]

His first task was to call in all outstanding debts by placing advertisements in the New York newspapers,[26] and when this failed to bring a quick response, by pursuing the debtors in the courts.[27] His efforts were largely successful, which testifies to his devotion to the Warren interests, the soundness of the credit of the Warren debtors, and to the improved economic conditions of the late 1750s.[28]

One of the interesting debts that DeLancey was able to recover for the Warren heirs was owed by settlers on Warren's Mohawk–Schoharie valley tract, called Warrensburg. In October 1736 he had given six Palatine families supplies to the value of NY£200, and in addition had loaned them NY£177 in cash, for which he took their joint bond.[29] The loan was interest-free for the first two years, a rare example of consideration by Warren in such matters, and thereafter at the rate of seven per cent, when the maximum allowable under New York law was eight. By 1752 two of the six settler families had run off without paying their share of the debt, moreover neither principal nor interest had yet been received from the rest. However, in 1767 two of the remaining four families began regularly to pay their debt, and by 1776 had made payments to DeLancey amounting to NY£360.[30] This was not the entire sum due to the Warrens, if the interest due since 1736 is added, but the repayment of such a significant part of the debt testifies both to DeLancey's tenacity as a money collector, and to the prosperity of the frontier New York farmers who in the years immediately before the outbreak of the War of Independence were able to pay off a debt contracted in the 1730s.

Besides calling in debts outstanding before 1753, DeLancey undertook new loans in Lady Warren's name and in the name of her children between 1753 and 1769. His records show that between 5 October 1753 and 19 May 1759, NY£8,837 12s. 1d. was invested in new bonds.[31] Details for the period after May 1759 are not complete, though it is known that the last bonds taken by DeLancey in his sister's name were dated March 1769 and amounted to NY£4,219.[32] No new debts were contracted after Lady Warren's death in 1771; and her heirs, all living in England, decided not to continue her policy of lending money in New York. It was then Oliver DeLancey's task to recover as much as possible of the outstanding debts, which he estimated in 1772 at NY£9,495.[33] Of this sum, he reckoned that almost NY£1,400 was beyond recovery owing to the long insolvency of the debtors, whose economic difficulties cannot be associated in any way with the Anglo-American trial of strength. By the time war engulfed New York in 1776, DeLancey had collected NY£1,100, thus reducing the outstanding principal to about NY£7,000.

It is remarkable how little of the NY£7,000 investment was lost as a result of the war and its aftermath. Most of the Warren debtors were Loyalists and stayed in New York City until 1783 and then settled in England. DeLancey was able to collect more than NY£4,250 without great difficulty. When he was exiled to England in 1783, he left John Watts Jr. in charge of the interests of the Warren heirs. Between 1785 and 1805 Watts spent part of his time overseeing the sale of the Warren real estate in New York and elsewhere in America, and in tracing the few remaining debtors. In 1795, urged on by the Warren heirs (the Earl of Abingdon, Viscount Gage, and Lord Southampton), Watts prepared a report showing that of the NY£2,750 in principal then outstanding, only NY£292 10s. was beyond recovery.[34] As this amount had been considered safe in 1776, its loss must be attributed to the effects of the war. As evidence after 1795 is lacking, it is not possible to know if Watts was successful in collecting the balance of the principal and interest owing to the Warren heirs. However, the 1795 report showed that it was possible to collect pre–1776 debts from Americans, even if the creditors were members of English aristocracy, and so long as the creditors were patient and were served by able and devoted agents on the spot. Though the Warren heirs were closely connected with two leading New York Loyalist families — the DeLanceys and the Johnsons — and though one of the heirs, Viscount Gage, was the son of General Thomas Gage, for whom no American could feel much affection, still the debt obligations contracted before the war survived its aftermath.

It should be remembered that both the peace treaty of 1783 as well as the treaty of London in 1794 dealt in part with the repayment of debts owed by Americans to British creditors.[35] In general, the collection of such debts was objected to by the various state legislatures; and only with the adoption of the federal constitution in 1789, by which states were prevented from passing laws impairing obligations of contracts and by which a federal judiciary was established to decide, among other things, all matters between Americans and citizens of foreign states, were Americans forced to make good these long-standing obligations.

A number of more specific conclusions can be drawn. The first relates to the effectiveness of the colonial laws relating to the rate of interest. No credit was ever advanced on behalf of the Warrens which exceeded the legal ceilings. Such a policy also characterized their money-lending behaviour elsewhere: in New England, South Carolina, Ireland, and England. Whether their practice was exceptional or commonplace in New York or elsewhere in colonial America is not known, for the general question has yet to be studied. If their behaviour was indeed exceptional as many eighteenth-century commentators would have found it,[36] then it could be argued that the Warrens' best interests were not being served by their agents. Instead of putting out money within the legal ceiling on interest rates, the agents ought to have asked whatever the traffic would bear. By contrast, if their behaviour was commonplace, as was probable, then the general law of political economy applied. When demands for loans forced interest rates to the legal ceiling, would-be borrowers had to content themselves with borrowing less than they wanted as liquid funds dried up. At times of extreme demand, borrowing virtually became impossible. This, however, is not to suggest that the usury laws were invariably followed; in periods of prolonged illiquidity there always could be found those prepared to conclude illegal transactions.[37]

Furthermore, though the Warrens adhered to the law, they were nevertheless in the habit of charging the maximum rate of interest and rarely granted their debtors an interest-free interval. Between 1731 and 1769 only sixteen debtors are known to have been given preferential treatment of this sort. Analysis of the New York economy at various moments in this period produces no explanation for this phenomenon. Wherever there are examples of such favourable treatment being granted, usually at a per cent or per cent and a half below the ceiling, there are many more contemporaneous instances of loans made at the maximum rate. The explanation must be in Warren's personal relationship to his debtors. For instance, his desire to find settlers for his Mohawk valley tract in the 1730s inspired him to lend money to newly-established families at seven instead of eight per cent interest, with an interest-free interval of two years. Another example of such favourable treatment concerns Warren's nephew, William Johnson, whose first bond was interest-free for four years and the second for twelve years.[38] There is also some evidence that larger loans were made at privileged rates. Thus NY£1,200 was loaned to Nicholas Bayard in 1743, NY£700 to the Dongans in 1747, and NY£1,000 to the Willets in 1748, all at six per cent when the prevailing rate was seven. Oliver DeLancey in partnership with Beverley Robinson in 1759 also were made a large loan of NY£1,285 at a rate of interest below the legal ceiling.[39]

The financial interests of the Warrens in New York also cast light on the DeLanceys, a family of considerable importance in both the political and economic life of the province. Although their political activities have attracted much comment from historians, their economic empire remains largely unstudied.[40] From the evidence presented here it is obvious that part of the Warrens' capital came from the modest fortune created by Stephen DeLancey, and later assigned to the Warrens as part of their marriage settlement. This capital took the form of bonds and mortgages from New York and New Jersey businessmen. Only rarely did the Warrens themselves intervene to designate those to whom loans should be made. For the most part, Warren debtors were men known to the DeLanceys in the daily course of their own business pursuits.

In particular Oliver DeLancey profited from his role as Warren agent. Though he made no formal charge for his services, he was always able to draw on Lady Warren for short-term funds, and as Warren income and capital gathered in his hands, he had the use of it, while he made remittances to her only about every fifteen months. On occasion he floated a long-term loan from his sister at an interest rate well below the legal ceiling, and without first securing her authorization. Such financial security, in a period of considerable economic anxiety in New York, afforded him a very special advantage. It is therefore in no way surprising that his claim after 1783 for compensation amounted to one of the half-dozen largest submitted by a Loyalist to the British government. Furthermore, by being able to direct the flow of Warren capital with a free hand between 1753 and 1769, DeLancey was able to show favour to his particular business associates, thus strengthening his own position among them.

On a more general level, the analysis of the Warren's money-lending interests in New York draws attention to an unnecessary lacuna in

American colonial historiography. Though the general features of the credit system of the British seaborne empire are well known, neither the pattern of inter-colonial credit nor of private credit advanced between individuals without necessarily involving an exchange of goods has yet been examined. Scattered evidence suggests that a credit system pervaded the economy of each colony, New York included, wherein almost everyone, even with the smallest amounts of capital, extended credit and took bonds and mortgages as security even for minute sums.[41] Yet neither the pattern of this type of credit nor its importance in comparison with credit advanced from abroad are yet determined.[42] It might, for instance, be assumed that the principal American ports—Boston, Newport, New York, Philadelphia, and Charleston—as well as other centres, such as Albany, were creditors to their rural hinterlands, but the evidence to establish such a pattern has yet to be collected. Nor are the financial relationships between such towns properly understood. For instance, Boston's position as an entrepôt declined relatively from at least the 1730s, while New York and Philadelphia underwent a corresponding advance.[43] Yet the extent to which Boston's net financial position was actually undermined by this relative decline in trade is a matter still inadequately studied. Such study may illuminate the reasons for the great variety in rates at which money could be loaned within neighbouring American provinces. In Georgia and South Carolina the legal ceiling was 10 per cent, while on the other end of the scale Virginia established a ceiling of six per cent and in 1748 reduced this to five per cent.[44] Only by further research can it be known if these legal rates actually reflected the cost of money, and whether or not the laws were effective in protecting the borrower from excessive rates. Such work will perhaps also demonstrate the relationship between the rate of interest and the price of land, the state of trade and the general stage of economic development of each colony at different times.[45] It should also help establish the relationship between public borrowing by colonial governments and private borrowing by individuals.[46] Even if some of these questions can be only partially answered, knowledge of the colonial American economy will have been considerably advanced.

Chapter 6

Money Lending

in New England

1739-1805

Peter Warren was an untypical source of credit for the businessmen of New England. He was not himself a merchant, though as a naval officer he had dabbled in trade.[1] He was not a native New Englander, though he was by no means ignorant of New England. He had commanded the Royal Navy station ship at Boston between 1736 and 1741, and later had participated closely with the Yankees in the capture of Louisbourg in 1745 and lived with them through a period of appalling disease in the winter of 1745-46. The following summer he left Louisbourg for Boston where he planned with them the assault on Canada.[2] Later when he returned to England and became a Member of Parliament, he did not forget New England. He employed whatever influence he possessed to hasten the ministry's decision to indemnify the several New England governments for a significant part of their expenses during the siege of Louisbourg. Ultimately in the summer of 1749 when the government agreed to make payment, Warren acted as one of the trustees on behalf of Massachusetts.[3]

Warren's New England interests were thus solidly based in personal knowledge of the colony. Nevertheless, his absentee status after 1746 made the use of agents there as necessary as in New York. Agency, as usual, was changeable and costly. Messrs. Frankland, Apthorp, and Thomas Hancock of Boston were Warren's original agents, though Henry Frankland retired from business in 1754 and Apthorp died in 1759. When Thomas Hancock died in 1764, the Warren affairs passed into the hands of his nephew, John Hancock, to whom he left his entire fortune. John Hancock wanted no part of the agency, and no suitable replacement was found. Henry Lloyd Jr. was approached but declined the offer of the agency.[4] Eventually Samuel Fitch, a Boston merchant, became agent for a short time. He was found to be ineffective and in 1775 John Watts Jr. went to Boston in an unsuccessful attempt to find a suitable alternate. The onset of the war left the Warren affairs in a state of suspension; only in 1787 did Watts resume contact with Boston on behalf of the Warren heirs. In the next few years, until 1805 when the Warren interests in New England were liquidated, Watts employed a number of agents, the most prominent of whom was the Boston lawyer, John Lowell Jr.

Warren made his first loan in New England in 1739 to William Bollan, an English-born Boston lawyer, who married Governor William Shirley's daughter, and became advocate general for Massachusetts in 1742.[5] Warren took Bollan's note for £105 at six per cent. Warren received the first interest payment from Bollan in September 1740.[6] When Warren was next in Boston in August 1741 he loaned Bollan a further £100, but this time took his bond, the first note being paid off at this time.[7] In 1744, Warren took another £100 bond from Bollan, the arrangement being concluded in his absence by Messrs. Frankland, Apthorp, and Hancock.[8] Both were paid off by the summer of 1746.

These loans were the forerunners of a far larger investment by Warren in 1746 and 1747. The total capital outlay amounted to £6,470. His funds came from his share of prizes taken the year before at Louisbourg. He had first intended to use the money to finance the purchase of the Lloyd's Neck estate on Long Island.[9] This scheme failed to develop; and faced with the prospect of returning to England with a large amount of cash, Warren decided to put part of it to use in New England. This did not strike him as a great risk, for he fully expected to return to America the following spring in command of a great squadron for the conquest of Canada. He was then in the midst of the previously mentioned negotiations with George Clinton, the New York governor and connection of the Duke of Newcastle and Henry Pelham, to purchase the governorship for an annuity of £400 a year.[10]

All but two of the new loans made in Boston were in sterling. The two exceptions were in Massachusetts Old Tenor. On 14 November

1746 he loaned the Reverend Charles Brockwell, the assistant minister at King's Chapel, Boston, м£100 Old Tenor, taking his note which read: "I Promise to Pay Peter Warren Esq[r]. or Order on Demand the Sum of One Hundred Pounds Old Tenor, with Legal Interest from the date hereof."[11] Five days later he loaned Captain Robert Cummings, a merchant ship's commander м£400 Old Tenor for the account of his nephew, Captain Warren Johnson, newly arrived in Boston from Ireland.[12] These were the only two loans in New England which Warren and his heirs failed to recover, a loss in terms of sterling of £83 6s. 8d. Brockwell died insolvent never having paid any interest or principal, while Cummings soon after left Boston, leaving the note unpaid, and was never heard of again.[13]

Other loans made by Warren in New England before he left Boston in November 1746 included a £900 mortgage at five per cent taken from Estes and Nathaniel Hatch on 1 October 1746.[14] Two more loans were concluded on 14 November 1746: £2,500 at six per cent to Captain Godfrey Malbone[15] and Jahleel Brenton,[16] of which £2,000 was secured by mortgage and £500 by means of a bond; £1,000 also at six per cent to Colonel Daniel Updike[17] and Jahleel Brenton also secured by a mortgage. In addition, on 18 November 1746 Warren loaned £75 to Captain Jonathan Bagley[18] and £30 to Colonel Israel Williams,[19] in both cases being satisfied with their notes of hand as sufficient security. Before leaving Boston on 28 November 1746 Warren told his agents to use whatever interest they collected for "other bonds or mortgages as you shall judge most for my advantage at the legal interest of 6 p.C[t]. ascertaining the money to Sterling."[20] He also referred to specific loans which he had not time to bring to a conclusion before sailing. His letter is a good example of the business-like manner in which he typically conducted his affairs:[21]

Having agreed to Lend M[r]. George Cradack £800 St[g]. at 5 p[r]. C[t] Interest, to be paid in England or here at my option, upon his and M[r]. Brinley's bond, and also to lend M[r]. Brinley two hundred pounds Sterling at 6 p[r]. Cent Interest, upon his bond, for which sum as well as for the other . . , M[r]. Brinley agrees to give me any Collateral security that I shall think proper to desire, I must therefore pray the favour of you, when M[r]. Brinley and M[r]. Cradack shall have executed the said Bonds, and a general Mortgage upon M[r]. Brinleys whole estate as a Collateral security to your and my Lawyer, M[r]. Auchmutys satisfaction, after the records are duly

TABLE 12 *New England Loans 1739-1751*

Date	Debtor	Principal	Interest	Paid Off
Sept. 1739	William Bollan	£ 105	6%	1741
August 1741	William Bollan	100	6%	1746
16 Jan. 1744/45	William Bollan	100	6%	1746
1 Oct. 1746	Estes and Nathaniel Hatch	900	5%	Nov. 1759
14 Nov. 1746	Rev. Charles Brockwell	17	6%	Bad Debt
14 Nov. 1746	Capt. Godfrey Malbone and Jahleel Brenton	2,000	6%	1754
14 Nov. 1746	Jahleel Brenton and Malbone	500	6%	May 1760
14 Nov. 1746	Col. Daniel Updike and Jahleel Brenton	1,000	6%	July 1760
18 Nov. 1746	Captain Jonathan Bagley	75	6%	By 1752
18 Nov. 1746	Colonel Israel Williams	30	6%	By 1752
19 Nov. 1746	Captain Robert Cummings	67	6%	Bad Debt
29 Dec. 1746	Major Leonard Lockman and John Jones	50	6%	Sept. 1763
30 Dec. 1746	Francis Brinley and George Cradock	800	5%	Bad Debt*
30 Dec. 1746	Francis Brinley and George Cradock	200	6%	Bad Debt*
4 Feb. 1746/47	Jonathan Belcher	800	5%	1757
20 Feb. 1750/51	Daniel Ayrault Jr. and Jahleel Brenton	32	6%	1752

Source: Gage Papers.

*Secured by mortgage on land.

examin'd, and no other incumbrances found thereupon, and the Mortgage to me shall be properly executed, acknowledg'd and recorded, that you will draw Bills upon me for the abovemention'd sums, payable at 60 days after sight.

The £1,000 loan to Brinley[22] and Cradock[23] was concluded on 30 December 1746, while the day before Frankland, Apthorp, and Hancock took a £50 bond from Major Leonard Lockman[24] and John Jones,[25] at six per cent interest.[26]

Only two further loans were made in New England between 1747 and Warren's death in 1752. One of £800 to Jonathan Belcher, who, in the spring of 1747, had secured, after years of soliciting the Duke of Newcastle for an appointment, the governorship of New Jersey.[27] The loan was secured by a mortgage on Belcher's 200–acre farm at Milton, Massachusetts; and interest payments were to be made in

Boston by Belcher's son. The second loan was for £31 16s., made in February 1750/51 to Brenton and his son-in-law, Daniel Ayrault Jr.[28] This small loan, Bollan's bonds, and Col. Williams's note of £30 were the only debts that had been cleared by the time Warren died. Table 13 summarizes the details of all the New England loans.

Lady Warren was anxious to wind up her husband's New England interests and gave her brother, Oliver DeLancey, instructions to call in all outstanding obligations due the estate. Here she experienced great frustration. She soon discovered that unless Sir Peter Warren's will was probated in Boston and unless Frankland, Apthorp, and Hancock were given power to discharge mortgages, they would lose any suit they might initiate in a Massachusetts court for the recovery of debts.[29] It was not until the spring of 1754 that her Boston agents had the necessary powers of attorney and a start could be made to collect these debts.

Lady Warren's frustrations were shared by a least one of her debtors: Colonel Estes Hatch. Hatch had been obliged to mortgage his farm at Dorchester, Suffolk County as well as land in Worcester County; and upon learning of Warren's death was anxious to redeem his mortgage. He had not paid any of the £900 in principal, and only £45 in interest.[30] In October 1751 he had given Warren a bond to cover the £183 9s. in interest arrears. He was advised in 1753 to collect enough capital to pay off the mortgage. This he did with great difficulty, only to be told by Frankland, Apthorp, and Hancock that "the Lady Warren's powers tyes up their hands that they cannot give me a proper discharge of the mortgage."[31] His son Nathaniel then drafted a release and sent it to Chief Justice DeLancey for authorization before a New York justice of the peace in the hope that it would be accepted in Boston.[32] However, he was soon informed that this procedure was not acceptable and would have to wait the arrival of the new power of attorney from England. By the end of April 1754 he had paid off the £900 mortgage, but the final payment of the interest due was delayed until November 1759, when the estate of Colonel Hatch was settled by his heirs.[33]

Another of Warren's debtors prepared to pay off part of his debt was Godfrey Malbone. To secure his £2,000 bond Malbone had mortgaged his house and farm near Newport. His first interest payment for £120 was made in May 1749, and in December 1751 he gave Warren a new bond for £525 to secure the unpaid interest.[34] No further payments were made before Warren's death, but in the spring of 1754 he paid

Hancock £2,837 1s. 9d., the balance of the debt.[35] Malbone had incurred a £500 debt in November 1746 in addition to the £2,000 mortgage; and this he was far slower to pay off. The final payment appears to have been made only in May 1760, by which time Apthorp and Hancock had received £746 15s.[36]

Governor Belcher was rather more prompt in repaying his £800 mortgage. In April 1750, his son paid Apthorp three years' interest: £120. The principal was repaid in 1754 after the marriage of his son Andrew to Miss Elizabeth Trale, his step-sister, who brought with her a £1,500 dowry. Part of this was used to recover the mortgage on the farm at Milton.[37] Lockman and Jones long delayed in paying off their bond. Interest was at first paid regularly, but when news of Warren's death reached them, interest payments were not again made until 1760. The balance of the interest and the entire principal were paid only in September 1763.[38] Colonel Daniel Updike of Kings County, Rhode Island, was equally tardy in repaying his debts to the Warrens. To secure his loan of £1,000 he had mortgaged his house and farm, yet took until July 1760 to clear the debt, by which time he had paid the Warren agents £1,581 5s. 4½d.[39]

These delays were nothing compared to the difficulties occasioned by the mortgage taken from Francis Brinley and George Cradock in 1746. The property mortgaged was an 862–acre farm at Framingham, about twenty-five miles from Boston on the road to Worcester. In April 1748, Brinley and Cradock made their first interest payment of £52.[40] In November 1751 Warren, through his agents, obliged them to give a separate bond to cover the unpaid interest then amounting to £224 17s. 6d.[41] No further payments were received before Warren's death in 1752. However, Oliver DeLancey thought the prospect of repayment so good that he told his sister, Lady Warren: "I think you may safely leave Mr. Brinleys debt provided he is punctual in paying the interest."[42] The advice was accepted but, as neither Brinley nor Cradock were regular in their interest payments, by 1757 Lady Warren pressed DeLancey to get this, and all outstanding obligations in New England, paid off promptly.[43] Despite pressure from Apthorp,[44] Brinley merely wrote DeLancey a letter expressing his intention of conforming to Lady Warren's "most Equitable demand" and added:

As the Sum is pretty Considerable (as well as heavy on me) being only a Security for an unfortunate Gent[n]. Mr. Cradock. I hope both her Ladyship, and you won't press on me too hard, but be as favourable as you can. The Honbl S^r. Peter Warren Deceas'd Ever Assur'd me He'd be Favourable, now as that Gent: M^r: Cradock has putt into my hands landed Estate sufficient, but these Times of warr and Difficulties make it hard to sell is my Burthen. Who have been setting out five Sons in the World, and am Growing Old, wanting the time above from my Lady to be more particular.[45]

DeLancey thereupon ordered Apthorp "to get the Money in the best Way possible."[46] However, by the time Apthorp died a year later nothing more had been received from Brinley or Cradock. The Warren affairs then passed solely into Thomas Hancock's hands, and though he too failed to raise any money from Brinley and Cradock, he managed to increase the security of the debt. He obliged them in December 1759 to give a £100 bond for part of the unpaid interest due, and the following June as further security he got from them a mortgage on two farms owned by Brinley, one at Needham and a large one in Leicester.[47] He was still unable to make them pay off any of the debt by the time of his own death in 1764.

Thomas Hancock's death marked a decline in the level of attention which the Warren affairs received in Boston. Frankland, Apthorp, and Hancock all had known Admiral Warren and had maintained some personal interest in Warren's affairs after his death in 1752. With Thomas Hancock's death, this personal link was broken, and Oliver DeLancey never found an adequate substitute. Thomas's heir, John Hancock, refused to handle the agency, and instead recommended another Boston businessman, Samuel Fitch, to whom John Hancock gave all the Warren New England documents, after repeated requests from Oliver DeLancey.[48] Fitch managed to collect some of the outstanding interest owed by Brinley and Cradock, for by 1776 he owed the Warren estate £222 16s. 3d.[49] He also filed suit against the pair, the result of which was that the Brinley farm at Framingham passed into the hands of the Warren heirs. Oliver DeLancey thereupon leased the Framingham farm to Edward Brinley at a yearly rent of £30. In 1776 DeLancey attempted to sell the Framingham farm for £1,000. Articles of agreement were drawn up between himself and John Taylor of Northborough and John Emms of Framingham, payment to be made in two equal sums in March 1777 and 1778. The war prevented the deal from being completed.

It was a decade before the Warren interests in New England again received any attention. In 1787 John Watts Jr., who since 1783 had been solely responsible for the interests of the Warren heirs in America, wrote to John Hancock asking that a debt, owed by his uncle Thomas Hancock, be paid to the Warren heirs, and added "I think it reasonable some Interest should be paid."[50] The debt was merely £47 19s. 4d., the balance in the Warren–Hancock account since 1763. He also asked a New York merchant and friend, Daniel Ludlow, who was on his way to Boston, to collect the debt and to investigate the state of the Warren farm at Framingham.[51] Ludlow secured the help of the Boston attorney David Sears, who discovered that the Framingham farm was held by Levi Thayer, who claimed to have a deed of sale from Oliver DeLancey.[52] It was not until 1794 that Watts was in a position to get writs of ejection filed against the then tenants of Framingham. When the principal tenant refused to abandon his holding, claiming a valid deed from Thayer, the opinion was solicited of one of Boston's ablest attorneys, John Lowell Jr. After studying the dispute, Lowell took a great interest in the property. He told Watts in New York of the spoiling that the estate had suffered: "The depredations already committed have reduced the farm to a deplorable condition, and the misfortune is, that both the past and the present tenants are as unable to compensate for the injuries as they have been shameless in y^e. commission of them."[53]

Lowell complained that much good timber was being cut and sold in Boston for firewood and lumber. John Watts merely advised that either he or Edward Brinley, who also acted on behalf of the Warren heirs in Boston, should contact Admiral Warren's only surviving daughter, Ann, the wife of Lord Southampton. Brinley wrote and found out that neither she nor her husband knew much about their New England interests, but let it be known that if an offer for the Framingham farm was made it would be accepted.[54] A decade later, in July 1805, Lowell purchased the Framingham farm for £900 from Lady Southampton and Montagu, fifth Earl of Abingdon, Admiral Warren's grandson, the only other of his heirs with a legal interest in his estate in America.[55] With this Warren's last connection with New England was severed.

What conclusions can be drawn from this evidence? In the first instance, money lending was both a profitable and secure form of investment, even when an ocean separated the debtor and creditor and despite the absence of a continuing business arrangement, such as that which characterized the normal relations between merchants of England and New England. Bad debts amounted to £1,083, but of this all but £83 was secured by mortgage, the loss being only 1.3 per cent of the total capital outlay of £6,470.

However, assets in the form of loans were not nearly as liquid as they appeared. The bonds taken by Warren, for instance, were almost invariably for twelve months, and legally, unless they were repaid on time, the creditor could demand a penal sum of twice the original principal. In fact there is no example either of such bonds being repaid within the specified interval or of Warren demanding the penalty. Moreover, though he was not anxious to recover the outstanding loans, his widow was, and it took her agents from 1753 to 1760 to collect all debts that were capable of being repaid. That the debtors were usually remiss in paying their interest regularly or in paying off the principal was of course a matter of some embarrassment to Lady Warren and her agents, for the debtors were not small businessmen or farmers. They were men prominent in their communities, against whom the agents were reluctant to bring law suits for the recovery of debt, except in the case of Brinley and Cradock who had obviously become by the 1760s incapable of meeting obligations made in the 1740s.

In New England, as elsewhere, Warren adhered strictly to the laws governing interest rates, which in Massachusetts had a ceiling of six per cent.[56] Several loans were made at rates below this ceiling but whether this was a reflection of the market for loans in 1746, or merely the result of Warren's friendship with his debtors is unclear.[57] Nor does any pattern emerge if loans made on the security of bonds are compared with those secured by mortgages.

The real economic significance of Warren's money-lending activities in New England could be estimated properly only if the use to which his loans were put was known. His debtors in New England formed part of the economic and social elite; yet they were for the most part not builders of family fortunes, but men who enjoyed the benefits of wealth that had been accumulated a generation earlier. Though evidence is lacking, it would appear that the funds borrowed from Warren were used for consumption rather than investment, a pattern already well known to students of eighteenth-century England, but only beginning to be investigated in New England.[58] This view would help to explain the difficulties they faced in repaying their loans. This contrasts with the decidedly mercantile character of Warren's investments in New York.

Exceptions may have been Godfrey Malbone and Jahleel Brenton. It is known that both invested in privateers between 1739 and 1747, and, though at first very successful, disaster overtook their ventures in 1746 and 1747. In 1746 two large privateers, the *Duke of Cumberland* (30 guns), owned wholly by Malbone, and the *Prince of Wales* (22 guns), jointly owned by Malbone and Brenton were cast away in what has been described as "one of the greatest calamaties that ever befell Newport."[59] The next year Malbone's privateer *Charming Betty* (10 guns) was captured. This triple disaster seems to have substantially undermined the financial position of both men, while Warren's loans were crucial in shoring up their affairs.[60]

Finally, as in the case of Warren's New York investments, the American Revolution had little real impact upon the final dispositon of the Warren assets in New England. The war certainly prevented the intended sale of the 862–acre Framingham farm, and permitted a fraudulant claim to delay for a decade the return of the property to the admiral's heirs. In 1805 the farm fetched £900, whereas in 1776 it might have sold for £1,000. The loss was not just the difference of £100, for in the intervening thirty years inflation had undermined the purchasing power of sterling, so that an additional loss of at least £400 must be estimated.[61] Yet this last asset held by the Warren heirs in New England had not been forfeited, even though for years it had been virtually forgotten. It is somewhat ironical that eventually the claims of the absentee English landowners, then members of the aristocracy, were made good by the efforts of John Lowell, a well-to-do Boston lawyer, against the interests of small New England farmers, in whose interests the American Revolution presumably had been fought. Only further study of such examples of post-war assets held by British subjects will show if the Warrens were exceptional or part of a larger group. Even if they are shown to be exceptional, their example shows that behind the rhetoric which kept Americans and British apart at that time, there was a strong effort on the part of the economic elites of both nations to carry on as if no political gulf divided them. Evidence arising from the study of the Warren's New England interests thus adds to the general impression that the American Revolution had an essentially conservative impact on Anglo-American economic relations.

Chapter 7

South Carolina

Interests

1731-1771

Besides investments in New York and New England, Warren had a limited interest in the province of South Carolina. His career as a naval officer had brought him to Charleston on three occasions, and in all he lived there for more than a year. In 1728, as captain of the *Solebay,* he was en route to England from Vera Cruz, where he had negotiated the release of South Sea Company ships seized by the Spanish authorities at the outbreak of war two years earlier, when his frigate was battered by a hurricane and Warren put into Charleston for repairs. On that occasion he remained four months and established a lifelong friendship with Captain George Anson, commander of the South Carolina station ship.[1] Warren was next in Charleston in the winter of 1731-32, as commander of the station ship. He fully expected to spend at least a couple of years there, but the sharp reduction in naval forces by Parliament in 1732 obliged him to return to England after only seven months' duty there. His last visit to Charleston occurred in the winter of 1739-40, at the outbreak of war with Spain, when for some months he commanded the small squadron protecting South Carolina and Georgia from possible Spanish attack. It was during these months that preparations were made for the siege in the summer of 1740 of St. Augustine, the principal Spanish fortress in Florida. When the attack failed Warren left South Carolina for the last time, his brief association with the colony surviving only in a Charleston street name. The South Carolina that Warren knew was experiencing remarkable expansion, after a decade of political upheaval and economic depression.[2] The first permanent settlement in 1670 had developed slowly under the threat of attack by the Spanish, who were closer than the nearest substantial English settlements on the Chesapeake. The 1703 population of about 8,000 had grown to 30,000 by 1732. Two-thirds of the settlers were black slaves.[3] The disproportion between white settlers and black slaves remained the most important demographic characteristic of colonial South Carolina, despite a bounty since 1716 of sc£25 paid for every white indentured servant brought into the colony. Moreover a series of laws, the first of which was passed in 1703, imposing duties on blacks imported for sale in the colony, proved equally ineffective in creating a more balanced racial mixture. In time South Carolina merchants established "the largest and most widely developed slave trade of any of the English continental colonies."[4] Besides the slave trade, the colony's wealth was built upon its overseas trade in rice, first grown successfully in the 1690s and greatly stimulated after 1730, when it was for the first time permitted to be shipped directly to European ports south of Cape Finisterre.[5] Next to rice came naval stores, lumber, indigo, and from the 1740s, leather and deerskins, the principal items of the lucrative Indian trade.

Charleston, with its excellent harbour despite the bar which was passable by large ships only at high tide, prospered and grew to become by the 1760s the largest colonial city south of Philadelphia.[6] Though the capital of the province, it was without public buildings until the assembly erected a state house in 1756. Its prosperity was expressed in the stately private houses erected from the 1730s onwards, well-spaced on broad straight streets, lined with pine, cedar, and cypress trees. Like New York, the city had the well-merited reputation of being devoted as much to pleasure as to business.

A proprietary charter had been the basis of South Carolina's government until 1729, when, after a revolt in Charleston and much wrangling between rival factions, a royal charter was granted and Robert Johnson was named first royal governor. Johnson found the leading political agitators of the previous decade prepared to compromise. Restoring political harmony to the province, he launched South Carolina on an economic boom, which lasted until the outbreak of war with Spain in 1739, and was characterized principally by a remarkable expansion in rice production. Prosperity in the rice market created a land boom as rice planters inceased the area under cultivation. It also stimulated the slave trade, as cheap labour stood in high demand. It was Johnson's rationalization of the province's land system that became his most enduring contribution to South Carolina's history. He found the land system by 1730 in virtual chaos. The land office had been closed since 1719, no accurate roll of grants existed, and the quit rents demanded varied greatly from grant to grant. Johnson persuaded the colonists to accept a new land law, by which all proprietary land claims were recognized, if they were registered within two years. Landholders had to pay a uniform quit rent of 1s. per 100 acres, due on Lady Day of each year. If the quit rent fell in arrears for more than five years, the grant became void and the land could be granted anew. Finally the law remitted all quit rent arrears. The land office was reopened in November 1731 and soon 1,450,000 acres were confirmed in the possession of the claimants. The new law, however, did not deal with royal land grants made after 1730; but in practice Johnson and his council refused to grant lands until the patentee swore that the land was not for speculation. Under this system some 900,000 acres were newly granted in the 1730s in tracts ranging in size from 400 to 1,000 acres. In addition some 240,000 acres were granted according to a township plan proposed by Johnson and approved by the colony in 1730. Twelve new townships, each of 20,000 acres, were laid out, with 250 acres reserved for the development of the principal village, the rest being allotted in parcels of 100 and 75 acres to settlers. The settlers, poor Protestants from Europe, were also supplied with tools to help them get established. As a result colonies of Swiss, German, Irish, and Scottish immigrants were settled on the southern and western frontiers of the province, greatly adding to its security.

Under the reformed land system, Warren applied for and received two separate grants, the first in 1733 and the next in 1736. In March 1732, Robert Johnson issued a warrant permitting a survey to be made of 1,000 acres in Colleton County, lying west of Charleston. Three months later the survey was conducted under the direction of James St. John, Surveyor General of South Carolina, and a plan drawn of it.[7] The tract was long and narrow, some four miles in length from east to west, and a half mile deep. Almost a third, comprising most of the eastern portion, was marshy land through which Fishpond Creek meandered. Elsewhere the tract was heavily forested with oak, pine, hickory, beech, and dogwood trees, with cypress growing in the marsh. Lying south of a similar grant made to Thomas Arnold, a naval captain who had served with Anson on the South Carolina station, Warren's tract was officially patented in July 1733.[8] As with all such grants, one-tenth of all precious metals as well as all white pine timber was reserved for the crown. In addition, the grant was made with the usual condition that Warren, "within three years next . . . Clear and Cultivate at the rate of one Acre every five hundred acres of land and so in proportion according to the quantity of acres contained or build a Dwelling house thereon and keep a stock of five head of Cattle for every five hundred Acres upon the Same and in proportion for a greater or lesser quantity."[9]

Warren's second grant was made in September 1736, under letters patent signed by Lieutenant Governor Thomas Broughton, who had succeeded to the role of chief executive after Johnson died in 1735.[10] The grant amounted to 950 acres and was situated in Craven County lying north of Charleston. The same conditions applied to this grant as to the first. Warren was not then in South Carolina, and the circumstances surrounding his request for the new grant are not known. Both grants were assessed the usual quit rents. Yet Warren apparently only made two such payments, during the winter of 1739-40, amounting to sc£20 2s. 3d.[11] Though no other payments ever appear to have been made, Warren did not suffer loss of his land as the Quit Rent Act of 1731 had threatened. In fact, crown officials did well if they collected as much as half of what was due them, for as land was sold by the original patentees, the new buyers avoided registering the sales, as no regulation to do so existed. The result was that as land changed hands the quit rent roll dwindled.

There is little indication that Warren made any attempt to develop these tracts in line with the terms of the grants. Certainly he could have had no direct hand in the business, for he was absent from South Carolina from July 1732 until September 1739. In the interval his affairs were under the care of Anson so long as he served at Charleston, Christopher Gadsden, the Collector of Customs, and James Graeme, then judge of the Vice Admiralty Court and later Chief Justice of South Carolina. Gabriel Manigault,[12] one of Charleston's leading merchants, was also concerned in Warren's affairs there. If any development actually took place on the Warren tracts it was these men who saw to it. The evidence is simply that Warren retained in the 1730s for varying lengths of time a number of white indentured servants. That these servants were connected with South Carolina is uncertain, but they are not found either as members of his crews nor related to his New York interests. Moreover, the sc£25 bounty for each such servant offered by the South Carolina government would have acted as a serious inducement to Warren to settle bondsmen on his lands. The men are mentioned last in a financial statement which he prepared for his wife's use in March 1737.[13]

In 1751 Warren disposed of these properties for the nominal sum of 5s. to his nephew Richard Tyrrell, then a captain in the Royal Navy, "in consideration of the naturall Love and Affection which he hath and beareth to his said Nephew."[14] The deeds spoke of the property as, "All the Estate and Lands of the said Sir Peter Warren situate lying and being in the Province of South Carolina in America containing by estimation Two Thousand Acres . . . and also all houses edifices Buildings Gardens Orchards Lands Meadows Commons Pastures feedings . . . which are now or formerly were therewith used occupyed or enjoyed." Whether this was merely legal jargon or was meant truly to indicate that some real improvements had been made on the tracts remains uncertain. It seems doubtful that Warren would have put his signature to such a deed, if in fact the tracts were still the same unimproved marshy wildernesses he had been granted more than fifteen years earlier.

No further mention was made of the South Carolina grants until after Lady Warren's death in 1771, when her heirs suddenly raised the matter with Oliver DeLancey. As they imagined the property "must be of considerable value,"[15] they wrote to DeLancey for information about the estate. The answer they received was not very satisfactory, for DeLancey told them that he still held the original patents, and that he had once been offered £100 for them, and had written to Lady Warren about it, but that she had taken no action. He admitted that he was "quite Ignorant of the State of Lands in that Country and Know few People there."[16] He suggested that they contact Mr. Ralph Izard, a grandson of Governor Robert Johnson, normally a resident of Charleston, who had married DeLancey's niece, Alice DeLancey. The Izards were then in England and had met Lady Warren during her last months, being present at her final illness.[17] Taking DeLancey's advice, the Warren heirs spoke to Izard, who promised to write to Charleston for information; but the replies to his queries never reached him, the mail in which they came being robbed near Rochester on their way to London in May 1774.[18] There the matter was left, the war in America soon overshadowing all other events. At the war's end, when the division of the Warren estate in America took place, there was no mention of the South Carolina properties.

The fact of Tyrrell's ownership must have at length been appreciated by the Warren heirs. Tyrrell had died at sea in June 1766 after a distinguished naval career. His wife, the former Mrs. Russel Tankard Chester of Antigua, rightly considered the South Carolina tract as his property, and shortly afterwards leased it to one of the Middletons, a prominent family in South Carolina.[19] It was to them, presumably, that the land was eventually sold.

In 1732, when Warren took up his appointment as commander of the South Carolina station ship, he not only set about securing a grant of land, but he began lending money privately. By his marriage contract with the DeLancey family in July 1731 he had received NY£3,000 for his own use, independent of the NY£6,000 jointure.[20] About one-third of this sum was used for money-lending purposes at Charleston. Only the shortness of his stay prevented him from making a larger investment, while the fact that he became interested both in land and money lending indicated that he had planned to stay sometime in the province. He loaned £100 in March 1732 to James Graeme, the future chief justice, and £150 to Alexander Vander Dussen, the future commandant of the South Carolina militia in the abortive siege of St. Augustine in 1740.[21] Vander Dussen's loan was secured by a mortgage, the only one Warren held in the province. He also loaned James St. John, the Surveyor General, SC£200 (about £29), Mungo Welch, a Charleston merchant, SC£357 (£51), and two loans to another Charleston merchant, Matison by name, amounting to SC£1,089 (£156). These were all secured by bonds payable within six months. All were at ten per cent interest, the maximum rate allowable under South Carolina law.[22] When Warren left Charleston in July 1732 Anson owed him a small amount of money (£12), and agreed to sell goods valued at SC£395 (£56) which included 100 gallons of French brandy, and a black slave.

So long as Anson remained stationed at Charleston he was principally concerned with Warren's affairs and made various remittances to Warren, the last in October 1735, in the form of bills drawn on the Navy Board and credited to Warren's account by his London agent, Edward Jasper. All debts, except Vander Dussen's, were cleared by the time Warren returned to Charleston in September 1739. At that time he did not again invest in the Charleston money market, even though he managed to take two Spanish prizes during the siege of St. Augustine. Both were condemned by the Charleston Vice Admiralty Court, one valued at £180 and the other £1,715, his share being above £390.[23] The Vander Dussen mortgage was not paid off until July 1760, the affair being closed by Gabriel Manigault,[24] who had handled Warren's interests in South Carolina after Anson's departure in 1735. With this final transaction the Warren interests in South Carolina, very limited compared to his investments either in New York or New England, came to an end (see table 13).

TABLE 13 *American Investments 1732, 1742, 1752*

Assets	Value					
	1732	%	1742	%	1752	%
New York Loans	£2,480	75.7	£ 8,208	53.9	£8,174	28.9
New York Land	313	9.6	6,780	44.4	13,670	48.3
New England Loans	—	—	100	0.7	6,408	22.3
South Carolina Loans	486	14.7	150	1.0	150	0.5
Total	£3,279	100.0	£15,238	100.0	£28,402	100.0

Source: Miscellaneous Gage Papers and Warren Papers.

With almost 15 per cent of his assets in South Carolina in 1732, Warren gave every indication of solid interest in the prospering province. Opportunity to develop this interest failed to materialize and decline was rapid, so that a decade later no more than one per cent of his American assets was left in South Carolina. Nevertheless they are worth mentioning as they highlight a dimension of his affairs which in 1732 at least, promised to grow considerably. At that time he seemed confident that his term of serivce on the South Carolina station would last much longer than it actually did. With cash in hand he was reluctant to let it lie idle, and so put it to work at once. The attractive ten per cent interest rate in South Carolina, compared to eight per cent in New York where he had just begun lending money, had great appeal for him. Moreover, he must have been influenced by the stability of South Carolina's political life under Governor Johnson, which contrasted so markedly with the decade of chaos and revolution that had preceded it. Nor can he have failed to be impressed with the sc£25 bounty offered for immigrant white indentured servants. To profit by this regulation, he felt he must acquire some land on which the indentured men could work. He had arrived in Charleston at a moment when the chaos of South Carolina's land system had but recently been rationalized, the governor and council being eager to make new grants of land to those prepared to carry out improvements. This fortuitous beginning came abruptly to an end as a result of the Admiralty's orders to return to England in 1732. Warren's subsequent appointments in the navy brought him only once more to South Carolina, at which time he declined making further investments, as his American interests by then were concentrated in New York. By conveying his land grants to his nephew in 1751 — the only direct benefit Richard Tyrrell enjoyed from Warren's American estate — he had terminated all connection with South Carolina, except for one debt eventually paid off in 1760.

Part III

England and Ireland

Chapter 8

Estates in Ireland

1712-1791

Land ownership in Ireland underwent dramatic changes between the rebellion in 1641 and the beginning of the eighteenth century. The struggle left the Irish Catholic majority largely dispossessed, supplanted either by alien English Protestant settlers or absentee landowners or by native Irish converts to the established church. In 1641 Catholics held about sixty per cent of the land, by 1688 only twenty-two per cent, and by 1703 not more than fourteen.[1] Thereafter until 1782, when Catholics were once again formally allowed to buy land, the Catholic hold on Ireland further diminished through the workings of the penal laws, Catholic indebtedness, and the conversion of Catholic landowners to Protestantism. Arthur Young's estimate that by the end of the eighteenth century nearly the whole of Ireland was owned by five thousand Protestant landlords has largely been accepted by historians. Many were absentees living in England and Scotland who never crossed the Irish sea. Yet, even they were not immune to the economic fluctuations of the century, and some were obliged to sell their Irish lands because of growing debt or the failure of the male line.

Peter Warren, though born into an Irish Catholic family of small landowners, did not inherit a single acre of Irish land. The Warrens, like so many Irish Catholic families, twice forfeited their estate, first in the Cromwellian settlement after the civil survey of the 1650s and later by the bills of attainder of the English Parliament in 1689 directed against Irish Jacobites. Unlike many others among the Anglo-Irish Catholic gentry, they twice recovered their land, first by the 1663 restoration and secondly by the terms of the Treaty of Limerick in

1691. Peter Warren, by then a Protestant, acquired the entire family estate from his Catholic brother by two purchases in 1730 and 1749, thus ending the ancient Catholic line of ownership, which was not re-established until 1806.[2]

The restored estate of Warrenstown was in county Meath some twenty miles northwest of Dublin, lying between the hamlets of Summerhill and Dunshaughlin and the ancient town of Trim. It stood in the midst of good arable land, lush pastures, and a few scattered copses. Well-drained by a rivulet, the Skane, which led to the nearby river Boyne, its 433 acres lay on the southeast slopes of a shallow valley on the opposite side of which stood the eminence of castle Killeen, the principal seat of the Plunkett family, Earls of Fingal. According to Cromwell's civil survey of 1654-56, the estate was largely enclosed, with six acres of meadow, 112 of pasture, and the rest arable.[3] For Ireland generally it was a small holding, though in the Barony of Deece and county Meath it was of middling size. The civil survey distinguished between dwellings by employing these terms: castle, stonehouse, farmhouse, cottage, and cabin. In Deece there were eighteen castles and nine stonehouses, but Warrenstown was merely one of seventeen farmhouses. A later description of Warrenstown, made in 1700 for the trustees of forfeited estates arising from the rebellion of 1688, has survived:

> Warrenstown has a Very good large Farme house, A Barne, Maulthouse & Stable, all Thatch & Mud Walls. In good repair. The Barne & Haggard, Mudd Wall'd in good Order. Two Orcharts and a Kitchin Garden of about 3 Roods, There is about 150 Large Ash Growing Some Distance one from y[e]. other, It's all Arable, & Meddow, Most part under Tillage, The lands one with another are worth 10 sh pr acre p annum.[4]

The estate also had the most celebrated "holy well" in county Meath, which from remote times had been associated with miraculous cures. In 1708 the Irish House of Commons felt obliged to pass an act prohibiting pilgrimages to the well, a custom on the Feast of St. John the Baptist. In the words of the Catholic historian of the diocese of Meath, this was "because those bigoted despots pretended to fear that the poor pilgrims were assembled in that place to the great hazard and danger of the public peace and safety of the kingdom."[5]

Michael Warren, Peter's father, was fortunate indeed to recover his land, but this did not prevent him from gradually slipping deeply into debt. His father had put a £500 mortgage on the estate in 1673, the funds being advanced by a neighbour, Thomas Hussey, Baron of Galtrim.[6] On three occasions Michael Warren was obliged to add to his debt, so that by the time of his death in 1712 it stood at £1,850.[7] The heavily encumbered land passed to his eldest son, then a minor, who had become a Protestant when he entered the navy. His income, partly from rents and partly from naval pay, proved insufficient to sustain the debt charges, with the result that in 1723 he agreed to sell 200 acres or almost half of Warrenstown.[8] In order to redeem most of the Hussey debt two hundred acres were sold for £2,100 to Henry Rowley, one of his tenants who also owned land elsewhere in Meath. The purchase price was insufficient to meet both the principal and accumulated unpaid interest, so even after this arrangement was concluded a £400 mortgage remained on what was left of Warrenstown, the mortgage being held by Rowley.

Lieutenant Oliver Warren died unmarried in August 1724 while on half-pay in Ireland, his estate passing to his brother, Christopher, who in February 1730 sold it to Peter Warren for the sum of £500.[9] Warren was particularly anxious to pay off the £400 mortgage especially after his marriage in 1731, which brought him a sizeable dowry. Rowley proved uncooperative, insisting first that Warren confirm the sale made by his elder brother in 1723.[10] Warren not only refused but filed a suit against Rowley claiming that his brother had had no right to sell the land in the first place. He was not successful; and a solution was reached only after Rowley's death in 1744 by which time Warren's fortune was sufficiently large not only to pay off the mortgage but to finance the repurchase of the alienated part of Warrenstown.

When Warren learned of Rowley's death he was stationed in the West Indies, so he wrote at once to his London agents, Samuel and William Baker to use his investments in the London stock market to finance Rowley's part of Warrenstown, should it be offered for sale.[11] He also contacted his Dublin agent, the attorney Boleyn Whitney, to act with speed should the occasion present itself to buy the land. However, it was not until four years later, in 1748, that Whitney was in a position to act, a lengthy legal battle over the terms of Rowley's will having delayed matters.[12] Whitney first of all negotiated the settlement of the £400 mortgage on that part of Warrenstown owned by Warren. In May 1748 he paid Rowley's executors £592, which included six years of unpaid interest.[13] That summer the Warrenstown property was put up for public auction with Whitney being declared highest bidder at £2,464.[14] Still the matter was not settled. It took another eighteen months to convince the executors to execute the necessary deeds of release, and Whitney was obliged to make a major concession by agreeing to pay Rowley's widow an £80 annuity left to her in his will and charged to the land.[15] The exorbitant charge on a property of that value was obviously acceptable to Warren only in view of his determination to recover the land that had once belonged to his family. This ambition was fully realized when in March 1750 the title to the 200 acres held by Rowley since 1723 was transferred from Whitney's name to Warren's.[16]

Although determined not to settle in Ireland, Warren made land purchases there in addition to Warrenstown, so that by 1752 he owned 1,482 acres. In addition he invested in a lucrative rent charge. The land which caught his attention came on the market as a result of the growing debts of two families, one Catholic and the other Protestant.

The Catholic debtor was the Hussey family, his neighbour in Meath to whom both his father and grandfather had been indebted until 1723. By remaining Catholics the Husseys had experienced the same vicissitudes of fortune as the Warrens, except that they were considerably larger landowners and their debts were much larger, amounting to £7,500 by 1750. Stafford Hussey, the head of the family, decided to clear the debts by taking a path familiar to many landowners: retrenchment and the sale of part of his estate. Late in 1750 an agreement was concluded between him and Whitney, acting on behalf of Warren, by which for £7,679, Hussey sold four farms in county Meath amounting to 890 acres.[17] As security against any future action by any other member of the Hussey family who might believe himself entitled to a share in the estate, Whitney also obliged Hussey to convey to a trustee a further 1,014 acres in the same county.

Warren's last investment in Irish land occurred in 1752 and concerned estates formerly belonging to the family of Sir Richard Kennedy, Bart., who had died in 1688. By 1710 there was no direct male heir except Sir Richard's brother, William, an exile in France, outlawed for his adherence to the cause of James II and his property forfeited to the crown. In 1730 Sir Richard's great grand-daughter, Lady Elizabeth Dudley, the wife of Sir William Dudley, Bart., of Clapton, Northamptonshire, established her claim to part of the Kennedy estates in Ireland. The Westminster Parliament passed a private act by which she and her husband were made tenants in common of the estates with rights to raise portions for their children on the property.[18] This apparent success brought the Dudleys a great deal of trouble. Firstly, they had to share the proceeds of the estate with several other successful claimants, while secondly they lost several important and expensive suits in the courts of Ireland to Edward Keen of Dublin, who by 1752 had gathered into his hands most of the debts owing on the estates. Heedless of their financial difficulties the Dudleys gave their one daughter a £4,000 dowry on the estate in 1745, but soon were obliged to borrow money from their three sons. They also experienced difficulty in collecting rent from one of their principal properties, Ballydowde, a 159–acre farm on the outskirts of Dublin.[19]

Only in 1752 did Dudley agree to dispose of some of his Irish assets to free himself of debt; and Warren through two agents, Robert Macky, a London merchant, and Gabriel Johnston, a solicitor, at once became involved as a potential buyer. Warren's interest focused on four parts of the Kennedy estates: Ballydowde, a £500 annual rent charge on Mount Kennedy in county Wicklow, the Mount Kennedy estate itself, and several Dublin properties including Sir Richard Kennedy's former home. He was successful only in acquiring the first two. His death in Dublin in July 1752 interfered with his remaining plans, which his widow chose not to pursue. Agreement to purchase Ballydowde was concluded between Dudley and Johnston in March 1752, at twenty-four years' purchase amounting to £2,625.[20] In addition Dudley was paid £745 arrears in rent owing on the property. On this part of the sale Warren lost heavily for only £465 of this sum was ever collected from the tenant.[21] The rent charge on Mount Kennedy, valued at £500 annually, was held in part by Sir William Dudley and partly by his eldest son, Obrien. Robert Macky concluded separate agreements with them, paying the son £3,720 for his 80 per cent share in February 1752, and the father £930 for the rest in July.[22] Warren's total investment in the Kennedy estate thus came to £8,020.

Warren's sudden death three weeks after this last deal was concluded put an abrupt halt to his plans to acquire a greater interest in the Kennedy estates. In particular he had been attracted to certain properties on Nicholas Street in Dublin and to the Mount Kennedy estate itself, not just the rent charge. Warren's last surviving letter, written from his Jervis street lodgings in Dublin, provides the evidence for his interest in Mount Kennedy. In it he told his London solicitor, Gabriel Johnston, that he had offered to pay off Sir William Dudley's debts owing to his principal creditor, Edward Keen, on the condition that "there is not more due to him then the Value of the Estate after deducting y^e. Rent Charge of £500 a year, and I own I think it may be come at prety reasonably und^r. Such an Incumbrance."[23] But that was the last either Keen or Dudley heard of the offer.

Negotiations relating to the Dublin properties went a good deal further. The matter was first discussed between Dudley and Johnston in March. Early in April Dudley sent Johnston a detailed description of the property.[24] All leases were to fall in in 1790, and until then the income would be £80 a year. Haggling over price continued until the end of May, when the pair again got together. Dudley backed away from his first demand of twenty-four years' purchase, and Johnston, having first mentioned eighteen, insisted on sixteen years' purchase. To this Dudley agreed on the condition that, of the purchase price of £1,280, £800 would be the minimum down payment.[25] There matters stood when Warren's death obliged Johnston to extricate himself from his verbal commitment.

Between 1730 and 1752 Warren employed a variety of agents for his affairs in Ireland, and several of these were his kinsmen. In general they served him and, after his death, his heirs, with great devotion. His first agent was Patrick Aylmer, a cousin, who like himself was born a Catholic but underwent conversion to the established faith, forsaking the strong Jacobite sympathies of his father, Sir Gerald Aylmer, Bart.[26] When Aylmer died in 1739, Warren replaced him by Boleyn Whitney, a Dublin solicitor, who played an important role in Warren's land purchases and money-lending activities between 1748 and 1752.[27] Rent collection and the overseeing of the estates were at first the responsibility of Warren's Catholic brother-in-law, Christopher Johnson, who was aided by his eldest son, William, until the young man was sent by Warren to America to superintend his Mohawk estate in New York.[28]

In time Christopher Johnson was superseded by another of his sons, John Johnson, also a Catholic. Warren summoned him to England in 1750 asking him both to assume the responsibility of land agent and to become the tenant of Warrenstown. As Johnson explained to his brother in America: "He has been pleased to appoint me his receiver not only for what he has already purchased but for what he may hereafter purchase, in which station I shall endeavour to make it my

Chiefest study to keep up to the great duty we all owe so good an Unckle."[29] John Johnson retained this position after Warren's death in 1752, sending Lady Warren annual accounts and arranging for the necessary bills of exchange to be sent to London.[30] In 1791 when he retired, his son, John Johnson Jr., succeeded him and served the Warren heirs so long as they retained an interest in Ireland.

From the start Warren's Irish estate provided him with a steady income, though its extent is somewhat difficult to establish. In the 1730s Warren referred to his estate (then only 233 acres) as "Commonly lett at 1£150 p^r. annum."[31] This was a rough estimate of the gross rents receivable for by 1741 his expectations had risen above 1£168 per annum or twelve per cent as table 14 illustrates.

TABLE 14 *Warrenstown Rent Roll 1735 and 1741*

Tenants	Rents Receivable	
	1735	1741
Thomas Carr and John Darrahm (Daramy) Gaffney	1£ 60	1£ 70 10s.
Christopher (and William) Johnson	30 12s.	30 12s.
Richard and Anthony Brady	17 16s. 9d.	18 6s. 9d.
Henry Rowley	13 15s. 6d.	
Kearny		18 18s. 6d.
John and Nicholas Kennedy	11 16s. 11d.	12 6s. 11d.
Hugh and Thomas Coffey	7 6s. 6d.	8 15s. 9d.
Patrick Cael	6 2s. 6d.	6 2s. 6d.
James Brady	1 10s.	1 10s.
James Rooney	1 5s.	1 5s.
Total	1£150 5s. 8d.	1£168 7s. 5d.

Source: Gage Papers, G/Am/1, G/Am/12, pp. 14, 25-26.

Against this anticipated income there were certain expenses of which only the quit rent charge of 1£4 6s. 8d. and 1£1 1s. 8d. for the Warrenstown fair are known.[32] It was unlikely that Warren himself paid the tithe, for many Irish landlords insisted when giving leases to their tenants that it be paid by them. Certainly among Warren's papers there is no indication that he made such regular payments of this sort.

Information about the leases of the Warren tenants is scanty.[33] Christopher Johnson and the Coffeys held their land at Warren's pleasure. The leases held by the Bradys and Kennedys expired in May 1737, but how long they had been for or the length of the new ones is not known. Patrick Cael was the only one among Warren's tenants in the 1730s with a relatively long prospect of undisturbed tenancy, for his lease expired in 1754. Even the cottiers, Brady and Rooney, had leases. That Warren gave leases even to his least important tenants appears to conflict with the usual statements about the lowly cottiers. Dr. Connell, for instance, speaks of the "perhaps occasional existence of a lease which the peasant could enforce and which defined the rent."[34] There is no evidence to indicate whether the leaseholders cultivated their holdings themselves or sublet the land, a practice then well established in Ireland.[35]

In 1750, Warren laid the basis for the prosperity of his nephew, John Johnson, by allowing him use of all of Warrenstown at £160 a year. There was no lease involved but the arrangement was confirmed by the terms of Warren's will in July 1752, which in part stated: "I direct that my Nephew John Johnson may hold the Lands of Warrenstown Containing four hundred and forty Eight Acres or thereabouts which he is now in possession of at the yearly Rent of one hundred and Sixty pounds untill my Eldest Daughter may attain her full Age."[36] Miss Ann Warren came of age in 1759, and until then Johnson was guaranteed a rent which was at least £40 undervalued, for the land could easily have fetched fifteen shillings an acre had Warren thrown it open to the highest bidder, a practice widely followed in Ireland. This is no exaggeration for as early as 1741 he had received 1£168 for only 233 acres or 14s. 6d. an acre. In 1759 the rent went up to £280, which John Johnson's son years later acknowledged was moderate.[37] Only in 1771 was Johnson given a lease for thirty-one years, the maximum allowed a Catholic under Irish law. The rent was then raised to £406.[38] The lease did not run its full course, for in 1791 John Johnson retired, and his son, John Johnson Jr. was summoned to London by the Warren heirs, where he agreed to end his old lease and make a new one. Under the new lease the rent rose to £506 a year, which meant no real increase, for henceforth Johnson was to be paid £100 a year as agent, where before his father had performed this service without making any charge "on account of the friendship and relationship subsisting"[39] between the two families, the Johnsons and the Warren heirs.

When Warren acquired his other Irish properties they were on long leases. One of the farms, Phepockstown, amounting to 430 acres in the barony of Deece and the parish of Kilmoor, enjoyed virtually a perpetual lease and can hardly be said to have been Warren's property at all. In 1727 Hussey had leased it to Francis Prentice for fifty-two years at £120 a year, but to raise £250 cash in 1747 Hussey had granted Prentice a 999 year lease when the current lease expired in 1779.[40] The annual rent remained unchanged; so that when it became Warren's property, his interest in the property was more like that of a holder of a rent charge than that of a landowner. A second farm, Great Ardrums, of 312 acres, also in the barony of Deece and with its southern boundary on a great bog at the headwaters of the Rye Water and the Blackwater River, was on a thirty-three year lease from May 1741 at the annual rent of £115. In 1774, when this lease was due to expire, advertisements were placed in the Dublin newspapers for a lease of thirty-one years to the highest bidder. As a result the rent shot up to £400.[41] The two other farms purchased from Hussey were called Hainstown and Creemore, of eighty-two and sixty-six acres respectively; the first in the barony of Deece, parish of Culmillin, and the other in the neighbouring barony of Ratooth and parish of Rathregan. Both were on a twenty-eight year lease of £56 a year, held by Matthew White, a Dublin merchant, who probably sublet the farm in small plots rather than till the soil himself.[42] When the leases fell in by 1765, John Johnson took over the land, being granted a lease only in 1771 at the annual rent of £93.[43] Finally the two interests held by Warren in the Kennedy estates, Ballydowde in county Dublin and the rent charge on Mount Kennedy, county Wicklow, produced an annual income in 1752 of £110 and £500 respectively. The rent charge on Mount Kennedy was a fixed sum, but the rental income from Ballydowde rose sharply to £295 in 1791, when a new lease was negotiated.[44]

In this way rents receivable on Warren's Irish estates rose from £1,061 in 1752 at the time of his death, to £1,320 in 1772 when Lady Warren's affairs were settled, and to £1,914 in 1791 when John Johnson Sr. handed over the agency to his son. If inflation is not taken into consideration this was a rise between 1752 and 1791 of more than 80 per cent, and compares with increases exacted by other Irish landowners in the same period. For instance, rental income on the estates of the Earls Fitzwilliam rose by 86 per cent between 1746 and 1783.[45]

Over a shorter period, from 1758 to 1776, the rents on the estates of the Earls of Upper Ossory rose 49 per cent, while in a single decade from 1769 to 1779, the rental income of the Earl of Fingal rose 38 per cent. In view of the thirty-one year lease found so widespread in eighteenth century Ireland[46] and the acute competition for land owing to population pressure,[47] some rise in rents was to be expected especially in a period of rising prices for agricultural produce, all of which characterized the last half of the century in Ireland.[48] Despite the increase in rents, historians have estimated that the rise in Ireland was not significantly out of step with the contemporaneous situation in England.[49]

If allowances are made for inflation these income rises are much less impressive. Estimates of Irish inflation remain very general, for historians have yet to construct the indices necessary for precise commentary. However, the problem is less acute for the historian of the absentee landowner than for one interested in the domestic Irish economy. Since the absentee English holder of Irish land was interested principally in what funds remitted from Ireland could buy in England, the year to year movements in Irish commodity prices are of only marginal interest. What is of importance in this context is the rate of exchange between Irish currency and sterling, as well as the movement of prices in England. The controversy over the rate of exchange was settled in 1737 when Irish currency was established on a mint ratio identical to that of sterling, which effectively stabilized the rate of exchange at an $8\frac{1}{3}$ per cent premium on English currency in terms of Irish currency.[50] The arrangement survived until 1797 when the Bank of England suspended specie payments which had the effect of ending Ireland's separate monetary system.[51] There are useful indices of eighteenth-century English prices, both for consumers' and producers' goods, which allow for a much more precise estimate of annual inflation than

TABLE 15 *Irish Adjusted Rents Receivable*

Date	Nominal Rent	Price Index	Adjusted Rent
1752	£1,061	93	£1,141
1772	1,320	117	1,128
1791	1,914	121	1,582

Base: 1701 = 100

Source: Schumpeter, "English Prices and Public Finances," p. 35.

is possible for Ireland in the same period.[52] The impact of inflation on Warren's Irish estates can thus be calculated as shown in table 15. Thus the real rise in rents receivable between 1752 and 1791 was 38.6 per cent or less than half the rate of the nominal growth, which exceeded 80 per cent. Compounded annually this meant a real rise in rents receivable of less than one per cent.

The improved estimated value of the Warren Irish estates in the last half of the eighteenth century reflected this rise in anticipated rental income. The landed property had cost Warren roughly £18,790, yet by 1759, when his eldest daughter came of age, they were valued at £22,931.[53] After Lady Warren's death the property was again appraised, the estimate this time amounting to £37,145.[54] Inflation, as table 16 shows, again accounted for much of these advances.

TABLE 16 *Adjusted Value of Irish Estates*

Date	Nominal Value	Price Index	Adjusted Value
1752	£18,790	93	£20,204
1759	22,790	100	22,790
1772	37,148	117	31,750

Base: 1701 = 100

Source: Schumpeter, "English Prices and Public Finances," p. 35.

Thus the real rise in the estimated value of the Warren Irish estates in the two decades between 1752 and 1772 was 57 per cent, considerably less than the figure of 97.7 per cent that does not adjust for the inflation.

The gross rate of return on this investment was not out of line with other forms of capital. The real or adjusted rents produced a 5.6 per cent return on the real value of the estates in 1752 and a 3.5 per cent return in 1772.

The approximate net revenue of the estates can be calculated by deducting certain fixed charges. Quit rent charges and the annual fee for the fair at Warrenstown[55] remained constant throughout this period and amounted to I£28 10s., as follows:[56]

Warrenstown fair	I£1	1s. 8d.
Warrenstown quit rent	8	6s. 8d.
Phepockstown quit rent	8	16s. 5d.
Great Ardrums quit rent	6	4s. 5d.

Hainstown and Creemore quit rent   2 14s.
Ballydowde quit rent   1   6s. 8d.

In addition, the portion of Warrenstown purchased from Rowley's heirs had an annual charge of £80 during the widow Rowley's lifetime; and she survived until 1754. There was also the agent's commission. At first this was paid simply by letting Warrenstown to John Johnson at a reduced rent, which amounted to at least £40 per annum until 1759 and as much as £100 thereafter. In 1791 when the £100 commission was paid the agent, he then had to pay an economic rent for the land held. All other charges, including the tithe, appear to have been borne by the Warrens' tenants. Thus in 1752 all charges amounted to £146 10s. and by 1772 had declined to £126 10s. Thus the approximate net income in 1752 was 4.9 per cent, and in 1772 it had declined to 3.2 per cent. Even with the diminished return of 1772 the investment compared not unfavourably with the large Irish landowners, whom Large has studied. (In 1775 they were receiving 2½ per cent from their property.)[57]

All of Warren's Irish estates passed into the hands of his grand-daughter by 1790. By his will in 1752 the property was left jointly to his daughters, his wife having one-third use of the income until they married or came of age. Shortly after Lady Warren's death in 1771, her youngest daughter, Charlotte, Countess of Abingdon, expressed the desire to sell her one-third interest. The property was appraised and the sale effected in July 1773, purchased by the other two sisters, Ann Fitzroy and Susanna Skinner.[58] The Abingdons received £12,382. To finance their £6,191 share of the cost, the Fitzroys borrowed the entire sum from Colonel William Skinner at 4 per cent interest.[59] The principal on the debt was repaid in 1790 when Fitzroy, by this time Lord Southampton, sold his share in Warren's property to Susanna Maria Gage, the only daughter of Colonel William Skinner. The price was the same as that in 1773: £12,382 plus the £6,191 debt, or £18,573.[60]

After the 1798 Irish rebellion, which took its toll on the Warren estates, the Gages decided to liquidate their Irish assets. In 1801 Lord Rossmore offered £9,250 for the rent charge on Mount Kennedy.[61] In 1805 Ballydowde was sold for £8,575.[62] A year later a bid of £13,340 was refused for the farm at Ardrums.[63] In 1807 Warrenstown, Hainstown, and Creemore were sold to John Johnson Jr. for £18,000.[64] How

Johnson financed such a purchase is not known, but it was an amazing accumulation of capital for a Catholic tenant farmer, whose father sixty years earlier had very modest means. No offers were made for the last of Warren's five farms, Phepockstown, as the title to it though sound was not attractive. Its virtually perpetual lease and fixed income made it difficult to dispose of. It was still owned by the Gage family in the 1860s.[65]

Warren never expressed a desire to settle in Ireland, yet as a native son he had ambitions to acquire land there. By purchasing Warrenstown, his family's farm for several generations, he fulfilled his principal objective. His wealth gained at sea enabled him to rescue the estate from heavy debt and depletion, and to restore it to its ancient boundaries. Although his parents and their forbears had been Catholics, Warren conformed to the established church, and thus when Warrenstown became his, the "Catholic" stake in the land of Ireland was perceptibly diminished, a phenomenon clearly seen by contemporaries and later historians alike. Yet in Warren's case, this consideration is merely incidental, for there was nothing in his role of an Irish landowner lacking a male heir which made his religion significant.

What was of far greater importance was the role he assigned his Catholic nephew, John Johnson. By making him one of his principal tenants, by allowing him highly favourable terms, and by appointing him his agent for all his Irish estates, Warren laid the foundation of the Johnson family fortune in Ireland. The family greatly prospered and though their rise from the status of tenant farmer to gentry had much to do with their abilities as farmers, their role as middlemen, and the marriages they made, yet the vital first step towards affluence was given by Warren and his heirs. Their rise heralded the revival of Irish Catholic wealth based on land, facilitated by the land laws of 1778 and 1782, and the beginnings of a new Catholic Irish gentry, indistinguishable, except for religion, from their Protestant land-owning neighbours.[66]

That Warren was prepared to buy land other than Warrenstown is also of some interest. Unlike his land purchases in England, there was certainly no social merit for an Englishman in owning land in Ireland. Several Irish peers owned not a single acre of Irish land, deriving their income entirely from English estates and other English assets. When Warren's grand-daughter, Susanna Maria Skinner, married into the

Gage family in 1789, she brought them their first Irish lands, though they had held an Irish peerage since 1720. If Warren's principal motive in buying Irish land was neither his own social advancement nor that of his children, it was presumably economic; and it proved sound. In a strictly economic sense, suitably chosen Irish land proved for Warren in the second half of the eighteenth century to be a rather more attractive investment than land in England. By buying cheap in Ireland and collecting rent regularly, he was able to realize a 4.9 per cent net return by the end of his life. This compared favourably with his experience in England, which the next chapter will discuss, where land was more expensive and consequently the rate of return more modest than in Ireland.

Finally it is to be noted that with the economic advance in Ireland in the last decades of the eighteenth century, with its rising rents and land values, the Warren heirs enjoyed the full fruits of the investment. Initially the heirs were concerned primarily with rental income which, under the devoted care of their agents, was regularly paid, and raised sharply whenever leases expired.[67] However, unlike Warren, whose taste for Irish land was far from satisfied by 1752, his heirs declined reinvesting their Irish income in more Irish land. Instead, like so many other absentee landowners who apparently never visited Ireland after 1752, they merely gave orders for the transfer of their income as quickly as possible to their London bankers at the most favourable rate of exchange. This uninterrupted and steadily rising income was one of the principal investments inherited from Warren, the value of which they only fully appreciated when much of the land was sold during the wartime boom in the first decade of the nineteenth century.

Chapter 9

Estates in

Hampshire

1747-1789

Between 1747 and 1752 Warren paid £14,800 for six farms in Hampshire. Comprising some 1,070 acres, they lay together in the upper Meon Valley some sixteen miles north of Portsmouth and just west of where the Portsmouth–London road passed through Petersfield. Only his early death prevented him from adding substantially to this investment in land. The property remained in the hands of his heirs and their descendants until the 1860s.

Eighteenth-century agriculture and land ownership in Hampshire has been so little studied that it is difficult to generalize about either the rate of agricultural change or the state of the land market when Warren became an active buyer.[1] Historians interested in counties other than Hampshire have drawn conclusions which must be borne in mind when studying the Warren lands.[2] These conclusions may be summarized as follows. In the first half of the century there was an active market in land with a discernible tendency for landed property to concentrate in fewer hands. As very large estates increased in numbers and size there was a corresponding decline in the proportion of land owned by small freeholders and lesser gentry. After the mid-century these tendencies were less marked and less land came on the market. This relative shortage of land led to a sharp rise in its price whereas in the earlier part of the century prices were more or less stable or rising only moderately. At the beginning of the century land was usually valued at twenty years' purchase; by the last quarter of the century thirty years' purchase or even more was the customary valuation. Correspondingly the net return on land declined from about four per cent to no more than two and a half per cent. Secondly, the decades after the Peace of Utrecht were marked by agricultural depression which was at its worst between 1730 and 1750. The depression was characterized by falling prices for farm produce, resulting from high yields due to good harvests and hence relative over-production at a time when population was growing only very slowly. The depressed price situation put great strain on small landowners, especially those lacking non-agricultural income. It also hit hard at the tenant farmer who found himself unable to meet his rent, forcing many landlords to concede reductions or temporary abatements of rent, while assuming additional costs hitherto borne by tenants, such as payment of land tax, tithes, or poor rates. The depression forced farmers to work their land more intensively, and when this failed to bring the necessary cash return, they were forced off the land, and many farms were temporarily deserted. Lastly, though still a much sought-after asset, land no longer was without a serious rival among the safe long-term investments open to a man of wealth. From the late seventeenth century onwards they had to compete with government borrowing. By the mid-century the National Debt had proved itself not only a sound and safe investment, easily acquired and easily disposed of, but one which yielded a higher income than land and held out hopes of capital gain. Many squires could and did argue that this turned wealth away from land and hence affected its value.

The wealth that Warren brought to the English land market, though made at sea, was in essence not unlike that of a city magnate, West India merchant, or returning Nabob. Investment in land helped to confer that degree of social respectability which such men almost inevitably sought. However, because of his earlier claim to gentility in Ireland, Warren, unlike most of the nouveaux riches, believed his wealth merely enabled him to play in England a role that he was bred to play in Ireland.

Until 1747 Warren had no inclination to buy land in England, though since 1745 he had had sufficient capital. His naval career had kept him almost continuously employed abroad, principally in the West Indies and America, where most of his ambitions were then focused and where he had acquired much property very cheaply. When home on leave in 1726-27, 1732-33, 1735-36, and briefly in 1742 he spent his time either in Ireland or in lodgings in Portsmouth or London. Even in 1747, when he was next in England with plenty of ready cash, he felt no pressing need to make such an investment for he fully expected to return to North America that spring for the conquest of Canada.

These plans were laid aside at the end of March 1747, and instead he was ordered to serve under Anson in the Western Squadron. The change in plans apparently convinced him that he should bring his family from New York to join him in England, for early in April he inquired of the secretary of the Admiralty about the possibility of getting a warship from Louisbourg to carry out this task. He even had Anson write to the Duke of Bedford, the First Lord of the Admiralty, in support of the request. In the end a warship was sent from Portsmouth.[3] Warren and Anson were at that moment preoccupied with arrangements to outfit their fleet for sea; and it was not until the end of May, when they returned victorious to Spithead, that Warren was able to buy a suitable house.

The property he fixed on was called Westbury Manor and was purchased in June 1747 from the widow of Admiral Philip Cavendish, under whom Warren had briefly served in 1742 and who had died in 1743 after a successful if undistinguished career.[4] As early as March 1747 Warren had considered buying the estate, but only after the great addition to his fortune resulting from the victory over the French in May did he consent to Mrs. Cavendish's price: £8,500 with a further £1,000 for the furniture.[5] He thought it "a very dear bargain" as he told Anson, "which nothing but being your neighbour could have Induced me to Come into."[6]

Westbury was the principal estate in the parish of East Meon. The Domesday Survey assessed it at three hides, when it formed part of the barony of Hugh de Port.[7] It was at Westbury that the treaty between Henry I and his elder brother, Robert, was signed in 1101 to arrange the succession to the crown. In the thirteenth century the manor with the rest of the Port barony passed to the St. John family and then to the Poynings. Later it was owned by Robert le Ewer, who in 1322 received permission from Edward II to fortify the place. Through failures in the male line the property then passed to Nicholas le Devenische of Winchester and then to the family of John Golafre. Late in the fifteenth century the Fawconer family acquired title to the property. There they lived for two centuries, one of the few Catholic families surviving in the area. The estate was purchased from the Fawconers by John Holt of Portsmouth, whose son, Colonel Richard Holt, sold it in 1694 for £4,000 to Richard Markes of Petersfield.[8] It was probably Markes who rebuilt the house in the palladian style of Queen Anne, for by the time his widow sold to Admiral Cavendish in 1722, the price of the entire property had risen to £7,400.[9]

Despite the high price that Warren paid for it, the property had many attractions. The handsome brick house, insured by the Sun Fire Office for £2,000, was ample without being lavish.[10] It stood in a richly timbered park, while behind the house was a large pleasure garden laid out by Charles Bridgeman, the outstanding professional garden architect of his day.[11] Standing on rising ground above the Meon, it had a lovely view of the valley and the downs. The tree-lined avenue, which led up to the house from the East Meon–West Meon road, crossed a small bridge over the rivulet, which had been artificially broadened and given regularly shaped banks and at one point made into a pond. Nearby stood a chapel dedicated to Saint Nicholas, dating from the twelfth century.[12]

Westbury manor was freehold land enclosed in numerous large fields.[13] Some 554 acres, it was rather narrow and stretched for almost three miles from the downs south of the Meon northwards beyond the Winchester–Petersfield road. It had notable stands of timber in three principal woods covering 126 acres and valued in 1747 at £818. The Warrens added to these stands with purchases of young oak, elm, ash, walnut, and beech in 1750, 1751, 1752, and 1761. By 1772 the timber was valued at £1,180 and produced an income in excess of £60 per annum.[14]

When Warren bought Westbury manor he also acquired rights to a small parcel of land, which rounded out the west end of the park. It had been devised to Mrs. Cavendish in 1745 for a term of five thousand years by the lord of the manor of West Meon, Henry Foxcroft. In August 1747 Foxcroft assigned the same plot to Warren and thereafter it became part of the Westbury estate.[15] To this in 1748 he added ten acres of arable land and meadow bought from his bailiff, Thomas Earwaker, for £100. It was copyhold land held by the lord of the manor of West Meon.[16] Also in 1748 he added two other small parcels of land, bought from Mary Earwaker, who ran the Red Lion Inn at West Meon. Like the rest, it lay along the banks of the Meon River. The land was not paid for until after Warren's death, when interest owing on the debt brought the purchase price to £60. This was considered a steep price, but since part of the land lay opposite the entrance gates to Westbury Park, it was thought worth having.[17]

These two small purchases from the Earwakers were hardly more than attempts to make more convenient a couple of corners of the Westbury estate. The rest of Warren's acquisitions in the Meon valley were more significant and a conscious attempt to accumulate a number of small farms to establish a large estate. The scheme was brought to a sudden halt by Warren's death in July 1752, by which time he had bought a further five farms and a corn mill and had laid plans to make a much larger purchase, which would have brought his rental income to almost £1,000.

His first significant purchases after Westbury took place three years later in the autumn of 1750, when Warren acquired two farms: Dray ton farm and Peck farm. Drayton was purchased from Martha Trodd and John Rogers. This freehold land lay adjacent to Westbury in the parish of East Meon, partly in the tithing of Borden and Meon. From 1639 to 1734 it had belonged to the Pink family, but then had passed to Adam Churcher, who left it jointly to his two daughters. One of them, Martha Trodd, together with her brother-in-law, John Rogers, conveyed the land in two parcels by deeds dated 27-28 September 1750 and 1 April 1752.[18] The cost was £403 for twenty-four acres; and the farm consisted of two fields, a meadow along the Meon, and an orchard. The farm of Thomas Peck was also in East Meon parish, being mainly copyhold held of the manor of East Meon. Its several fields, most of them more than eight acres in size, were widely scattered though enclosed. There was a brick and tile farm house, a cottage, and barns. The farm had rights of common for 270 sheep on Old Down. Comprising 112 acres, it lay across the Meon valley from Westbury and contained a fine twenty-acre copse. The farm cost Warren £1,432, which included a fee to East Meon Court.[19] Two further farms were added in 1751: Palmer's farm and Langrish farm. On 28 May 1751 Warren paid Anthony Palmer £420 for his small farm, amounting to thirty-one acres with rights of pasture for sixty sheep on Old Down, by drawing bills on his London bankers, Messrs. Honeywood and Fuller.[20] It was held from the lord of the manor of East Meon, and had been owned by Palmer only since March 1744. Situated in the tithing of Riplington, it was a compact holding about two miles from West-bury House. Before 1752 Warren had financed the erection of a small barn on the farm, which earlier had neither house nor barn on it.

Later in the year Warren bought a more important farm called Langrish, from Richard Baker. The 247–acre farm lay in the parish of East Meon in the hamlets of Ramsdean, Oxenbourn, Langrish, and Meon. Much of it was freehold, the copyhold portions being held by four manors: East Meon, East Meon Church, held by the Bishop of Winchester, Langrish manor, owned by Sir Thomas Ridge, and Riplington. In 1772 Thomas Browne said it had a "very good farm House, 3 Barns, Stable, Cart house, Malting, and other buildings all in pretty good repair."[21] There was a hop garden and an orchard near the house and out-buildings. Most of the fields were distant from the house, and many were still in strips, particularly those in copyhold tenure, lying in what was called the west common field. However, both freehold and copyhold land had undergone much enclosure, for there are to be found in the description of the farm many references to fields formerly separated but by 1750 laid together. Ransfield, for instance, the largest field of twenty-seven acres was described as formerly "in the Six Closes with fosters Mead but now all laid into two Closes."[22] The principal meadow on the farm was described as "Pidham Mead and Bottom Mead . . . now Laid together." Another field of fifteen acres, called Bartons Ham, Bartons Stiles, and Little Ham was described as "being formerly in three fields but now laid altogether."

Baker had wanted £3,000 for the farm, and had declined an offer of £2,700 before Warren became involved with his offer of £2,400.[23] He actually paid £2,580, payment not being completed until 1757, five years after his death.[24] By Lady Day 1752 he had paid only £174. Late in April he paid a Mr. T. Pickering £1,256, which was the principal and interest owing on a mortgage that Baker had on the property, the funds originally coming from Pusey Brooke, Esq., the commissioner for sick and wounded seamen at Portsmouth. The rest of the purchase money was unpaid at the time of Warren's death. Of this, £300 was in the form of a note of hand given Baker by Warren at 4 per cent interest which Lady Warren paid in November 1752, together with interest due. The rest, according to the agreement between Warren and Baker, was left in the Warrens' hands to provide a £25 annuity to Richard Baker's mother for the rest of her life. Mrs. Baker died in 1757 having received £125, at which time the remaining £625 plus interest was paid, to bring the total cost to £2,580.

In 1752 Warren purchased the last of his Hampshire farms and a corn mill. The farm Warren acquired in April 1752 from William Buckle, Esq., for £1,023[25] was copyhold land of the manor of East

Meon. As it paid but a small quit rent of 6s. 8d. with a fine of two shillings and no heriot at the death of the holder, Thomas Browne considered it in 1772 "nearly equal to freehold."[26] Comprising 124 acres in the tithing of Riplington, most of its fields were enclosed, while it contained three small copses and fifty-four acres of down-land.[27] The timber in 1772 was valued at £26. The corn mill, Warren's last purchase in the Meon valley, stood near Drayton's farm, and contained two pairs of stones. Until 1752 it was owned by Henry Hunt. Warren had loaned him £255 in September 1748, taking as security a mortgage on the mill.[28]   This was too good a bargain for Hunt to resist, for he made only one £5 interest payment on the loan, and in 1752 it was forfeited to Warren. After Warren's death the mill, with its small parcel of land and a cottage, was made over to Miss Ann Warren, who paid £18 to repair it. It was let at various rates from £12 12s. to £6 6s. a year. The mill paid an annual quit rent of fifteen shillings to the manor of East Meon. The £250 that it cost Warren was considered about twice its real value, but as Browne observed in 1772, it was thought "to be convenient for the Estate and therefore purchased."[29] Table 17 summarizes the details of these purchases in Hampshire.

TABLE 17 *Hampshire Property Cost*

Date	Purchase	Cost
1747	Westbury manor (with furniture)	£ 9,500
1748	Earwaker's 10 acres	100
1748	Mary Earwaker's plot	60
1750	Drayton farm	403
1750	Peck's farm	1,432
1751	Palmer's farm	420
1751	Langrish farm	2,580
1752	Buckle's farm	1,023
1752	The mill	250
Total		£15,768

Source: Gage Papers.

Though Hunt's mill was Warren's last purchase, he had at least one other property under negotiation, which his heirs broke off after his death. Shortly before his last trip to Ireland in June 1752, Warren became party to an agreement between the Right Honourable Henry Legge, John Bonham Smith, Elizabeth Bridges, and Robert Andrewes relating to certain farms and cottages in the manors of Farlington and Drayton.[30] The rent roll amounted to £705 12s., twice that of all his other property in Hampshire. The property had belonged to one Thomas Smith; and at his death it passed to his widow, Elizabeth, who upon her marriage to Wakefield Bridges had agreed to sell the property for £15,000 to John Bonham Smith. The articles of agreement were signed on 24 March 1748, and the sale concluded on 11 December 1750. John Smith acted only as trustee of the Right Honourable Henry Legge, and went so far as to make an initial payment to Bridges of £120 of the purchase money. As there were a number of lawsuits then before the High Court of Chancery between Bridges and Thomas Dacros, which Dacros would not withdraw, Bridges found himself unable to convey the property to Smith. Moreover, on learning this, Bridges's attorney, George Baskerville, refused to proceed with the matter until his accounts had been paid by Bridges. Henry Legge was then prevailed upon to pay off Baskerville, and provided Bridges with a £2,000 mortgage on the property. Early in January 1751, Bridges suddenly died; whereupon Legge determined to proceed no further with the purchase. There the matter stood until the twice-widowed Elizabeth Bridges succeeded in capturing Warren's interest in the property. The first task was to secure Smith's and Legge's formal renunciation of the original articles of agreement. This was done by means of a new agreement signed on 18 June 1752; but Warren's death six weeks later obliged them to find an alternative, since Lady Warren had no desire to pursue the matter.

From 1747 until the spring of 1755 the Warrens cultivated their entire Hampshire estate themselves.[31] In 1755 Lady Warren let two of the farms comprising the estate: Palmer's and Langrish. A further reduction in the acreage of the home farm was effected in 1760, when all but 202 of the 1,070 acres were let. Of this 126½ acres were woodland.[32] To cultivate the estate for themselves was a unique experience for the Warrens. So long as Warren was actively engaged at sea he had had no leisure to involve himself directly either with his farm at Warrenstown in Ireland or at Greenwich and Warrensburg in New York, though his experience as a landowner had afforded him opportunity enough to become acquainted with the usual problems of agriculture.

Despite the advantages of good woodland, fertile arable land, lush meadows, downland suitable for sheep, healthy livestock, and buoyant prices for farm produce, the Warrens' estate was a steady, though by no means large, drain on their other resources. This conclusion derives from a study of the account book kept between 1753 and 1762 by the bailiff, Thomas Earwaker.[33] Unfortunately the bailiff made no satisfactory distinction between "farm" and "house" expenses, thus making impossible an acceptable division between such important items of expenditure as tradesmen's bills and labour costs. Nor is it possible to evaluate that part of the farm's produce which was used either by the household at Westbury or for the London house. To maintain an adequate amount of cash in the bailiff's hands, and to balance his accounts, the Warrens had regularly to remit funds from London to Hampshire. The average annual amount of these remissions, between 1749 and 1752, came to £545,[34] and between 1753 and 1762 to £313. Table 18 provides details of expenditure and income and takes into account these cash inputs.

TABLE 18 *Hampshire Estate, Income and Expenditure 1753-1762*

Year	Income	Cash Input	True Income	Expenditure	Loss
1753	£558	£102	£456	£541	£ 85
1754	842	485	357	648	291
1755	456	128	328	629	301
1756	683	316	373	635	262
1757	987	402	585	931	346
1758	853	308	545	843	298
1759	744	283	461	683	222
1760	690	273	417	587	168
1761	835	281	554	577	23
1762	987	554	433	674	241
Average	£764	£313	£451	£675	£224

Source: Gage Papers, GA 728.

The principal sources of income were corn, livestock, wool, and wood, besides rent which will be considered separately later.[35] Annual surplus of wheat averaged 65½ quarters between 1753 and 1762, with a high of 109½ quarters in 1754 and a low of 11 qrs. in 1762. The average annual sales of barley amounted to 36 qrs. with a high of 61 qrs. in 1755 and a low of 2 qrs. in 1762. Only once (in 1759) were oats sold, as the farm usually didn't grow enough for its own needs. On one other occasion (also in 1759) too much wheat and barley was apparently sold, for the bailiff was forced to buy 3½ qrs. of barley and one qr. of "French wheat." The cereal sales averaged £150 per annum, with a high of £286 in 1757 and a low of £22 in 1762.

Of the livestock the most important were sheep and lambs. An average of 78 sheep and 92 lambs were sold each year, though the average for sheep is somewhat misleading as 312 sheep were sold in 1753 alone. If this figure is excluded the average of the sheep sales for the nine years between 1754 and 1762 was 52, which meant a flock of about 200 ewes if one quarter was offered for sale annually.[36] Besides sheep and lambs the farm also sold 19 cows, 53 calves, 2 bulls, and 30 pigs during the decade.[37] The average annual value of all livestock sales amounted to £89.

Wool and wood were next in importance as sources of farm income. Average sales of wool amounted to 837 pounds (of which 182 pounds on average were lambs' wool), for an annual value of £23. The chief product of the woodland was faggots, of which 3,100 were sold annually at 11s. or 12s. per 100. Only occasionally during the decade under study were trees felled for sale, which brought the average income for wood to £21. There was in addition a variety of products of less value. A few pounds of tallow and butter (after 1759), sheepskins, sainfoin and clover seed, and hay (7 tons in 1754, 5½ tons in 1757) were the most prominent items of a miscellaneous nature sold by the farm, and whose value only three times exceeded £15 per annum. Table 19 summarizes much of this information.

The most important items of expenditure included tradesmen's bills for the supply of the farm and house, labour costs, a variety of taxes, tithes, quit rents, and poor rates, feed costs, and finally the cost of seed. Tradesmen's bills formed probably as much as 40 per cent of the total expenditure. Most bills came from the inhabitants of the nearby villages of West Meon and East Meon, and included the butcher, malster, turner, blacksmith, locksmith, collarmaker, stonecutter, mason, carpenter, glazier, bricklayer, ironmonger, and farrier. If as much as half of these bills related to the household, the losses sustained by the farm would be greatly reduced; but as has been pointed out such a distinction is impossible to make. As the Warrens undertook no

TABLE 19 *Income: Farm Produce 1753-1762*

Year	Corn		Livestock	Wool		Wood	Balance*	Total**
	Value £	Quantity qrs.	Value £	Value £	Quantity lbs.	Value £	Value £	Value £
1753	151	106	234	25	1,012	23	23	456
1754	173	153½	64	21	909	17	82	357
1755	153	140½	57	18	662	22	78	328
1756	139	94½	39	25	984	24	146	373
1757	286	131	77	28	919	36	156	585
1758	184	85½	117	34	1,022	21	189	545
1759	138	101½	96	35	1,075	24	168	461
1760	168	133½	105	25	858	18	101	417
1761	78	70	67	14	542	21	374	554
1762	22	13	37	10	397	—	364	433
Ave.	150	101½	89	23	837	21	168	451
%	33.3%	—	20%	5%	—	4.7%	37%	100%

Source: Gage Papers, GA 728.

*After 1756 the balance rose largely from rental income.

**See True Income column in table 18.

important building at Westbury, there are no extraordinary expenditures noted by the bailiff which would provide evidence for such a distinction.

Next to tradesmen's bills came the cost of labour and management; this amounted to 28.6 per cent of total expenditures. The bailiff received £20 a year, while Henry Foxcroft, the lord of the manor of West Meon, received £30 for his trouble in transferring funds from Lady Warren to the bailiff. The principal labourers included the shepherd, gardener, woodsman, headcarter, and dairymaid. The shepherd received £15 12s. a year, the headcarter £8 8s., the dairymaid £4 10s. The gardener, woodsman, and other labourers were paid 1s. a day. All took the opportunity to earn extra wages haymaking, harvesting, washing and shearing sheep, winding wool, clearing ditches, and hedging, so that some managed on occasion to earn more than £20 a year. In addition all had free beer, no small matter in view of the size of the malster's annual invoice.[38]

The various taxes, tithes, quit rents, and poor taxes were next in importance and constituted 15.3 per cent of expenditures. They were both numerous and quite heavy owing in part to the fact that in the middle of the eighteenth century much of the estate was still copyhold land, and partly because the decade under study, 1753 to 1762, was one of high taxes resulting from war and a sharp rise in the poor rate. Most of these expenses were born by the estate, tenants at the most being required only to meet the window tax.[39] Thus the estate had to pay annually £22 10s. in tithes, £9 15s. window tax for Westbury and 3s. for one of the cottagers, land tax of £35 3s. 6d. at 4s. (and £26 7s. 9d. at 3s.), and poor rates which varied from year to year, as high as £19 4s. 8½d. in 1759 and never below £16. In addition, quit rents remained fixed at £12 5s. 8d. with an additional 5s. for the use of water on Drayton farm. Thus at worst almost £100 a year went to this uncontrollable form of expenditure, while the average for the decade was £98. It is well known that the burden of the land tax fell unevenly throughout England, with the heaviest load falling upon landowners in the southeastern counties, and very lightly on those in the north.[40] When the land tax stood at 4s., only the southeastern counties could expect to pay the full 20 per cent of the rented assessment of the landed property. By paying £35 3s. 6d. the estate owned by the Warrens was assessed as though its rental income amounted to £175 17s. 6d., when privately Westbury manor alone was valued at £200 per annum.[41] High though the taxes were in wartime, still the estate was taxed at only about 15 per cent of its value when the land tax called for a 20 per cent rate.

The last significant category of farm expenditure related to the cost of feed and seeds, the one constituting 6.8 per cent and the other 6.7 per cent of the total, an average of £46 and £45 per annum respectively. The principal feed cost was oats of which an average of 52 qrs.

TABLE 20 *Purchases of Seeds 1753-1762*

Year	Wheat qrs.	Barley qrs.	Oats qrs.	Grass qrs.	Clover lbs.	Sainfoin qrs.	Turnip lbs.	Vetch bush.
1753	15	—	—	18	—	—	30	—
1754	19	17	36	16	200	—	30	13
1755	7½	21	10	17	342	—	30	12
1756	35	—	11	—	266	—	20	6
1757	6½	10	—	12½	—	—	33	7
1758	19	5½	4	—	220	—	42	8
1759	14½	18	—	3½	212	—	41	11
1760	10½	8	10	16	600	6	29	7
1761	8½	3	—	6	100	19	20	10
1762	—	5	—	—	—	1	15	—

Source: Gage Papers, GA 728.

was purchased annually between 1753 and 1762. Occasionally hay and straw were also purchased, but they never formed an important part of the cost. The bulk of the seed cost went to purchase seed wheat, seed barley, and seed oats. A flexible rotation of crops[42] (though the exact nature of that rotation is not known) was achieved by growing turnips[43] and legumes, expecially clover and sainfoin, along with the usual grass seeds. Table 20 gives details of the relative quantity of seed used on the farm.

Finally, there was always a miscellaneous body of expenses, Of these the most important was the purchase of livestock.[44] Usually this consisted of the annual purchase of ten or twelve wethers for fattening, at a cost of from £7 to £9. However in 1757 at least £43 was spent on livestock for a bull, two cows, four calves, a ram, thirty wethers, thirty chickens, and two pigs. Another regular though small expense related to the cost of carting grain to market and fetching seed from neighbouring farmers. Table 21 provides the most important details of these costs.

One significant item not considered above was rental income which was of special importance to the estate only after 1761 when most of

TABLE 21 *Principal Farm Expenses 1753-1762*

Year	Labour	Taxes	Feed	Seed	Balance*	Total**
1753	£161	£ 68	£ 40	£35	£237	£541
1754	173	71	25	93	286	648
1755	239	93	18	59	220	629
1756	236	128	59	21	191	635
1757	239	149	50	26	467	931
1758	190	177	127	47	362	843
1759	160	78	69	58	318	683
1760	205	124	34	54	170	587
1761	200	89	13	27	248	577
1762	127	110	24	26	387	674
Average	£193	£103	£46	£45	£288	£675
%	28.6	15.3	6.8	6.7	42.6	100

Source: Gage Papers, GA 728

*Largely tradesmen's accounts.

** See Expenditure column, table 18.

the farm was let to tenant farmers. There was a consequent decline in production on the home farm. The question of how well Lady Warren fared as a *rentier*, when compared to the previous owners of the Westbury estate and to landowners generally at that time, now presents itself. Before any answer can be proffered the real value of the estate must be computed. Though Warren had paid £15,768 for the estate, its value for the purposes of calculating its yield was rather less. From the £9,500 purchase price of Westbury manor must be subtracted the £1,000 cost of the furniture as well as £2,000 for the house, pleasure garden, vegetable garden, and outbuildings.[45] To the £6,000 that remains must be added £800 as the value of the timber on the estate for a total of £6,800. The rest of the estate was appraised in 1772 at £6,000, somewhat below the £6,268 that Warren had paid for it. Thus the estate can be said to have been valued at £12,800 at anytime between 1752 and 1772.[46] Rental income after 1760 amounted to £302 1s., and by 1772 the timber was thought to be worth £60 7s. 6d. a year in contrast to the £21 average income from it between 1753 and 1762 (see table 22).

TABLE 22 *Hampshire Rent Roll 1761-1772*

Property	Tenant	Rent	
Westbury farm (less house, garden, timber, etc.)	John Green	£101	
Peck and Drayton farms	John Green	56	15s.
Buckle farm	John Green	26	
Langrish farm	Richard Eames	94	10s.
Palmer farm	Thomas Pink	14	
Hunt's mill	Randall Clark	6	6s.
Cottage	John Triggs	2	5s.
Cottage	William Ford	1	5s.
Timber (in 1771)		60	7s. 6d.
Total		£362	8s. 6d.

Source: Gage Papers, G/Ha/66 (20)

On the £12,800 value the £362 8s. 6d. income represented a 2.8 per cent gross yield. This contrasted unfavourably with what the previous owners of Westbury had achieved. They had bought the estate in 1722 for £7,400, which could have been valued, after discounting the house, furniture, garden, and outbuildings, at £4,400. They let the entire farm for £180 to one John Stone to which sum was added £20 a year for timber, making a total of £200 income, and a gross yield of 4.5 per cent.[47] This decline in gross yield was not unique, for the return on landed investments tended to decline throughout the eighteenth century.[48] At the beginning of the century, land was habitually priced at twenty years' purchase, a yield of 5 per cent gross, which after deductions for repairs, taxes, and cost of administration meant a net yield of perhaps 4 per cent. By the late eighteenth century land often commanded thirty years' purchase. This large price rise meant naturally that yield dropped, perhaps generally to 3–3½ per cent, which after deductions for expenses meant in fact about a 2–2½ per cent net yield. In fact the 1772 valuation of the Warren estate in Hampshire in general based its calculations upon a formula of twenty-eight years' purchase for copyhold land and thirty years' purchase for freehold.[49] It would seem that return on the estate fell slightly below this norm; and this was recognized by those making the appraisal, who felt that the £101 rent for Westbury farm was a "very low rate indeed."[50] An additional £50 for that part of the farm would have placed the estate comfortably within the broad movement of rents which historians have identified as normal for the period.

Warren spent as much time as he could spare at Westbury, yet in the five years between 1747 and his death in 1752 he managed to live there for only about forty weeks. Once the war was over in 1748 he planned to spend as much of the summer and autumn months in the country as his parliamentary responsibilities at Westminster allowed. Thus in 1749 he and his family were at Westbury for three months and in 1750 for five. In 1751 his health obliged him to take the waters in Scarborough, and though the family returned from Yorkshire to London in September, as Lady Warren was then with child it was decided not to go to the country. In 1752 Warren again intended to return to Hampshire; and when he left for Ireland in June on business he had already made arrangements for his family to leave London. It was at Westbury at the beginning of August that they learned of his death in

Dublin. After his death, his widow and young family continued to spend much of the summer and autumn months in the country, until the children had grown and married and ill-health kept Lady Warren at home in her Grosvenor Square house.

Between 1747 and 1752, Warren's days at Westbury were mixed with the pleasure of sport and social gatherings and the business of seeing to the home farm and extending his purchases in the Meon valley. He hunted and tried his hand at shooting,[51] which caused him to bemoan his ill-luck to Anson, "there are a good many Partridges, but so wild y^t. wee Berd Gunners Cant kill one."[52] Warren also bought fishing rods to try the trout in the several rivers, the Meon included, that took their source from the hills around Petersfield. Moreover he displayed enough interest in cricket to purchase both bat and balls. Perhaps the formation in 1750 of a cricket club at nearby Hambledon had something to do with his interest in this sport.[53]

Warren's Hampshire estates remained intact throughout the lifetime of his widow. She enjoyed, by the provisions of his will, one-third of the income of the estate, the rest being divided among her three surviving daughters as they married or came of age. At her death in November 1771, all her property was equally divided among them, as was her husband's property of which she had had part use. This obliged the heirs to carry out a thorough evaluation of the Hampshire property. Though Warren's estate had cost almost £14,800, its value twenty or more years later was reckoned only at £14,300. It was felt that the estate might possibly sell for somewhat more "if a purchaser liked the Situation, distance from London etc."[54] In fact one of Lady Warren's sons-in-law Colonel William Skinner, who had married her second daughter, Susanna, decided to buy the entire estate himself. Skinner, a short time before, had bought an adjoining estate, called Riplington, of 694 acres.[55] Deeds of sale were completed between Skinner and the other two Warren sons-in-law, Colonel Charles Fitzroy and the Earl of Abingdon, in April 1772. When Skinner died in 1780, a widower, the entire estate, then amounting to 1,764 acres, passed to their only child, Susanna Maria. Upon her marriage in 1789 to Major Henry Gage, the future third Viscount Gage, the estate passed into the Gage family, who steadily added to it. When Susanna Maria died in 1821, the estate, then amounting to 1,942 acres, was valued at £39,735.[56] In 1865, grown to 2,512 acres, it was put up for sale by her younger son, the Honourable William Henry Gage, whose only son had predeceased him. The auction was not a success, Gage refusing bids that ranged from the first of £45,000 to the last of £75,000.[57]

Warren's desire to acquire land in England had little to do with investment. The prices he paid for his six farms — about £14,800 — he felt were for the most part very high. In this he was probably correct for in 1772, twenty-five years after the purchase of Westbury manor, the property was valued only at £14,300: thirty years' purchase for the freehold and twenty-eight years' for the copyhold. It took many more years, and additional costs associated with enclosure, new buildings, and reforestation, before the estate was assumed to have improved its value substantially. Moreover, the property yielded gross income only at the rate of 2.8 per cent. Although this was more than the American estates (2.6),[58] it was less than the 3.2 per cent from the Irish estates, and considerably less than investments in government stock and private money lending. As Habakkuk has observed: "A very wealthy merchant or lawyer, a distinguished soldier or sailor, was prepared to incur a loss of income of 1 or 1½ per cent in order to acquire an estate and establish himself as a landowner. It was the fee he paid for admission into the charmed circle of English landed society. But to purchase additional estates beyond that minimum involved a significant fall in income and brought little additional prestige."[59] By confining himself to a group of small properties in one district, and by retaining large investments elsewhere, he was typical of many wealthy men of his generation.[60] He had become part of the landed gentry while also providing his family with an agreeable home in the country, to be used during several months of the year when Parliament rose and fashionable society left London.

Had his Hampshire property been his only investment, he would have ranked, according to the usual methods of categorizing the landed classes in the eighteenth century, only as a member of the lesser gentry, hardly above the "better sort" of freehold farmer.[61] That he thought of himself in quite different terms goes without saying. Indeed, by 1747, his considerable wealth and naval distinction led him to aspire to the ranks of the nobility. As he told his friend, Anson, whose peerage had just been announced, "Pray when Shall I have the Honour to address you in a Noble Stile. 'Tis Publicly Said here Sober-town is to be one of your Tytles which I think a very pretty one. Who knows, but this Cruize may bring forth Lord Westbury."[62] Warren's ill-health prevented him from further earning the nation's gratitude, and no Lord Westbury emerged. Instead he had to content himself as lord of the manor of Westbury, and the principal personage of the parishes of West and East Meon. In this capacity he established himself in a circle of friends from among the landowning families of the district, not a few of whom were naval officers. There he entertained his London friends and visitors from America. Having no male heir, he chose not to build a grand house, as so many of his contemporaries were tempted to do, so the expenditure on his estate was not extravagant. Though without family connection with Hampshire, as a naval officer who frequented Portsmouth he found no difficulty in identifying himself with his adopted county. Such was the ease with which wealth, tempered somewhat by earlier claims to gentility in Ireland, allowed him happily to pass from the role of fighting admiral to that of country gentleman.

Chapter 10

Money Lending in

England and Ireland

1727-1774

Borrowing between individuals in the eighteenth century was carried on principally by means of mortgages or bonds, though notes of hand were also common, especially for small amounts. The mortgage had evolved by the beginning of the century into a "long-term instrument of debt,"[1] and had become an effective alternative to land as a sound investment. Though the usual mortgage in Warren's day only rarely contained references to a fixed rate of interest for a defined number of years, and in theory either party of the contract could withdraw or insist on an adjustment to the rate of interest after giving six months' notice, in fact the mortgage had acquired much greater security for both borrower and lender than it had had a century earlier.

In addition there was a steady decrease in the rate at which money could be legally loaned. In England the ceiling was ten per cent until 1625, thereafter eight per cent until 1651 when it was further reduced to six per cent; from 1714 it was five per cent until the Usury Laws were repealed in the mid-nineteenth century.[2] In Ireland, as in America, the maximum rate of interest allowed was higher than in England, standing at ten per cent until 1703, then at eight per cent until 1722, then at seven per cent. In 1731 the ceiling was reduced to six per cent, where it remained for the rest of the century.[3] In both England and Ireland the interest rate on both mortgages and bonds tended to follow with a lag of some six months the rate of yield on government securities.[4] The rates for private lending were almost invariably higher owing to the "greater elements of risk in lending to private individuals than in entrusting money to the state."[5] The higher rate also compensated the lender for the fact that, although the mortgage and bond market was not without flexibility, both mortgages and bonds were far more trouble to liquidate than investments in government stock either in England or Ireland. It is against this background that the ensuing discussion of Warren's money lending must be set.

From his first months as a post captain in 1727 Warren became a money lender to members of his crews. Seamen were habitually short of money owing to the inefficient system by which wages were paid. Upon entering a ship, a seaman was assigned a ticket number by his purser against which was recorded all wages, as well as deductions made for tobacco, clothing, and contributions to Greenwich Hospital or Chatham Chest.[6] Just as warships were on the point of leaving their homeport the crews were normally given two months' pay, no further wages being paid or pay tickets issued until the ship was de-commissioned and paid off. The seamen then presented their tickets to the naval pay office in London or to the dockyard commissioner at the homeport. The interval between the initial distribution of wages and the final settlement might be many months and even several years, during which the seamen were desperate for cash. To satisfy the need seamen exchanged their tickets at a discount to anyone who could supply the cash. Though the Admiralty officially disapproved of seamen selling their tickets, they could suggest no cure; and in Warren's day, the practice was common. The cash was advanced not only by professional dealers in pay tickets but also by naval officers, expecially captains. It was a very secure type of loan, the only difficulty arising when seamen complained to the authorities if an exorbitant discount rate was demanded.

That Warren was a supplier of cash to his seamen is readily seen from a study both of the pay books of the ships he commanded and of his own private accounts. Nowhere, however, is it indicated at what rate he discounted the tickets; if his customary adherence to the usury laws is any real indication, he would have insisted on no more than the legal maximum. Warren did not himself appear at the pay office to claim his debts once the tickets were paid off but employed his London agents: at first Edward Jasper and later the Bakers. He did not confine himself to pay tickets of seamen on ships he himself commanded, but also invested in tickets of seamen from ships of his squadron, and on one occasion at least the pay ticket of a seaman serving on an East Indiaman.[7] During the Louisbourg siege in 1745, for instance, in order to encourage men to volunteer to serve on the *Vigilant,* the warship just captured from the French, Warren advanced cash to many of the crew in return for their pay tickets.[8] Table 23 provides all available evidence of Warren's dealings of this sort.

TABLE 23 *Loans on Seamen's Tickets 1726-1750*

Year	Description	Amount		
1726	Pay tickets for *Falkland*	£ 27	11s.	3d.
1728	Pay tickets for *Grafton*	136	6s.	9d.
1729	Pay tickets for *Leopard*	15	15s.	
1730	Pay tickets (misc.)	50	17s.	7d.
1731	Pay tickets for *Solebay*	15	16s.	
1731	Pay tickets (misc.)	196	12s.	7d.
1732	Pay ticket for *Aldborough*	26		6d.
1734	Pay ticket of John Smith [*Solebay*]	6		
1735	Pay tickets for *Leopard*	62	15s.	
1735	Pay tickets for *Tartar*	1	6s.	6d.
1735	Pay ticket for *Happy*	7	12s.	6d.
1735	Pay ticket for *Decker* (East India ship)	7		
1735	Pay ticket for *Solebay*	94	1s.	6d.
1735	Pay ticket for *Hector*	15	5s.	4d.
1736	Pay tickets for *Scarborough*	40	4s.	
1737	Pay tickets for *Squirrel*	152	4s.	5d.
1738	Pay tickets for *Squirrel*	673	19s.	
1739	Pay tickets for *Squirrel*	27	17s.	10d.
1740	Pay tickets for *Squirrel*	243	16s.	2d.
1745	Pay tickets for *Squirrel*	75	7s.	
1750	Pay tickets for *Superbe*	93	7s.	6d.
1750	Pay tickets for *Vigilant*	153	16s.	10d.

Source: Jasper–Warren accounts, 1730-40, 1742-45, Gage Papers, G/Am/1, G/Am/13, p. 6, 8, 10, 13; Warren Papers, WLCL; Pay books, Adm. 33/277, Adm. 33/289, Adm. 33/328, Adm. 33/393, Adm. 33/409, PRO.

Warren also loaned his seamen money on the security of their anticipated prize money. Though his private accounts do not provide a complete story of this aspect of his investments, they reveal that he adopted this policy as soon as prize money began to flow into his hands in 1740, continued it throughout the war and even after peace was concluded, so long as prize funds were still owing to his men.[9]

Warren also acted as capitalist for his fellow naval officers, at least from 1730, but particularly between 1749 and 1752. By January 1732 he had advanced £150 to Lieutenant John Ambrose, who served with him in America.[10] At the same time he loaned £25 to a Lieutenant Watkins, whom he described as a "relation of Sir John Norris."[11] These and other such early loans were secured only by a note of hand. Most of the larger loans made between 1749 and 1752 were short-term and all but one were at four per cent. He loaned £700 to Captain Warwick Calmady, who had served under him in the West Indies and who commanded the *Launceston* at Louisbourg in 1745. It was repaid in May 1749 with £12 1s. 6d. interest. Captain Forbes of the marines repaid his £500 note of hand, also of short duration, in May 1751. In November 1749 Warren loaned £1,000 to Captain William Holburne, who had served with him in the West Indies, commanded the *Vigilant* at Louisbourg in 1745, and subsequently served under Warren in the Western Squadron in 1747 and 1748. The loan was repaid the following March with £14 6s. 6d. interest. In July 1750 he loaned £300 to another officer who had served with him at the 1745 siege of Louisbourg, Captain John Brett.

The only loan made by Warren to his fellow officers secured by mortgage was advanced to Captain Henry Cosby, the son of the one time governor of New York, Colonel William Cosby. Cosby commanded the station ship at New York from 1751 until his death in 1753. In May 1751, on the eve of Cosby's departure for New York, Warren and Admiral Anson loaned him £1,986 at five per cent secured by a mortgage on Cosby Manor, a 19,000–acre estate on the Mohawk River in frontier New York.[12] Warren had advanced £662 and Anson the balance. It would appear that Warren was at least as interested in acquiring the mortgaged estate as the annual interest and eventually the principal. Anson's involvement, obviously stimulated by Warren's knowledge of the New York land market, was perhaps inspired by the same concern. In fact the property never came into either Warren's or Anson's hands. The manor was sold first to William Johnson, who in 1762 resold it to a New York consortium led by Oliver DeLancey. The New York partnership was then anxious to get a clear title to the land and applied to Cosby's executor, his mother the Honourable Mrs.

Grace Cosby. The matter dragged on for another six years, for only in 1768 were the Warren heirs credited by Oliver DeLancey with both repayment of principal and interest: £1,233, a profit of £571 on the original investment of £662.[13]

One of Warren's "loans" to his fellow officers involved no outlay of cash on his part. On 30 April 1748 he was sent a bond for £200 by Captain John Wickham, who had served in the Western Squadron. Wickham had received £640 freight money for carrying bullion from Lisbon to England; and Warren had laid claim to one-third. Wickham not wanting to offend his admiral at once sent Warren a bond with a promise to pay by 20 June, or sooner if his accounts with the Navy Board were quickly passed, and a letter of mild protest: "As I never Once heard of a Commanding Officer's sharing with any Captain whom before went that voyage I realy look't upon the whole freight as My right, Otherwise should have tenderd it you long since & have been more spareing in furnishing a little house and buying some things which I should have longer done without, altho necessary and much wanting."[14] For the details of this and other loans to officers and seamen, table 24 acts as a summary.

Another sector of Warren's money lending activities comprised loans to his Irish relations. In July 1731 he loaned his cousin, Sir Gerald Aylmer, third baronet, £400 at seven per cent.[15] Fifteen months later he loaned him a further £100, this time at six per cent. In both cases the only security offered was bonds. When Sir Gerald died in 1745 he still owed £400, a sum which was unpaid when Warren died seven years later.[16] Though Warren did not forgive the debt in his will, it seems never to have been repaid. Warren also loaned the Johnson family in Ireland various sums of money. As early as December 1733 he had loaned his brother-in-law, Christopher Johnson, £100 at six per cent, taking his bond as security.[17] Interest was paid regularly until at least 1744. It may then have been paid off, though evidence is lacking. Certainly neither Warren nor his executors complained of lack of payment; nor is there reference to it in Warren's final will. Warren may have excused the debt, for when he began to collect a fortune in the early 1740s he displayed considerable generosity to the Johnsons. Two of Christopher Johnson's sons in Ireland also benefited from Warren's fortune. Warren Johnson had borrowed before June 1749 £400 from Warren, and that month Warren advanced him a further £650 to purchase a commission in the English army. On 22 June Johnson gave Warren his bond for £1,050.[18]

TABLE 24 *Miscellaneous Loans to Officers and Seamen*

Year	Description	Amount	Paid Off	Yield on 3% Funds
1730-31	Lieut. John Ambrose's note	£150	before 1740	3.1%
1730	Lieut. Watkins' note	25	?	3.1
pre-1740	Midshipman Archer's note	5 5s.	?	—
pre-1740	Lieut. Wakeman's note	31 10s.		—
1740	Seamen Holderm, Hall, and Hughes	19 5s.		3
1745	Lieut. Riggs' bond	100		3.3
1745	Midshipman Winslow	25	1751	3.3
1748	Capt. Wickham's bond	200	1748	3.6
1748	Capt. Calmady's bond @ 4%	700	1749	3.6
1749	Capt. Forbes' note @ 5%	500	1751	3.2
1749	Seaman Gurdett's note	11 11s.	?	3.2
1749	Seaman Flood's note	10	?	3.2
1749	Capt. Holborne's note @ 4%	1,000	1750	3.2
1750	Capt. Brett's note @ 4%	300	1752	3.0
1750	Gunner Hook and Boatswain Percy	100	1750	3.0
1750	Seamen Vivian, Wendover, and Biddlecomb	150	1750	
1751	Capt. Cosby's mortgage @ 5%	662	1768	3.0
1752	Seaman Briger's note	5 5s.	?	2.9

Source: Warren accounts, 1749-52, Warren Papers, WLCL; Gage Papers, G/Am/1, G/Am/2, G/Am/40a and 40b. Ashton, *Economic Fluctuation*, p. 187.

Two years later Warren Johnson's younger brother, John Johnson of Warrenstown, borrowed £462 from Warren giving his bond as security.[19] Both loans were at 4 per cent interest; but none of the capital was recovered as Warren forgave the debts by his final will, which stated: "I hereby discharge the said several Debts and desire that whatever Bonds of theirs I have may be given up having taken their Bonds not with an Intent to be paid but to make them diligent."[20]

Warren also helped finance the brief business career of another nephew, Captain Richard Tyrrell, whose naval fortunes Warren had fostered. In 1751 when Tyrrell decided to take extended leave from the navy to pursue his fortune in the sugar business in Antigua, Warren not only gave him an initial loan of £2,600 at four per cent, but also subsequently acted as his banker by accepting his bills of exchange.[21] Warren's death put an end to this convenient source of credit for Tyrrell, who then stood indebted to his uncle in the amount of £3,814. This debt Warren did not excuse; when Tyrrell returned to England in 1754 he paid off the principal, as well as £249 in accrued interest. Though the debt had not been excused, Warren willed that the proceeds be divided between Tyrrell's two sisters and the children of Christopher Johnson, except his eldest son, William.[22] He planned to compensate Tyrrell by naming him heir to one-third of his entire estate, should all Warren's children die unmarried before coming of age. As this eventuality never materialized, of all Warren's relations, Tyrrell profited the least from his uncle's fortune. The details are found in table 25.

TABLE 25 *Loans to Irish Relations 1731-1752*

Year	Description	Amount	Paid Off	Yield on 3% Funds
1731	Sir Gerald Aylmer's bond @ 7%	£400	?	3.1%
1732	Sir Gerald Aylmer's bond @ 7%	100	before 1752	3.1
1733	Christopher Johnson's bond @ 6%	100	before 1752	3.0
[1747]	Warren Johnson's bond @ 4%	400	forgiven	3.5
1749	Warren Johnson's bond @ 4%	650	forgiven	3.2
1751	John Johnson's bond @ 4%	462	forgiven	3.0
1751	Capt. Richard Tyrrell @ 4%	2,600	1754	3.0
1752	Capt. Richard Tyrrell @ 4%	1,214	1754	2.9

Source: Gage Papers, Warren Papers, WLCL and NYHS; Ashton, *Economic Fluctuations*, p. 187.

This capital in the form of loans to Irish relations thus represented more an exercise in philanthropy than strict economic investments. Without doubt the credit extended to his three nephews helped them in their careers, while the return on the earlier loans to Christopher Johnson and Aylmer was almost negligible.

An eighteenth century maxim held that "the man who buys land has principal without interest; he who lays out his fortune in the funds has interest without principal: but he who lends on mortgage has both principal and interest."[23] Doubtless Warren would have agreed with this for he put more than two-fifths of his outlay in loans between 1748 and 1752 into mortgages. Though there were only six of these loans, their capital value amounted to £14,950.

Two of the mortgages were taken from Warren's neighbours in Hampshire. He first loaned £250 to Henry Hunt in September 1748

on the security of a water mill not far from Warren's home at Westbury. Only one payment of interest was ever received from Hunt, and
by April 1752 the mill had been forfeited to Warren. Its value even in
1772 was reckoned at only £100, and must be considered a poor
investment.[24] The second mortgage was taken from Warren's bailiff,
Thomas Earwaker, on his land in the parish of West Meon, as security
on £250 cash advanced him in January 1752.[25] Like Hunt's mortgage,
Earwaker's was at four per cent. It is not known when this debt was
paid off, but certainly not before 1762, when the Westbury accounts
stop.

The four other mortgages held by Warren were for much larger
amounts and involved substantial landowners. In June 1749 Warren
loaned Sir Thomas Robinson, Bart., £1,700 at five per cent interest,
on his Whitehall house.[26] A year later Warren advanced him a further
£100, for which he merely took a bond at five per cent interest. Warren
had known Robinson well, when Sir Thomas was governor of Barbados between 1742 and 1747. The arrangement, which grew from
this acquaintance, was not without risk, for Robinson was noted for
his extravagance, both in London and on his Yorkshire estates at
Rokeby.[27] An amateur architect, he had rebuilt the family mansion and
had managed to waste a great deal of money. Moreover, while in
London his entertainments were as frequent as they were magnificent.
It was the precarious state of his finances which apparently had forced
him to accept the post of colonial governor. So lavish was his spending
on his official residence and other buildings in Barbados that he was
obliged to meet part of the cost himself. Upon his return to England
in 1747 he resumed his extravagance, ultimately being rescued only by
selling Rokeby. By then his debt to Warren had long been settled; and
Warren escaped without having burned his fingers.[28]

In December 1751 Warren loaned the Earl of Egmont £3,000 at four
per cent, secured by a mortgage on 2,800 acres of Egmont's estates in
county Cork, whose rent roll amounted only to £270 per annum.[29] The
mortgage was recovered only after 1758.[30] Here, too, Warren might
have been influenced both by political and economic considerations,
for Egmont, as lord of the bedchamber in the household of the Prince
of Wales, was one of the leading opponents of the Pelhams for many
years. When Warren's own political ambitions faded after 1749, he
moved towards the opposition, and was actually counted among the
adherents of Leicester House. In 1749 Egmont thought him a suitable
candidate for the Westminster constituency in the election to be held

after the death of George II and the accession of his son, Frederick, "if Sir Peter keeps a character by his conduct in the House."[31] Warren was even listed among the members of the new Admiralty Board to be established under Frederick.[32] After the prince's sudden death in March 1751, Egmont was the only one of his principal adherents not to make his peace with the Pelhams.

The last two mortgages acquired by Warren were negotiated in February and May 1752. The first was a loan of £4,650 to William Graves, secured on his estate in county Meath.[33] The other was a £5,000 loan to George Armstrong, Esq., secured on an estate in Middlesex and Hertfordshire.[34] Both loans were at four per cent interest. Graves's loan was still unpaid by 1791, though regular interest payments were made to John Johnson. The mortgage must have eventually been recovered, for it is nowhere mentioned in the Irish land papers of the Warren heirs up to the first decade of the nineteenth century. The money loaned to Armstrong was to purchase an estate near Tullamore in Kings County, Ireland, whose annual rent roll amounted to £250. The agreement signed in London stipulated that Warren would give up the mortgage if within six months Armstrong could raise more than £5,000 from other sources. It also contained the condition that if the principal was not repaid within that short interval, the rate of interest would rise from four to five per cent. In fact Lady Warren recovered the £5,000 early in November as well as £94 interest, either as a result of her desire to call in as many of her husband's outstanding loans as possible following his death in July, or because Armstrong had succeeded in finding a larger creditor elsewhere.[35]

It is interesting to see that Warren was equally prepared to lend money on the security of either English or Irish land. Many other sources of credit, London bankers and London insurance companies for instance, were very reluctant to finance mortgages on Irish property and insisted, whenever possible, on English land as security. It is also a matter of some interest that of the six mortgages taken by Warren, four were negotiated in a period of six months from December 1751 to May 1752. This switch to mortgages may have resulted from the rise in price of government stock after the war, with its consequent decline in yields. Furthermore, the government's intention to reduce interest rates on the National Debt must also have helped to induce this important alteration in his portfolio. Warren's death put an end to such investments in England and Ireland, for his widow invested almost exclusively in the Funds. It was there, for instance, that she placed the £5,000 principal received from Armstrong in November 1752; and this established her investment pattern for the rest of her life. The details of these mortgages are summarized in table 26.

TABLE 26 *English and Irish Mortgages*

Year	Description	Amount	Paid Off	Yield on 3% Funds
1748	Henry Hunt @ 4%	£ 250	bad	3.6%
1749	Sir Thomas Robinson @ 5%	1,700	1751	3.2
1750	Sir Thomas Robinson @ 5%	100	1751	3.0
1751	Earl of Egmont @ 4%	3,000	after 1758	3.0
1752	Thomas Earwaker @ 4%	250	after 1762	2.9
1752	William Graves @ 4%	4,650	after 1791	2.9
1752	George Armstrong @ 4%	5,000	1752	2.9

Source: Gage Papers and Warren Papers, WLCL; Ashton, *Economic Fluctuations*, p. 187.

Though bonds were much less secure than mortgages, Warren was often satisfied with this form of security. In Ireland he took the additional precaution of having those who had given him their bonds declare themselves as "judgment debtors," by registering their indebtedness in the Dublin Registry of Deeds.[36] Between June 1749 and July 1752 Warren made sixteen loans secured by bonds both in England and Ireland. The capital involved amounted to £12,015; and of this only £310 had been repaid by the time of his death. The sums involved ranged from £2,000 down to £25, the rate of interest varying between four and five per cent.[37]

Warren's most important loans, secured by bonds, were made to English and Irish landowners, some of them politicians and some who had once been active Jacobites. In 1749 Warren loaned Thomas, Viscount Gage, £500 at five per cent. Gage was master of the household of the Prince of Wales from 1747 until the prince's death in 1751. The possible political motives in this case are similar to those already referred to in relation to the Earl of Egmont's mortgage. The loan was still outstanding in 1758, despite Lady Warren's attempts to recover it. She had been anxious to see Gage in the summer of 1754 before Parliament rose, but had missed him and never saw him again, for Gage fell ill that autumn and died in the following December. His son and heir, William Hall, Viscount Gage, was in no hurry to pay off his father's obligations or indeed even to pay the interest.[38] In 1750 Warren loaned the Honourable Henry Bilson Legge, a junior member of the Admiralty Board in 1745 and 1746, an adherent of the Duke of Bedord's, and a future Chancellor of the Exchequer, £260 on his bond at five per cent interest.[39] The debt was repaid almost right away, thus being one of only two such bonds recovered before Warren's death.

Warren's loans to three former adherents of the Jacobite cause form a curious aspect of his money-lending activity. In 1750 he loaned £500 to the Honourable Theobald Taaffe, £2,000 to Viscount Taaffe, and £1,000 to Viscount Dillon. The Taaffes were Irish born, Dillon was born in France. Viscount Taaffe's parents had left Ireland, and he had been educated in Lorraine, then entered the Austrian army. When Warren first met him he was Imperial Ambassador to the Court of St. James.[40] Dillon served in the French army in a regiment commanded both by his father and elder brother. In 1744, he abandoned French service, returned to England, and laid successful claim to the forfeited Dillon estates in Ireland.[41] He married the eldest daughter of the Earl of Litchfield and, through her, his elder son inherited as well the entire Litchfield estate. These three loans, amounting to £3,500 were at five per cent interest, and were all eventually repaid. Viscount Taaffe paid £2,273 in March 1753, Dillon £1,108 in December of the same year.[42] The loan to Taaffe's kinsman was more difficult to recover, for Lady Warren had "given him great offence by puting his bond in Sute" in 1754; the debt was still unpaid in 1758.[43]

The remaining landowners to whom Warren lent on bond were also Irish. In November 1749, £2,000 at four per cent went to Miss Rebecca Forster, the only woman among Warren's debtors. In March 1750 Colonel Robert Longfield borrowed £419. In May 1749 and June 1751 Noah Webb borrowed at first £50, repaid it, and then borrowed £1,000, both at 4½ per cent. Finally, John O'Connor was loaned £1,000 at the same rate in December 1751.[44] None were paid off, except Webb's initial loan, during Warren's lifetime. The loan to Noah Webb, who lived at Dunshaughlin near Warrenstown, county Meath, was recovered only after 1770, the debtor proving himself a considerable nuisance. Until 1762 Webb made regular interest payments on his loan, but then instituted legal proceedings in Dublin claiming a substantial part of Warren's Irish investments on the grounds that the admiral had failed to adhere strictly to the requirement of Irish land law, when making his various purchases between 1749 and 1752.[45] In particular he claimed that Warren's parents were known to have died as Catholics, and that Warren himself had failed to take the necessary oaths of allegiance and conformity on each occasion that land was transferred to his name. Webb used Edward Shank, a cordwainer of Dublin, as the principal in the suit. Neither Lady Warren nor her sons-in-law even bothered to reply to the suit, though Webb thought his interest in it sufficiently well-established to convey in his final will, drawn up in 1767, whatever rights he possessed in the dispute to his heir, Henry Webb of Westphalstown, county Dublin. After considerable negotiations, Henry Webb in February 1770 gave up his pretensions to the Warren estates in Ireland by conveying his "rights" in the case to the Warren heirs. The dispute had delayed the recovery of the loan to Webb by more than eight years, and is a typical instance of the difficulties which the Irish land law in the eighteenth century created even for the most robust adherents of the established church. The only profit went to the lawyers of the warring parties.[46]

TABLE 27 *English and Irish Miscellaneous Bonds*

Year	Description	Amount	Paid off	Yield on 3% Funds
1749	Noah Webb @ 4½%	£ 50	1751	3.2%
[1749]	Viscount Gage @ 5%	500	after 1754	3.2
1749	Miss Rebecca Forster @ 4%	2,000	after 1758	3.2
1750	Col. Longfield and son @ 5%	419	after 1754	3.0
[1750]	Theobald Taaffe @ 5%	500	after 1758	3.0
1750	Viscount Taaffe @ 5%	2,000	1753	3.0
1750	Viscount Dillon @ 5%	1,000	1753	3.0
[1750]	Gabriel Johnston @ 4%	700	after 1754	3.0
1750	Henry Legge @ 5%	260	1751	3.0
1751	Harman Verelst @ 5%	300	bad debt	3.0
1751	Noah Webb @ 4½%	1,000	after 1770	3.0
1751	Smith, Andrews, and Pace @ 4½%	150	1753	3.0
1751	John O'Connor @ 4½%	1,000	after 1754	3.0
[1752]	Gabriel Johnston @ 5%	1,300	after 1754	2.9
1752	Samuel Leake @ 5%	100	bad	2.9
1752	Crofton & Meares @ 4%	651	1753	2.9

Source: Gage Papers and Warren Papers, WLCL; Ashton, *Economic Fluctuations,* p. 187.

In contrast to the money-lending activities carried on in his name in New York by the DeLanceys, Warren made few loans to merchants in England or Ireland. When he did, he was satisfied by bond security; the capital involved amounted only to £1,200. The largest loan was to the Dublin merchants Messrs. Crofton and Meares for £651 at four per cent in July 1752, the last such arrangement concluded before Warren's death a fortnight later. The previous October he had loaned the London merchants, Messrs. Smith, Andrews, and Pace £150 at 4½ per cent, which was repaid in July 1753.[47] Two other loans to merchants were not recovered. One for £300 was given to Harman Verelst, who until 1751 was accomptant to the Trustees of the Colony of Georgia. The loan was made in January 1751 when, perhaps unknown to Warren, Verelst was in grave financial straits. By 1754 Lady Warren said he was in jail without hope "of his ever being able to pay a farthing."[48] The Warrens not only never received any of their principal loaned but not even a single interest payment. The other bad debt involved Samuel Jeake of London and Jamaica. Warren had loaned him £100 at five per cent in May 1752, when Jeake was employed by the Society for a Free British Fishery, in which Warren had invested; the two had probably first met there. Verelst was also sufficiently aware of Warren's affairs to know of his plans, which proved abortive, to purchase a large Hampshire estate. Shortly after borrowing from Warren, Jeake left for Jamaica where he acquired a modest fortune; but despite the demands made on him by Lady Warren, he refused to repay his £100 loan. A typical answer was one he sent Lady Warren in April 1769, which is worth quoting as a rare example of correspondence between the Warren estate and its debtors: "I am very sorry it hath not yet been in my Power to acquit my self of it. I had hope to have done it long since out of the demands I have upon Alderman Beckford but have by the great Delays in the Prosecution of those Demands arising partly from the Nature of Proceedings in Law and partly from Want of Money to expedite Proceedings, I have still been unable to acquit my self as I ought of that Debt."[49]

The debt was still unpaid by the time Lady Warren died in 1771. After some deliberation her heirs thought it worth their while to pursue Jeake. In 1754 a power of attorney was sent to a Mr. Gordon in Jamaica enabling him to collect the loan, but without apparent success.[50] The loss was not only the £100 but also the interest which had not been paid since the debt had first been contracted in 1752.

The last bond debt to be considered was that incurred by Warren's London attorney, Gabriel Johnston, who had borrowed £700 in 1750 and £1,300 in 1752. After Warren's death Lady Warren was keen to recover the principal as quickly as possible, but immediately encountered difficulties from Robert Macky, who had been associated with

Johnston and her husband in the 1752 negotiations for the purchase of various Irish estates. She explained her predicament to her brother, Oliver DeLancey: "Mr. Macky says he made an agreement wth. You that he should receive his proportion of Councellor Johnstons Debt and threatens that if I pursue to secure my Debt by Law that I shall have one if not two bills in Chancery filed against me so you see how I am treated at all sides."[51] Lady Warren's need of her husband's firm hand in business affairs was nowhere more in evidence than in her attempts, so often unsuccessful, to recover quickly the principal he had laid out in bond debts both in England and Ireland. Table 27 provides a summary of these bond loans.

For Warren, money lending always formed an important segment of his investments. As his fortune grew so his activities multiplied. Beginning modestly by discounting seamen's pay tickets, more as a convenience to his crews than to himself, he became a lifelong creditor both of seamen and their officers. The climax was reached at Louisbourg in 1745 when he was responsible for paying part of the crews of several ships in his squadron. He also loaned money to both his men and officers on the security of the prize money due them, particularly when lengthy legal disputes inordinately delayed the prize processes.

It was his own prize fortune which enabled him, especially in the years after the war, to expand his money-lending activities. £36,000 was put out at interest in this way in England and Ireland, of which no less than £30,800 was still outstanding at the time of his death in 1752. This yielded an income of £1,270 (3.5 per cent), excluding those loans on which neither interest nor principal were ever received. This income declined after Warren's death, partly because of the loans to his two nephews, the Johnson brothers, whose obligations were cancelled by the terms of his will, and partly by the repayment of certain other loans. By 1754 the income stood at £947, of which £403 was remitted annually from Ireland by John Johnson, the family's agent there.

Warren's lending on bonds displayed an apparent indifference about whether the debtor lived in England or Ireland, whether they were staunch supporters of the government or leading opponents of the Pelhams, whether they were great landlords or his humble neighbours in Hampshire. His loans to the two merchants who defaulted, Verelst and Jeake, appear foolhardy especially since one was in difficulty and the other in indifferent circumstances. Yet there might have been ties of friendship which made him ignore their credit rating, which a strict business arrangement would have demanded. Loans on mortgage were fewer though larger than bond loans. There are only six examples, and a seventh if the £662 loan made to Captain Cosby, secured by a mortgage on his New York frontier tract, is included. In general loans which were on mortgage received a more favourable rate of interest. The only mortgage at the maximum rate, to Sir Thomas Robinson, was soon paid off. In view of Warren's death, and the difficulties his widow experienced in calling in his private loans, the real differences between mortgages and bonds, other than the rate of interest, became blurred. On the one hand the mortgagor borrowed his money at a lower rate than the bond-debtor; on the other hand the bond-debtor, for the most part, experienced as much undisturbed security as if he had mortgaged his property. From the viewpoint of Lady Warren and her daughters this was of course less than satisfactory. One has the feeling that had Warren not died prematurely, his bond-debtors would not have been allowed such independence. This is not to suggest that he would have been free of bad debts. No expedient has yet been devised to remove that risk from the money lender, and certainly none was known to the men of Warren's day. It was this risk, which Warren apparently accepted lightly, that enabled the creditor to demand a return on his investment higher than that on either land or the Funds.

Only in a few cases is it known why the borrowers reviewed here became indebted. The £5,000 loaned to Armstrong in 1752 was to be used to purchase land in Ireland. Much of the funds advanced to Warren Johnson was used to purchase a captaincy in the British army. The money loaned to Tyrrell was employed in setting up his sugar business in Antigua. The loans to seamen served merely to supply them with the bare necessities of life, which the delay in both their wages and prize money made exceedingly grim. For the majority, however, nothing certain can be said.

Finally, whether Warren loaned money in England or Ireland, he always kept within the ceiling imposed by law on the interest rate. Only in the early 1730s did he demand the maximum rate in Ireland. Thereafter nothing in his activities indicates that his loans in Ireland were determined by the higher ceiling allowed there, for after 1734 he never loaned at a rate above five per cent. Indeed, at times he loaned money in Ireland at four per cent, when at the same time in England he demanded five per cent. Although friendship and kinship can explain in part the favourable rates at which he sometimes appears to have loaned money, general market factors undoubtedly dictated to a large extent the terms of the loans. Most of his important lending occurred at a time of unusually low interest rates both in England and Ireland.[52] Between 1748 and 1752 the Funds were selling almost at par, then at par, and finally above par, thus forcing yields for the first time in two decades below three per cent. Thus, while Warren was earning an impressive capital gain by selling part of his investment in government Funds to finance both land and money lending, he was also having to accept at times lower interest rates on bonds and mortgages than would have been the case had the Funds not been selling at a premium. On balance these circumstances suited him well, while the eventual recovery by his heirs of almost all the capital laid out by him between 1748 and 1752 fully justified the risks he had accepted in laying out so large a portion of his wealth in private loans.

A View of New York from the North West.

A view of New York from the northwest. From the *Atlantic Neptune* (c. 1773) by Frederick William DesBarres. "Warren's Wharf is on the extreme left. The principal spire is that of Trinity church, while Fort George is on the right." Courtesy of the I. N. Phelps Stokes Collection, Prints Division, The New York Public Library, Astor, Lenox, and Tilden Foundations.

The Naval Nurse; or Modern Commander. Courtesy of the British Museum.

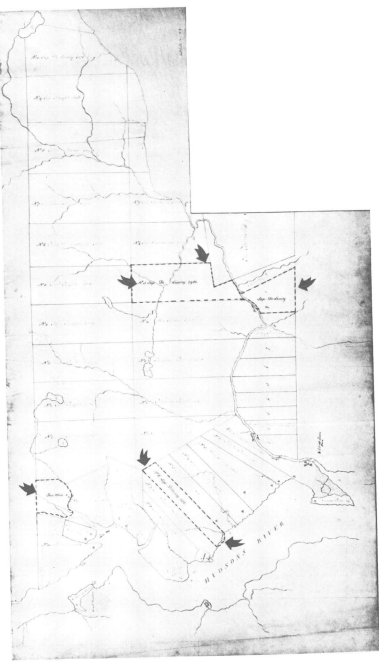

Cortlandt Manor in 1734, with iron works and Warren family holdings indicated. Courtesy of the William L. Clements Library, University of Michigan.

Warrensburg 1739

According to Edward Collins

▨ Squatters

▲ Future site of Johnson's house

--→-- Road to Fort Hunter

Warrensburg 1739. Adapted with permission from Edith M. Fox, "William Johnson's Early Career as a Frontier Landlord and Trader." Prepared by David Farnsworth, University of Ottawa.

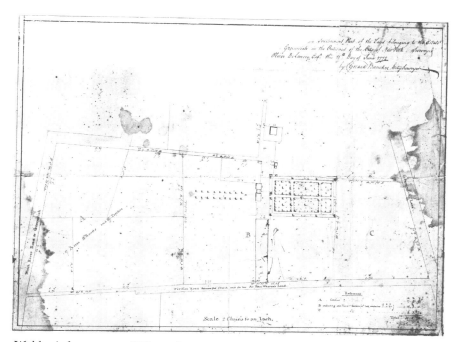

Webber's farm, part of Warren's estate at Greenwich, Manhattan Island, surveyed by Gerrard Bancker, June 1772. Courtesy of the New-York Historical Society.

Opposite page
A plan of the city of New York surveyed in the years 1766 and 1767 for Sir Henry Moore, Bart., by B. Ratzer. Courtesy of The New-York Historical Society. Arrows indicate property owned by Vice Admiral Warren.

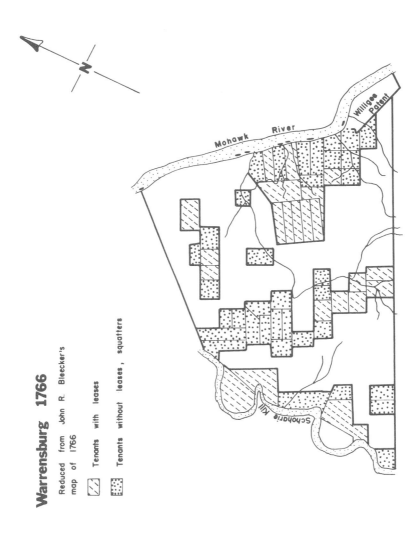

Warrensburg 1766. Adapted with permission from Edith M. Fox, "William Johnson's Early Career as a Frontier Landlord and Trader." Prepared by David Farnsworth, University of Ottawa.

miral Warren's estate at Greenwich, Manhattan Island, surveyed in August 1773 by Gerrard
ıcker. Courtesy of the I. N. Phelps Stokes Collection, Prints Division, The New York Public
rary, Astor, Lenox, and Tilden Foundations.

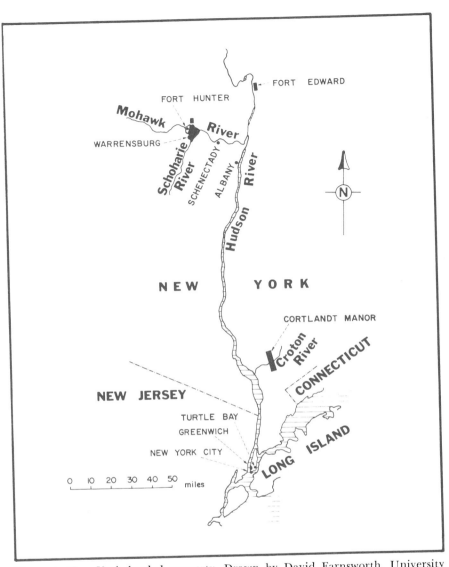

Warren's New York landed property. Drawn by David Farnsworth, University of Ottawa.

Opposite page
A plan of Westbury house and gardens together with the offices, farmyard, barns stabling, and lands adjacent. Courtesy of Viscount Gage and the Sussex Archaeological Society, Lewes.

A Plan of
Westbury House & Gardens
Together with the Offices Farm yard
Barns stabling and Lands adjacent

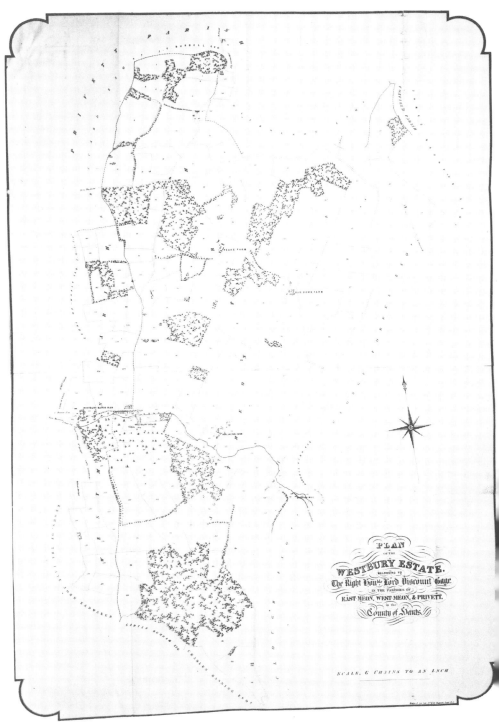

Plan of the Westbury estate belonging to Viscount Gage, offered for sale by auction August 1865, in part inherited originally from Vice Admiral Warren. Courtesy of the British Museum.

Part of Ballydowde, county Dublin, surveyed in April 1778. Courtesy of the National Library of Ireland, Dublin.

Warrenstown, county Meath. Courtesy of Jack Leonard, Esq.

Sir Peter Warren. By Faber after Hudson. Courtesy of the National Maritime Museum, London.

Vice Admiral Sir Peter Warren by François Roubilliac (d. 1762). Supposedly his wife on the right. Courtesy of the Dean and Chapter of Westminster Abbey.

Chapter 11

Investments in the

London Money Market

1728-1772

Like other men of wealth in the eighteenth century, Warren did not confine his investments to land and money lending, but found the stock of the great trading companies, the new insurance companies, and particularly the funded debt of the government in England, extremely attractive. His interest in this type of investment developed in the midst of impressive financial expansion and inventiveness, especially in the field of public credit. Massive borrowing by the English government had begun only in the late seventeenth century. By the 1720s, despite the recent experience of the South Sea "Bubble" and considerable nervousness over the size of the National Debt, the government was administering with considerable competence a successful and well-organized fiscal system, which ultimately enabled it "to spend on war out of all proportion to its tax revenue."[1] During the War of the Spanish Succession, government expenditure had reached £93.6 million, of which £29.4 million (or 31.4 per cent) had been raised by loans. This unprecedented achievement was repeated in the war with Spain and France between 1739 and 1748, which cost Britain £95.6 million, of which £29.7 million (or 31.1 per cent) was again raised by loans. As only a part of these debts were redeemed, the National Debt rose from £12.8 million in 1702 to £77.5 million in 1749. This revolutionary development occurred at a time of general price stability, thus enabling the government to borrow without either causing inflation or cornering the investment market. With this growth had developed an effective market in securities in the city of London, thus simplifying dealings in government debt and short-term government obligations such as Army debentures, Navy bills, and Exchequer bills.[2]

The enormous growth in government indebtedness, aided by a sound economy, was a new phenomenon attractive to those even with very limited amounts of capital to invest. Moreover, it offered an attractive alternative to land, private money lending, and industrial or commercial investment. By 1752 the National Debt alone was held in some 53,000 separate accounts, which because of institutional accounts and holdings by trustees (especially executors), involved a somewhat larger body of the economic elite. Most investors were bankers, insurance brokers, officials of the trading companies, merchants of all sorts, stock brokers, and jobbers, as well as women, members of the Church and professions, members of parliament, and government officials. Perhaps a tenth of the National Debt was held by foreigners, principally Dutch and Swiss, but most of the domestic capital came from those living in the London area.

Warren's investments in this market began modestly with the so-called "South Sea Old Annuities." The debt of the South Sea Company had undergone two significant changes since the great collapse of 1720-21. In 1723, the £33,802,203 capital of the company had been divided into two equal portions, one representing the trading capital, and the other described as the joint stock of the South Sea Annuities. In 1733 a further division took place when the company's trading capital was reduced by two-thirds to £3,662,784. The remainder of the trading capital of 1733, amounting to £10,988,319, became a fixed interest stock bearing 4 per cent interest, and known as South Sea New Annuities. The South Sea Old Annuities of 1723 originally bore 5 per cent interest, but in 1727 had been reduced to 4 per cent. Both old and new were administered at South Sea House, and "for all practical purposes they were government stocks like those administered by the Bank of England."[3]

Warren's first ventures into the London stock market were on a relatively small scale, and were interrupted by his being posted abroad. In March 1728 he bought £1,000 South Sea Old Annuities, the capital doubtless arising from his share of freight money for carrying South Sea Company bullion from Jamaica in 1726. In the spring of 1730, upon sailing for New York, he instructed his agent, Edward Jasper, to sell the investment; and this was done in July.[4] Warren again bought South Sea Old Annuities to the value of £400 in 1735.[5] These he held for a very short time, and sold them in February 1736, upon leaving for Boston in command of the ship appointed to the New England station. In both instances there was no market reason for selling. Warren probably felt uneasy about leaving capital in this form so remote from his control. The news of any decline in the stock market would have reached New York or Boston too late for him to escape a capital loss. It was far less risky for him to leave a favourable balance in his account with Jasper, from whom he received 5 per cent per annum.[6]

It was only upon his return to England in 1742 that Warren again invested in South Sea Old Annuities. By that time his position was much more secure as a result of his success at sea and the prize money he had earned. In January 1742, for £1,127 Warren acquired £1,000 stock from Lewis Vanden Enden. The transfer was managed by Messrs. Samuel and William Baker, with whom Warren had been dealing since 1738 and whose fortunes he considerably strengthened in 1745 when he helped to secure for them the contract for the supply of the Louisbourg garrison.[7] The Baker cousins eventually made three further purchases for Warren, who was again absent from England until 1746. In each case an additional £1,000 was bought. The first, in March 1743, cost him £1,153; the next, in the September following, £1,155; and the third, in August 1744, £1,129, the price of the stock having fallen upon the outbreak of war with France earlier in the year. Thus for £4,565, Warren had a £4,000 investment producing £160 in interest annually. He retained this stock until June 1749, though as early as 1745 he had hinted to the Bakers his intention of selling in order to buy land in Ireland.[8] Warren sold the stock for £4,235, thereby incurring a capital loss of £330, the most serious he was to experience.[9] By then he had much larger investments in other government securities, some of which were selling at a premium far above what he had paid for them, so he could have liquidated one of these instead to finance his Irish land venture. Why he chose to sell the South Sea Old Annuities is not clear, though it probably had something to do with the government's conversion scheme then pending by which the interest rate on the stock would eventually be reduced to three per cent from four.

Warren also invested in East India Company stock. He was able to consider such an investment as early as 1741 when prize money from

his successes off the Florida coast and in the West Indies began to
reach him and his London agents. From Jamaica in March 1741 Warren suggested to Messrs. Baker to invest "In Such Publick Fund as you
and my Good Friend M^r. Norris Son to Sir John Norris Shall Think
safest in my Name, to whom I have wrote on this Occasion, to Pardon
me for such Trouble. But if you have Laid out any of the Money I have
remitted you for my Use and in my Name, I would have it Remain So
till my Return. But this money or Any Other I may hereafter Remitt
you I would have Laid Out in the Manner I have now Directed."[10] In
September the Bakers made their first purchase, £500 in East India
stock, the minimum necessary for voting qualification.[11] Warren never
sold this investment nor added to it, nor did his widow after his death.
It ultimately passed into the hands of their three daughters' trustees
in 1772. It was a sound investment, paying a 3½ per cent dividend
until 1744, when it rose to 4 per cent and ultimately to 6 per cent. By
the time of his death in 1752 Warren had received £445 dividends.
Though the stock had not then regained its market value of the early
1740s, it achieved spectacular levels in the 1760s.

Warren also invested in East India Company bonds and annuities,
but on a far larger scale. East India bonds were almost like large
denomination currency, easily acquired and easily disposed of, but had
the additional merit of continuously earning interest, together with the
possibility of capital gains. A widely read pamphlet of the time explained their value, in language made simple for the layman:

India bonds are the most convenient and profitable security any
person can be possessed of, who has any quantity of cash unemployed, but which he knows not how soon he may have occasion
for; the utility and advantage of these bonds is so well known to
the Merchants, and Traders of the City of London, that it is wholly
unnecessary to enlarge upon it; . . . There is as little trouble with
an India Bond, as with a Bank Note; it is not indeed current in the
common course of business, but may always be sold in office-
hours, at any of the public offices, as well as at Jonathan's Coffee-
House. . . . When you want to buy, you have no further trouble
than to agree on the price, for the seller is to make out the
bill. . . . These Bonds are usually for £100 each; and the seller
receives the interest of the purchaser, up to the day he sells.[12]

They were transferable to the purchaser by endorsement and delivery.

Warren first bought an East India bond in May 1745, the Bakers paying £99 for one £100 bond.[13] This remained an isolated venture until 1749 when Warren acquired another £10,100 bringing his total to £10,200. In 1750, East India bonds were subject to a conversion scheme proposed by the company under pressure from the government. Of the £4.2 million of the government's debt to the company, £3.2 million paid interest at four per cent and the rest at three per cent. Under the leadership of First Lord of the Treasury, Henry Pelham, the government was determined to reduce nearly all of the National Debt to three per cent. Its inducement to get the reluctant East India Company to agree was permission for the latter to fund part of its bond debt. In 1750 bond-holders subscribed £2,992,440, three quarters of which became stock (the so-called East India Annuities), and the remaining quarter became 3 per cent new bonds.[14] Accordingly, on 14 June 1750 Warren subscribed £10,000 of his £10,200 East India bonds, receiving in return certificates for £5,000 4 per cent annuities, £2,500 3 per cent annuities, and £2,500 new bonds.[15] The 3 per cent annuities were sold in February and March 1752, while the £5,000 4 per cent annuities, reduced by January 1756 to 3 per cent, became, after the settlement of his wife's estate in the spring of 1772, the property of Warren's three surviving daughters, in the name of their respective trustees.[16]

Warren added to the £2,500 in new East India bonds and the £200 in old bonds that he still retained. By the end of 1751 he owned altogether £13,000 of these bonds. The £10,300 acquired in 1751 had cost him £10,875, an average price of £105 11s. 9d. including brokerage fee, per £100.[17] Of the £13,000 owned by Warren at his death, £10,000 were sold by Lady Warren's broker, John Shipston of Cornhill, to help finance her £11,900 subscription in the 1757 Government Loan.[18] Later, as Lady Warren's daughters married or came of age their shares of the 1757 Government Loan were transferred either to their names or those of their guardians.

Following her husband's lead, Lady Warren invested heavily in East India annuities after his death, her first purchase being in November 1752: £5,000 at 104⅝ per £100, which, with the brokerage fee, cost her £5,238.[19] Her old friend, William Baker, thereupon advised her: "I think your Ladyship cannot do better than lay the mony you have by you out in the same three p Cent Annuities as you brought last, which may be done and paid for in the Same Manner, wither by writing to me with an order to Mess.[rs] Honeywood & Fuller to pay for them or else by writing to M[r]. Shipston yourself."[20] She chose to deal with Shipston directly, though her interest on the stock was invariably collected by William Baker on her behalf.[21] By the time her daughter, Ann, married in July 1758, Lady Warren held a nominal £22,400, which had cost her £21,648, the market having fallen significantly with the outbreak of hostilities with France in 1755.[22] She continued investing in this stock for many years, her last recorded purchase being made on 19 December 1768; at her death in November 1771, she held £16,800 East India annuities, even after having made over £34,800 to her daughters as they had married or had come of age.[23] The residue was divided in April and May 1772.

If Peter Warren's investment in East India securities was considerable, his stake in the government's debt administered by the Bank of England was formidable. The 1745 3 per cent annuities attracted a great part of Warren's prize fortune. It was the second of the large long-term loans floated by the government since the outbreak of war with France in 1744. As Dr. Dickson explains: "Until 1744, new English government long-term loans were relatively small, and 3% stock remained at par or just below it. When France officially entered the conflict against her in March 1744, and the real struggle began, the 3 per cents at once sank to 92-93, and the scale of long-term borrowing sharply increased. Larger and larger loans became needed each year."[24]

Whereas the government had raised £1.8 million from the public in 1744, £2 million were called for in 1745, £3 million in 1746, £5 million in 1747, and £6.3 million in 1748.[25] This was not the full extent of growing government indebtedness, but it represents the greater part of government borrowing by means of publicly subscribed loans.

The 1745 loan of £2 million was announced on 19 March. The rate of interest was to be 3 per cent. The increased interest charge which the government would have to meet was to come from an additional duty of £8 a tun on French wine and £4 a tun on other imported wines. Of the £2 million subscribable, £1.5 million was to be raised by issue of stock, and the rest by a lottery. The stock subscribed for was to be paid in four instalments, while the lottery tickets at £10 each were to be paid for at once. Everyone who purchased ten lottery tickets was allowed a 4½ per cent Exchequer annuity for his own life or for a nominee's.

The decision to invest in the 1745 loan was taken by the Baker cousins, who fully explained their reasons to Warren in a letter of March 1745:

> We have determined and made a bargain accordingly to invest your money which now is, and will be, in our hands in the New Funds established this Year, which we think will be more for your Advantage than buying old four p^r. Cent Annuities, of the Government continue to have a very high Premi^m. now as soon as a Peace is made, without which none of the Funds will be worth anything, the Government will, nay they must, reduce the Interest of those Debts for which they pay 4 p^r. Cent to three, either by paying them off in which case all y^e. Premium will be Lost to the proprietors, or else by reducing the Interest by a Law, and then great part of the Premium will be lost; this year they have Established New three p^r. Cent Annuities which are now come to Market, the Conditions are to pay one fourth part down, and the remaining three fourths at three quarterly payments, so that at Xmas next, the whole principal Sum will be paid, and then become a transferrable Stock receiving three p^r. Cent per Annum, and the Proprietors have Interest from this present Lady Day on the whole Capital Sum.[26]

They then went on to say that they had committed Warren to the purchase of £4,000 of the annuities, which they were to acquire at a discount of 12⅛ per cent, or £3,520 with brokerage fee. They then added:

> Should there come a Peace there will be Premium in all probability very Considerable thereon; We have done as for ourselves and doubt not your approbation; we must observe only this to you, that if you have occasion to turn any of your Stocks into Money, it will be most to your advantage to sell out any other, rather than the new ones, because the advantage of these arises from a future Certainty of their rising in value, whereas immediately it's very likely they may be at a larger, or at least at y^e. same Discount.[27]

This advice proved to be sound, though the funds took longer to recover after the peace than they had hoped.

Warren was not pressed for cash and did not need to liquidate any of his holdings. On the contrary, his success at Louisbourg very rapidly swelled his account with the Bakers, and without waiting to receive his specific orders they bought heavily: £6,000 stock in February, £10,000 in March, and £7,000 in April 1746.[28] The cost of this additional £23,000 was £17,695, the fund then selling at a discount even lower than the subscription rate, owing largely to the Jacobite threat. Despite the state of international tension, and the uncertainty of the direction which the war with France might take, confidence in the fund remained strong as far as the Baker cousins were concerned. This they explained to Warren in a letter carried to him at Louisbourg by Oliver DeLancey: "This is the fund which is by much the most advantageous to lay your money out in because as you will not want to alter the Situation of it there is no doubt but when a peace comes these three p[r]. cents will be at or above parr and by that means you will have an encrease of your principal equall to the present discount, this is the Concurrent Opinion of Mr. Anson, Mr. Norris, and ourselves."[29]

Anson and Norris were concerned because Warren had asked them in 1745 to act with the Baker cousins as trustees for him while he remained abroad. The real burden, however, fell on the Bakers and their broker, John Shipston, who arranged the buying: £6,000 in September, £13,000 in October, and £4,000 in November 1746. When Warren returned to England he ordered a further purchase of £4,000 worth of 1745 3 per cents in February and March 1747.[30] The exact price that Warren paid for the last £27,000 of stock is not known, but an estimate of £22,260 can be made from the unofficial stock market quotations listed by John Castaigne, the Huguenot broker, and his son-in-law, Richard Shergold.[31]

Thus, altogether Warren's £54,000 worth of 1745 3 per cents had cost him £44,226, an average of £81 18s. per £100. Of these he retained but £20,000 by the time of his death in July 1752. He began selling in 1750 in order to buy land, and continued until June 1752; only his death put a stop to this transfer of assets. Since between 1750 and 1752 the 1745 3 per cents were selling at a premium, Warren realized a substantial capital gain. His brokers' expectations were thus fully realized. The stock recovered as soon as the peace preliminaries were announced in 1748, but did not reach par for another year. The price actually reached £103 in October 1749, but then weakened during the last two months of the year and the first five months of 1750. Thereafter, until the clouds of war again gathered in 1755, this fund sold at a premium, reaching a high point of £106½ in June 1752.

The £34,000 of 1745 3 per cents, disposed of between February 1750 and June 1752, brought Warren £34,476, after the brokerage

fees had been subtracted.[32] In theory these were the first of the 1745
3 per cents that he had purchased, which had cost Warren £25,601,
thus giving him a capital gain of £8,875, a comfortable fortune in itself.
In addition between Christmas 1745 and Christmas 1751 he received
interest amounting to £9,300; and at his death was owed £300 for the
midsummer 1752 payment.[33] It had been an important segment of his
income during the last seven years of his life, and by far the most
significant of his investments in the National Debt.

Lady Warren never sold the remaining £20,000, which in due course
became part of the Consolidated 3 per cents, when the government's
conversion plan was completed in December 1753. At her death in
1772, her share was equally divided among her children. Warren's
eldest daughter, Ann, married in July 1758, but not until May 1759 was
£4,444 5s. 7d. transferred to the Right Honourable Francis, Earl of
Hertford, one of her guardians.[34] The next transfer, for the same
amount, less a penny, was in June 1765 to Miss Susanna Warren,
Admiral Warren's second daughter, upon her coming of age.[35] Warren's third daughter, Charlotte, was married in July 1768, the transfer of her share of the remaining 1745 3 per cents taking place in
September 1769, in the name of her guardian, Matthew, Lord Fortes-
cue.[36] The remaining £6,667 3s. 4d. was divided equally in April and
May 1772, each sister getting £2,222 7s. 9d. with Ann being given the
odd penny.[37] Thus the investment made by their father in the 1740s
sustained them throughout the rest of their lives.

Warren did not again invest in a new long-term government loan
until 1748. In February 1748 the government announced the largest
loan of the war: £6.3 million to be raised at 4 per cent interest, the
interest for which was to be secured by increasing tonnage and pound-
age by one shilling. Each subscriber of £100 would receive a free £10
lottery ticket. The lottery tickets, both blanks and prizes, were then to
be funded, thereby increasing the government's liability to
£6,930,000.[38] Warren subscribed £15,000, but he must have got rid
of the investment almost at once because when the ledgers were
opened his balance was nil.[39] In 1750, £1,000,000 had to be raised
"towards the Supply granted to his Majesty, for the Service of the Year
1750." The "million loan," as it was called, was not publicly subscribed but was farmed out to a number of large government contractors, who then distributed it to whom they pleased. The 3 per cent
interest was charged on the sinking fund. Warren purchased £5,000
from Samson Gideon, one of the foremost government agents for

loan-subscriptions and a man at the very heart of the financial life of the nation.[40] Warren made payment in five instalments, between April and December 1751.[41] On 14 March 1751 Warren received three-quarters of a year's interest to Christmas 1750, amounting to £112 10s.[42] It was the only dividend he received, for in May 1751 through John Shipston he liquidated this asset, receiving only £4, 993 9s., for a loss of £6 11s.[43]

In 1749 the government began an elaborate series of negotiations in what proved to be a very successful conversion of nearly all its long-term loans to 3 per cent. The original plan of 1749 called for all holders of any of the 4 per cent fund to undergo a reduction to 3½ per cent from December 1750 and 3 per cent after December 1757. The bill became law on 20 December 1749. Some investors resisted; and among the most recalcitrant were South Sea annuitants. Individuals holding this fund refused to accept the conversion, and thereby forced the government to buy them out, in part by raising a new loan of £2 million. Of this £1.4 million was raised by subscription and the rest by lottery, and tickets for which were to be funded in 1752 in South Sea 3 per cents of 1751.[44] Though Warren put £3,400 into the subscription and £1,700 into lottery tickets, he disposed of this fund almost at once.[45]

Besides investing in the funded debt of the government, Warren also showed interest in its floating or short-term debt. In April 1748, when he received payment for the prizes taken at the May 1747 victory over the French off Cape Ortegal, both he and Anson put part of their share of the flag's eighth into Navy Board bills. Such bills, along with those of the Victualling Board, and seamen's wage tickets, were the principal components of the navy debt. Navy bills, made out to contractors for ships and ships' stores, were orders to the treasurer of the navy from the board to pay a named person for goods or services supplied. Six months after the bill was issued the holder became entitled to quarterly interest, which from 1713 to 1748, was 5 per cent. The bills, which became "a barometer for naval credit,"[46] were assignable. In this way Warren acquired bills totalling £21,140, which at a 2 ½ per cent discount cost him £20,611.[47]

By late 1746 the rapid enlargement of the navy debt alarmed the ministry. Temporary solutions were found in 1746 and 1747 by extra parliamentary grants of £1 million. Still, by 1749, the debt stood at £3,072,472; and on 21 March Parliament decided to fund the debts. Holders of navy and victualling bills, and of ordnance and transport debentures, were to take them to the appropriate departmental office by 20 April, to be cancelled and exchanged for a certificate assignable until Michaelmas. On or before Michaelmas the certificate was to be surrendered to the Bank of England, which would then credit the holder with 4 per cent annuities.[48] Warren held bills amounting to £29,669 1s. 10d., of which £12,363 19s. 11d. were in his wife's name, making them together one of the largest subscribers.[49] Warren sold £10,000 of his £17,305 7s. 11d. share in January and February 1751, but a year later, shortly before his death, purchased a further amount of £330 12s. 2d. to give him a balance of £7,636 1d.[50] When added to Lady Warren's share this amounted to exactly £20,000. This investment Lady Warren kept throughout her life.[51] In May 1759, her eldest daughter received rights to one-third of the two-thirds left for the Warren children, £1,696 17s. 9d. The same amounts were assigned to Miss Susanna Warren in June 1765 and to the trustees of Charlotte, Countess of Abingdon, the youngest daughter, in December 1768, leaving Lady Warren with £2,545 6s. 10d., her one-third share of her husband's estate. This, like her other assets, was divided among her three daughters in 1772.[52] The interest, at first at 4 per cent, was reduced to 3½ per cent in 1750 and in 1757 to 3 per cent. For the Warrens it represented, after the 1745 3 per cents, their largest investment in the public debt. It was the largest single item of Lady Warren's income, and sustained her throughtout nineteen years of widowhood.

Warren did not limit his activity in the London money market to government funds and the stock of the large companies. He invested as well in the shares of the Sun Fire Office. The Sun Office, established in 1710, by the mid-century was one of the three principal London concerns offering insurance against the hazards of fire.[53] The other two, the Royal Assurance[54] and London Assurance, then had a larger financial stake in the business, and it was not until the 1790s that the Sun Office established a dominant position in the field. Originally there had been twenty-four managers with one share each. In 1720, for each share 100 new shares were issued, and in 1740 this was doubled to a total of 4,800. In 1726 the capital of the office was £48,000, to which another £24,000 was added in July 1741, and yet another £28,800 in January 1752.

In December 1749 Warren paid £1,800 for 50 shares in the Sun Fire Office, or £36 a share.[55] He purchased them through John Boult, the attorney to Ann Jasper, the widow and executrix of Edward Jasper, formerly Warren's agent in London.[56] It would seem that the initiative to become a Sun Office shareholder came, not from the Bakers, but from Warren himself. The transfer of shares took place on 21 December 1749,[57] with Warren putting his signature to the arrangment at the Craig Court branch of the Sun Office. Warren held the shares for only a year, before transferring them on 20 December 1750 to William Braund for £38 apiece, thus making a quick profit of £2 a share or £100.[58]   It appears that Warren regretted the move, for on 4 April 1751 he again became a shareholder in the Sun Fire Office, by purchasing two lots each of twenty-five shares, through Richard Chilton, from two shareholders recently dead, Ann Croft and William Darling.[59] These fifty shares were transferred at his death to his wife and daughters. Lady Warren, at the marriage of each of her surviving daughters, transferred eleven shares, retaining seventeen for herself. After her death two shares were sold and the remaining fifteen divided equally among her heirs.[60]

The shares of the Sun Fire Office proved a remarkably good investment. It is difficult to estimate the appreciation of the share value, as they were not quoted on the Exchange, as were the shares of the London Assurance and Royal Exchange Assurance. That they grew in value is certain, for the rate of increase in dividends made them very attractive to holders. When Warren made his initial purchase in 1749 there were two yearly dividends of 12s. 6d. each, paid at midsummer and Christmas.[61] Steadily the twice yearly dividends increased, until in midsummer 1783 they reached 45s., reflecting the real growth of the company's assets and business strength.[62] In addition, numerous extraordinary dividends of £2 a share were announced, so that by midsummer 1772, the extra dividends alone had covered the cost of the Warrens' original investment of £1,800.[63]

Another of Warren's smaller investments, though far from profitable, was in the Society for a Free British Fishery, established by royal charter in October 1750.[64] The charter permitted a number of London and provincial merchants and Members of Parliament to raise £500,000 capital by voluntary subscription, to be invested in fishing boats and wharves in a serious attempt to challenge the Dutch grip on the white herring fishery. The charter guaranteed subscribers a three per cent annual return on their investment "out of the Customs." Subscribers could not transfer, however, their holdings for five years, except through death or bankruptcy. The Prince of Wales, an ill omen perhaps, was the first governor, Alderman Slinglsey Bethell the president, and Alderman Stephen Theodore Janssen the vice president. They were supported by a 30–member council, which counted among its numbers Admiral Vernon, one of the prime movers in the scheme. Warren had not been initially concerned in the venture, but in December 1750 subscribed £500.[65] His widow sold the shares exactly five years later, after dividends of £75 had been received, and at a capital loss of £145 16s.[66]

The last of Warren's investments to be noticed here was the least important, and also concerned fish. In 1750 he bought two £40 subscriptions for the establishment of a Westminster fish market.[67] The subscription campaign had been launched following an act of Parliament in 1749, based on a bill "For Making a Free Market for the Sale of Fish in Westminster."[68] The scheme was an overt attempt to bring down the price of fish by opening a rival to Billingsgate; and the act created a board of trustees to oversee the establishment and operations of the new market. A public subscription was launched to create the necessary capital and to undertake construction, and a dividend was to be paid based upon the income deriving from fees paid by the fisherman and fishmongers who used the market. The venture did not survive long, though the market was still in existence fifteen years later. There is no record of when the Warrens' shares were sold, or how many dividends were paid beyond the first. Perhaps since Warren was Member of Parliament for Westminster, it was expected that he would join in the subscription; though, by the small amount of capital that he was prepared to risk he had no great hopes of getting his money out.

When Warren died in July 1752, he held investments of the sort described which had cost him £58,917, with a nominal value of £60,980. Had these been liquidated at any time in 1752 they would have been worth more than an additional £6,000, in view of the premium which most of the government's funded debt then enjoyed. He had begun modestly in 1741 and his investments reached a peak in 1749, as table 28 shows:

Several observations are worth making. In the first place though Warren had been able to invest almost £9,000 by the end of 1745,

TABLE 28 *Stock Exchange Investments 1741-1752*

Date	Purchases and Sales	Accumulated Cost
1741	£500 East India stock	£ 807
1742	£1,000 South Sea Old annuities for £1,127	1,934
1743	£2,000 South Sea Old annuties for £2,309	4,243
1744	£1,000 South Sea Old annuities for £1,129	5,372
1745	£4,000 1745 3%s for £3,250; £100 East India bond for £99.	8,991
1746	£46,000 1745 3%s for £37,615	46,606
1747	£4,000 1745 3%s for £3,361	49,967
1748	Bought and sold £15,000 1748 4%s; bought £21,140 in 5% Navy Bills for £20,611.	70,578
1749	Bought £8,529 Navy Board Bills for £8,316; sold South Sea Old annuities, which had cost £4,565. Bought Sun Fire Office shares for £1,800; bought £10,100 East India bonds, for net increase of £15,864.	86,442
1750	Sold Sun Fire shares and £12,000 1745 3%s which had cost £9,565; sold £10,000 Navy Board 5%s which had been bought at a 2½% discount, or £9,750; bought £5,000 in Million Loan, £500 Free British Fishery, and £80 in Westminster Fish Market, £10,000 East India bonds converted to £5,000 4% annuities £2,500 new bonds, for net decrease: £15,535.	70,907
1751	Sold £8,000 1745 3%s, which had cost £6,107; sold 1750 Million Loans; bought 50 Sun Fire shares;* bought East India bonds costing£10,875; bought 1751 government loan, £5,100, for net increase: £6,768.	77,775
1752	Sold £14,000 1745 3%s, which had cost £11,589; sold £5,100 1751 loan, and £2,500 East India 4% annuities, bought £331 Navy Board 4% 1749 annuities, for net decrease: £18,858.	58,917

Source: Data taken principally from ledgers in BERO and IOR.

*The cost of the 50 Sun Fire shares is not known, so it is assumed that he paid as much as he had earlier sold them for: £1,900.

before his large prize earnings from Louisbourg began to reach his agents, the Louisbourg wealth quite altered his situation, so that he became one of the largest investors in the 1745 Government Loan. The Louisbourg wealth was credited to his account with the Bakers throughout 1746, and continued to reach their hands at least until 1751. In 1747 though Warren shared in numerous prizes, much of the money came to him only in 1748 and this he invested in Navy Board Bills. It must be remembered, however, that though he invested only £3,361 in the stock market in 1747, he had the same year put £9,500 into an estate in Hampshire, paid £2,200 towards the cost of his election campaign for Parliament, and paid the Duke of Bedford £4,800 to secure an adequate qualification to stand as a candidate.[69] Prize money still flowed into his hands throughout 1749 which enabled him to add almost £16,000 to his investment in the stock market while lending more than £3,600 to private individuals. It was in 1749 that his investments in stock reached their peak of almost £86,500, though the nominal value was much greater: £96,169. The year 1749 also marked the beginning of the large-scale diversification of his interests. He began to lend money on a lavish scale both in England and Ireland, and to make considerable additions to his estates both in Hampshire and Ireland. To finance these schemes he used, between 1749 and 1752, some £25,000 net of his holdings in stocks, together with the large capital gain he had received from the sale of the 1745 3 per cents.

Warren had come comparatively late to the London money market after abortive ventures in 1728-30 and 1735-36, and after having devoted his early modest fortune to inexpensive land purchases in New York and money lending there, in New England, South Carolina, and on a small scale in Ireland. Yet at the time of his death he held more of his wealth in the funds than in either land or private money lending, though his interest in both these other forms of investment had greatly developed after 1747. It implied on his part great confidence in government securities, and an ample desire to feed the machine of credit by which England was able to carry on her worldwide struggle with France and Spain. In return the funds afforded him a profitable, secure, and simple means of absorbing the wealth he had gained by the fortunes of war. Among his fellow naval officers, Warren, with £58,000 nominal value, was undoubtedly one of the largest investors in government stock. Anson, a man of greater fortune, had only £30,000 invested in five prominent stocks examined by Dickson, and Anson's nearest rivals in turn were Admiral Isaac Townsend with £19,000, Sir

Challoner Ogle with £14,000, William Rowley with £11,000, Lord Vere Beauclerk with £3,200, and George Clinton with £3,000.[70] Moreover, Warren was not satisfied at leaving his large investments undisturbed, comforted with the three per cent return they were destined to produce. Though he intended to maintain a large stake in the funds, his great activity between 1749 and 1752 shows that he was anxious to liquidate some of his safe investments in order to undertake more imaginative ventures of greater risk. He also displayed a willingness to make small investments in securities somewhat out of the ordinary, which he must have felt were less likely to show an immediate return, and were certainly less secure than the stock of the great companies or the National Debt funded by them and the Bank of England. From all this he emerges as a successful, well-organized opportunist, who had the remarkable good luck to make a fortune in prize money at a moment when the government had greatly expanded its borrowing, and thus depressed the price of securities.

Lady Warren, by the terms of her husband's will, was not free to dispose of any of his assets. She had full use of his fortune until her three surviving daughters either married or came of age, when she would retain one-third for her own use throughout her lifetime. She was very attentive to business, though very conservative in her decisions. She bought no land except for a few acres in Hampshire. She moved house only once in 1763 from Cavendish to Grovesnor Square. She discontinued her husband's practice of private money lending, except in New York where her brother, Oliver DeLancey, managed her affairs with great devotion. She sold her husband's investment in the Society for a Free British Fishery, certainly a wise move. She built up her holdings of East India annuities, which she particularly favoured, and entered one major new venture: a £11,700 investment in 1757 3 per cents.[71] By the time her youngest daughter had received her full share of Admiral Warren's estate, Lady Warren still retained an impressive portfolio, with a nominal value of £44,756, as shown in table 29.

By 1770 her daughters had all come of age and received their share of their father's stock market investments. In the spring of 1772, a few months after her death, Lady Warren's share of her husband's investments, as well as all stock outstanding in her name, was divided among the three co-heirs. There was one exception, for two Sun Fire Office shares of the seventeen she had retained were sold so that the remainder could be equally divided. By the spring of 1772, the nominal value

TABLE 29 *Stock Exchange Holdings: Lady Warren 1771*

Security	Nominal Value
East India stock	£ 167
East India annuities	16,800
Ditto in Warren's name	1,667
1745 3%s	6,667
1749 Navy Board Bills	12,364
Ditto in Warren's name	2,545
Sun Fire shares (17)	646*
1757 3%s	3,900
Total	£44,756

Source: Stock ledgers in BERO and IOR as well as Sun Fire Office papers in Guildhall Library.

* Since the 1771 value in unknown this represents the cost of shares to Warren and is certainly an underestimate of their worth.

TABLE 30 *Stock Exchange Holdings 1752 and 1772*

Security	Nominal Value	
	1752	1772
East India stock	£500	£500
East India bonds	5,000	—
East India annuities	13,000	56,600
Navy Debt	20,000	20,000
1745 3%s	20,000	20,000
1757 3%s	—	11,700
Sun Fire Office shares	1,900*	1,824**
Free British Fishery	500	—
Westminster Fish Market	80	—
Total	£60,980	£110,624

Source: Ledgers in BERO and IOR; Sun Fire Office MSS, Guildhall Library, London.

*1752 value is not known; amount here represents cost to Warren, which even by 1752 was perhaps an underestimate.

**Represents the cost to Warren for 48 shares.

of the Warren holdings stood at £110,624 compared to £60,980 in 1752, as table 30 shows. The nominal value of the portfolio had thus grown at a fraction over 4 per cent per annum.

Far from dissipating the fortune Warren had gathered, his widow, by living well within her income, which was limited by the terms of his will, and by converting to the funds all her husband's outstanding capital in the form of loans, almost doubled the family's investments in the London stock exchange. This shift of emphasis is illustrated in table 31.

Warren's fortune, though large, was a good deal less than contemporary rumour put it. Horace Walpole wrongly believed Warren "richer than Anson,"[72] while his nephew, Warren Johnson, thought him "one of the Richest men in England . . . worth three or four Hundred Thousand Pound Sterling."[73] Warren, knowing better, had confided to Oliver DeLancey in 1750 that his wealth was "not near so much as the World Imagine nor More than the Necessary parade here Obliges me to Live up to."[74] At the time of his last illness he probably had no precise notion of the market value of all his assets, especially his New York estates, but doubtless he had a clear idea of his income. The subsequent rise in income during the next two decades, from £5,332 to £6,432, was, owing to inflation, illusory. In so far as inflation can be accurately gauged, then it can be said that income from the Warren fortune in real terms actually declined by 1772, as table 32 shows.

This obvious failure to maintain or advance the level of income between 1752 and 1772 needs some elucidation. The principal explanation is to be found in the transfer to government securities after 1752 of capital in the form of personal loans. As loans, such capital had earned between 4 and 6 per cent in England, Ireland, and New England, 7 per cent and 10 per cent elsewhere in America. Lady Warren's general reluctance to venture capital in loans, except on a reduced scale in New York, and her decision instead to invest in the most conservative offerings of the London stock market meant a safer but relatively lower income. This is particularly true in view of the general decline after 1752 in the rate of interest on such government securities. In 1752 Warren still held several stocks which paid more than 3 per cent at par value, while in 1772 no such securities held by Lady Warren exceeded 3 per cent. This loss of income was only partially offset by the rise in income from both the Sun Fire Office and East India stock; for the amount of capital involved, compared to that in

TABLE 31 *The Warren Fortune 1752 and 1772*

	1752				1772			
	Nominal Value		Income		Nominal Value		Income	
	£	%	£	%	£	%	£	%
Land								
New York	13,670	8.6	166	3.1	35,762	16.0	817	12.7
New England	—	0.0	—	0.0	1,000	.05	—	0.0
Ireland	18,663	11.7	1,061	19.9	37,145	18.3	1,380	21.5
England	14,800*	9.3	—	0.0	14,300*	7.0	362	5.6
		29.6		23.0		31.35		39.8
Loans								
New York	8,174	5.1	313	5.9	4,375	2.1	284	4.4
New England	6,470	4.1	305	5.7	—	0.0	—	0.0
South Carolina	150	0.01	15	.03	—	0.0	—	0.0
England–Ireland	30,494	19.2	1,281	24.1	4,650	2.3	193	3.0
		28.4		35.73		4.4		7.0
Others								
Stock Market	60,980	38.3	1,891	35.7	110,624	54.2	3,396	52.8
Duke of Bedford	4,800	3.0	300	5.6	—	0.0	—	0.0
Merchant Ships	1,000	.06	—	0.0	—	0.0	—	0.0
		41.4		41.3		54.2		52.8
Total	159,100		5,332		204,856		6,432	

Source: Warren Papers, Gage Papers, ledgers in BERO and IRO, Sun Fire Office MSS.
*Excludes £1,000 value of furniture at Westbury.

TABLE 32 *Adjusted Income 1752 and 1772*

Date	Nominal Income	Price Index	Real Income
1752	£5,332	93	£5,733
1772	£6,432	117	£5,497

Base: 1701 = 100

Source: Schumpeter, "English Prices and Public Finances," p. 35.

government securities, was small. Even this modest influence was further limited after 1772 since the Warren heirs sold two of their fifty Sun Fire Office shares. Finally, the decline in income can be explained in part by the loss of the 6.3 per cent annuity from the Duke of Bedford, and the forfeiture by Warren's early death of what had appeared to be an attractive investment.

In so far as one can refer to a growth in the nominal capital of the Warren fortune between 1752 and 1772, it can be seen that the appreciation in New York and Irish land values was the principal factor involved. In addition it should be noted that Lady Warren, by living well within her income added at least £1,000 in capital to her husband's fortune for each of the nineteen years of her widowhood.

Chapter 12

Conclusion

There is a tension between the advocates of what may be called macro-history and micro-history, the one taking a large, comprehensive view of the past, touching, as it were, the mountain tops, the other concentrating upon a narrow front but penetrating deeply into the valleys. Both approaches have their usefulness, though neither on its own will entirely satisfy the historian. Pioneer historians have usually aimed at the first; later generations of historians, especially in economic history, attempt the latter. Professor Wilson's remark that it is "the lot of research to blur the clear outlines drawn by the historical pioneers, to make history more complicated and maybe duller in the process of getting it right"[1] expresses concisely the point that micro-history acts as a valuable check on large views of the past, and ultimately reshapes them.

It is in this way that the study of the fortune of Admiral Sir Peter Warren, though narrow in itself, has value for the light it throws on general issues. First, there is his remarkable rise in status. As the youngest of three sons, in a family of small Irish Catholic landowners, he had few evident prospects other than the declining economic condition of his class. Yet he broke out of this trap by conforming to the established church after his father's death in 1712, and by making a career in a relatively new profession—the Navy—under the patronage of his relations, Admirals Aylmer (a convert from Catholicism like himself) and Norris. His naval career opened the path, at first, to modest affluence, and later, with war, to great wealth. His status as gentleman–officer and Irish landowner, with important connections, enabled him to make an advantageous marriage in New York, which in turn added considerably to his happiness, confidence, wealth, and business opportunities. From the outbreak of war in 1739 he showed himself amply prepared both as a professional sailor and as a man of business to take advantage of the new and excellent openings which war presented. The former prospects of stagnating in Ireland or even of taking service with France or Austria, had by this stage long been forgotten. Warren's rise thus focuses attention on the Navy as a means to wealth of unprecedented dimensions. It also displays the Irish element among eighteenth century naval officers, hitherto a neglected subject. It is clear that Warren was merely the most successful of several naval officers from Ireland, such as Henry Aylmer, John Forbes,[2] John Ambrose, Christopher Pocklington, Richard Tyrrell, and Christopher Parker, all of them Warren's contemporaries. It is curious that we are relatively well-versed in the services of Irish officers to various continental states in the seventeenth and eighteenth centuries but relatively ignorant of their role in England.

That war was big business caused neither Warren nor any of his fellow naval officers much worry. He never felt the reluctance or horror of some gentlemen to mix with merchants. Like other naval officers on foreign stations, he made use of his opportunities to trade on a small scale in wines and spirits (especially rum and brandy), in tea, and in slaves. Later in retirement he invested as well in two merchant ships trading to the West Indies.[3] He often spoke with pride of his good relations with merchants at Boston, New York, Charleston, Jamaica, Antigua, and London. It may be noted that he was not the only naval officer in this period to advance his fortune by marrying well abroad, carried there by naval service. His contemporaires Vincent Pearce, Matthew Norris, Charles Knowles, and his nephew, Richard Tyrrell, for instance, all made alliances of this sort. It took no great effort for such men to become as familiar with the state of the international economy as many merchants. Their contribution to the development of mercantile wealth, as Warren's career demonstates, could be significant, and not merely as guardians of the sea lanes. Warren undoubtedly stimulated the prosperity of the DeLanceys of New York, while his early patronage of the Bakers, by the assistance he gave them in securing the contract to provision of the garrison of Louisbourg between 1746 and 1749, helped to establish them as one of the principal London houses trading to America. At a more general level, it can be argued that Warren's case illustrates mercantilism in action, for the wealth of Spain and France, seized on the high seas, was rerouted into English bond issues, which helped hold Spanish and French power in check. Warren, while remaining part of a class of permanent professional naval officers bent on the pursuit of wealth through war, may be considered as a "war entrepreneur" significantly stimulating the general process in his own class interest.

What is also of general importance in Warren's case is the international character of his investments. He did not merely plough back the wealth from his prizes into the English economy. Instead he made use of his experience both in America and Ireland; and his investments there ultimately proved more lucrative than those made in England. The impression one has of him when he was thus acting as an international financier is quite remote from the traditional conception of the younger son eking out a rather grim existence on the meagre wage of a naval officer. Warren evidently had great confidence in the economies both of the American colonies and of his native Ireland, a confidence that was well placed. His activities there draw attention to aspects both of the land market and the money market, especially in America, which historians have largely ignored. In America most of his money lending was to merchants, while his interest in the Mohawk valley stimulated the early development of one of the richest agricultural areas in the middle colonies. It is also interesting to observe the impact of the War of Independence upon the interests of the Warren family. The defeat of the British did not result in the confiscation of Warren property, either in the form of debts or land, while the rights of the Warren heirs to these assets were guaranteed by both the peace treaty of 1783 and the London Treaty of 1794. The loans proved to be recoverable, while some of the tenants resumed payment of rents in 1783, after several years of neglect, as if no political gulf now separated them from the absentee landowners. In the 1780s and 1790s both tenants and debtors were obliged to adhere strictly to the law by well-to-do New England and New York agents of landlords and creditors, who, in the case of the Warren heirs, were all members of the supposedly despised English aristocracy. This calls to mind the comment by Halifax, "When the people contend for their liberty they seldom get anything by their victory but new masters."[4] The evidence undoubtedly underlines the very conservative nature, in economic terms, of the War of Independence. It should also be noted that Warren's case shows that while the yield on American land was less than on Irish or English, corrupt or incompetent agents, frontier wars, and the poverty of tenants all reduced this return considerably. The result was that the real return was achieved only when the land was sold; and here the War of Independence acted as a political catalyst, for despite the excellent economic prospects of the new republic, the Warren heirs disposed of their potentially highly profitable American estate.

The situation in Ireland was somewhat different. As far as Irish land was concerned, Warren's principal aim—like Warren Hastings with Daylesford[5]—was the recovery of his family's seat of Warrenstown; and this gave a purposeful direction to his early activities in the Irish land market. Thereafter his land purchases in Ireland showed him able to take advantage of the economic plight of Protestant and Catholic landowners alike. Religion in this context was clearly a matter of indifference to him, so long as the price was right and the prospects of capital appreciation reasonable. These investments, limited by Warren's sudden death when he was in the midst of negotiating further purchases, not only produced a return higher than similar investments in England, but also, in contrast to his American assets, were sold at the top of the wartime market at great profit to his heirs. His interest in Ireland was of value not only to his heirs but also to the Johnson family who acted as his agent. Here too religion was of less importance to him than family ties for the Johnsons were Catholics. Warren laid the basis of much of their prosperity not only by employing them as his agents but also by letting much of his Irish estate to them at very advantageous rates, a policy continued after his death. The Johnsons on their part elevated themselves in two generations, partly by tilling the soil themselves and partly perhaps by acting as middlemen; they quickly rose from the ranks of the tenant farmer to that of the landowner. Their rise in status clearly shows that for well-placed Catholic families in Ireland the opportunities created for them by the relaxation in laws governing Catholic ownership of land in the late eighteenth century had very tangible benefits. Their rise coincided with a general upswing in the Irish economy before the over-rapid population growth of the first half of the nineteenth century imposed severe strains on Irish society.

It was only after Warren had established a stake in America and Ireland that he invested in England on any scale. It was perhaps inevitable after his election to Parliament in 1747 and his failure to secure a colonial appointment that much of his fortune would be permanently invested in England. Ultimately, it should be noted, the entire Warren fortune was repatriated to England from Ireland and America, and the international character given to it by Warren was lost. Warren's English investments were of two main kinds: in land (for pleasure) and in public and private loans (for profit). His choice of Hampshire as a suitable place to buy land seems to have been determined by the proximity of Portsmouth and a seat of his friend, Admiral Anson.

Here, as in Ireland, Warren, probably influenced by having no sons, was not tempted to build a great house. In this probably fortunate economy he contrasts with many of his contemporaries, Admiral Boscawen for instance, who at Hatchlands near Guildford used his prize fortune to transform a small Tudor house into a modern red brick mansion.[6] Warren's land purchases in the upper Meon valley reflect on a small scale the general pattern of eighteenth century land ownership, namely land becoming increasingly concentrated in larger units and fewer hands. However, by confining himself to a relatively small estate in one district and by retaining large investments in other forms of capital, Warren was no doubt typical of many wealthy men of his generation. In such purchases prestige rather than return on capital was probably the main determinant. Thus Warren's willingness to pay such high prices for his Hampshire farms undoubtedly resulted from his anxiety to become a well-located English landowner. Had he been less keen to do this, he might have bargained more conscientiously. When negotiating his Irish purchases, for instance, he did so through agents and those who sold to him never realized they were dealing with a man of reputed great wealth. By contrast, in Hampshire the sellers always knew that Warren was the other principal involved, which put them in a relatively strong position: knowing both that he wanted the land, and that he could afford to pay dearly for it.

Warren's money-lending activities in England and Ireland show that private bonds were still as important as mortgages in this period, and that the distinction between them, in fact if not in law, was very little. Warren's bond debtors were allowed to carry on for years without repaying the principal, while their debts were considered evidently as secure a form of investment as mortgages, without their bother and risk to the lender. Moreover, when Warren lent on land he did so with apparent indifference to whether the borrower was Irish or English. In this he differed from many institutional lenders, such as the Sun Fire Office, which in this period refused to lend on Irish land.

Warren's large interests in the London stock market raise certain general questions about the soundness of this sort of investment. Like so many others of his generation, Warren had great faith in governmental credit and an ample willingness (bred of expectations of capital gain) to feed the machine by which Britain was able to fight her wars so successfully. By buying into the stock market at a discount during war-time uncertainties, Warren realized a capital gain, equivalent to a further series of prize money, when in the 1750s the Funds recovered and were selling at their highest eighteenth-century level. In addition to government securities, Warren put money into the East India and the Sun Fire Office; one the most successful British overseas trading company; the other the most successful insurance company in the country. Yet after his death, his widow and his heirs largely concentrated their capital in government securities, even selling part of the excellent Sun Fire Office investment. As capital in the form of private loans was called in it was tranferred to government stock. Yet, with the mild price inflation of the third quarter of the eighteenth century and the depressed price of the Funds after 1755, this form of investment became much less attractive than it had been in Warren's heyday. Inflation ate at the real value of revenue, the long-term fall in stock prices ate at the capital value of their portfolio. Yet Lady Warren and the Warren heirs held on to their investments. In theory (and perhaps this encouraged their policy) these assets were liquid; yet they were not sold. Instead, much less liquid capital in the form of land in America and Ireland, which, despite political turmoil, had greatly appreciated in value and, in the case of America, held great promise of further growth, was sold. This set of decisions illustrates the very impermanence of a fortune such as Warren's: mortality clearly played a crucial part in a non-corporate entrepreneurial situation. Warren was obviously a keen businessman. His wife and heirs, though careful in their financial dealings, were too cautious and quite without imagination and daring, the stuff needed for continued success in this field. Their knowledge of America and Ireland, always very limited, grew less, until, for instance, they had wholly forgotten that they even owned an estate in New England, or where exactly their Irish estates were. Their experience was confined to England, their ambition a three per cent return in the stock market and two per cent on land. By the end of the eighteenth century the Warren fortune had more or less fallen asleep.

Appendix A

Warren Genealogy

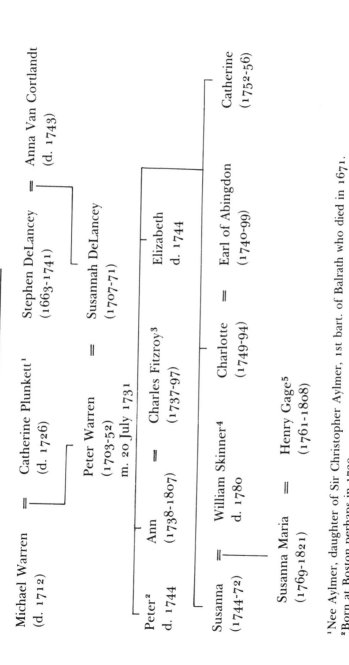

Michael Warren (d. 1712) = Catherine Plunkett[1] (d. 1726)

Stephen DeLancey (1663-1741) = Anna Van Cortlandt (d. 1743)

Peter Warren (1703-52) m. 20 July 1731 = Susannah DeLancey (1707-71)

Peter[2] d. 1744

Ann (1738-1807) = Charles Fitzroy[3] (1737-97)

Elizabeth d. 1744

Charlotte (1749-94) = Earl of Abingdon (1740-99)

Catherine (1752-56)

Susanna (1744-72) = William Skinner[4] d. 1780

Susanna Maria (1769-1821) = Henry Gage[5] (1761-1808)

[1] Nee Aylmer, daughter of Sir Christopher Aylmer, 1st bart. of Balrath who died in 1671.
[2] Born at Boston perhaps in 1739.
[3] Baron Southampton in 1780, younger brother of the Duke of Grafton.
[4] Captain in 85th Foot 1759; Lt. Col. in 1763; Col. August 1777.
[5] Became 3rd Viscount Gage in 1791.

Appendix B

New York Bond Loans

DATE OF LOAN	DEBTORS	PRINCIPAL NY £	INTEREST RATE	DATE PAID OFF
29 Nov. 1725	Thomas and John Smith	54	8%	1742
3 Jan. 1725/26	Edward Burling	324	8%	Before 1750
8 July 1731	Richard Riggs	100	8%	Aug. 1733
17 Aug. 1731	Richard Riggs	200	8%	Aug. 1733
8 Sept. 1731	Timothy Bagley	100	8%	July 1742
11 Sept. 1731	Wm. Crowe and L. Garner	150	8%	Nov. 1733
14 Sept. 1731	Joseph Kniffen & Co.	100	8%	Nov. 1733
16 Sept. 1731	Jonathan Whithead & Co.	100	8%	Before 1742
18 Sept. 1731	Rip Van Dam	300	8%	Before 1742
6 Oct. 1731	Richard Riggs	200	8%	Nov. 1733
14 Oct. 1731	Jeremiah Fowler & Co.	200	8%	Before 1742
20 Oct. 1731	David Minville & Co.	125	8%	Before 1750
5 Nov. 1731	Thomas Smith Jr. and Wm. Smith	500	8%	Before July 1741
29 Nov. 1731	Jonathan Peasly & Co.	113	8%	Before 1742
24 Feb. 1731/32	Henry Beekman	300	8%	Before 1750
9 Oct. 1732	John Lyndesay & Co.	30	8%	Before 1750
19 Nov. 1732	Samuel Bayard	150	8%	July 1734
13 June 1733	Col. Nathaniel Gilbert	400	8%	Before 1750
20 June 1733	Hendrick Vroom	15	8%	Oct. 1754
2 Aug. 1733	William Kingsland & Co.	100	8%	Before 1750
23 Aug. 1733	Samuel Bayard	100	8%	Before 1750
15 Oct. 1733	James DeLancey	300	8%	Aug. 1734 and Mar. 1738
1733	John Corbett	100	8%	May 1734
23 Nov. 1733	John Bell and L. Garner	50	8%	Before July 1741
27 Nov. 1733	Jack Haviland & Co.	53	8%	Aug. 1734
27 Nov. 1733	Richard Seaman & Co.	100	8%	Before 1742
29 Nov. 1733	Jeremiah Latouch & Co.	100	8%	Dec. 1734
19 Dec. 1733	Robert Farrington & Co.	50	8%	Before 1742
4 Jan. 1733/34	John Lyon and George Goram	50	8%	Before 1750
1 Feb. 1733/34	Henry Dusenberry & Co.	77	8%	Before 1742
30 April 1734	James Clement & Co.	70	8%	Before 1742
8 May 1734	Jacques Denys & Co.	100	8%	May 1735
19 June 1734	Wm. Ludlow & Co.	75	8%	June 1735
26 July 1734	Sylvanus Palmer & Co.	100	8%	June 1737
29 Sept. 1734	Rev. Wm. Skinner & Co.	250	8%	1750
29 Sept. 1734	Benjamin Thorn & Co.	62	8%	Before 1742
3 Dec. 1734	Edward Hicks & Co.	108	8%	Before 1742

DATE OF LOAN	DEBTORS	PRINCIPAL NY £	INTEREST RATE	DATE PAID OFF
14 Dec. 1734	John Glover & Co.	75	8%	1736
12 May 1735	Daniel and Benjamin Whitehead	100	8%	Before 1750
15 May 1735	Samuel Fitz Randal	89	8%	Before 1750
25 June 1735	William Fowler & Co.	40	8%	Before 1742
27 June 1735	Gabriel Ludlow & Co.	80	8%	Before 1742
5 Aug. 1735	Adam and Jacob Van Allen	100	8%	Before 1750
12 Nov. 1735	John and Isaac Noe	100	8%	Before 1750
29 Jan. 1735/36	Nicholas Bayard	116	8%	Before 1740
1736	Luens & Co.	500	8%	Before 1742
1736	Hume & Co.	100	8%	Before 1742
7 Aug. 1736	John McEvers	300	6%	Before 1750
9 Oct. 1736	John Heurter and Palatines	178	7%	Before 1776
14 Dec. 1736	John Glover & Co.	75	8%	Before 1742
24 Dec. 1736	John Groosbeg	100	8%	Before 1750
1736	Daniel	45	8%	1737
1737	Daniel Purdy and Syl. Palmer	150	7%	Before 1742
5 Feb. 1736/37	Samuel Brown	86	7%	Before 1750
2 March 1736/37	James Ellwood	10	7%	Bad debt
12 March 1736/37	Benjamin Birdsell	79	7%	Before 1742
2 April 1737	Nathaniel Fish	300	7%	Before 1750
15 April 1737	Isaack Van Aken & Co.	125	7%	1743
19 April 1737	Couenhoven & Co.	1,000	7%	Before 1750
29 April 1737	Nathaniel Kniffin	49	7%	Before 1750
29 April 1737	Jonathan Lynch	43	7%	Before 1750
6 June 1737	Walter Butler	100	8%	May 1754
3 July 1737	Samuel Moor Sr. and Jr.	50	8%	Before 1742
1 Aug. 1737	James and Samuel Bodman	213	6½%	Before 1750
16 Sept. 1737	David Usile	117	7%	Before 1750
27 Oct. 1737	Edward and Henry Holland	200	7%	Before 1742
27 Oct. 1737	Daniel Bennett	200	8%	Before 1750
5 April 1738	Anthony Rutgers Sr. and Jr.	600	7%	Before 1750
14 April 1738	Hendrick Snock	17	7%	Bad debt
15 April 1738	Lucas & Co.	517	7%	Before 1750
6 June 1738	Joseph Forman	600	6%	Bad debt
16 Sept. 1738	David Usile	117	7%	Before 1750
4 May 1739	Richard Annelly & Co.	600	6%	Before 1750
8 May 1739	James Henderson	300	7%	1743
20 June 1739	James Hude & Co.	325	7%	1754
1739	William Prince	10	7%	1740
16 Sept. 1739	David Usile	116	7%	Before 1750
8 Dec. 1739	John Glover & Co.	180	7%	Before 1750
6 Feb. 1739/40	Abraham Huisman & Co.	300	7%	Before 1750
29 March 1740	James and Thomas Duncan	40	7%	Before 1750

DATE OF LOAN	DEBTORS	PRINCIPAL NY £	INTEREST RATE	DATE PAID OFF
7 April 1740	Samuel Bernard & Co.	100	7%	Before 1750
28 April 1740	John Bagley & Co.	50	7%	Before 1750
1 May 1740	Adam Mott & Co.	200	7%	Before 1750
14 May 1740	Joseph Reynolds & Co.	94	7%	Before 1750
19 Aug. 1740	William Johnson	600*	7%	Bad debt
6 Oct. 1740	Nicholas Bayard	250	7%	Before 1750
21 Oct. 1740	Jonathan Brown & Co.	100	7%	1754
1 Jan. 1740/41	Joseph Sherwood Sr. and Jr.	100	7%	Before 1750
29 March 1741	Volkert Dirickson	45	7%	Bad debt (?)
2 June 1741	Cornelius Wyckoff Sr. and Jr.	200	7%	After 1754
July 1741	James Ellwood	40	7%	Bad debt (?)
1741	Mohawk Valley tenants	244	7%	Bad debt
15 July 1741	William Johnson	300*	7%	Bad debt
29 July 1741	John Wright & Co.	24	7%	Bad debt (?)
11 Aug. 1741	Richard Minville	54	7%	Before 1750
24 Nov. 1741	James Doughty	375	7%	July 1758
29 Nov. 1741	William Smith	99	7%	Oct. 1757
Jan. 1741/42	John Merzey & Co.	100	7%	Before 1750
18 Feb. 1741/42	Stephen and Augustine Hicks	100	7%	Before 1750
2 April 1742	Samuel Balden and Jurian Huff	75	7%	Before 1750
9 April 1742	Samuel Hunt & Co.	150	7%	Aug. 1755
1 Nov. 1742	John Forrest	100	7%	Bad debt(?)
1 Nov. 1742	William Johnson	200	7%	Bad debt(?)
2 Nov. 1742	John Cain	50	7%	1752
8 Dec. 1742	Jonathan Ogden & Co.	52	7%	Bad debt (?)
24 Dec. 1742	Matthew Stewart	286	7%	Bad debt
1742	John Connum	100	7%	Before 1750
1742	Messrs. Shedwell and Kniffin	100	7%	Before 1750
1742	Messrs. Denton and Swedecker	354	7%	Before 1750
1742	Peter Rutgers	200	7%	Before 1750
1742	William Willet	161	7%	Before 1750
8 Jan. 1742/43	George Gorum and Thomas Lyon	100	7%	Before 1750
9 March 1742/43	Nicholas Bayard	1,200	6%	Oct. 1758
1743	Abraham Darie	100	7%	Before 1750
9 April 1744	Josiah Milliken & Co.	100	7%	Before 1754
6 March 1744/45	Stephen Van Cortlandt	250	7%	1758
26 April 1745	David, Samuel, and George Merrit	100	7%	Dec. 1754
3 May 1745	David Lane & Co.	100	7%	After 1754
6 May 1747	William and Lawrence Roome	100	7%	Jan. 1759
25 Aug. 1748	John and Thomas Willet	1,000	6%	After 1752
17 Feb. 1748/49	Daniel Purdy	50	7%	Before 1752

DATE OF LOAN	DEBTORS	PRINCIPAL NY £	INTEREST RATE	DATE PAID OFF
24 July 1749	Edward Prendergras & Co.	100	7%	Before 1754
21 March 1749/50	Gerardus Duyekinck	100	7%	After 1758
19 April 1750	Jacob Hoff Sr. and Jr.	350	7%	1754
1 May 1750	Mathew Staples & Co.	25	7%	Bad debt (?)
1 May 1750	Dr. John Bard	106	7%	45 owing in 1795
13 Sept. 1750	Hugh Winterworth & Co.	100	7%	Aug. 1754
17 Oct. 1750	Francis Lewis & Co.	400	7%	1754
28 Nov. 1750	Joseph and Samuel Holmes	400	6%	July 1754
2 April 1750	Oliver DeLancey	106*	7%	March 1752
4 Oct. 1751	John and Thomas Willeg & Co.	800	7%	June 1759
21 Oct. 1751	Thomas Clarke	200	7%	Dec. 1754
March 1752	Oliver DeLancey	200*	7%	June 1753
July 1752	James DeLancey Sr. and Jr.	752*	7%	May 1761
20 Oct. 1752	Allen Moore and John Hallick	200	6%	Jan. 1759
20 Oct. 1752	Nathaniel and Benj. Birdsell	200	7%	April 1773
1753	John and Jonathan Anderson	600	7%	May 1759
1753	John Richards	70	7%	Before 1772
5 Oct. 1754	Nicholas Bayard	400	7%	May 1758
12 Nov. 1754	Andrew and John Smith & Co.	200	7%	Aug. 1781
4 April 1755	Phillip French	130	7%	Bad debt (?)
1757	Lewis and Richard Morris	400	7%	Feb. 1759
1757	John Brady	20	7%	April 1758
1757	David Lance & Co.	100	7%	May 1759
29 May 1759	O. DeLancey and B. Robinson	1,285	6%	After 1783
14 Sept. 1764	Dr. Lewis Johnston	163	7%	Bad debt (?)
15 Oct. 1765	David Ogden	719	7%	March 1773
14 July 1767	Daniel Purdy & Co.	156	7%	July 1772
6 Aug. 1767	Stephen Crane Sr. and Jr.	287	7%	March 1773
24 Nov. 1767	John Roxeran	42	7%	Bad debt
25 March 1769	Beverley Robinson	2,120	6%	After 1783
25 March 1769	James Parker	2,120	6%	After 1783
1769	John Oostroom	175	7%	Bad debt

*sterling

This list contains only those loans known to have been secured by means of a bond. It is incomplete especially for the period after 1753. For instance between 1753 and 1759, some NY £8,838 in new loans were made, yet only NY £5,122 can be accounted for: NY £1,917 in mortgages and NY £3,205 in bonds. After 1759 the details are even more scarce, and hence the list less accurate.

Notes

Chapter 1

1. All the American manuscripts in the Gage collection at Lewes are now available on microfilm. See Julian Gwyn, ed., *The American Manuscripts in the Gage Papers* (EP Group of Companies, Microform Division, Yorkshire, 1972), 3 reels. This edition was prepared as part of *Micro-form Publications of British Records Relating to America,* for the British Association for American Studies, under the general editorship of Professor Walter H. Minchinton.

2. David Spinney, *Rodney* (London, 1969), esp. pp. 226-49. Other naval officers, whose careers had ended before Nelson achieved prominence, and about whom historians have been particularly interested, include Anson, Boscawen, Byng, Cook, Cornwallis, Hawke, Howe, Norris, Saunders, and Vernon.

3. Lucy S. Sutherland, *A London Merchant 1696-1774* (London, 1933) and Richard Pares, *A West-India Fortune* (London, 1950).

Chapter 2

1. There is no record of his birth. His monument in Westminster Abbey says he died "in the 49th year of his age" in July 1752. His coffin's inscription says he was forty-eight, *The Dublin Gazette*, no. 205, 1-4 Aug. 1752. One authority claims, without evidence, that he was born on 11 Mar. 1703/04, Franz V. Recum, *The Families of Warren and Johnson of Warrenstown, County Meath* (New York, 1950), p. 3.

2. Gage Papers, G/Am/2 (68), p. 40.

3. Sir Fenton Aylmer, *The Aylmers of Ireland* (London, 1931), p. 158.

4. In Irish acres the estate measured only about 430 acres. By 1717 the mortgage amounted to £2,376, Gage Papers, G/Ir/2 (68), p. 2.

5. An abstract of Michael Warren's will, proved 20 Feb. 1712/13 is in the Genealogical Office, Dublin, Irwin vol. 437, p. 359. A copy of Catherine Warren's will, proved 20 Dec. 1726, is in the Public Record Office of Ireland, Wills Prerogative, 1726-28, 1A/2/3, fol. 119b-120.

6. For details of Aylmer's career see Aylmer, *The Aylmers of Ireland,* pp. 168-95.

7. For details of Norris's career see D. D. Aldridge, "Admiral Sir John Norris 1670 (or 1671)-1749: His Birth and Early Service, His Marriage and His Death," *The Mariner's Mirror,* 51 (1965); 173-83.

8. 18 Apr. 1716, from the Pay Book of the *Rye,* Adm. 33/307. Her muster book has not survived. In a letter dated 6 Feb. 1742/43, Warren said he had then served 28 years in the navy, but there is no evidence that he joined in 1715, Adm. 1/2653.

9. See Paul S. Fritz, "Jacobitism and the English Government

1717-31"; Ph.D. thesis, Cambridge University 1967.

10. From the *Rye* Warren transferred to the *Rose* (20 guns) as a volunteer per order in Feb. 1717/18, Adm. 6/12, p. 114. His lieutenant's examination was held in London, 5 Dec. 1721, Adm. 107/3, p. 113.

11. See Warren's lieutenant's log, Adm/L/F/14, National Maritime Museum.

12. See Admiral Norris's journal, 19 June 1727; Norris Papers, Addit. MSS. 28130, fol. 26, British Museum (hereafter BM).

13. Warren to Burchett, 24 Apr. 1728, Adm. 1/2650; Admiralty to Warren, 2 Apr. 1730, Adm. 2/52, p. 591; Admiralty to Warren, 20 Mar. 1735/36. Adm. 2/54, p. 579.

14. Woodes Rogers to James Craggs, 24 Dec. 1718, Adm. 1/4102, p. 43; Duke of Portland to Carteret, quoted by Frank Cundall, *The Governors of Jamaica in the First Half of the Eighteenth Century* (London, 1937), p. 110.

15. Gage Papers, G/Am/13, p. 1, 18; G/Am/1, p. 14, 18; Warren to Oliver DeLancey, 30 Dec. 1742. Warren Papers 22, New-York Historical Society (hereafter NYHS).

16. Burchett to Warren, 7 May 1726, Adm. 2/458, p. 436.

17. Memorial no. 42,633, Deed Book 63, Register of Deeds, Dublin; 19 Feb. 1729/30.

18. For the DeLanceys see D.A. Story, *The Delanceys: A Romance of a Great Family with Notes on Those Allied Families Who Remained Loyal to the British Crown during the Revolutionary War* (London, 1931).

19. For the Van Cortlandts see George W. Schuyler, *Colonial New York, Philip Schuyler and His Family* (New York, 1885), 1, 187-205.

20. For the Delancey–Heathcote connection, see Stanley Nider Katz, *Newcastle's New York: Anglo-American Politics, 1732-1753* (Cambridge, Mass., 1968), pp. 111-13.

21. The marriage contract is in the John E. Stillwell Collection, NYHS, 20 July 1731.

22. The details are found in a number of sources, principally, DeLancey Papers, doc. 40.19.162, Museum of the City of New York; Deeds Book, XIV, pp. 110-11. Department of State, Albany; Warren Papers 27, NYHS; Gage Papers, G/Am/11, G/Am/66, G/Am/80a.

23. Warren to Clinton, 22 Aug. 1742, George Clinton Papers, 1, William L. Clements Library, Ann Arbor, Michigan (hereafter WLCL).

24. Warren to Anson, 2 April 1745, Anson Papers, Add. MSS 15957, fol. 152, BM.

25. See Chapters 6 and 9.

26. *The St. Augustine Expedition of 1740: A Report of the South Carolina General Assembly* (Columbia, S.C., 1954). Reprinted from the Colonial Records of South Carolina with an introduction by John Tate Lanning.

27. Warren to Samuel and William Baker, 5 March 1740/41, Gage Papers, G/Am/21.

28. Vernon to Burchett, 31 Oct. 1741, Adm. 1/233, p. 49.

29. Warren to Corbett, 19 March 1741/42, Adm. 1/2653; Admiralty to Warren, 14 Aug. 1742, Adm. 2/58, p. 439.

30. *The Gentleman's Magazine*, August 1744, p. 424; Corbett to Capt. Charles Knowles, 18 Aug. 1744, Adm. 2/484, p. 196.

31. Shirley to Warren, 29 Jan. 1744/45, Adm. 1/3817. For Shirley's career see John A. Schutz, *William Shirley, King's Governor of Massachusetts* (Chapel Hill, 1961).

32. Warren to Corbett, 8 Sept. 1744, Adm. 1/2654; his earlier letter was dated 6 Feb. 1742/43, Adm. 1/2653.

33. Warren to Anson, 2 Apr. 1745, Anson Papers, Addit. MSS. 15957, fol. 147, BM.

34. Corbett to Warren, 9 Aug. 1745, Adm. 2/492, pp. 4-10; Warren to Anson, 2 Oct. 1745, Anson Papers, Addit. MSS. 15957, fol. 160, BM; For Pepperrell's career see Byron Fairchild, *Messrs William Pepperrell: Merchants at Piscataqua* (Ithaca, N.Y., 1954).

35. Warren to Corbett, 18 June 1745, Adm. 1/2655; Warren and Pepperrell to Newcastle, 4 July 1745, Belknap Papers 61c, Massachusetts Historical Society (hereafter MHS), Warren to Newcastle, 23 Nov. 1745, C.O. 5/44, fol. 105-114v.

36. Arthur H. Buffinton, "The Canada Expedition of 1746: Its relation to British Politics," *American Historical Review* 45 (1940): 552-80.

37. Guy Frégault, "L'expédition de duc d'Anville," *Revue d'histoire de l'amérique française*, 2 (1948): 27-52.

38. 12 Jan. 1746/47, Sir Herbert Richmond, *The Navy and the War of 1739-1748*, 3 vols. (Cambridge, 1920), 3: 49-50; Warren to Newcastle, 17 Jan.

1746/47, Halifax Papers in Egerton MS. 929, pp. 168-72, BM.

39. Admiralty to Warren, 5 Mar. 1746/47, Adm. 2/69, p. 178.

40. Admiralty to Anson, and to Warren, 30 Mar. 1747, ibid., 267-69.

41. Daniel A. Baugh, *British Naval Administration in the Age of Walpole* (Princeton, 1965), p. 112; Richmond, *The Navy and the War of 1739-1748*, 3: 81-94.

42. Ruddock Mackay, *Admiral Hawke* (Oxford, 1965), pp. 53-62.

43. Warren to Corbett, 12 Aug. 1748, Adm. 1/88; for the 1748 sea campaign, see Richmond, *The Navy and the War of 1739-1748*, 3: 226-37.

44. The two principal acts governing the distribution of prize money were: 6 Anne, c. 13 (1708) and 13 Geo. II, c. 4 (1740).

45. Warren to Corbett, 6 Feb. 1742/43, Adm. 1/2653, and 8 Sept. 1744, Adm. 1/2654.

46. Warren to Corbett, 8 Jan. 1741/42, Adm. 1/2653.

47. Warren to Corbett, 9 and 25 Feb. 1744/45, Adm. 1/2654.

48. Warren to Pieter, Dutch governor of St. Eustatius, 28 Jan. 1744/45, and Warren to Corbett, 7 Feb. 1744/45, Adm. 1/2654.

49. Warren to Anson, 5 July 1747, Anson Papers, Add. MSS. 15957, fol. 200.

50. One of many such letters, see Warren to Corbett, 9 Apr. 1744, Adm. 1/2654.

51. Schutz, *William Shirley*, p. 105, thoroughly misinterprets a letter from Shirley to Pelham, 23 Sept. 1745, which mentions the incident. HM 9707, Huntingdon Library, San Marino, California.

52. Warren to Corbett, 27 Sept. 1744, Adm. 1/2654. In 1743 Anson had taken the Acapulco galleon, which for a time became the norm by which the value of all rich prizes was judged.

53. James Graeme to Corbett, 23 June 1744, Adm. 1/2878. See also 12 July 1740, Gage Papers, G/Am/1, and Warren–Baker accounts, 1738-46, Warren Papers, WLCL.

54. The evidence for this relates to a dispute over a Spanish prize taken by one of Warren's squadron, the *Woolwich,* commanded by Edward Herbert. As late as 1760 Lady Warren and Knowles were still in pursuit of what they believed was their share in this prize. Knowles to John Cleveland, Weybridge, 15 June, 26 July, 4 Aug., 6 Aug. 1760, Adm. 1/578; Cleveland to Knowles, 22 July 1760, Adm. 2/529, p. 111; Cleveland to Sir Peircy Brett, 5 Aug. 1760, Adm. 2/529, p. 163. Proceedings against Herbert had been initiated by Warren in 1749, with half the expected cost and profit to be Knowles's, Warren's account book 1749-52, 20 June 1749, Warren Papers, WLCL.

55. Warren to Corbett, 6 Feb. and 30 Mar. 1747/48, Adm. 1/88. Also Warren's account book 1749-52, Warren Papers, WLCL.

56. Warren to Burchett, 18 Nov. 1739, Adm. 1/2652. Also Adm. 1/3787 for papers of the Vice Admiralty Court of Charleston, South Carolina. Gage Papers, G/Am/1.

57. One of the prizes was the sloop *St. Charles,* taken in February 1741 with 2,000 pieces of eight

and 500 pistoles on board. Warren to Vernon, 23 Feb. 1740/41, Vernon–Wager Papers, 4601-19, Library of 1750-1845,Washington, D.C.

58. Warren to Samuel and William Baker, 5 Mar. 1740/41, Jamaica, Gage Papers, G/Am/21.

59. Warren's accounts with Messrs. Baker, 1738-1746, 1 and 2 Mar. 1742, Warren Papers, WLCL.

60. Ibid, 10 Nov. and 4 Dec. 1742, 25 Feb. 1744.

61. Ibid., 22 August 1742 and 28 Sept. 1743 respectively. "By my bill on Messrs. Bell, Jasper, and the rest of the Agents for the *Peregrina.*"

62. From a list of prizes condemned at New York from 25 Dec. 1739 to 29 Sept. 1745, C.O. 5/1061, Gg 216. The *San José* was condemned on 29 Apr. 1743.

63. Warren's accounts with Messrs. Baker, 1738-1746, Warren Papers, WLCL, credited to his account, 17 Feb. 1743/44.

64. Ibid, 7 Apr., 5 May, 4 and 21 Sept., 2 Oct., 28 Dec., 1744, and 6 Feb. 1745.

65. C.O. 5/1061, Gg 216.

66. Warren's accounts with Messrs. Baker 1738-46; 11 Jan. 1746; Warren Papers, WLCL. See also, Warren's account book, 1749-54, for 27 April and 9 June 1750, Warren Papers, WLCL.

67. A detailed account of the prize, called the *Saint François Xavier,* less the value of the bullion, is found in the Warren Papers, WLCL. The piece of eight had a value of 4s. 5d.

68. On board the *Vigilant* also were 1,454 oz. of silver plate, 125 gal. of brandy, 2,905 gal. of wine.

For detailed account see Warren Papers, WLCL. See also Board of Ordnance to Warren, 20 Oct. 1747, Warren Papers, WLCL.

69. Warren to Wickham, 20 Aug. 1745; Adm. 1/2655.

70. Shirley to Pelham, 27 Sept. 1745, HM 9707, Huntingdon Library.

71. Warren accounts with Messrs. Baker, 1738-1746, Warren Papers, WLCL.

72. Warren to Admiral Sir John Norris, 7 June 1746, Gage Papers, G/Am/6.

73. Baugh, *British Naval Administration in the Age of Walpole*, p. 112.

74. Warren's accounts with Lord Anson, 16 June 1747 to August 1748, Anson Papers, Add. MSS. 15955, fol. 16-17, BM.

75. Abstract of Prize Money received by Philip Stephens on Account of Anson and Warren, ibid, fol. 22.

76. Warren accounts, 1749-52, Warren Papers, WLCL.

77. Warren to Clinton, 26 Oct. 1742, George Clinton Papers, 1, WLCL. Warren never took his seat as Councillor, E.B. O'Callaghan, ed., *Documents relative to the Colonial History of the State of New York* (Albany, 1855), 6: 165.

78. Warren to Anson, 2 Apr. 1745, Anson Papers, Addit. MSS 15957, fol. 152. BM.

79. Warren to Clinton, 24 June 1746; Clinton to Warren (Aug. 1746), George Clinton Papers, 2, WLCL.

80. The best published account of the background is by Katz, *Newcastle's New York*, pp. 164-244.

81. Warren to Clinton, 18 Oct. 1747, Gage Papers, G/Am/6;

Warren to Clinton (Dec. 1747), partly extracted, Clinton to Cadwallader Colden, 11 Mar. 1747/48, *The Letters and Papers of Cadwallader Colden*, 3: 364, Collections of the New-York Historical Society for 1919 (New York, 1920).

82. Ibid.

83. Nicholas Varga, "Robert Charles: New York Agent, 1748-1770," *William and Mary Quarterly*, 3rd series, 18 (1961): 211-35.

84. Warren to Charles Knowles, 10 Nov. 1746, Gage Papers, G/Am/6; Admiral Edward Vernon had been an MP since 1722.

85. Sir Lewis Namier and John Brooke, eds., *The History of Parliament: The House of Commons 1754-1790* (London, 1964), 22: 336. For a brief account of Warren's parliamentary career see the article by Dr. Edith Cruickshanks in Romney Sedgwick, ed., *The History of Parliament: The House of Commons 1715-1754,* 2 vols. (London, 1970), 2: 522-23.

86. Bedford to Anson, 20 June 1747, Anson Papers, Addit. MSS., 15955, fol. 141, BM.

87. Warren had 2,858 votes, *The Gentleman's Magazine,* 1747, p. 307; for note on Trentham, see Namier and Brooke, *The History of Parliament*, 3: 38-39.

88. Warren to Anson, 26 Aug. 1747, Anson Papers, Addit, MSS., 15957, fol. 222, BM.

89. Warren to Anson, 3 Dec. 1748, Warren Papers, 1, WLCL.

90. Sir Lewis Namier and John Brooke, *Charles Townsend* (London, 1964), p. 26; W.S. Lewis, ed., *Horace Walpole's Correspondence,* 20

(New Haven 1960), Walpole to Horace Mann, 26 Dec. 1748: 16-17.

91. Letters patent for the new Admiralty Board, 24 Dec. 1748, Adm. 4/25.

92. Letters patent for this new addition to the Board, 18 Nov. 1749, Adm. 4/26.

93. The bill was entitled: "A Bill for amending, explaining and reducing into One Act of Parliament, the Laws relating to the Government of his Majesty's Ships, Vessels, and Forces by Sea."

94. The bill was introduced by Lord Barrington, *Journals of the House of Commons*, 25: 708.

95. See *Considerations on the Bill for the Better Government of the Navy; Remarks on a Pamphlet Called Considerations . . .* ; [Augustus Hervey], *A Detection of the Considerations of the Navy Bill;* [Temple West], *An Examination and Refutation of a late pamphlet intitled, Considerations . . . ; A letter from a Friend in the Country . . . ; Objections to the Thirty-fourth Article of the Navy Bill;* all published in London in 1749.

96. David Erskine, ed., *Augustus Hervey's Journal* (London, 1953), p. 80.

97. Adm. 3/60 gives the text of the petition.

98. Feb. 1748/49, ibid.; Erskine, ed., *Augustus Hervey's Journal*, p. 80.

99. The original petition with the signatures is dated 23 Feb. 1748/49, Adm. 1/578.

100. The bill received royal assent on 26 May 1749, 22 Geo. II, c. 33.

101. Warren to Anson, 7 Oct. 1750, Anson Papers, Addit. MSS., 15957, fol. 312, BM.

102. On 25 Apr. 1750 he was known to have dined at Leicester House. See John Carswell and Lewis Arnold Dralle, eds., *The Political Journal of George Bubb Dodington* (London, 1965), pp. 66-67; for list, see Egmont MSS, 47097/6, BM.

103. *Journals of the House of Commons*, 25: 1007, 1017, 1049, 1095.

104. Ibid, pp. 785, 808, 809, 838, 842. For Warren's share in this venture see Chapter 11.

105. For his parliamentary speeches see William Corbett, ed., *The Parliamentary History of England*, 14: 613-19, 711-13, 27 Nov. 1749 and 5 Feb. 1749/50; Horace Walpole, *Memoirs of the Reign of George II* (London, 1847), 1: 243.

106. For a general survey see David Owen, *English Philanthropy, 1660-1960* (Cambridge, Mass., 1965).

107. John Dalton, *A Sermon preached before the Governors of the Middlesex Hospital* (London, 1751), pp. 10-11. Warren accounts, 1749-52, Warren Papers, WLCL. Between 1749 and 1752 his gifts amounted to £171.

108. Warren–Jasper accounts, 1742-44, Warren Papers, WLCL. Warren–Anson accounts, Anson Papers, Addit. MSS. 15955, fol. 26-27, BM. £258 in such gifts are recorded.

109. £20 to King's Chapel, Boston, in 1749, Henry Caner and John Gibbons to Warren, 29 Jan. 1748/49 in Henry Wilder Foote, *Annals of King's Chapel* (Boston, 1896), 2: 50-51, 63, £100 to St. George's Chapel, New York in 1751, Morgan Dix, *A History of the Parish of Trinity Church in the City of*

New York (New York, 1898), 1: 258.

110. For a detailed account see Andrew McFarland Davis, *Currency and Banking in the Province of the Massachusetts Bay,* reprint edition (New York, 1970), 1: 203-43, 437-40.

111. Warren to Josiah Willard, 12 Aug. 1749, Massachusetts Archives, 20: fol. 559-60.

112. See Pepperrell's memorial to the Massachusetts General Court, 28 Jan. 1750/51, Massachusetts Archives, 1: fol. 296-98. Also Warren accounts 1749-53, Warren Papers, WLCL, 9 Aug. 1750.

113. Warren to Willard, 30 Mar. 1751, *Massachusetts Archives,* 13: fol. 245-47, and 22 Mar. 1752, fol. 297-99. The fund lay unused until 1761 when Eleazar Wheelock, a Congregationalist minister and later founder of Dartmouth College, received permission to use the income for his Indian school at Lebanon, Connecticut. See James Dow McCallum, *Eleazar Wheelock: Founder of Dartmouth College* (Hanover, New Hampshire, 1939), pp. 143-44.

114. Susan Warren to William Johnson, 21 Apr. 1744, James Sullivan, ed., *The Papers of Sir William Johnson* (Albany, 1921), 1: 21-22.

115. Hugh Phillips, *Mid-Georgian London* (London, 1964), p. 302 says their house was no. 15. In 1763 Lady Warren moved to Grosvenor Square. For the Hampshire estate, see chapter 8.

116. The Dublin press was shocked by his passing. See the *Dublin Gazette,* nos. 204-5 and *The Dublin Journal,* nos. 2649-50.

117. Alice Izard to her mother, Elizabeth DeLancey, 17 Nov. 1771, Delancey Papers, doc. 42.315.617; Museum of the City of New York. For Warren's children and descendants, see Appendix A.

118. George Edward Cokayne and others, eds., *Complete Peerage,* 12 (London 1953): 135-36. See also Bernard Falk, *The Royal Fitz Roys, Dukes of Grafton through Four Centuries* (London, 1950).

119. Thomas Jones, *History of New York during the Revolutionary War* (New York, 1879), 1: 662-63. Skinner was captured at Oswego in 1756 and taken to France before being released, whereupon he settled in England. In 1759 he purchased a commission in the 85th Foot, serving first at Bellisle and later at Lisbon, reaching the rank of colonel in 1777.

120. Cokayne, *Complete Peerage,* 5: 597-98.

121. Cokayne, ibid., 1: 48-49.

122. There is some doubt about the date of Catherine's death. See Gage Papers, G/Am/103 and G/Ir/2 (70).

Chapter 3

1. Tripartite agreement signed 20 July 1731. John E. Stillwell Collection, NYHS.

2. Nicholls, of Welsh extraction, had come to New York about 1715. An attorney at law, he also acted as a credit broker. Elected coroner in 1737, he was appointed Registrar of the New York Vice Admiralty Court in 1744, and later became Postmaster. He died in 1775.

3. S. and W. Baker to Warren, 2 Nov. 1745, Warren Papers, 1, WLCL.

4. Warren to O. DeLancey, 11 Aug. 1750, Warren Papers 37, NYHS.

5. 6 May 1772, Robert Watts Papers, box 2, NYHS.

6. Warren heirs to O. DeLancey, 2 May 1772, Gage Papers, G/Am/135.

7. DeLancey to Warren heirs, 8 Aug. 1772, Gage Papers, G/Am/137.

8. DeLancey to Warren heirs, 10 June 1772, Gage Papers, G/Am/136.

9. J. Potter, "The Growth of Population in America, 1700-1860" in *Population in History,* ed., D.V. Glass and D.E.C. Eversley (Chicago,1965), pp. 631-63, upon which the paragraph is based.

10. Ibid., p. 662

11. The best estimate is 256,400 blacks between 1701 and 1780. See Philip D. Curtin, *The Atlantic Slave Trade: A Census* (Madison, Wisconsin, 1969), p. 140, Table 40.

12. Potter, "The growth of population in America, 1700-1860," p. 654.

13. Charles W. Spencer, "The Land System of Colonial New York," New York State Historical Association, *Proceedings,* 16 (1917): 151-62; Ruth L. Higgins, *Expansion in New York, with Especial Reference to the Eighteenth Century* (Columbus, Ohio, 1931), pp. 24-25; Ulysses P. Hedrick, *A History of Agriculture in the State of New York* (New York, 1933), pp. 56-57; Stella Helen Sutherland, *Population Distribution in Colonial America* (New York,

1936), p. 82; Irving Mark, *Agrarian Conflicts in Colonial New York, 1711–1775* (New York, 1940), pp. 73-74; David Maldwyn Ellis, *Landlords and Farmers in the Hudson-Mohawk Region 1790-1850* (Ithaca, 1946). Ray A. Billington, *Westward Expansion: A History of the American Frontier* (New York, 1949), pp. 85-89.

14. Sung Bok Kim, "A New Look at the Great Landlords of Eighteenth Century New York," *The William and Mary Quarterly,* 3rd. series, 27 (1970): 581-614.

15. Ibid, p. 614.

16. Ibid.

17. Ibid, pp. 589-92.

18. Potter, The Growth of Population in America, 1700–1860," p. 641.

19. Sutherland, *Population Distribution in Colonial America,* pp. 64-96, for details of New York's population; also Evarts B. Greene and Virginia D. Harrington, *American Population Before the Federal Census of 1790* (New York, 1932), pp. 88-105.

20. Pehr Kalm, *Travels in North America* (Warrington, 1770), 1: 248; trans. John Reinhold Forster.

21. For biographical details see Edward Porter Alexander, *A Revolutionary Conservative: James Duane of New York* (New York, 1938), pp. 3-13. Deeds dated 27-28 June 1731, Warren Papers 12, and Warren Deeds 3, NYHS.

22. Deeds dated 3-4 June 1737 and 17-18 Aug. 1741, DePeyster Deeds, 1 and 14, NYHS. There is a 1772 plan of the Webber farm in Watts Papers 10, NYHS.

23. 24-25 Sept. 1744, Warren Deeds 6, NYHS.

24. Warren to O. DeLancey, 11 Aug. 1750, Warren Papers 37, NYHS.

25. 11 Sept. 1744, *Minutes of the Common Council of the City of New York 1675-1776* (New York, 1905), 5: 125-26. For a plan of the grant see Warren Papers 30b, NYHS. In July 1743, through Richard Nicholls, Warren had asked for the land.

26. There is a 1773 plan of the estate in the Prints Division, New York Public Library, Stokes Cat. No. 1773 B-77. For the fullest history of the ownership of the entire estate see I.N. Phelps Stokes, *The Iconography of Manhattan Island* (New York, 1928), 6: 157-69.

27. See Edmund T. DeLancey, *New York's Turtle Bay Old and New* (Barre, Mass., 1965), pp. 3-4; also Stokes, *The Iconography of Manhattan Island*, 6: 172-76.

28. Deed signed 22-23 Mar. 1749/50, Warren Papers 1, NYHS.

29. Warren to DeLancey, 11 Aug. 1750, Warren Papers 37, NYHS.

30. For the correct account see Martha J. Lamb and Mrs. Burton Harrison, *History of the City of New York* (New York, 1877), 2: 84-86.

31. Gage Papers, G/Am/13.

32. 5-6 Nov. 1736 and 27-28 Feb. 1737/38, DePeyster Deeds, 2, nos. 4 and 9; 9, nos. 5 and 6. There is a plan of this whole area, measuring 81 feet by 427 feet in Warren Papers 53a and 77, NYHS.

33. Gage Papers, G/Am/11.

34. The property had 142 feet of frontage on Broadway and 110 on Little Queen Street. See deeds 3-4 Sept. 1734, and 8 July 1736,

DeLancey Deeds and DeLancey Papers, NYHS.

35. There is a plan of the lot in Warren Papers 30a, NYHS. For a description see the original deed of mortgage, 23-24 Sept. 1731, DeLancey Papers, 10 and 11, NYHS.

36. Gage Papers, G/Am/69.

37. Deeds of sale dated 25-26 Feb. 1750/51, Gage Papers, G/Am/62 and GA 840. For details of expenses relating to sale see Gage Papers, G/Ha/43.

38. DeLancey to Charles Fitzroy, 6 Apr. 1774, Gage Papers, G/Am/160.

39. 13-14 Aug. 1741, Warren Deeds 5, DePeyster Papers 6, no. 3, NYHS.

40. New York Council Minutes, 5: 299; 6: 2.

41. Schuyler, *Colonial New York: Philip Schuyler and His Family,* 1: 192, 199. An excellent study has recently been completed by Sung Bok Kim, "The Manor of Cortlandt and Its Tenants, 1697-1783."

42. Kim, "The Manor of Cortlandt," p. 91.

43. Deed Book XIV, pp. 110-11, 21 Oct. 1743, Department of State, Albany, New York.

44. 3-4 Aug. 1744, Warren Papers 27, NYHS. See also Watts Papers 10, NYHS.

45. 6-7 Sept. 1744, DeLancey Papers 20 and DeLancey Deeds 24, NYHS.

46. Died 17 Sept. 1745; will proved 26 Sept. 1746. See *Abstract of Wills on File in the Surrogate's Office, City of New York, 4, 1744-1753.* Collections of the New-York Historical Society for 1895 (New York, 1896), p. 92 for

an abstract of his will. For an
inventory of items sold at the sale
on 27 Feb. 1746/47 see DeLancey
Papers doc. 40/190.32., Museum
of the City of New York.

47. 2 June 1738; E.B.
O'Callaghan, *Documents relative to
the Colonial History of the State of
New York* (Albany, 1855) 6: 116.

48. 12 April 1750; 23 Geo. II,
c. 29.

49. Arthur Cecil Bining, *British
Regulation of the Colonial Iron
Industry* (Philadelphia and London,
1933), p. 3.

50. See his Appendix B, ibid.,
pp. 128-32.

51. Ibid., p. 18. In 1757 James
DeLancey had told the Board of
Trade: "Several works have been
begun but were dropt through the
mismanagement or inability of the
undertakers; of these there were
two Furnaces in the Manor of
Cortland and several Bloomeries;
but they have not been worked for
several years past." O'Callaghan,
*Documents relative to the Colonial
History of New York,* 7: 335.

52. Warren–Stephen DeLancey
accounts, 1743-44; DeLancey
Papers 19, NYHS; Warren–Oliver
DeLancey Accounts, Gage Papers,
G/Am/27. They had a
one-quarter share in one iron
works and one-sixth in the other.

53. 5 May 1737, *Calendar of New
York Colonial Manuscripts: Endorsed
Land Papers in the Office of the
Secretary of State of New York*
(Albany, 1864), p. 228.

54. 6 Dec. 1737, Warren Papers
17, NYHS.

55. Gage Papers, G/Am/66.
The description is Warren's.

56. Henry Lloyd Sr. to his
agent, Robert Temple, 1 Sept.

1746, *Papers of the Lloyd Family of
the Manor of Queens Village, Lloyd's
Neck, Long Island, New York* (New
York, 1927), 1: 377.

57. Temple to Lloyd Sr., 21-24
Sept. 1746, ibid., pp. 378-79.

58. 11 Aug. 1750, Warren
Papers 37, NYHS.

59. Thomas to Warren, 11 June
1751, Warren Papers, WLCL.
Warren's letter to which this was a
reply has not survived.

60. Evidence is taken from a
variety of accounts and letters
among the Warren Papers, NYHS,
and Gage Papers.

61. Oliver DeLancey to Lady
Warren, letters of 1753 and 1754,
Gage Addit. 1201.

62. Warren to O. DeLancey,
11 Aug. 1750, Warren Papers 37,
NYHS.

63. DeLancey to Lady Warren,
29 Nov. 1762, Gage Addit. 1201.

64. Catherwood to Clinton,
2 Apr. 1750, George Clinton
Papers, 10, WLCL. In May 1750
Warren received £264 14s. 2d.
from Clinton. Warren accounts
1749-52, Warren Papers, WLCL.

65. O. DeLancey to S. Warren,
23 Oct., 1 and 25 Dec. 1753,
Gage Addit. 1201.

66. Richard Nicholls to Susan
Warren, 12 July 1753, ibid.

67. O. DeLancey to S. Warren,
20 July 1754, ibid.

68. O. DeLancey to S. Warren,
6 Mar. 1757, ibid.

69. O. DeLancey to S. Warren,
4 Oct. 1757, ibid.

70. O. DeLancey to S. Warren,
19 July 1759, ibid.

71. He had originally planned
only NY£425 in improvements. He
claimed to find the house "Much
Convenient for My Family . . .

than . . . Bloomendal." O.
DeLancey to S. Warren, 19 July
and 29 Nov. 1762, 14 May 1763,
ibid. His detailed instructions to
the builders, Staunton and
Tembrock are dated 7 May 1763,
DeLancey Papers 29, NYHS.
Stokes incorrectly believed they
applied to the Henderson house,
The Iconography of Manhattan Island
6: 167-68.

72. Plan of the new road is in
DeLancey Papers 32, with a
description in Warren Papers 54a,
NYHS. See also 26 May 1762,
*Minutes of the Common Council of the
City of New York 1675-1776*,
6: 288-89.

73. 1769 Rent Roll, Warren
Papers 55, NYHS.

74. O. DeLancey to S. Warren,
13 Apr. and 20 July 1754, Gage
Addit. 1201. See also the accounts
sent John Kempe by DeLancey,
23 Dec. 1766; and J. T. Kempe to
O. DeLancey, 20 Dec. 1766,
Kempe Papers, box 1, D-E,
NYHS.

75. Stokes, *The Iconography of
Manhattan Island*, 6: 168.

76. 1769 Rent Roll, Warren
Papers 55, NYHS.

77. See the lease dated 4 June
1765, Warren Papers 58, NYHS.

78. Fitzroy to DeLancey, 6 May
1772, Gage Papers, G/Am/135.
DeLancey had wanted to buy
either the Duane or the
Henderson house and was
consequently disappointed by this
decision. DeLancey to Warren
heirs, 8 Aug. 1772, Gage Papers,
G/Am//137.

79. Ibid.

80. DeLancey to S. Warren,
1 Feb. 1772, Gage Papers,
G/Am/131.

81. Skinner to DeLancey,
25 Jan. 1774, Gage Papers,
G/Am/157.

82. Skinner to DeLancey,
15 Apr. 1775, Gage Papers,
G/Am/174-75.

83. Warren to DeLancey,
11 Aug. 1750, Warren Papers 37,
NYHS.

84. O. DeLancey to Lady
Warren, 1 Feb. 1772, Gage
Papers, G/Am/130.

85. DeLancey to William
Skinner, 22 Mar. 1776, Gage
Papers, G/Am/181.

86. Gage Papers, G/Am/62 and
Gage Addit. 845.

87. O. DeLancey to Lady
Warren, 20 July 1754, Gage
Addit. 1201.

88. 20 Dec. 1755, ibid. In 1753
a storm demolished the wharf at
Turtle Bay; the rebuilding cost
was NY£137 10s., Gage Papers,
G/Am/82.

89. Oliver DeLancey to Lady
Warren, 4 Oct. 1757, Gage Addit.
1201. For references to small
income from Turtle Bay in 1757
see Gage Papers, G/Am/82.

90. See Gage Papers,
G/Am/79a, G/Am/82, G/Am/89,
G/Am/142, G/Am/158 and
G/Am/170 for references to
income from Navy Board to 1775.

91. See statement by John Watts
Jr., 1 Sept. 1789, Gage Papers,
G/Am/192b.

92. Gage Papers, G/Am/69,
1 May 1750.

93. Warren Papers, 55, NYHS.

94. Warren Papers, 68, NYHS.

95. Warren Papers, 55, NYHS.

96. DeLancey to Col. William
Skinner, 22 Mar. 1776, Gage
Papers, G/Am/181. For reference
to the burning see Warren Papers
68, NYHS.

97. Stephen Jenkins, *The Greatest Street in the World: the Story of Broadway, Old and New, from Bowling Green to Albany* (New York, 1911), pp. 38-39.

98. The first lease dated from 1 May 1751, Gage Papers, G/Am/64, G/Am/95, G/Am141.

99. Warren Papers 68, NYHS.

100. *Minutes of the Common Council of the City of New York 1675-1776* (New York, 1905), 6: 2, 16 Jan. 1755.

101. Ibid., 6: 120, 127; 19 Dec. 1757 and 13 Mar. 1758. The wharf initially measured 40 feet by 15 feet. The cost was NY£52 4s. 7d. Gage Papers, G/Am/82.

102. The deed has unfortunately been divided into two parts, one classified as Warren Papers 42, the other as DeLancey Papers 37, NYHS.

103. DeLancey to Lady Warren, 25 Apr. 1758, Gage Addit. 1201.

104. Gage Papers, G/Am/64, G/Am/69, G/Am/82, G/Am/107, and Warren Papers 68. NY£46 14s. 11d. was spent on repairs between 1755 and 1760. One of the Dock Street houses burned down apparently in 1776.

105. Gage Papers, G/Am/82 and G/Am/89.

106. DeLancey to Col. Fitzroy, 6 Apr. 1774, Gage Papers, G/Am/160.

107. Skinner to DeLancey, 15 Apr. 1775, Gage Papers, G/Am/175.

108. DeLancey to Skinner, 9 Aug. 1775, Gage Papers, G/Am/176. For 1772 valuation see Gage Papers, G/Am/141.

109. Warren Papers 68, NYHS.

110. From 1 Jan. 1748/49, see Pierre Van Cortlandt's Receipt Book, Sleepy Hollow Restorations, MS. V. 1689.

111. Warren to Oliver DeLancey, 11 Aug. 1750, Warren Papers 37, NYHS.

112. O. DeLancey to Lady Warren, 20 Dec. 1755, Gage Addit. 1201.

113. Gage Papers, G/Am/82.

114. O. DeLancey to Lady Warren, 4 Oct. 1757, Gage Addit. 1201. The appointment was made sometime early in 1758, and first rents were received in May 1758. See Van Cortlandt's Receipt Book, Sleepy Hollow Restorations, MS. V. 2301.

115. Gage Papers, G/Am/79a, G/Am/129.

116. Gage Papers, G/Am/142, G/Am/158, G/Am/170.

117. DeLancey to William Skinner, 4 Nov. 1775, Gage Papers, G/Am/178.

118. These were properly speaking "tenants-at-will," whom DeLancey described as on "parole." Warren Papers 55, NYHS.

119. The three tenants were David Montross, Symon Maybee, and Nathaniel Whitney on South Lot 5, lots 1, 2, and 7 respectively.

120. Gilbert Totten, tenant of Lot Nine (lot 3), was succeeded by his widow, Mary, while William Pearce, tenant of Lot Nine (lot 4) was succeeded by his son, Richard.

121. The revisionary work of Dr. Kim, cited earlier, is of particular importance here. Unfortunately the value of his work has not been appreciated by

Patricia U. Bonomi, *A Factious People: Politics and Society in Colonial New York* (New York, 1971), especially chapter 6, "New York's Land System: Problems and Opportunities."

122. See especially Staughton Lynd, *Anti-Federalism in Dutchess County, New York: A Study of Democracy and Class Conflict in the Revolutionary Era* (Chicago, 1962), and Irving Mark, *Agrarian Conflicts,* pp. 137-39.

123. Kim, "The Manor of Cortlandt," pp. 230-31.

124. Ibid., pp. 233-67.

125. Ibid., p. 188.

126. Ibid. pp. 166-69, 188, for details of what follows.

127. For details see Watts Papers, NYHS. Also DePeyster Papers, 1, items 17 and 21.

128. Ruth L. Higgins, *Expansion in New York, with Especial Reference to the Eighteenth Century* (Columbus, Ohio, 1931), p. 80. See also William H. Hill, *Old Fort Edward* (Fort Edward, New York, 1929).

129. The surveyor was Dirck Swart; his account is in Warren Papers 59.

130. Map of Washington County in *Atlas of the State of New York* by David H. Burr (New York, 1829) shows the lots.

131. William Sherriff's receipt from DeLancey, 19 July 1768; Warren Papers 71a; see also 1768-69 accounts, Gage Papers, G/Am/89. Payment was made in two instalments, one for NY£162 3s. 1d. on 5 April, the second for NY£140 9s. 8d. on 19 July 1768.

132. Smyth to DeLancey, 26 Mar. 1768, DeLancey Papers 55, NYHS.

133. DeLancey to Smyth, 27 May 1768, Warren Papers, 71b.

134. DeLancey to Silvester, 18 Oct. 1768, Warren Papers 50, to inform him of his arrangement with Smyth.

135. Dunham to DeLancey, 28 May 1767, DeLancey Papers 51, NYHS.

136. DeLancey to Col. Skinner, Col. Fitzroy and Abingdon, 5 Sept. 1774, Gage Papers, G/Am/167.

137. DePeyster Deeds 2, item 31, p. 15, 31 Mar. 1787, NYHS.

138. See chapters 8 and 9.

139. See various accounts sent to Lady Warren and the Warren heirs, Gage Papers, G/Am/79a, G/Am/82, G/Am/129, G/Am/142, G/Am/158, G/Am/170.

140. For details of New York commodity prices, which moved in the same direction though more sharply than those in England, see Herman M. Stoker, "Wholesale Prices at New York City, 1720 to 1800," part II of *Wholesale Prices for 213 Years: 1720 to 1932,* pp. 201-22 (Cornell University Agricultural Experiment Station, Ithaca, 1932); and George F. Warren, Frank A. Pearson, and Herman M. Stoker, "Wholesale Commodity Prices at New York, 1720-1861," pp. 9-24, being chapter 2 of *Wholesale Commodity Prices in the United States, 1700-1861,* ed. Arthur H. Cole (Cambridge, Mass., 1938).

141. Elizabeth B. Schumpeter, "English Prices and Public Finances, 1660-1822," *Review of Economic Statistics* 20 (1938): 35.

142. Information on New York's exchange rates with sterling has in part been supplied by Professor

Joseph A. Ernst and Dr. John M. Hemphill, who have studied a wide variety of merchants' letter-books and papers. Other information was also found in the *Letter Book of John Watts, Merchant and Councillor of New York, January 1, 1762 – December 2, 1765,* Collections of the New-York Historical Society for the Year 1928 (New York, 1928), and in William S. Sachs, "The Business Outlook in the Northern Colonies, 1750-1775" (Ph.D. dissertation, Columbia University, 1957). Perhaps the best study of any American colony's exchange rates is found in Anne Bezanson, Robert D. Gay, and Miriam Hussey, *Prices in Colonial Pennsylvania* (Philadelphia, 1935), chapter 13, "Sterling Exchange," pp. 314-36. Further information was found among the Warren Papers and Watts Papers, NYHS, and the Gage Papers.

The amount of New York currency that was paid for £100 bills rested fundamentally on the rating given by New York merchants to the Spanish dollar. Between 1730 and 1775 this varied between 6s. and 9s. 6d., when the sterling rate established by law in 1704 was 4s. 6d. In practice, actual bills of exchange on London available in New York depended on the quantity of goods and services exported to Great Britain, and the price they attained when sold abroad. This ultimately had some relation to the price of the same goods and services in New York. In addition New York had an indirect supply of sterling bills drawn on London mercantile houses through its trade with other colonies, and with southern Europe. Where New York traded favourably, such as in the West Indies, a net increase in sterling bills in New York resulted; and the favourable trade balance was settled by means of bills of exchange on London.

143. When Richard Nicholls became one of the Greenwich tenants, he charged the estate NY£125 for repairs to the house and property, which included new fences. DeLancey to Lady Warren, 1753-54 letters, Gage Addit. 1201. The same house in 1775 was given a new roof; and the cost was NY£64. Earlier the Warren estate had been charged NY£89 for fencing and NY£41 for a new road at Greenwich. Gage Papers, G/Am/82, G/Am/89, G/Am/142, G/Am/158. In 1753 ice damaged the Turtle Bay Wharf; and the cost of repairs was NY£138. Over the next five years another NY£34 was spent in keeping it in proper order. Gage Papers, G/Am/82. The old houses on Pearl Street and Bridge Street needed constant upkeep. Gage Papers, G/Am/170.

144. John Christopher Schwab, "History of the New York Property Tax," *Publications of the American Economic Association,* 5 (1890): 410-12. This is no more than an introductory survey, so that the general subject of New York taxation in the colonial era remains neglected. For a survey touching all colonies see Aaron Morton Sakolski, *Land Tenure and Land Taxation in America 1607-1879* (New York, 1957), pp. 250-51.

145. John H. Hickcox, *A History of the Bills of Credit or Paper Money Issued by New York from 1709 to*

1789 (Albany, 1866), pp. 26, 34-35, 40.

146. Charles Worthen Spencer, "Sectional Aspects of New York Provincial Politics," *Political Science Quarterly*, 30 (September 1915): 397-424, for a general discussion of the politics of land tax assessment in New York from 1691 to 1760. For quit rents see Beverley Waugh Bond, *The Quit-Rent System in the American Colonies* (New Haven, 1919).

147. DeLancey to Elliott, 28 Jan. 1774, original MS, in an extra-illustrated edition in NYHS of John Wakefield Francis, *Old New York: or, Reminiscences of the Past Sixty Years* (New York, 1895); for reference to payment see Gage Papers, G/Am/170.

148. Details taken from DeLancey's 1768-69 accounts prepared for Lady Warren, Gage Papers, G/Am/89.

149. See rough drafts of Watts's accounts prepared for the Warren heirs between 1789 and 1791, DePeyster Papers, box 1, nos. 17, 19, 21; and Watts Papers, NYHS.

150. Gage Papers, G/Am/89, G/Am/142.

151. See DePeyster Papers, box 1, and Watts Papers, NYHS for details of rental income remitted after 1783.

152. See table 2.

153. Article 9: Samuel Flagg Bemis, *Jay's Treaty: A Study in Commerce and Diplomacy* (New Haven, revised edition, 1965), p. 466. Jay's original draft was adopted verbatim in the final treaty.

154. 31 Mar. 1787, DePeyster Deeds, 2, NYHS. Miss Skinner's guardian was the Rev. John

Aylmer of East Greenwich, Kent, her cousin, and the sole surviving trustee of her parents' marriage settlement of 1767, Gage Papers, GA 846.

155. Details noted on an abstract of the 1787 deed in John Watts's hand, Warren Papers 68, NYHS.

156. 5 May 1791, Clinton Papers, doc. 54.215.1., Museum of the City of New York. See letter to Viscount Gage, who married Miss Skinner in 1789, from Peter Kemble, 15 Apr. 1791, Gage Papers, G/Am/206.

157. 21 Oct. 1791, Stokes, *The Iconography of Manhattan Island*, 6: 174. John Watts to Gage, 22 Oct. 1791, Gage Papers, G/Am/214.

158. Warren Papers 68, NYHS. The date of sale is not known. Varion continued to pay the city an annual quit rent of NY£10. *Minutes of the Common Council of the City of New York 1784-1831* (New York, 1917), 11: 559, 614, 735, 2 April, 14 May, and 23 July 1821 for the last mention of Warren by the corporation.

159. Watts Papers, 5, NYHS for indenture of sale.

160. *Thoughts on the Letters of Edmund Burke, Esq., to the Sheriffs of Bristol on the Affairs of America* (Oxford, 1777); reprinted in Paul H. Smith, comp., *English Defenders of American Freedoms 1774-1778: Six Pamphlets Attacking British Policy* (Washington, 1972), pp. [193]-[203]. The survival of the placename, Abingdon Square, in Greenwich Village, on land formerly owned by the Earl, may be considered a direct consequence of his one attempt at pamphleteering.

161. Edith M. Fox, *Land Speculation in the Mohawk Country* (Ithaca, 1949) is largely a consideration of Clarke's grandiose scheme to develop the New York frontier from Schenectady to the Genesee Valley. I am indebted for information about the later generation of Clarkes to Professor William A. Kearns, who is preparing an analysis of the Clarke estates in New York from 1791 to 1834.

162. Katz, *Newcastle's New York*, p. 147.

163. John B. Pearse, *A Concise History of the Iron Manufacture of the American Colonies* (Philadelphia, 1876), pp. 44-52. See also Bonomi, *A Factious People*, pp. 71-75.

164. See tables 4 and 8.

165. In particular see Mary Beth Norton, *The British-Americans: The Loyalist Exiles in England, 1774-1789* (Boston, 1972), Wallace Brown, *The King's Friends: Composition and Motives of the American Loyalist Claimants* (Providence, 1965).

166. Oscar Zeichner, "The Loyalist Problem in New York after the Revolution," *New York History*, 21 (July, 1940): 284-302; Harry B. Yoshpe, *The Disposition of Loyalist Estates in the Southern District of the State of New York* (New York, 1939); Julius Goebel, ed., *The Law Practice of Alexander Hamilton*, 2 vols. (New York, 1964-69).

Chapter 4

1. Colden to Clark, 14 Feb. 1738, "Observations on the . . . Province of New York," E. B. O'Callaghan, ed., *Documents relative to the Colonial History of the State of New York* (Albany, 1855), 6: 121-25.

2. He paid her £25 cash giving a bill for the rest on his London agent Edward Jasper, 9 July 1736, Warren-Jasper Accounts, 1732-1738, Gage Papers, G/Am/13, p. 9.

3. *The Letters and Papers of Cadwallader Colden*, 2: 152. The New-York Historical Society Collections for 1918 (New York, 1919).

4. John R. Bleecker to Oliver DeLancey, 7 Dec. 1765, Warren Papers 60, NYHS.

5. The mortgage refers to the tract as amounting to 534 acres, having been originally granted to Henry Huff, whose son John had sold it to Butler. Cowley paid Butler NY£350. See Warren Papers 15, DePeyster Deeds 1, no. 5, NYHS; and Gage Papers, G/Am/1.

6. To William Johnson, 20 Nov. 1738, Milton W. Hamilton, ed., *The Papers of Sir William Johnson* (Albany, 1965), 13: 2.

7. See comment by Oliver DeLancey on rent roll of Warren estates in New York, 1 June 1759, Gage Papers, G/Am/107.

8. Gage Papers, G/Am/1, from a statement prepared by Warren of the state of his finances and investments, May 1740.

9. David H. Burr, *An Atlas of the State of New York* (New York, 1829), Map 17: Montgomery County.

10. Warren's relationship with Johnson has been considered in some detail by each of Johnson's

several biographers. It is therefore surprising in view of the many documents readily available both in Albany and New York City how carelessly this relationship has been interpreted. Thirteen volumes of Johnson papers were published between 1921 and 1967, yet only two scholars have made consistently careful use of them. One, Dr. Milton W. Hamilton, the last editor of the Johnson Papers, has published nothing about Warren. The other, Mrs. Edith M. Fox, formerly curator of the collection of regional history at Cornell University Library, wrote an excellent, though little known, study of Johnson's early frontier career, and correctly analysed the bases of Warren's role in Johnson's success. See "William Johnson's Early Career as a Frontier Landlord and Trader" (Master's essay, Cornell University, 1945). Johnson's original biographer, William Stone, by contrast, made errors of fact and judgment which have been repeated in later works. *The Life and Times of Sir William Johnson, Bart.* (Albany, 1965), 2 vols. A potted version of this was later written by William Eliot Griffis, *Sir William Johnson and the Six Nations* (New York, 1891). Augustus C. Buell, an unreliable historian, wrote a biography that was so dishonest that where he could find no evidence he manufactured it. See Augustus C. Buell, *Sir William Johnson* (New York, 1903), also Milton W. Hamilton, "Augustus C. Buell, Fraudulent Historian," *Pennsylvania Magazine of History and Biography*

14 (October 1956): 478-92. The first really useful biography of Johnson appeared in 1930, but the authors went seriously astray whenever they wrote of Warren. Arthur Pound and Richard E. Day, *Johnson of the Mohawks* (New York, 1930). The same year there appeared a lamentably unsatisfactory biography by Flora Warren Seymour, *Lords of the Valley, Sir William Johnson and His Mohawk Brothers* (New York, 1930). The most recent of Johnson's biographers used the abundance of material quite carelessly, which reviewers unfortunately failed to detect. James Thomas Flexner, *Mohawk Baronet, Sir William Johnson of New York* (New York, 1959). Most thought Warren equally ignorant of agriculture, trade, and the keeping of accounts, while ascribing to Johnson all the singular qualities of the successfully rapacious entrepreneur as well as those of the honest, neighbourhood shopkeeper, an impossible mixture! Only Miss Fox made sense of the financial arrangements between Warren and Johnson and correctly identified the source of Johnson's fortune. Besides Dr. Hamilton, the only other scholar to have used Miss Fox's thesis intelligently is Dr. Charles Roscoe Canedy, III, "An Entrepreneurial History of the New York Frontier 1739-1776" (Ph.D. dissertation, Case Western Reserve University, 1967). He devoted two chapters to Johnson's fortune and entrepreneurial skills.

11. Several letters passed between Warren and Johnson

before the arrangements were complete, though none of this early correspondence has survived. The reference to Boston as the port of arrival is in Johnson to Oliver DeLancey, 3 Nov. 1753, Warren Papers 43, NYHS.

12. Three horses and a wagon were purchased from the patroon, Jeremiah Van Rensselaer. Johnson to Warren, 26 Oct. 1738, which letter has not survived. Reference is found in Warren to Johnson, 20 Nov. 1738, Hamilton, ed., *Johnson Papers*, 13: 3.

13. At Schenectady they stopped at Major Jacob Glen's, Warren to Glen, 3 Sept. 1738, ibid., 9: 1.

14. Warren to Glen, ibid.

15. Warren may also have held out hope to his nephews of assigning the home farm to them in his final will. In fact none of Warren's surviving letters give the least hint of such an offer. For his 1740 will, see Gage Papers, G/Am/1. For partial transcript of his 1746 will, see Horace Lyman Weeks MSS, New York Public Library. See also Johnson to O. DeLancey, 3 Nov. 1753, Hamilton, ed., *Johnson Papers*, 1: 907.

16. A later survey indicated a lot of 203¼ acres. A simple plan of the farm shows that it stood on the Schenectady road, about a half mile deep and two-thirds of a mile long. Warren Papers 35, NYHS. It was later known as lots 78–79, Warren Papers 74, NYHS.

17. Johnson to DeLancey, 3 Nov. 1753, Warren Papers 43, NYHS. Johnson's son-in-law, Daniel Claus, spoke of the farm as "the Land he slaved himself for and injured his health upon."

Claus Papers 14, Public Archives of Canada.

18. Warren took Tyrrell to Jamaica as part of his crew, Adm./L/S/404, see also Tyrrell to Johnson, 28 May 1741, Hamilton, ed., *Johnson Papers,* 1: 10-14.

19. Warren Papers 18 and 19, NYHS and Gage Papers, G/Am/1.

20. Gage Papers, G/Am/11, and Warren Papers 18 and 19, NYHS.

21. Edgar J. McManus, *The History of Negro Slavery in New York* (Syracuse, N.Y., 1966), p. 25. By 1746 the 9,000 slaves formed some 15 per cent of the population. By a 1755 census only seven slaveholders owned 10 or more, pp. 45-46.

22. Ibid., p. 41.

23. Hamilton, ed., *Johnson Papers,* 13: 4-6.

24. Annual cost for the hire of slaves in 1695 was about NY£5, in 1725 NY£20, by 1760 NY£60, and by the 1770s NY£100, yet by 1760 "slave labour cost employers only about half as much as the going rate of free labour." McManus, *The History of Negro Slavery in New York*, p. 54. What Johnson charged is not known, though he sold his slaves for between NY£40 and NY£72. Warren Papers 18 and 19, NYHS.

25. Johnson built not only his farm house but a barrack for the slaves and workers. There were also outbuildings which included a stable and a barn. Warren Papers 18 and 19, NYHS.

26. Michael Tyrrell to Johnson, 28 May 1741, Hamilton, ed., *Johnson Papers,* 1: 14.

27. Warren to Johnson, 20 Nov. 1738, Hamilton, ed., *Johnson Papers* 13: 2-3.

28. Warren Papers 35, NYHS.

29. Warren to Johnson, 20 Nov. 1738, Hamilton, ed., *Johnson Papers* 13: 1-3. In 1741 and 1743, for instance, Johnson sent altogether one barrel of pork, 255 bushels of peas, and 45 bushels of maize to Warren at New York, as well as 4 cwt. of flour, the total value of which was NY£80 7s. 6d.

30. Warren to Johnson, Boston, 20 Nov. 1738, Hamilton, ed., *Johnson Papers*, 13: 1-2.

31. Ibid., p. 1.

32. Warren Papers 18 and 19, NYHS; see also Michael Tyrrell's letter to Johnson, 28 May 1741, Hamilton, ed., *Johnson Papers* 1: 14. Their value was merely NY£23 15s.

33. The trade goods included Madeira, axes, molasses, cod, wearing apparel, and rum. The first batch was shipped to Boston by Arthur Middleton, possibly from Ireland, and thence to Albany via New York. Warren paid by drawing bills on his London agent, Edward Jasper, Warren–Jasper accounts, Gage Papers, G/Am/1. See also Warren Papers 19, NYHS, and Warren–Baker accounts, Warren Papers, WLCL.

34. The goods from Boston were valued at M£1,555 10s. or NY£513, one-third of which was NY£171. Those shipped from England came to £1,533 15s. 5½d. (or NY£2,761) including shipping and insurance costs. Warren actually claimed only to have spent £1,440 6s. 7d. having inadvertently omitted £46 16s. for insurance and an item costing £46 12s. 10d. Ibid.

35. The rum came from New England and was shipped through Nicholas Bayard of New York City. Rum and molasses were valued at NY£57 15s. 3d. Warren Papers 19, NYHS.

36. Johnson to Warren, 10 May 1739, Hamilton, ed., *Johnson Papers* 1: 6-7.

37. Walter Allen Knittle, *Early Eighteenth Century Palatine Emigration: A British Government Redemptioner Project to Manufacture Naval Stores* (Philadelphia, 1937).

38. See an example of one lease, Oct. 1736, DePeyster Papers 14, no. 5, NYHS.

39. Some of the family names were Heuster, Saltzer, Kleyn, Lucs, Wallislow, and Snoks. The bond was dated 7 Oct. 1736, Gage Papers, G/Am/1 and G/Am/20. One settler bought a Warren slave paying with a NY£40 bond, Warren Papers 18 and 19, NYHS.

40. Warren to Johnson, 20 Nov. 1738, Hamilton, ed., *Johnson Papers* 22: 2.

41. Johnson to Warren, 10 May 1739, Hamilton, ed., *Johnson Papers* 1: 5.

42. Collins was one of Colden's deputy-surveyors, an Albany lawyer, onetime Indian commissioner, and involved in the illegal trade to Canada on behalf of the DeLanceys and Schuylers, to whom he was related. Johnson to Collins, 2 Sept. 1739, ibid., p. 8; Fox, "Early Career of William Johnson," pp. 33-34. The survey cost Warren NY£54, while Johnson charged the Warren heirs NY£12 for his services. Gage Papers, G/Am/1 and G/Am/20, Warren Papers 19, NYHS.

43. The loans included NY£50 to John Kain, NY£24 to John Ewarts, and NY£32 to Jacob Bonnel. Gage Papers, G/Am/26.

44. 19 June 1743, O'Callaghan, ed., *Documents relative to the Colonial History of New York*, 6: 225.

45. Lionel Groulx, *Roland-Michel Barrin, marquis de La Galissonière* (Toronto, 1971). Only five new families settled at Warrensburg between 1748 and 1755: James Allen in 1748, and Christian Ernst, James Phillips, Christopher McGraw, and Patrick Connolly in 1752, Warren Papers 55, 69, and 74, NYHS.

46. 20 Dec. 1755, Gage Addit. 1201.

47. DeLancey to Lady Warren, 1 Feb. 1755, ibid.

48. The will has been printed in Hamilton, ed., *Johnson Papers* 13: 19-23.

49. Warren Papers 19, NYHS.

50. 18 Oct. 1752, Gage Papers, G/Am/2.

51. Warren Papers 18 and 19, NYHS.

52. The cost of supplying a slave then was NY£21 per annum: NY£15 for maintenance, and NY£6 for clothing.

53. Chambers–Nicholls memo., 20 Mar. 1754, Hamilton, ed., *Johnson Papers,* 13: 33-35.

54. DeLancey to Susan Warren, 13 Apr. 1754, Gage Addit. 1201.

55. Ibid.

56. Warren Papers 19, NYHS.

57. Further details of the dispute which went on for years will be considered in chapter 4.

58. Warren Papers 55. See DeLancey's note under lots 78 and 79.

59. DeLancey to Susan Warren, 6 Mar. 1757, Gage Addit. 1201.

60. Johnson to DeLancey, 7 Nov. 1765, O'Callaghan, ed., *The Documentary History of the State of New York* 2: 825-26.

61. DeLancey to Johnson, 28 Feb. 1762, ibid., p. 800.

62. DeLancey to Johnson, 25 Dec. 1765, ibid., p. 827.

63. DeLancey to Lady Warren, 1 Mar. 1770, Gage Papers, G/Am/93.

64. It is known that Johnson collected rents from the tenants on Miln's tract, at all times refusing to give DeLancey an account of them. DeLancey in 1772 reckoned he owed the Warren estate about NY£35 from such sources, DeLancey to the Warren heirs, 8 Aug. 1772, Gage Papers, G/Am/137. See also Warren Papers 55, NYHS.

65. For which he charged Lady Warren £6 8s. 11d. 25 Sept. 1760, Gage Papers, G/Am/82.

66. DeLancey to Bleecker, 17 Oct. 1765, Warren Papers 56, NYHS. See also Bleecker to DeLancey, 2 Sept. 1765, DeLancey Papers 41, NYHS.

67. DeLancey to Johnson, 26 Oct. 1765, O'Callaghan, ed., *The Documentary History of the State of New York,* 2: 823.

68. Ibid., pp. 823-24.

69. Johnson to DeLancey, 7 Nov. 1765, ibid., p. 826.

70. Although Glen as early as November 1766 was being sent instructions by DeLancey, his official agency at NY£15 a year began in June 1767; see his accounts, Warren Papers 76, NYHS.

71. DeLancey Papers 43, NYHS, 31 May 1766, Bleecker to DeLancey.

72. Bleecker to DeLancey, 7 Dec. 1765, Warren Papers 60; DeLancey to Bleecker, 15 Jan. 1766, Warren Papers 62; a plan of Remsen's subdivision is in Warren Papers 16; the legal opinion of William Cockburn and Christopher Yates of Schenectady, 31 July 1766 is in Warren Papers 61b, NYHS.

73. Bleecker to DeLancey, 7 Dec. 1765, Warren Papers 60, NYHS.

74. Details taken from the 1769 rent roll, Warren Papers 55, NYHS.

75. See DeLancey's instructions to Glen, 13 Nov. 1766, Warren Papers 61, NYHS.

76. Gage Papers, G/Am/142.

77. Paid 1 Nov. 1742 to cover arrears to 29 Aug. 1742, Gage Papers, G/Am/1.

78. Beverley Waugh Bond, *The Quit Rent System in the American Colonies* (New Haven, 1919), chapter 9, "Royal Quit Rents in New York," pp. 254-85.

79. This was the opinion of James Duane, retained by Oliver DeLancey in 1772. Duane had a large estate near the Mohawk, Gage Papers, G/Am/145.

80. See *The Colonial Laws of New York from the Year 1664 to the Revolution* (Albany, 1894), 4: 584-601, 612-14, 1036-38.

81. DeLancey to Warren heirs, 8 Aug. 1772, Gage Papers, G/Am/138.

82. Details taken from Duane's legal opinion prepared in 1773, Gage Papers, G/Am/145.

83. Bradstreet to DeLancey, 5 July 1772, DeLancey Papers 69, NYHS.

84. Details taken from DeLancey's "Memorandum about the Land sold at Vendue . . . for arrears of Quit Rent," Watts Papers, NYHS.

85. Edward P. Alexander, *A Revolutionary Conservative: James Duane of New York* (New York, 1938). There is a recent study of Scott by Harry M. Dunkak, "John Morin Scott and Whig Politics in New York City (1752-1769)" (Ph.D. dissertation, St. John's University, 1968).

86. The letter is reproduced in Gage Papers, G/Am/145.

87. DeLancey Papers 67, NYHS; witnessed by Bradstreet. See Don R. Gerlach, *Philip Schuyler and the American Revolution in New York, 1733-1777* (Lincoln, Nebraska, 1964), pp. 218-25, which devotes part of chapter 6 to the affair. Gerlach confuses Warren's tract with Cosby Manor.

88. DeLancey to Schuyler, 5 Aug. 1772, original MS bound into an extra-illustrated edition of John W. Francis, *Old New York* (New York, 1895), in NYHS.

89. DeLancey Papers 70, NYHS.

90. Gage Papers, G/Am/145 for details. The opinion is undated, but in a letter from DeLancey to Skinner, 24 Feb. 1773, Duane is reported to be preparing it; Gage Papers, G/Am/143; on 15 Aug. 1773, Skinner told Stephen DeLancey and John Watts Jr. that he had read it, Gage Papers, G/Am/152.

91. Ibid.

92. William Skinner and Charles Fitzroy to DeLancey, 29 Nov. 1772, Gage Papers, G/Am/139.

93. Ibid.

94. Forrester's opinion, Gage Papers, G/Am/145a.

95. Skinner called Scott this in a letter to DeLancey, 25 Jan. 1774, Gage Papers, G/Am/157.

96. DeLancey to Skinner, 24 Feb. 1773, Gage Papers, G/Am/143; Skinner to DeLancey, 19 Apr. 1773, Gage Papers, G/Am/147; DeLancey to Skinner, 10 Nov. 1773, Gage Papers, G/Am/157; see also the 1773-74 accounts, Gage Papers, G/Am/158, payment was made by Duane on 8 Aug.

97. Scott to DeLancey, 26 June 1774, Gage Papers, G/Am/165; DeLancey to Scott, 4 July 1774, ibid.

98. DeLancey to the heirs, 4 Aug. 1774, Gage Papers, G/Am/166.

99. See the 1774-75 accounts, Gage Papers, G/Am/170. Skinner's dismay at the additional costs was expressed in a letter of 15 Apr. 1775 to DeLancey, of which there were two distinct drafts, Gage Papers, G/Am/174 and 175.

100. Skinner to DeLancey, 25 Jan. 1774, Gage Papers, G/Am/157.

101. DeLancey to Skinner, 24 Feb. 1773, Gage Papers, G/Am/143.

102. Gage Papers, G/Am/107, G/Am/141.

103. Warren Papers 68, NYHS.

104. See rent roll for 1788, Warren Papers 74, which lists the arrears against each tenant, and from which the total rent can be calculated.

105. Abingdon and Southampton to Watts, 30 June 1788, DeLancey Papers 90, NYHS. See Watts's rough notes which indicate that a trickle of rental income was reaching him, Watts Papers, NYHS, and DePeyster Papers 1, nos. 17, 19, 21.

106. I have not found a complete map of the tract, but one for the Gage section is in the Watts Papers, NYHS, while a map of the Southampton section is in the Executive Department, Office of General Services, Albany, O.G.S. Map No. 439.

107. Watts–Abingdon accounts, 1789, Watts Papers, NYHS.

108. "Lot A of the Estate of Sir Peter Warren in the State of New York in America, now Miss Skinner's, 1 Sept. 1789," Gage Papers, G/Am/182b.

109. 5 Sept. 1774, DeLancey to the Warren heirs, Gage Papers, G/Am/167.

110. DeLancey to Skinner, 4 April 1775, Gage Papers, G/Am/173.

111. Alexander, *A Revolutionary Conservative*, chapters 4 and 10, pp. 52-67, 215-36.

Chapter 5

1. Two useful, unpublished accounts still worth noticing are, Arthur Shelburn Williamson, "Credit Relations between Colonial and English Merchants in the Eighteenth Century" (Ph.D. dissertation, State University of Iowa, 1927), and Benjamin Redford Baldwin, "The Debts Owed by Americans to British Creditors, 1763-1802" (Ph.D. dissertation, Indiana University,

1932). By far the most thorough study, the product particularly of research during the past twenty years, relates to the southern plantation economy, especially the Virginia tobacco trade. Jacob M. Price, "The Rise of Glasgow in the Chesapeake Tobacco Trade," *William and Mary Quarterly,* 3rd series, 11 (1954): 179-200; Price, "The Economic Growth of the Chesapeake and the European Market, 1697-1775," *Journal of Economic History,* 24 (1964): 496-517; Price, "Capital and Credit in the Chesapeake Tobacco Trade, 1750-1775," in Virginia Bever Plat and David Curtis Skaggs, *Of Mother Country and Plantations: Proceedings of the Twenty-Seventh Conference in Early American History* (Bowling Green, Ohio, 1971), pp. 7-36; John M. Hemphill, "Virginia and the English Commercial System, 1689-1733" (Ph.D. dissertation, Princeton University, 1964); Samuel M. Rosenblatt, "The Significance of Credit in the Tobacco Consignment Trade; A Study of John Norton & Sons, 1768-1775," *William and Mary Quarterly,* 3rd series, 19 (1962): 383-99; Emory G. Evans, "Planter Indebtedness and the Coming of the Revolution in Virginia," *William and Mary Quarterly,* 3rd series, 19 (1962): 511-33; Aubrey C. Land, "Economic Behavior in a Planting Society: The Eighteenth Century Chesapeake," *Journal of Southern History,* 33 (1967): 469-85.

2. "Book debts" are debts on account current. For the consignment agent in Britain they were accounts receivable; for the American debtor, accounts payable. The conversion of such debts into bonds and mortgages was by no means universal. The example of the House of Lascelles is such an exception. "The partners allowed the debts on account current to run into thousands without asking for a bond or a mortgage . . . it was generally believed that a planter's credit was blasted by a mortgage." Richard Pares, "A London West India Merchant House 1740-69," in Richard Pares and A.J.P. Taylor, eds., *Essays Presented to Sir Lewis Namier* (London, 1956), p. 99.

3. This was the legal ceiling on debts in England. An act to reduce the rate of interest, without any prejudice to parliamentary securities. 12 Ann c. 16. *The Statutes at Large* (London, 1768), 4: 45-46. For an excellent analysis of one serious liquidity crisis, see Richard B. Sheridan, "The British Credit Crisis of 1772 and the American colonies," *The Journal of Economic History,* 20 (1960): 161-86.

4. English factors also of course invested in "American" shipping. For a recent study, see John J. McCusker, "Sources of Investment Capital in the Colonial Philadelphia Shipping Industry," *The Journal of Economic History,* 32 (1972): 146-57.

5. *The Remarkable Case of Peter Hasenclever* (London, 1773); Bining, *British Regulation of the Colonial Iron Industry,* p. 18.

6. The Beekman family is an obvious exception. See Philip L. White, *The Beekmans of New York in Politics and Commerce 1647-1877* (New York, 1956) and Philip L.

White, ed., *The Beekman Mercantile Papers, 1746-1799*, 3 vols. (New York, 1956).

7. *The Colonial Laws of New York from the Year 1664 to the Revolution* (New York; 1894), 1: 1004-5. In May 1717 the rate had been fixed at 6 per cent, but within a very short time was raised to 8 per cent. Ibid., pp. 609-10. For the new law in 1737, ibid., 2: 980-81.

8. The original deed is among the John E. Stillwell Collection, NYHS; 21 July 1731.

9. See Appendix B, for the list of Warren's New York bond debtors, 1725-69.

10. See chapter 3.

11. There were few notes of hand. For instance, in 1731 Warren took a NY£50 note from Peter DeLancey for a slave, Gage Papers, G/Am/13, p. 13. In 1733 he took a note for NY£19 11s. 1d. from James DeLancey for goods purchased in England for the Chief Justice, Gage Papers, G/Am/20.

12. Details taken from Gage Papers, G/Am/1, G/Am/13, p. 13 and G/Am/18a. All these obligations had been paid off by Sept. 1750, according to a report sent Warren by Richard Nicholls, Gage Papers, G/Am/64.

13. Gage Papers, G/Am/70. The act was passed 24 March 1772. *Colonial Laws of New York* 5: 440-50.

14. The Butler–Cowley agreement to sell was dated 13 Nov. 1736, Warren Papers 15, Cowley borrowed most of the purchase money from Abraham Lodge, 13 June 1737, DePeyster Papers 1, no. 8, NYHS.

15. The properties fetched NY£700. Warren held a NY£500 mortgage, while Richard Nicholls held a second mortgage for NY£298. As Nicholls was repaid in full, Warren therefore recovered only the difference or NY£402, of his loan, thus adding NY£98 to the purchase price. The deed of release is dated 24 Sept. 1736, DeLancey Deeds, NYHS.

16. Gage Papers, G/Am/13, p. 13.

17. Two loans each of NY£100, 23 Aug. 1733 and 15 Oct. 1733, were repaid on 23 Aug. 1734 and 18 Mar. 1737/38. Gage Papers, G/Am/18a, G/Am/20.

18. This was repaid by 1750. Gage Papers, G/Am/64.

19. Repaid in two amounts of NY£673 and NY£211 on 20 Jan. and 23 Feb. 1750. See Warren account book 1749-52, Warren Papers, WLCL.

20. Gage Papers, G/Am/2, the loan was made 20 Mar. 1752. See settlement of the Warren estate in 1752, Gage Papers, G/Am/103.

21. 6 Mar. 1744/45, @ 7%; 23 July 1752, Gage Papers, G/Am/98a.

22. Oliver DeLancey to Lady Warren, 1 Feb. 1755, Gage Addit. 1201.

23. 2 June 1752, NY£410 was repaid in February 1755, NY£645 in December 1759, NY£233 in May 1761. See O. DeLancey to Lady Warren, 1 Feb. 1755, 19 Dec. 1759 and 7 May 1761, Gage Addit. 1201.

24. Warren Papers 18, NYHS.

25. DeLancey to Lady Warren, 23 Oct. 1753, Gage Addit. 1201.

26. "All persons indebted to the estate of Sir Peter Warren, are

desired to pay the same to Oliver DeLancey, to prevent Trouble," ran the advertisement, appearing in the *New York Mercury* from 22 Oct. to 19 Nov. 1753 and in the *New York Weekly Post Boy* from 8 Oct. to 3 Dec. 1753.

27. New York passed a great many laws between 1730 and 1775, relating to insolvent debtors. Most expired within a year of their being passed. In general they greatly favoured creditors, as debtors were required to submit detailed statements of their assets, real and personal (except clothing and bedding for their families and their tools of trade), as well as their debts. Creditors, through "Commissioners of Bankrupt," were assigned assets to meet the debts owed them. The costs of the suit and court costs were also paid off from the debtors assets. It is not known how rigorously the law was practised. *The Colonial Laws of New York,* 2: 669-75, 753-58; 3: 312, 694, 822, 835, 866, 924, 939, 1019, 1099; 4: 10, 18-19, 103, 182, 345, 370, 526, 533-34, 747, 862, 928, 949; 5: 63, 120, 126, 195, 206, 416-18, 451, 595-600, 618-21, 701-7, 807-33.

28. Let a selection from those debts that were paid off at this time suffice to show that the credit advanced by the Warrens though allowed to remain outstanding for many years, proved sound in the end. A NY£15 debt against Hendrick Vroom of Middlesex, New Jersey contracted in 1733 was paid off in Oct. 1754, Gage Papers, G/Am/72. A NY£100 bond taken from Capt. Walter Butler, dating from 1737, was paid 17 May 1754, Gage Papers,

G/Am/82. A NY£325 bond given by James Hude, Dirch Schuyler, and Jacob and William Ouke of New Brunswick, New Jersey, in June 1739 was paid off in Oct. 1745; see Wm. Ouke to Oliver DeLancey, 25 March and 7 Oct. 1754, DeLancey Papers 27, NYHS, and Gage Papers, G/Am/72. Three bonds, each for NY£125, given in 1741, 1742, and 1743 by James Doughty of Oyster Bay, Queens County, were cleared on 13 July 1758, Gage Papers, G/Am/79a. William Smith had been indebted to the Warrens since 1741 for the sum of NY£98 15s. which was paid off 11 Oct. 1757, Gage Papers, G/Am/82. In 1731 Smith borrowed NY£500 which was not repaid until 1741, Gage Papers, G/Am/13, p. 13 and G/Am/20. No mention is made of the Smith family's indebtedness in L.S.F. Upton, *The Loyal Whig: William Smith of New York and Quebec* (Toronto: 1969). A 1742 bond of NY£150 given by Samuel Hunt and Henry Dusenberry of Westchester County, was paid off 1 Aug. 1755, Gage Papers, G/Am/82. A NY£1,200 bond given by Nicholas Bayard in 1743 was paid off 10 Oct. 1758, Gage Papers, G/Am/79a. Two 1745 bonds of NY£100 each, one to David, Samuel, and George Merrit of White Plains, and the other to David Lane, Samuel Dean, and Thomas Waters of Northcastle were paid off 1 Dec. 1754, Gage Papers, G/Am/72.

29. Details found in Gage Papers, G/Am/1, G/Am/26 and G/Am/64.

30. See John Glen's accounts, Warren Papers 76, NYHS. Glen acted as DeLancey's agent for the DeLancey as well as the Warren interests on the Mohawk.

31. Gage Papers, G/Am/76a.

32. Gage Papers, G/Am/134.

33. Captain DePeyster Papers, NYHS; Gage Papers, G/Am/134, 10 April 1772.

34. Report dated 22 June 1795, DeLancey Papers 66, NYHS. See also Lord Southampton's letter to John Watts Jr., 5 Oct. 1795, Watts Papers, Box 9, NYHS.

35. Baldwin, "The Debts Owed by Americans," p. 215. See 1783 Treaty, Articles IV, V, VI, and VII; 1794 Treaty, Article VI. In 1802 an Anglo-American Convention was concluded by which some £600,000 was paid by the government of the United States to the British government in final compensation for debts still outstanding. For its part the British government undertook to distribute the sum among petitioning British merchants. With this the debt question, which had so adversely affected relations between the two powers, was settled.

36. Many such views are found in the pamphlets in Andrew McFarland Davis, ed., *Colonial Currency Reprints, 1682-1751* (New York, reprint edition; 1965), 4 vols. For instance, Benjamin Franklin believed that it was "impossible by any Laws to restrain Men from giving and receiving exhorbitant Interest, where money is suitably scarce. For he that wants Money will find out Ways to give 10 per cent, when he cannot have it for less, altho' the Law forbids to take more than 6 per cent." Benjamin Franklin, *A Modest Inquiry into the Nature and Necessity of a Paper-Currency* (Philadelphia, 1729), in Davis, *Colonial Currency Reprints,* 2: 336-37.

37. The effectiveness of the usury laws has been studied by British scholars. It is now generally agreed that from the 1770s onwards the laws were freely evaded by lending on annuities for the life of the seller. Sybil Campbell, "Usury and Annuities of the Eighteenth Century," *The Law Quarterly Review,* 44 (1928): 473-91. For other ways by which the usury laws were circumvented in England, cf. L.S. Pressnell, *Country Banking in the Industrial Revolution* (Oxford; 1956), pp. 317-19. See also his "The Rate of Interest in the Eighteenth Century," in L.S. Pressnell, ed., *Studies in the Industrial Revolution* (London, 1960), pp. 178-214. The evidence for the colonies is unsatisfactory. I have seen none for New York, though in New England Thomas Hancock at times advanced credit at 7 per cent, when the legal ceiling was 6 per cent. Thomas Hancock Papers, box 6, folder 4, Baker Library. For Virginia, see Joseph A. Ernst, "The Robinson Scandal Redvivus: Money, Debts, and Politics in Revolutionary Virginia," *Virginia Magazine of History and Biography,* 7 (1969): 146-73.

38. Gage Papers, G/Am/64.

39. Gage Papers, G/Am/79a, 29 May 1759.

40. Three studies concerned with the DeLanceys' land interests

merit attention: Harry B. Yoshpe, "The DeLancey Estate: Did the Revolution Democratize Landholding in New York?" *New York History,* 17 (1936): 167-79, and Sung Bok Kim, "The Manor of Cortlandt," as well as Bonomi, *A Factious People.*

41. For a list of small money lenders, probably quite typical, see Helen Wilkinson Reynolds, ed., *Eighteenth Century Records of Dutchess County, New York,* Dutchess County Historical Society Collections, 6 (Poughkeepsie, N.Y.; 1938). The list contains 519 mortgages (many for amounts of less than NY£10) registered by the county clerk between 1754 and 1800. Most of the capital came from New York City, Long Island, or Dutchess County. Lenders included "individual investors, trustees, executors of estates," p. 4. Among the Alexander Papers, box 1, NYHS, there is a list of bad debts totalling NY£3,137, dated 15 July 1768, of which the largest amounted to NY£68, with most sums ranging from NY£1 to NY£5. Information supplied by Professor Joseph A. Ernst. There is much good sense in Pressnell, *Country Banking,* who notes in reference to England: "Much lending and borrowing was small scale, local, and personal, to oblige friends and relatives and neighbours," p. 185. Land, "Economic Behaviour in a Planting Society," speaks of "the tissue of debt so striking to investigators. . . . In the records it appears that everyone owed everyone else — and that was not far from the case," p. 479. See also Alice Hanson Jones, "Wealth Estimates for the American Middle Colonies, 1774," *Economic Development and Cultural Change,* 18, No. 4, Part 2 (1970), p. 4: "Despite the absence of banks and of a uniform currency, there was a large volume of transactions by credit, and financial assets and liabilities were important elements in many estates, even ones of small size. Common entries include notes, bonds, book debts, money placed at interest with a given individual, accounts owing, and balance due."

42. See William S. Sachs, "The Business Outlook in the Northern Colonies, 1750-1775" (Ph.D. dissertation, Columbia University, 1957) for a most useful general analysis of the pre-revolutionary economy of the colonies to the north of Maryland. See also his "Interurban Correspondents and the Development of a National Economy before the Revolution: New York as a Case Study," *New York History* 36 (1955): 320-55. The one important work on New York merchants before 1776 refers only briefly to the subject of private credit. See Virginia D. Harrington, *The New York Merchant on the Eve of the Revolution* (New York, 1935) for such brief remarks as "Investments most preferred were those comprising personal financial engagements — bonds, notes, or mortgages were the most common as they combined mobility with security," p. 131. The most complete account of an individual merchant family of New York in colonial times makes equally unsatisfactory references to this sort of activity. See White, *The Beekmans,* pp. 215, 402-3, 434, 484, 501.

43. See Richard Pares, *Yankees and Creoles: The trade between North America and the West Indies before the American Revolution* (London, 1956), esp. pp. 24-29. Professor James G. Lydon of Duquesne University is preparing a comparative study of the ports of Boston and Philadelphia in the eighteenth century.

44. The 10 per cent ceiling was created by acts passed in South Carolina in 1720 and in Georgia in 1755, in *The Statutes at Large of South Carolina*, edited by Thomas Cooper (Charleston, 1838), 3: 104-5, 132-34; *Acts Passed by the General Assembly [of Georgia], 1755 to 1774, now first printed*, edited by George Wymberley-Jones de Renne (Wormloe, 1881), pp. 61-62. Virginia was unique among the colonies in establishing a 5 per cent ceiling in 1748 (reduced from 6 per cent), William Walker Hening, ed., *The Statutes at Large, being A Collection of All the Laws of Virginia from the First Session of the Legislature* (Richmond, 1819), 6: 101-4. Most colonies maintained a 6 per cent ceiling: Maryland in 1684 (confirmed by later acts in 1692, 1704 and 1715), Massachusetts in 1693, Pennsylvania in 1723 (having had since 1700 a ceiling of 8 per cent), Delaware in 1726 (likewise reduced from 8 per cent), North Carolina in 1741, Rhode Island in 1767, and New Hampshire in 1769. See respectively *Acts of the Assembly Passed in the Province of Maryland From 1692 to 1715* (London, 1723), pp. 27-28; *The Acts and Resolves, Public and Private, of the Province of Massachusetts Bay* (Boston, 1869), 1: 113; *The Statutes at Large of Pennsylvania from 1682 to 1782*, compiled by J.T. Mitchell and Henry Flanders (Philadelphia, 1896), 2: 17, 3: 338-39; *Laws of the State of Delaware From the Fourteenth Day of October, One Thousand Seven Hundred to The Eighteenth Day of August, One Thousand Seven Hundred and Ninety Seven* (New Castle, 1797), 2: 96; *The State Records of North Carolina*, edited by Walter Clark (Goldsboro, 1904), 23: 169; *Acts and Laws of The English Colony of Rhode-Island and Providence-Plantation in New England in America: Made and Passed since the Revision in June, 1767* (Newport, 1772), p. 304; *Laws of New Hampshire, including Public and Private Acts and Resolves, Royal Commissions and Instructions*, edited by Henry Harrison Metcalfe (Bristol, 1915), 3: 361-63, 515-17. New Jersey followed New York's lead by reducing its ceiling on interest rates from 8 to 7 per cent in March 1738/39, *Acts of the General Assembly of the Province of New Jersey, from 1702, to 1776*, edited by Samuel Allison (Burlington, 1776). I do not know the legal ceiling on the rate of interest in Connecticut, for the only act concerning usury which I have uncovered was passed in May 1734, entitled: "An Act in addition to an Act for Restraining Excessive Usury." It contains no reference to the legal rate of interest. The earlier act is not found in *The Public Records of the Colony of Connecticut*, edited by C.J. Hoadley (Hartford, 1873), vol. for 1726-1735.

45. For England, see H.J. Habakkuk, "The English Land Market in the Eighteenth

Century," in J.S. Bromley and
E.H. Kossman, eds., *Britain and the
Netherlands* (Oxford, 1960),
p. 161. See also his "Long-Term
Rate of Interest and the Price of
Land in the Seventeenth
Century," *The Economic History
Review,* 2nd series, 5 (1954):
26-45.
   46. In England the movement in
the rate of interest followed the
rate of yield on government
securities by roughly a six months'
interval, with the rates on private
lending almost invariably higher
owing to the "greater elements of
risk in lending to private
individuals than in entrusting
money to the state." T.S. Ashton,
*An Economic History of England: The
18th Century* (London, 1961),
p. 28; also his *Economic Fluctuations
in England, 1700-1800* (Oxford,
1959), p. 87.

Chapter 6

   1. In 1737 he was Peter
Faneuil's partner in a clandestine
shipment of foodstuffs to
Louisbourg. Faneuil to Warren,
19 Sept. 1737, in Faneuil
Letterbook 1737-1739, F-4, Baker
Library. He also traded in tea on
behalf of the DeLanceys of New
York. Warren to Oliver DeLancey,
30 Dec. 1742, Warren Papers 22,
NYHS. He imported trade goods
for his nephew, William Johnson,
as was seen in chapter 3. In 1750
he invested directly in two English
merchant ships. Gage Papers,
G/Am/2, G/Am/5, G/Am/97. See
chapter 12, n. 3.

   2. Between 1736 and 1739
Warren rented a house in Boston
from James Allen, a member of
the Massachusetts Council. Gage
Papers, G/Am/130. In 1746 his
Boston residence was the home of
the Louisbourg engineer, John
Henry Bastide; see Thomas
Hancock's letters to Bastide in
1746, Hancock Papers, box 11,
Baker Library. Two of Warren's
children were born in Boston, his
eldest daughter, Ann, in October
1738. *Boston Gazette,* 16 Oct. 1738
for announcement.
   3. See especially, Davis, *Currency
and Banking, in the Province of the
Massachusetts Bay,* 2 vols. (New
York, 1970), 1: 203-43, 437-40.
   4. Oliver DeLancey to the
Warren heirs (Charles Fitzroy, the
Earl of Abingdon, Col. William
Skinner), 10 Apr. 1772, Gage
Papers, G/Am/133.
   5. Bollan later acted as agent in
London for Massachusetts
(1745-62) and for the
Massachusetts Council (1768-75).
Born in 1710 he died in England
in 1782. See Malcolm Freiberg,
"William Bollan: Agent for
Massachusetts," *More Books,*
23 (1948): 43-54, 90-100, 135-46,
168-82, 212-20.
   6. 11 Sept. 1740, Gage Papers,
G/Am/11. Paid to Warren at New
York by John Peagrum, Surveyor
General of Customs in North
America (1732-42).
   7. 3 Aug. 1741, Gage Papers,
G/Am/22 and G/Am/38; also in
the Norcross Collection of the
Greenough Collection in the
Massachusetts Historical Society.
   8. Ibid., and Gage Papers,
G/Am/25; 16 Jan. 1744.

9. See chapter 3.

10. As early as August 1742 Warren had made Clinton an offer even before the governor had left England. For details see George Clinton Papers, vols. 1-4, WLCL. For details of Warren involvement in New York politics, see chapter 2.

11. 14 Nov. 1746, Gage Papers, G/Am/31. "Old Tenor" was the name given to Massachusetts colony bills of credit issued from 1702, until Feb. 1736/37, when a new act created "New Tenor" bills. Bills of Old Tenor were to be "in value equal to money," but suffered from depreciation, so the New Tenor bills were given a value equal to silver at 6s. 8d. per ounce. But massive depreciation, especially between 1744 and 1749, undermined the value of both Old Tenor and New Tenor. In 1702 a £100 bill cost M£133, in 1737 M£500, in 1746 M£760, in 1749 M£1,100. See Davis, *Currency and Banking,* 1: 20n, 126n, 168, 367, 369-70.

12. 19 Nov. 1746, Gage Papers, G/Am/34; witnessed by William Tattum, Warren's secretary.

13. These details were noted by Thomas Hancock on the two notes, 15 Dec. 1763, Gage Papers, G/Am/31 and G/Am/34.

14. See Gage Papers, G/Am/2, G/Am/5, G/Am/31-38, G/Am/85; also Norcross Collection, MHS; and Chamberlain Collection of the Hancock MSS. Ch.M.1.10., Boston Public Library. Hatch, the most prominent landowner in Dorchester, Suffolk County, Mass., led a company at Louisbourg in 1745. See Louis Effingham De Forest, *Louisbourg Journals 1745*

(New York, 1932), pp. 40, 54, 128, 131, 150, 151, 153. Nathaniel, his son, was a Harvard graduate in the class of 1742; John Langdon Sibley and Clifford Kenyon Shipton, *Harvard Graduates: Biographical Sketches of those who attended Harvard College,* 11 [1741-1745] (Cambridge, Mass., 1960): 150-52.

15. Malbone (1695-1768) was born in Virginia but settled in Newport and became a leading merchant with particular interest in the West Indies rum trade. See Howard W. Preston, "Godfrey Malbone's Connecticut Investment," *Rhode Island Historical Society Collections,* 16 (1923): 115-20; and Ruel Pardee Tolman, *The Life and Works of Edward Greene Malbone 1777-1807* (New York, 1958), pp. 4-7.

16. Brenton was an important inhabitant of Newport, Rhode Island, having inherited his fortune from his uncle and owning one of the chief homes in the town. See George Champlin Mason, *Reminiscences of Newport* (Newport, 1884), pp. 365-74.

17. Updike was born in Rhode Island and became attorney general of the province. His grandfather, a settler in New Amsterdam, had immigrated to Newport in 1664 and laid the foundation of the family fortune. *Dictionary of American Biography,* 19: 120-21.

18. Bagley, a native of Amesbury, Mass., commanded a company at Louisbourg in 1745-46. See DeForest, *Louisbourg Journals.* pp. 135, 143, 145, 148, 153, 154, 156, 166; also Rev. Everett S. Stackpole, *History of*

Durham, Maine with Genealogical Notes (Lewiston, Maine, 1899), pp. 10-11, 149.

19. Williams, a Harvard graduate, served as a selectman of Hatfield (1732-1763),and amassed "considerable wealth through trading, farming, and land speculation." *Dictionary of American Biography,* 20: 266.

20. Warren to Messrs. Frankland, Apthorp, and Hancock, 20 Nov. 1746, Gage Papers, G/Am/6.

21. Warren to Frankland, Apthorp, and Hancock, 24 Nov. 1746, ibid.

22. Brinley (1690-1765), whose mother was an Apthorp, was one of the founders of King's Chapel, Boston. He was born in England, educated at Eton; served as deputy surveyor general of Massachusetts; held a large estate at Roxbury, and was colonel of militia. He was cousin to Cradock. See Francis S. Drake, *The Town of Roxbury* (Boston, 1905), p. 327.

23. Cradock was collector of customs for the port of Boston, and a deputy judge of the Vice Admiralty Court there. Two of his daughters married Brinley's sons.

24. Lockman, a naturalized British subject, was made judge of the Vice Admiralty Court in Rhode Island through the patronage of the Duke of Newcastle, and came to the colony for the first time in 1743. See Gertrude Selwyn Kimball, ed., *ı ne Correspondence of the Colonial Governors of Rhode Island 1723-1775* (Boston, 1902), 1: 224, 227 ff. See also 5 Geo. II, c.1., private acts (1732).

25. Jones has been described in 1763 as being "not worth a farthing," Thomas Hancock to Lady Warren, 24 Nov. 1763, Hancock Letterbook 1762-1783, JH-6, Baker Library.

26. Gage Papers, G/Am/2, G/Am/5, G/Am/36.

27. 4 Feb. 1746/7, @ 5%, Gage Papers, G/Am/36. Belcher (1682-1757) was born in Massachusetts, educated at Harvard; was governor of Massachusetts (1730-41), and of New Jersey (1747-d); a great benefactor of Princeton. See Sibley and Shipton, *Harvard Graduates,* 4: 434-49.

28. Ayrault, born at East Greenwich, Rhode Island, was the son of a Huguenot who had received letters of denization in 1702. See Elisha R. Potter, *Memoire concerning the French Settlements and French Settlers in the Colony of Rhode Island* (Providence, R.I., 1879), p. 106. Gage Papers, G/Am/59. Repaid 14 Nov. 1751.

29. Oliver DeLancey to Susan Warren, 1 and 25 Dec. 1753, Gage Addit. 1201.

30. Paid by a bill on Commodore Charles Knowles in 1748, Gage Papers, G/Am/2.

31. Nathaniel Hatch to John Watts Sr., Boston, 10 Dec. 1753, Watts Papers 4, NYHS.

32. The unsigned and undated draft is in Warren Papers 44, NYHS. Also Watts Papers, box 4, NYHS.

33. Charles Apthorp and Thomas Hancock to Lady Warren, 1 May 1754, Warren Papers 47, by a bill drawn on William Baker of London, NYHS; Peter Warren–Thomas Hancock accounts, 1759-63, Hancock Papers, MHS.

34. Gage Papers, G/Am/2.

35. Apthorp and Hancock to Lady Warren, 1 May 1754, Warren Papers 47, NYHS, by Hancock's bill on Messrs. Kilby and Barnard in London.

36. Chamberlain Collection of Hancock MSS., Boston Public Library, Ch.M.1.10.

37. See various letters in Belcher Letter Book, MHS, especially Belcher to Warren, 8 June 1748 and 8 June 1751. See also Gage Papers, G/Am/2 and G/Am/5.

38. 11 July 1760 and 15 Sept. 1763, Warren–Hancock accounts, 1759-63, Hancock Papers, MHS.

39. 1 July 1760, Chamberlain Collection of Hancock MSS., Boston Public Library, Ch. M.1.10. See also Thomas Hancock to Lady Warren, 3 Dec. 1759, 20-21 May [June], 23 June, 4 July, and 5 Aug. 1760; Thomas Hancock Letterbook 1750-1762, TH-4, Baker Library.

40. 12 Apr. 1748, Chamberlain Collection.

41. 12 Nov. 1751, Gage Papers, G/Am/63.

42. DeLancey to Lady Warren, 15 Dec. 1754, Gage Addit. 1201.

43. DeLancey to Lady Warren, 4 Oct. 1757, ibid. Lady Warren's letter has not survived.

44. Apthorp to DeLancey, 10 Apr. 1758, Gage Papers, G/Am/101. Apthorp claimed to have been bothering the two about their debt for many years. "They have made some Payments towards the Principal and promise to finish it this Sumer; Coll⁰ Brinley I spoke to yesterday he promises to write you . . . don't chuse to sue him."

45. Brinley to DeLancey, 10 Apr. 1758, Gage Addit. 1201.

46. DeLancey to Lady Warren, 25 Apr. 1758, ibid.

47. Warren–Hancock accounts, 1759-1763, Hancock MSS., MHS.

48. 10 Jan., 24 May, and 6 July 1767, DeLancey to John Hancock, DeLancey Papers, Museum of the City of New York, doc. 49.9.4, Hancock to DeLancey, 5 Aug. 1767, Gage Papers, G/Am/110, Fitch to DeLancey, 6 Aug. 1767, Gage Papers, G/Am/86. See also John Hancock to Lady Warren, 25 July 1765, Hancock Letterbook 1762-83, JH-6, Baker Library.

49. John Watts Jr. to Daniel Ludlow, 20 Sept. 1787, Watts Papers, NYHS.

50. Watts to Hancock, 20 Sept. 1787, ibid.

51. Watts to Ludlow, 20 Sept. 1787, ibid.

52. David Sears to John Watts, 30 Aug. 1788 and 22 Apr. 1789, ibid.

53. John Lowell to John Watts, Boston, 19 Aug. 1794, Watts Papers 6. See also Edward Brinley's letter to Watts, 20 July 1794, Watts Papers 1, and Watts's reply to Lowell's letter, 8 Oct. 1794, Warren Papers 81, NYHS.

54. Edward Brinley to Watts, 26 May 1795, DePeyster Papers 1, no. 23, NYHS.

55. Deed dated 2 July 1805, F. L. Gay Collection, MHS.

56. 2 May 1693, *The Acts and Resolves, Public and Private of the Province of the Massachusetts Bay*, 1: 111.

57. The state of the loan market in 1746 is unknown. Thomas Hancock asked 7 per cent from Allan McLean in April 1746, and

5½ per cent from Henry Smith in November 1746. These are the only two such loans recorded in 1746 among his papers, the most complete collection of its type for Massachusetts. Thomas Hancock Papers, box 6 (folder 4), Baker Library.

58. See Alice Hanson Jones, "Wealth Estimates for the New England Colonies about 1770," *Journal of Economic History* 32 (1972): 98-127.

59. Howard M. Chapin, *Rhode Island Privateers in King George's War 1739-1748* (Providence, 1926), p. 173. The first displaced 180 tons and carried 130 men, the second 200 tons and 130 men, the last 80 tons and 70 men.

60. Malbone must have prospered in the next war, for by the time of his death he left his two surviving sons land in Connecticut and Rhode Island as well as 27 black slaves, and livestock comprising 80 cows, 45 oxen, 30 calves, 30 steers, 6 horses, 600 sheep, 180 goats, 150 pigs, and an unspecified number of poultry. See Preston, "Godfrey Malbone's Connecticut Investment."

61. In 1776 the commodity price index stood at 114, but by 1805 it had moved ahead 64 per cent to 187. See Schumpeter, "English Prices and Public Finances, 1660-1822,"p. 35.

Chapter 7

1. Edgar K. Thompson, "George Anson in the Province of South Carolina," *The Mariner's Mirror,* 53 (1967): 279-80.

2. This brief survey is based on M. Eugene Sirmans, *Colonial South Carolina, A Political History 1663-1763* (Chapel Hill, 1966); Richard P. Sherman, *Robert Johnson, Proprietary and Royal Governor of South Carolina* (Columbia, S.C., 1966); Robert L. Meriwether, *The Expansion of South Carolina 1729-1765* (Kingsport, Tenn., 1940); Sutherland, *Population Distribution,* the chapter on South Carolina, pp. 236-53.

3. Elizabeth Donnan, "The Slave Trade into South Carolina before the Revolution," *American Historical Review* 33 (1928): 804-28.

4. W. Robert Higgins, "The South Carolina Negro Duty Law" (M.A. essay, University of South Carolina, 1967), p. 1.

5. Ibid., p. 28.

6. Leila Seller, *Charleston Business on the Eve of the American Revolution* (Chapel Hill, N.C., 1934).

7. Warren's copy of the plan is in Gage Papers, GA 838. The official copy is in Colonial Plat, Book I, p. 400, South Carolina Archives, Columbia, S.C.

8. Royal Grants, Book 1, p. 167, South Carolina Archives. The letters patent were dated 7 July 1733, and the deed was drawn up on the 11th.

9. Gage Papers, GA 839.

10. Land Papers, Book 2, p. 467, Colonial Plat, Book 3, pp. 100-1, South Carolina Archives.

11. Quit Rent Ledgers, 1735-42, South Carolina Archives, 18 July 1739, sc£16 4s. 3d., p. 63, 26 Mar. 1739-40, p. 69. Other surviving ledgers, covering the years 1733-42, 1760-74 contain no

further reference to Warren's land.

12. Maurice Alfred Crouse, "The Manigault Family of South Carolina, 1685-1783" (Ph.D. dissertation, Northwestern University, 1964).

13. John Myer £10 per annum, John Mun £23 per annum, John Duck £2 per annum, Patrick Burnet at no wages, Jeremiah Rowbry £2 per Annum for two years "indentures are to be given up," John Wiseman and John Smith £2 for the first year and £3 thereafter, William Gaff £3 per annum, Thomas Headly, Henry Gray, and John Moorshead all £2 per annum "indentures to be given up." Gage Papers, G/Am/13, p. 21.

14. 22 March 1750/51, Gage Papers, GA 841. Tyrrell (d. 1766), was born in Dublin ca. 1717, entered the navy in 1730, and served much of his early service with his uncle at New York, Charleston, and Boston. He served at the sieges of St. Augustine, Cartagena, and with the Leeward Islands' squadron. In 1747 he married the widow of Edward Chester Jr. of Antigua. He retired temporarily in 1750 from the navy and entered the sugar trade. He returned to active service in 1754, was promoted to Rear Admiral of the White in 1762 and commanded the Leeward Islands' squadron. He died and was buried at sea in June 1766. There is a memorial inscription to him in Westminister Abbey. His will (dated 20 Feb. 1766, proved 5 Aug. 1766) mentioned estates in Antigua, Jamaica, and a £5,000 mortgage

on an estate owned by Henry Sharpe of St. Kitt's. No reference to the South Carolina properties was made. Vere Langford Oliver, *The History of the Island of Antigua,* 3 vols. (London, 1894-99).

15. Fitzroy to DeLancey, 6 May 1772, Gage Papers, G/Am/135.

16. DeLancey to the Warren heirs, 8 Aug. 1772, Gage Papers, G/Am/137.

17. Alice was the fifth child of Peter DeLancey and Elizabeth Colden. Thomas Jones, *History of New York during the Revolutionary War* (New York, 1879). Alice Izard's journal for 1771-72 is in the Museum of the City of New York, doc. 42. 315, 617, DeLancey Papers. Langdon Cheves, "Izard of South Carolina," *South Carolina Historical and Genealogical Magazine* 2 (1901): 214-17.

18. Skinner to DeLancey, 29 Nov. 1772 and 19 April 1773, Gage Papers, G/Am/139, G/Am/146. See also a letter to Skinner from a Mr. Kelly, 19 May 1774, Gage Papers G/Am/162.

19. Memorandum, Gage Papers, G/Am/109.

20. See chapter 3.

21. Gage Papers, G/Am/13, p. 18, and G/Am/1.

22. *The Statues at Large of South Carolina,* 3: 104. The act was passed 13 Feb. 1719/20.

23. Adm. 1/3878; see also Gage Papers, G/Am/1, and Warren to Josiah Burchett, 18 Nov. 1738, Adm. 1/2652.

24. Gabriel Manigault to Lady Warren, 1 July 1760, Gage Addit. 1201. In 1754 Manigault's son, Peter, on business in England, visited Lady Warren at her London home and discussed the

Vander Dussen debt. Peter
Manigault to Gabriel Manigault,
2 Mar. 1754, in Mabel L. Webber,
"Peter Manigault's Letters," *South
Carolina Historical and Genealogical
Magazine,* 32 (1931): 279.

Chapter 8

1. The best studies on Irish
landownership in the seventeenth
century are by Dr. J.G. Simms. By
contrast the eighteenth century
has largely been neglected. See
especially his article "Land Owned
by Catholics in Ireland in 1688,"
Irish Historical Studies,
7 (1950-51): 180-90; *The Williamite
Confiscation in Ireland 1690-1703*
(London, 1956), pp. 158, 162,
195-96; *The Treaty of Limerick*
(Dundalk, 1961), Irish History
Series, no. 2; and his *Jacobite
Ireland, 1685-1691* (London,
1969), pp. 3-4, 262-63.
2. Warren's grandfather, Oliver
Warren, who had inherited the
estate called Warrenstown from
his father John in 1638, suffered
almost total forfeiture between
1654 and 1663. Rev. Thomas
Warren, *A History and Genealogy of
the Warren Family,* p. 187. When in
1662 a court was created to hear
claims of those who had suffered
confiscation under Cromwell, both
Oliver Warren and his mother
appeared before the tribunal and
were restored to the 320 acres
that had been forfeited. 7 March
and 4 May 1663, Appendix to the
*19th Report of the Deputy Keeper of
the Public Records of Ireland* (Dublin,
1887), pp. 46, 52. Peter Warren's
father, by joining the army of

James II, automatically forfeited
the estates which he had inherited
from his father. Surrendering
under the terms of the Treaty of
Limerick, he was offered the
alternatives of going to France
and forfeiting his estates or of
remaining in Ireland, submitting
to William III, and being restored
to his property. Captain Michael
Warren chose to stay in Ireland. 1
July 1692, Trinity College, Dublin,
MS, N.1.3.; published in "Irish
Jacobite Lists," edited by J.G.
Simms, *Anelecta Hibernica,* 22
(Dublin, 1960): 104. All references
to acreage are by Irish measure.
See chapter 2, n. 4.
3. For a description of
Warrenstown in 1640 see *The Civil
Survey,* vol. 5, *County of Meath*
(Dublin, 1940), pp. 145, 152, ed.
by Robert C. Simington. See also
J. G. Simms, "The Civil Survey,
1654-56," *Irish Historical Studies,* 9,
no. 36 (1955): 253-63. An early
nineteenth century plan of the
estate is owned by Jack Leonard,
Esq. of Moortown, Drumree,
county Meath.
4. Add. MSS. 41159, fol. 112v,
BM; 26 August 1700. Estates were
sold and conveyed in 1702 and
1703, and in Meath raised
£73,339 less expenses of £8,263.
Only county Cork produced more
revenue.
5. Rev. Anthony Cogan, *The
Diocese of Meath Ancient and Modern*
(Dublin, 1867), 2: 351-52. For a
Protestant account see John
Healy, *History of the Diocese of Meath*
(Dublin, 1908).
6. 30-31 Jan. 1672/73, Gage
Papers, G/Ir/2 (68), p. 1.
7. £225 in Sept. 1703, £375 in
May 1708, £400 at a later date;
£150 in legacies for his widow and

two daughters. Dublin, Register of Deeds, memorial no. 23, book 1, pp. 45-46. His will was dated 3 Sept. 1711, and was proved 20 Feb. 1712/13, an abstract of which was made by Sir Alfred Irwin, Irwin Ms. vol. 437, p. 359, Genealogical Office, Dublin.

8. 31 May–1 June 1723, Register of Deeds, memorial no. 23,564, book 35, p. 525. By earlier agreement, 18 May 1717, with Hussey, the debt had been fixed at £2,367, interest on £830 being waived for five years. Gage Papers, G/Ir/2 (68). p. 2.

9. 19-20 Feb. 1729/30, Register of Deeds, memorial no. 42,633, book 63, p. 55. What became of Christopher Warren is uncertain. The historian of the Warren family believed that he was "the Very Reverend Christopher Warren, who was appointed Guardian of the Franciscan Convent of Kildare in 1729." Warren, *A History and Genaeology of the Warren Family*, pp. 187-88.

10. Details taken from Gage Papers, G/Am/1 and G/Am/23.

11. Bakers to Warren, 23 March 1744/45, Gage Papers, G/Am/7 (2).

12. The will was dated 22 May 1742. There is an abstract of it in Gage Papers, G/Ir/2 (68), pp. 9-10.

13. 23-24 May 1748, Gage Papers, G/Ir/2 (68) pp. 8-9.

14. Gage Papers, G/Am/5.

15. 2-3 Dec. 1748. Register of Deeds, memorial no. 93,274, book 133, p. 547, and 13-14 Dec. 1749, memorial no. 93,773, book 139, pp. 106-7.

16. 21-22 March 1749/50, Register of Deeds, memorial no. 104,412, book 156, pp. 217-18.

17. 29-30 Nov. 1750, Gage Papers, G/Ir/2 (68), pp. 16-19.

18. Details taken from ibid., pp. 22-28. 3 Geo. II, c.21, "An Act for the Relief of Dame Elizabeth Dudley relating to an Estate in Ireland Forfeited to the Crown during the Life of William Kennedy her Great Uncle." *Statutes at Large*, 6: 3 Geo. II, c. 21 (private).

19. There is a 1778 plan of part of Ballydowde in the National Library of Ireland, Map. 16.6.42 (20).

20. 18 March 1752, Register of Deeds, memorial no. 103,366, book 150, pp. 495-96. By the phrase "twenty-four years' purchases" is meant the property brought a price of twenty-four times the annual gross income.

21. See Dudley's statement of arrears in his letter to Gabriel Johnston, 5 Apr. 1752, Gage Papers, GA 1301. 1£500 was paid by John Johnson on behalf of the tenant, into the bank of William Lennox and George French; see Johnson–Warren Accounts, 1752-54, and Lady Warren's accounts with Lennox and French, Gage Papers, G/Am/69. This bank was bankrupt in March 1755, but Lady Warren was not listed among the creditors in "An Act for the Relief of the Creditors of the Bank lately kept by William Lennox and George French, of the City of Dublin" 20 Geo. II, c.21, *The Statutes at Large passed in the Parliament held in Ireland from the Third Year of Edward the Second, A.D. 1310, to the First Year of George the Third, A.D. 1761, Inclusive* (Dublin, 1765), 7: 397-425.

22. 13 Feb. 1752 and 9-10 July 1752, Gage Papers, G/Ir/2 (68), pp. 35-38. On 13 June 1753 Macky tranferred title of the property to Lady Warren, Register of Deeds, Dublin, memorial no. 108,887, book 161, pp. 335-36.

23. Warren to Johnston, 12 July 1752, Gage Papers, GA 1301 (13).

24. Dudley to Johnston, 5 April 1752, ibid.

25. Dudley to James Forster, Esq., Friday, 4 June 1752, ibid.

26. Sir Fenton Aylmer, *The Aylmers of Ireland* (London, 1931), pp. 250-51.

27. There is a complete list of the papers given by his widow, Williamza Aylmer to Boleyn in 1742, Gage Papers, G/Am/23. A second list was prepared by Whitney upon Warren's death, Gage Papers, G/Ha/37. Few of the documents in either list have survived.

28. There are references in 1734 and 1736 to William Johnson in Warren's accounts, Gage Papers, G/Am/13, p. 2, 16. See above, chapter 4.

29. John Johnson to William Johnson, 13 Jan. 1750, Sullivan, ed., *William Johnson Papers*, 1: 258.

30. Warren unsuccessfully tried to convince him to see the error of his ways and, like his two brothers, forsake the Catholic church. The letter, along with several others to John Johnson, was owned by Mrs. Annette Leonard (née Johnson) in 1925, and was referred to by a neighbour, Rev. Hamlet McClenaghan in a letter to Horace Lyman Weeks of New York City. Horace Lyman Weeks MSS, New York Public Library. These letters cannot now be located.

31. Gage Papers, G/Am/1.

32. Gage Papers, G/Am/12. For details of the fair, see below n. 55.

33. Details taken from Gage Papers, G/AM/2, G/Am/5, G/Am/12, G/Am/13. The lease of the Darramys expired in May 1738. It seems their part of Warrenstown was let to Gaffney thereafter. Henry Rowley's lease expired on 1 May 1740, which part of the estate was apparently leased thereafter by Kearny.

34. K. H. Connell, *The Population of Ireland, 1750-1845* (Oxford, 1950), p. 244.

35. Connell describes the typical Irish case: "The middleman endeavoured to take an estate on as long a lease as possible . . . and sub-let it for short periods; increasing land values would give the less extortionate middleman profit for his pains, and his unscrupulous fellow, each time a lease fell in, could put the land up to auction and extort over the period of his tenancy a steeply increasing rent." Ibid, p. 67. Some estimates put the middleman's income at three times that of the landlords.

36. The will had been published in Sullivan, ed., *William Johnson Papers*, 13:19-23

37. 23 May 1791, Gage Papers, G/Ir/1 (46a)

38. 26 July 1771, G/Ir/2 (68), pp. 12-13, Gage Papers.

39. Gage Papers, G/Ir/1 (46a)

40. Gage Papers, G/Ir/2 (68), p. 15.

41. Gage Papers, G/Ir/1 (25). See advertisements in the Dublin newspapers dated 21 Jan. 1774.

42. Gage Papers, G/Am/69.

43. Gage Papers, G/Ir/2 (68), pp. 13-14.

44. John Johnson Sr. to Lord Southampton, 26 Mar. 1791, Gage Papers, G/Ir/1 (43).

45. David Large, "The wealth of the greater Irish Landowners, 1750-1815," *Irish Historical Studies*, 15, no. 57 (1966): 21-47.

46. E. Wakefield, *An Account of Ireland, Statistical and Political* (London, 1812), 2 vols. discussed the length of Irish tenure, county by county, and found the most common to be either 21 or 31 years, though 61 was not uncommon, while many tenures were for life or several lives.

47. Connell, *The Population of Ireland, 1750-1845*, especially p. 69.

48. The question has recently been re-assessed by L.M. Cullen, "Problems in the Interpretation and Revision of Eighteenth-Century Irish Economic History," *Royal Historical Society Transactions*, 5th series, 17 (1967): 1-22.

49. Large believes that Irish absentee landholders raised rents at a rate "not very markedly greater" than their landowners did in England. Large, "The Wealth of the Greater Irish Landowners," p. 29. Connell states, "Rents rose probably even more spectacularly than in England." Connell, *The Population of Ireland, 1750-1845*, p. 69. For the period 1793-1815, Large adds: "Prices appear to have risen as much as rents and possibly rather more rapidly than rents did on some estates, so that favourably situated tenants–a minority no doubt–probably did not suffer any change in their economic condition and may even

have improved it." Large, "The Wealth of the Greater Irish Landowners," p. 31. In England between 1750 and 1790 rents rose 40 to 50 per cent, G.E. Mingay, *English Landed Society in the Eighteenth Century* (London, 1963), p. 52; and between 1790 and 1815 by about 90 per cent, F.M.L. Thompson, *English Landed Society in the Nineteenth Century* (London, 1963), p. 220.

50. L.M. Cullen, "The Exchange Business of the Irish Banks in the Eighteenth Century," *Economica*, new series, 25 (1958): 326-38; and also his *Anglo-Irish Trade 1660-1800* (Manchester, 1969), especially chapter 9, "Exchanges and Balances of Payments," pp. 155-86.

51. *The Irish Pound 1797-1826: A Reprint of the Report of the Committee of 1804 of the British House of Commons on the Condition of the Irish Currency*, with an introduction by Frank Whitson Fetter (London, 1955), pp. 7-11.

52. Schumpeter, "English Prices and Public Finances, 1660-1822." The indices were based on a then unpublished manuscript by Lord Beveridge, *Prices and Wages in England from the Twelfth to the Nineteenth Century* (London, 1939), 2.

53. Gage Papers, G/Am/5.

54. Gage Papers, G/Ir/1 (19).

55. Rev. G. Hansbrow, *An Improved Topographical and Historical Hibernian Gazetteer* (Dublin, 1835), p. 410. The fair was held 1 Jan., 26 Apr., 22 June, and 2 Sept.

56. In sterling this amounted to £26 10s. Gage Papers, G/Am/69.

57. Large, "The Wealth of the Greater Irish Landowners," pp. 29-30. He also estimated that

by 1793 the Irish landowner was getting about 4¼ per cent.

58. 16-17 July 1773, Register of Deeds, memorial no. 198,653, book 299, pp. 377-83.

59. 29 July 1773, Register of Deeds, memorial no. 198,655, book 300, pp. 50-54.

60. 1-2 June and 12-13 July 1790, Register of Deeds, memorial nos. 280,298, and 280,299, book 434, pp. 25-33.

61. Rossmore to Gage, 24 March 1801, Gage Papers, G/Ir/1 (75).

62. Thomas Metcalfe to Gage, Lincoln's Inn, 10 Oct. 1805, Gage Papers, G/Ir/1 (137).

63. Metcalfe to Gage, 22 July 1806, Gage held out for 1£15,000, Gage Papers, G/Ir/2 (4).

64. Metcalfe to Gage, 8 Oct. 1807, Gage Papers, G/Ir/2 (52).

65. Messrs. Lee and Pemberton to Gage, 19 Sept. 1861, Gage Papers, G/Ir/2 (61).

66. The creation of Catholic wealth in Irish trade has been studied elsewhere. See Maureen Wall, "The rise of a Catholic middle class in eighteenth-century Ireland," *Irish Historical Studies*, 11, no. 42 (1958): 91-115. She argued that the "laws which prevented Catholics from buying land, or from taking long leases, and which left Catholic landed families at the mercy of the informer, the unfaithful wife, and the undutiful child, drove many more Catholics to seek a living in trade," p. 98.

67. See the correspondence of John Johnson Sr. and Jr. with the Warren heirs, together with accounts, in Gage Papers, G/Ir/1 and G/Ir/2.

Chapter 9

1. The most useful studies on Hampshire are all rather general: Abraham and William Driver, *General View of the Agriculture of the County of Hants, with Observations on the Means of Its Improvement* (London, 1794); Charles Vancouver, *General View of the Agriculture of Hampshire Including the Isle of Wight* (London, 1813); Rev. John Wilkinson, "The Farming of Hampshire," *The Journal of the Royal Agricultural Society of England*, 22 (1861): 239-371; W. E. Tate, "Field Systems and Enclosures in Hampshire," *Papers and Proceedings of the Hampshire Field Club*, 16 (1947): 257-79; M.C. Naish, "The Agricultural Landscape of the Hampshire Chalk-lands, 1700-1804" (M.A. thesis, University of London, 1961); E. L. Jones, "Eighteenth-Century Changes in Hampshire Chalkland Farming," *The Agricultural History Review*, 8 (1960): 5-19.

2. H.J. Habakkuk, "English Landownership, 1680-1740," *The Economic History Review*, 1st. series, 10 (1940): 2-17; H.J. Habakkuk, "Marriage Settlements in the Eighteenth Century," *Royal Historical Society Transactions*, 4th series, 32 (1950): 15-30; H.J. Habakkuk, "The Long-Term Rate of Interest and the Price of Land in the Seventeenth Century," *The Economic History Review*, 2nd series, 5 (1952): 26-45; J.S. Bromley and E.H. Kossmann, eds., *Britain and the Netherlands* (Oxford, 1960), article by H.J. Habakkuk, "The English Land Market in the Eighteenth

Century," pp. 154-73; G.E. Mingay, "The Size of Farms in the Eighteenth Century," *The Economic History Review*, 2nd series, 14 (1962): 469-88; G.E. Mingay, *English Landed Society in the Eighteenth Century* (London, 1963); Christopher Clay, "Marriage, Inheritance, and the Rise of Large Estates in England, 1660-1815," *The Economic History Review*, 2nd series, 21 (1968): 503-18.

3. Warren to Corbett, 3 Apr. 1747, Adm. 1/88, Anson to Bedford, 5 Apr. 1747, Bedford MSS, XVI, fol. 53, Warren to Anson, 23 Apr. 1747, Addit. MSS. 15957, fol. 172-73, BM. See also Admiralty minutes for 1 June 1747, Adm. 3/57 and the orders to the captain of the warship sent to New York: Corbett to Robert Jeffries, 1 June 1747, Adm. 2/691, p. 214; Jeffries to Corbett, 3 June 1747, Adm. 1/1983. The ship was twice attacked by French privateers and forced to put in at Shannon, Ireland to undergo repairs. Lady Warren and her two children thereupon made their way to Dublin, thence to the Chester coast before reaching London in November by coach.

4. Post Captain 1701, Rear Admiral 1728, member of Admiralty Board from 19 March 1742 until his death. Officer commanding Portsmouth naval station from 1739 to 1742. Dying childless, he left his entire estate to his widow. His will, made 2 May 1728, was proved 15 July 1743; a copy in Gage Papers, G/Ha/29.

5. On 24 March 1747, the wife of Captain Edward Boscawen wrote, "Admiral Warren will certainly agree with Mrs. Cavendish about the villa," Cecil Aspinall–Oglander, *Admiral's Wife Being the Life and Letters of The Hon. Mrs. Edward Boscawen from 1719 to 1761* (London, 1940), p. 31. The property was conveyed to Warren on 28-29 June, the arrangements being carried out by Thomas Browne, a solicitor of James Street, Bedford Row, London. As Warren was then at sea, a local farmer, John Eames, acted on his behalf. Gage Papers, G/Ha/36, p. 2.

6. Warren to Anson, 31 May 1747, Anson Papers, Addit. MS. 15957, fol. 1971. In 1772 Browne himself remarked: "It was then thought to be sold very dear." Gage Papers, G/Ha/66 (20), p. 14.

7. Details taken from Miss Frances Brough's account of East Meon parish in William Page, ed., *The Victoria History of the Counties of England: Hampshire and the Isle of Wight* (Westminster, 1902-14), 3: 68-69. See also John Hurst and Frances Collins, *West Meon, Hampshire* (Petersfield, Hampshire, 1972).

8. Gage Papers, G/Ha/53; a statement relating to the title to Westbury prepared by William Pierce Williams of Middle Temple, Admiral Cavendish's attorney, 28 Aug. 1721. It is not known if the acreage was the same in 1694 as in 1747 when Warren bought the estate.

9. Deeds of lease and release dated 8-9 June 1722, Gage Papers, G/Ha/46, p. 2. The exact acreage of the estate in 1722 is not stated. There is no evidence that Cavendish either added to the

estate after 1722 or that his widow sold other parcels of land other than to Warren in 1747. In 1736 Cavendish put a £4,000 mortgage on the property, the money being advanced by Major General William Hargrave, the officer commanding the Gibraltar garrison, 28 May 1736, Gage Papers, G/Ha/28.

10. The furniture was insured for £1,000, the coach house for £100, the wheat barn £50, the oat barn £30, a granary £20, and other buildings £60 for a total of £3,500. The cost: £4 6s. a year. See Sun Fire Office policy, no. 136, 159, Guildhall MS. 11,936/101, pp. 482-83, Guildhall, London.

11. Christopher Hussey, *English Gardens and Landscapes 1700-1750* (London, 1967), pp. 36-37, does not list Westbury among Bridgeman's works, though Mrs. Cavendish refers to him in her detailed description of house and garden, Gage Papers, G/Ha/66 (2a). An original plan of the house, farm buildings, and park is in Gage Papers, G/Ha/42.

12. In 1703 the Hampshire antiquarian, William Povey, visited the chapel noting that no services were then held in it; British Museum, Stowe MSS. 845, fol. 56. Services were resumed by the third Viscount Gage who restored the chapel. Gage Papers, G/Ha/66 (63 and 74). It is now a ruin.

13. Details drawn from "A Particular of the Estate Late Adm'l. Cavendish's in Hampshire," Gage Papers, G/Ha/66 (2a).

14. Farm account book, 1753-63, Gage Papers, GA 728.

See also "An account and Valeyaition of the Timber belonging to Westbury Estate," prepared for Mrs. Cavendish in 1747, Gage Papers, G/Ha/66 (4); and Warren accounts, 1749-52, Warren Papers, WLCL.; Report prepared by Thomas Yeoman, 26 Sept. 1771, Gage Papers, G/Ha/66 (19a and 19b).

15. Gage Papers, G/Ha/46, p. 1., which described it as being "formerly part of Peek Meadow afterwards part of Mr. Cavendish's Garden lying in the west of said garden." It amounted to a mere 180 square yards.

16. Ibid., p. 2, described as: "three Closes of arable land called Hales and Longcroft with a little meadow plot adjoining."

17. Altogether about 2½ acres. The debt was paid on 29 Jan. 1753. Gage Papers, G/Ha/66. The comment on the high price was made by Thomas Browne who in 1772 prepared an evaluation of the entire estate: Gage Papers, G/Ha/66 (20), p. 4.

18. Gage Papers, G/Ha/46, pp. 3-4, 6. All measurements are statute measure.

19. For field by field description, see Gage Papers, G/Ha/66 (1). Payment was made 3 Oct. 1750, Warren accounts, 1749-52, Warren Papers, WLCL. Reference to the rights of common is in a note in Warren's hand, Gage Papers G/Am/5.

20. Warren accounts, 1749-52, Warren Papers, WLCL. For description of the fields see Gage Papers, G/Ha/66 (1), and reference to the rights of common pasturage, Gage Papers, G/Ha/46, p. 5.

21. Gage Papers, G/Ha/66 (20), p. 7. A detailed description of the farm was prepared by Baker in November 1750, Gage Papers, G/Ha/32.

22. Ibid.

23. John Bricknell to Thomas Browne, 30 April 1772, Gage Papers, G/Ha/66 (23).

24. Details of the transactions are taken from Gage Papers, G/Am/2, G/Ha/29, G/Ha/33.

25. Gage Papers, G/Am/2. Bricknell thought it "a dear bargain," Gage Papers G/Ha/66 (23), p. 6 and (23).

26. Gage Papers, G/Ha/66 (20), p. 6.

27. For a detailed field by field description, see Gage Papers, G/Ha/66 (13). Plans of the three copses are in G/Ha/62.

28. Gage Papers, G/Am/6 for reference to interest payment and loan. Mill was conveyed on 1 April 1752 to Warren, Gage Papers, G/Ha/46, p. 4; for details of repairs see Gage Papers, GA 728. Thomas Browne called it the "clock" mill, Gage Papers, G/Ha/66 (20), p. 14.

29. Bricknell to Browne, 20 April 1772, Gage Papers, G/Ha/66 (23), G/Ha/66 (20), p. 8.

30. See indenture dated 18 June 1752 for details upon which this paragraph is based. Gage Papers, G/Ha/31.

31. No rental income other than from cottagers was received by the Warrens until late in 1755. See Gage Papers, GA 728, farm account book, 1 Jan. 1753– 1 August 1763, for details.

32. See Gage Papers, G/Ha/66 (20), pp. 1, 3. The remaining 75½ acres comprised the house, outbuildings, pleasure garden, kitchen garden, orchard, water meadow, and two large fields of 20 and 14 acres.

33. Gage Papers, GA 728.

34. Warren accounts, 1749-52, Warren Papers, WLCL.

35. Details drawn from Gage Papers, GA 728.

36. In 1753 the estate paid 6s. 6d. labour for washing 520 sheep, ibid. The type of sheep is not certain. The usual flock then populating Hampshire was the ancient white-faced, horned variety, though South Down was beginning to be introduced. "Hampshire is considered as a great breeding county, and the stocks in most parishes are very large." Driver, *Agriculture of the County of Hants,* p. 23. "The lambs are put to the ram, at the Michaelmas twelvemonth after they are lambed; they are kept to breed when two, four and six, toothed. The full-mouthed ewes are regularly drawn out about the middle of August, and put to the ram, in order to get forward, for the graziers in the rich lands of this and adjoining counties. The wether lambs are sold off about Michaelmas to the same parts. . . . Ewes begin lambing early in February; they are fed on turnips, grass and vetches, till the weaning time, when they are weaned and turned upon the downs with the young sheep." Ibid., pp. 25-26.

37. In May 1750 Warren paid some £20 for "French cows," Warren accounts, 1749-52, Warren Papers, WLCL. By this he presumably meant Channel Island

cattle, usually known in the eighteenth century collectively as the "Alderney breed," and first introduced around 1700, with Southampton as the chief port of entry. By mid-century several hundred head, almost all either cows or heifers, were entering ports from Southampton westwards. Two-thirds or more came from Jersey. Hampshire and South Devon farmers were the principal importers. See Robert Trow-Smith, *A History of British Livestock Husbandry 1700-1900* (London, 1959), pp. 117-18, 263-64. The Warrens usually charged 3s. for the service of their bulls. The pigs were first bought in 1747, Warren accounts, 1747-48, Gage Papers, G/Am/5.

38. See Elizabeth W. Gilboy, *Wages in Eighteenth Century England,* reprint edition (New York, 1969). She studied Yorkshire, Lancashire, Devon, Somerset, Gloucester, Oxford, Middlesex, Surrey, and Kent. In the west she found stagnation in wages, though she was in doubt about real annual income, for much of her evidence referred only to daily wage scales, while evidence relating to perquisites was fragmentary. Details relating to total annual wages of individuals at Westbury and to their perquisites are taken from Gage Papers, GA 728.

39. Details from Gage Papers, GA 728.

40. For the land tax administration see W. R. Ward, *The English Land Tax in the Eighteenth Century* (London, 1953). See also G. E. Mingay, "The Land Tax Assessments and the Small Landowner," *The Economic History Review,* 2nd series, 14 (1964): 382, 384. That Warren did not pass on the cost of the land tax contrasts with the behaviour of Northamptonshire and Bedfordshire landlords, see H.J. Habakkuk, "English Landownership, 1680-1740."

41. Gage Papers, G/Ha/66 (20), p. 1. Excluding the timber, valued at £60 per annum in 1772, the Westbury manor portion of the estate was valued at £180 when the Cavendishes owned it, and at £200 in 1772.

42. "The fundamental improvement in eighteenth-century farming consisted in the spread of more flexible rotations of crops. . . . " J.D. Chambers and G.E. Mingay, *The Agricultural Revolution, 1750-1880* (London, 1966), p. 54.

43. At first the Warrens grew 7 acres and later 24 acres of turnips. Gage Papers, GA 728. See for instance a 1759 entry: "Paid for hoeing 24 acres of turnips 4.16.0."

44. Details from Gage Papers, GA 728.

45. In 1772 the house etc. was valued at £1,500, but the Sun Fire Office insured it for £2,000 and the outbuildings for £500. This did not include the insurance on the household goods and furniture which were separately insured for £1,000. Thus £2,000 is no less uncertain a figure than £1,500 for our purposes here. Guildhall MS. 11,936/101, pp. 482-83, policy no. 136159. See also Gage Papers, G/Ha/66 (20), p. 1.

46. Ibid., pp. 2, 3, 4, 6, 8, 12.

47. Gage Papers, G/Ha/66 (20), p. 1

48. Christopher Clay, "Marriage, Inheritance, and the Rise of Large Estates in England, 1660-1815," pp. 508, 513; also H.J. Habakkuk, "The Long-Term Rate of Interest and the Price of Land in the Seventeenth Century," *The Economic History Review*, 2nd series, 5 (1952): 26-45.

49. See Thomas Yeoman's, "A Survey and valuation of the Demesne and Copyhold Estates belong to the Right Honble, the Earl of Abingdon, the Hon. Lady Warren, Col. Fitzroy and Col. Skinner in the Parishes of St. Nicholas Westbury, East and West Meon in Hampshire." Gage Papers, G/Ha/19.

50. The comment was made by Thomas Browne, solicitor, who had sold the Westbury estate for Mrs. Cavendish and under whose supervision the 1772 valuation was carried out. Gage Papers, G/Ha/66 (20), p. 2.

51. The detailed bills for his hunting and shooting gear are found in Gage Papers, G/Am/3, a bill book kept for him by Captain William Holburne.

52. Warren to Anson, 16 Oct. 1747, Anson Papers, Addit. MSS. 15957, BM.

53. 20 and 29 June 1750, 23 Mar. 1751, Warren accounts, 1749-52, Warren Papers, WLCL.

54. Gage Papers, G/Ha/66 (20), p. 14.

55. Gage Papers, G/Ha/66 (3).

56. Gage Papers, G/Ha/46, valued in 1824.

57. A lithograph plan of the estate and printed detailed description with notation about the bidding is found in British Museum, Maps. 136.a.11 (14).

58. See chapter 3.

59. H.J. Habakkuk, "The English Land Market in the Eighteenth Century," p. 171.

60. Ibid., pp. 172-73.

61. G.E. Mingay, *English Landed Society in the Eighteenth Century*, p. 26.

62. Warren to Anson, 1 June 1747, Anson Papers, Addit. MSS. 15957, fol. 196, BM.

Chapter 10

1. H.J. Habakkuk, "The English Land Market in the Eighteenth Century," p. 161. See also his "The Long-Term Rate of Interest and the Price of Land in the Seventeenth Century." The comments in this paragraph are based on these two articles.

2. For a history of interest rates in England in the eighteenth century see Sidney Homer, *A History of Interest Rates* (New Brunswick, New Jersey, 1963), pp. 147-65.

3. L.M. Cullen, *Anglo-Irish Trade, 1660-1800* (Manchester, 1969), p. 20.

4. T.S. Ashton, *Economic Fluctuations in England, 1700-1800* (Oxford, 1959), p. 87, and L.M. Cullen, *Anglo-Irish Trade*, p. 184. It should be pointed out that a study of Sun Fire Office rates lends the hypothesis only qualified support. P.G.M. Dickson, *The Sun Insurance Office 1710-1960* (London, 1960), p. 257.

5. Ashton, *Economic History of England: The 18th Century*, p. 28.

6. Daniel A. Baugh, *British Naval Administration in the Age of Walpole* (Princeton, 1965), pp. 226-29, for a general discussion of the pay ticket system. Seaman indebtedness to officers deserves to be studied more fully. It is well-established that, on merchantmen, sailors borrowed from their captains, who, in turn, by the system of bottomry, borrowed funds by using the ship and the cargo she carried as security on a loan to be repaid with interest at the end of a voyage. See Pares, *Yankees and Creoles*, p. 22.

7. See Warren–Jasper accounts, 1731-45, Gage Papers, G/Am/1, G/Am/13, pp. 6, 8, 10, 12; and Warren Papers, WLCL.

8. See *Vigilant* pay book, Adm. 33/393, PRO.

9. Warren accounts, 1749-52, Warren Papers, WLCL; Gage Papers, G/Am/1, G/Am/2.

10. Ambrose was born in Dublin, the grandson of Sir Gerald Aylmer, Bart. of Balrath, and later married Charlotte, the youngest da. of Admiral Sir John Norris. He served as one of Warren's lieutenants between 1729 and 1732. See Aldridge, "Admiral Sir John Norris," pp. 177-78. The debt was repaid, but the date is uncertain, though before 1740. Jasper–Warren accounts, 1730-40, Gage Papers, G/Am/1.

11. Watkins's exact relationship with Norris is unknown. His debt to Warren was unpaid by May 1740. There was also at that time an additional £1 5s. in interest

owing. Before 1740 Warren also loaned a Lieutenant Wakeman £31 10s. to be repaid "if ever he gets a Command in the Navy." Gage Papers, G/Am/1. At Louisbourg in 1745 Warren loaned a Lieutenant Riggs £100 on his bond; the debt was repaid between May 1749 and October 1751, Warren accounts, 1749-52, Warren Papers WLCL. The information in the rest of the paragraph comes from the same source.

12. 1 May 1751, Gage Papers, G/Am/60.

13. 20 Sept. 1768, DeLancey–Warren accounts, 1768-69, Gage Papers, G/Am/89. See DeLancey's letters to Lady Warren, 12 and 17 July, 18 Sept., 29 Nov. 1763, 9 Jan., 13 Feb., 18 Sept. 1764, Gage Addit. 1201. 5 Mar. 1769, Gage Papers, G/Am/88. DeLancey to Mrs. Cosby, 18 Sept. 1763 and DeLancey to William Johnson, 20 Dec. 1764, in E.B. O'Callaghan, ed., *The Documentary History of the State of New York* (Albany, 1849), 2:804, 811-12. See Johnson to DeLancey, 24 Jan. 1764, in Richard E. Day, ed., *Calendar of the Sir William Johnson Manuscripts in the New York State Library* (Albany, 1909), p. 298.

14. Wickham to Warren, 30 Apr. 1748, Gage Papers, G/Am/40b.

15. 16 July 1731 and 12 Oct. 1732, Gage Papers, G/Am/13, pp. 2-3, 16. All loans made to those in Ireland were in sterling, unless otherwise indicated.

16. "Supposed to be bad" was the comment made by his executors on the inventory of his

assets and liabilities drawn up by them, Gage Papers, G/Am/10. See also Gage Papers, G/Am/97.

17. Gage Papers, G/Am/13, p. 6.

18. See reference to the commission purchase in Warren accounts, 1749-52, Warren Papers, WLCL, 16 June 1749. The bond was given up at Westbury, Hampshire, 18 Oct. 1752, Gage Papers, G/Am/2.

19. 22 Apr. 1751, 1£500 was paid by draft on Warren's bankers in Dublin; Messrs. Lennox and French, ibid.

20. 26 July 1752, Warren Papers 74, NYHS.

21. Details taken from Warren–Tyrrell accounts, 1751-54, Gage Papers, G/Ir/1 (9a). The initial bond was dated 20 March 1751, Gage Papers, G/Ir/1 (1), G/Ir/1 (7a), G/Ir/1 (8a and 8c) for further details.

22. 26 July 1752, Warren Papers, 74, NYHS.

23. Ascribed to Lord Mansfield. See John Holliday, *The Life of William Late Earl of Mansfield* (London, 1797), pp. 469-70.

24. 19 Sept. 1748; the one interest payment was for £5, paid 28 Apr. 1750. The mill became Warren's property on 1 Apr. 1752. See Gage Papers, G/Am/5, G/Ha/46, G/Ha/66 (20), p. 8, and Warren accounts, 1749-52, Warren Papers, WLCL.

25. 22 Jan. 1752, Gage Papers, G/Am/105b.

26. Gage Papers, G/Am/5, 13 June 1749 and 18 June 1750. Warren paid Robinson £15 to effect the bond, Warren accounts, 1749-52, Warren Papers, WLCL.

27. Robinson (1702?-1777), was an amateur architect, with special interest in Palladio; MP for Morpeth, 1727-34; gov. of Barbados, 1742-47; m. 1728, Elizabeth, eldest daughter of 3rd. earl of Carlisle; m. 2ndly, 1743, in Barbados, widow of Samuel Salmon, a successful ironmonger; after 1747 acquired shares in Ranelagh Gardens and became dir. of entertainments; built a house adjoining; brother of 1st. baron Rokeby, primate of Ireland. *Dictionary of National Biography*, 41: 49-51.

28. Gage Papers, G/Am/2 and G/Am/67; debt paid off in July 1751 with single payment of £1,901.

29. Gage Papers, G/Ir/1 (15), Register of Deeds, memorial no. 101, 366, dated 3 Jan. 1752.

30. From an undated note in Lady Warren's hand, Gage Papers, G/Ha/37.

31. Aubrey N. Newman, ed., "Leicester House Politics, 1750-60, from the Papers of John, Second Earl of Egmont," *Camden Fourth Series*, 7, *Camden Miscellany*, 23 (1969): 145.

32. Egmont MSS., 47097/8, BM. For details of Egmont's career, see Namier and Brooke, *A History of Parliament* 3: 266-68.

33. Registered 29 Feb. 1752, memorial no. 102,216, book 151, p. 475. Boleyn Whitney acted on Warren's behalf. The loan was actually for 1£5,000.

34. 13 May 1752, Gage Papers, G/Ir/1 (2). Gabriel Johnston acted for Warren in this affair.

35. 8 Nov. 1752, from a note in Lady Warren's hand, Gage Papers, G/Am/2. Conveyance of the

mortgage was effected in London, 18 April 1753, and registered in Ireland, Register of Deeds, memorial no. 109,515, book 161, p. 459.

36. See David Large, "The wealth of the greater Irish landowners, 1750-1815," for explanation of this process.

37. The two smallest, contracted for in October 1749 at 5 per cent, were for £25 and £60 to two of Warren's neighbours in Hampshire, a widow, Mary Abburrow of West Meon and the local butcher, John Andrews. Both loans were repaid in Jan. 1753 together with £14 interest. Gage Papers, G/Am/5.

38. See *Complete Peerage*, 5: 596-97. See also Lady Warren's letter to Oliver DeLancey, 20 June 1754, Warren Papers, 46b, NYHS.

39. 18 Dec. 1750, Gage Papers, G/Am/5.

40. John Lodge, *The Peerage of Ireland; or, a Genealogical History of the Present Nobility of that Kingdom* (Dublin, 1789), 4: 298-99.

41. Ibid., pp. 195-201.

42. The original loans were made 5 June and 14 July 1750, Gage Papers, G/Am/2 and G/Am/5.

43. Lady Warren to O. DeLancey, 20 June 1754, Warren Papers 46b, NYHS.

44. The Longfield loan was for 1£500; for details see Gage Papers, G/Am/2, G/Am/5, G/Ha/37 and G/Ha/64.

45. Details taken from various abstracted deeds in Gage Papers, G/Ir/2 (68), pp. 41-2.

46. There is no indication that the capital concerned was not recovered, though the actual date of recovery is not known.

47. 29 Oct. 1751 and 21 July 1753, Gage Papers, G/Am/2. The Crofton–Meares loan was for 1£700.

48. Lady Warren to O. DeLancey, 20 June 1754, Warren Papers 46b, NYHS.

49. S. Jeake to Lady Warren, Jamaica, 22 April 1769, Gage Papers, G/Ha/66 (77). This was in reply to Lady Warren's letter of 22 Dec. 1768.

50. Col. William Skinner to Mr. Gordon of Jamaica, 5 June 1774, Gage Papers, G/Am/163.

51. Lady Warren to Oliver DeLancey, 20 June 1754, Warren Papers 46b, NYHS.

52. For low interest rates in Ireland see Cullen, *Anglo-Irish Trade*, p. 185: "The market rates declined in the years of prosperity from the end of the 1740s. In the early 1750s the price of the 4 per cent Irish debentures had risen to 107 or 108." For England, see Ashton, *Economic Fluctuations*, p. 148.

Chapter 11

1. This introduction owes much to P.G.M. Dickson, *The Financial Revolution in England: A study in the development of public credit 1688-1756* (London, 1967).

2. The London Stock Exchange in 1728, when Warren first traded, offered the stock of two insurance companies: London Assurance and Royal Exchange Assurance; stock of the Bank of England, East India Company and South Sea Company; annuities of both the South Sea Company and the East

India Company and a variety of Bank of England annuities, such as the 1716 5 per cents, 1717 4 per cent debenture annuities, 1717 5 per cent lottery annuities, 1719 4 per cent benefit annuities, 1721 5 per cent Civil List, 1726 3 per cents, 1728 4 per cents.

3. Dickson, *The Financial Revolution in England,* p. 208.

4. South Sea Annuity Ledger, Bank of England Record Office (hereafter BERO). Bought 11 Mar. 1728/29, sold 7 July 1730. See note in Warren's account with Jasper, 6 March 1729/30 "By my South Sea Annuity which I have given him power to sell . . . £1000," Gage Papers, G/Am/13. For details of Jasper's career see P.G.M. Dickson, *The Sun Insurance Office 1710-1960: The History of Two and a Half Centuries of British Insurance* (London, 1960), pp. 241, 274 and 274n.

5. Warren–Jasper accounts, 1730-44, Gage Papers, G/Am/1 and G/Am/13.

6. In May 1740, Warren noted of Jasper, "if he was in My Debt he was to allow me 5 per cent interest," Gage Papers, G/Am/1. In December 1735, after his purchases of South Sea Old annuities were completed, Warren had a favourable balance with Jasper amounting to £172.

7. Warren Papers, WLCL contains the original receipt. For details of the sale see Warren–Baker accounts, 1738-46, 7 Jan. 1741/42, ibid.

8. For example see reference in S. and W. Baker to Warren, 10 Sept. 1745, ibid., and 1 March 1745/6, Gage Papers, G/Am/2.

9. 23 June 1749, Old South Sea Annuity Ledger (T-Z), 1744-51, fol. 494, BERO. The actual price Warren received is not known but the annuities were quoted at 105¾ that day, see [John Castaigne and Richard Shergold], *The Course of the Exchange,* for 1746, Library of London Stock Exchange.

10. Warren to Bakers, 5 Mar. 1740/41, Gage Papers, G/Am/2. Warren enclosed a bill of exchange for £250, and calculated that he had then deposited £2,275 with them, against which only a few small items had been debited. In fact by the end of July 1741 the Bakers had received £2,587, and paid out £371, for a balance of £2,316. Warren–Baker accounts, 1738-46, Warren Papers, WLCL.

11. The cost was £160 10s. per £100, which with the brokerage fee came to £807. The stock was registered in Samuel Baker's name, being transferred to Warren's in Feb. 1742 upon his return to England, Main Stock Ledger, 1738-1743, L/AG/14/5/8, India Office Records (hereafter IOR).

12. [Thomas Mortimer], *Every Man his Own Broker: Or A Guide to Exchange Alley, in Which The Nature of the Several Funds, Vulgarly Called the Stocks, is closely explained; and the Mystery and Iniquity of Stock-Jobbing laid before the Public in a New and Impartial Light* (London, 1761), 2nd edition, pp. 157-59.

13. 28 May 1745, Warren–Baker accounts, 1738-46, Warren Papers, WLCL.

14. Dickson, *The Financial Revolution in England,* p. 414.

15. Certificates are found in L/AG/14/5/354, IOR.

16. See L/AG/14/5/253, p. 647, for sale on 27 and 29 Feb. and 3 Mar. 1752; and L/AG/14/5/264, p. 400 for final disposal, IOR.

17. Details taken from Gage Papers, G/Am/2 and G/Am/5.

18. John Shipston to Susan Warren, 23 June 1757, which includes details of the sale, together with bond numbers, Gage Papers, G/Ha/43. They sold at £102 13s. per £100 for a loss of £264 which included the brokerage fee.

19. Shipston to Susan Warren, 16 Nov. 1752, ibid.

20. William Baker to Susan Warren, 19 Dec. 1752, ibid.

21. See Baker's letter to her on Feb. 1758, ibid.

22. Details taken from Shipston's letters to her, ibid.

23. Details taken from L/AG/14/5/253, pp. 649, 657; L/AG/14/5/258, pp. 528, 533, 535, 536; L/AG/14/5/261, pp. 557, 559, 562, 563, IOR.

24. Dickson, *The Financial Revolution in England,* p. 216.

25. Ibid., table 25, pp. 218-19.

26. Samuel and William Baker to Warren, 23 March 1744/45, Gage Papers, G/Am/7 (2).

27. Ibid.

28. Subscription Ledger, 1745 3% Annuities, 1745-1760, fol. 5, 7, BERO, provide details about dates the transfers took place, in what quantities, together with the name of the sellers. The stock was listed in the names of Warren's four trustees: Admiral George Anson, Admiral John Norris, Samuel and William Baker.

29. S. and W. Baker to Warren, 1 March 1745/6, Gage Papers, G/Am/7 (3-4).

30. Subscription Ledger, 1745 3% Annuities, 1745-60, fol. 5, 7, 12, 19, BERO.

31. [Castaigne and Shergold], *The Course of the Exchange,* for 1746 and 1747; Library of the London Stock Exchange. This sum includes brokerage charges.

32. Details of the sales are found in 3% Annuities: 1745 Subscription Ledger, 30 April 1745–11 Aug. 1760, fol. 2248, BERO.

33. Details taken from Gage Papers, G/Am/103 and Warren's accounts, 1749-52, Warren Papers, WLCL.

34. Ann was born in Boston in 1738, and married Col. Charles Fitzroy on 27 July 1758, Consols 3% 1752-59, fol. 4738, BERO.

35. Susanna was born 28 March 1744, and married Col. William Skinner in June 1768, Consols 3% 1764-69, fol. 10601, BERO.

36. Charlotte was born in May 1749, and married Willoughby, fourth Earl of Abingdon on 7 July 1768, ibid., fol. 10601, BERO.

37. Susannah, Lady Warren, died 19 Nov. 1771; the transfer took place on 15 April and 6 May 1772, Consols 3% ledger, fol. 11120, BERO.

38. Dickson, *The Financial Revolution in England,* p. 219.

39. 4% Annuities 1748, Subscription Ledger, BERO.

40. 3% Annuities 1750, Subscription Ledger, A-Z, 1750-1753, fol. 1073, BERO. The purchase was dated 18 Feb. 1750. For an account of Gideon's career see two articles by Dame Lucy

Sutherland, "Samson Gideon and the Reduction of Interest, 1749-50," *Economic History Review,* 1st series, 16, no. 1, (1946): 15-29; and "Samson Gideon: Eighteenth Century Jewish Financier," *Transactions of the Jewish Historical Society of England,* 17 (1951-52): 79-90.

41. Warren's accounts, 1749-52, Warren Papers, WLCL. Warren's bank book with Messrs. Honeywood and Fuller records the last four payments: "21 June, 2nd payment on £5000, £750; 18 Aug., 3rd payment on D°, £1250; 18 Oct., 4th payment 5000 Scrip, £1250; 18 Dec., 5 D°—D°, £1250." Gage Papers, G/Am/67, Warren Papers, WLCL.

42. Gage Papers, G/Am/2.

43. Gage Papers, G/Am/5; 3% Annuities 1750, Subscription Ledger A-Z, 1750-1753, fol. 1073, BERO, gives details of the sale.

44. Dickson, *The Financial Revolution in England,* p. 240.

45. Gage Papers, G/Am/67, Warren's Bank Book, 1750-52, paid in seven instalments between March and December 1751. Before selling he received interest of £76 10s. for three-quarters of a year to Christmas, 1751.

46. Dickson, *The Financial Revolution in England,* p. 400.

47. The arrangements were made by Anson's secretary, Philip Stephens, the future Secretary of the Admiralty Board. There were sixteen bills, all but one valued at £1,000, the other amounting to £6,140. All were dated 30 Sept. 1747, with interest being paid from 1 April 1747, when they became Warren's property. Anson Papers, Addit. MSS. 15955, fol.

24, 26-27, BM. The bills were numbered 163-66, 168-70, 178-83, 187, and 464.

48. Dickson, *The Financial Revolution in England,* p. 230.

49. Navy 4% Annuities 1749, 1st Subscription Ledger 9 Dec. 1749–10 Oct. 1753, fol. 223, BERO. Dickson, *The Financial Revolution in England,* p. 450, overlooks Warren's subscription though mentioning Lady Warren's.

50. For details see Navy 4% Annuities, 1749.

51. For details see Reduced 3% Annuities, 1771-1779, fol. 6151, BERO. The shares were for £4,121 6s. 7d. with the eldest daughter receiving two pence more.

52. The shares were worth £848 8s. 11d., ibid., fol. 6169.

53. For the background, see Dickson, *The Sun Insurance Office.*

54. Barry Supple, *The Royal Exchange Assurance: A History of British Insurance 1720-1970* (Cambridge, 1970), esp. Part A, pp. 1-100.

55. Gage Papers, G/Am/5.

56. Jasper was long associated with the Sun Office having served since 1724 as one of the Managers. Dickson, *The Sun Insurance Office,* pp. 274, 274n.

57. No. 1295, Share Transfer Book, Guildhall MS. 12,023/5.

58. No. 1306, Share Transfer Book, ibid. For William Braund's career see Lucy Sutherland, *A London Merchant 1695-1774* (London, 1962), reprint edition. See p. 135 for the cost to Braund.

59. Nos. 1311 and 1312, Share Transfer Book, Guildhall MS. 12,023/5.

60. This information is taken from the Sun Fire Office Dividend Book, 1744-1789, Guildhall MS. 12,020/3-4.

61. Ibid. It was available to be collected at the office usually late in July and January following.

62. At midsummer 1754 the dividend rose to 15s., to 20s. at midsummer 1757, to 25s. at midsummer 1771, to 30s. at Christmas 1773, to 35s. at Christmas 1776, to 40s. at midsummer 1778, and to 45s. at midsummer 1783, which is as far as I traced the matter. Ibid.

63. The first by which Warren profited was paid 6 Jan. 1752 and gave him £100. Though Warren had usually collected all dividends himself at the office, on this occasion his broker, John Shipston, received the payment. This was the fourth such extra dividend ever paid by the office; many more were to follow, so that during Lady Warren's lifetime it was virtually an annual affair. Extraordinary Dividend Book, 1745-73, Guildhall MS. 12,022/1-2, Extra dividends were paid in July 1753, Jan. 1756, July 1758, July 1759, July 1760, July 1761, July 1762, July 1763, July 1764, July 1765, July 1766, July 1767, July 1768, July 1769, July 1770, July 1771, July 1772, which is as far as I traced the phenomenon. See also Gage Papers, G/Am/2 and G/Am/5.

64. "His Majesty's Royal Charter . . . for Incorporating the Society for a Free British Fishery" (London, 1750), copy in Goldsmith's Library, University of London.

65. Paid to Messrs. Robert Surnam & Co., bankers in Lombard Street, in three instalments: 10 per cent on 18 Dec. 1750, the same on 23 Dec. 1751, the balance on 6 Mar. 1752. Gage Papers, G/Am/2 and G/Am/5.

66. Gage Papers, G/Am/97. Lady Warren noted, "Sold by Mr. Shipston our Shares of Free British Fishery for £354.4.-. and put in 3 pr Ct East India annetys."

67. Details in Gage Papers, G/Am/2, G/Am/5, G/Am/97. First instalment paid 17 Dec. 1750, next on 7 Feb. 1751 and last two on 7 Apr. and 7 May 1751. The first dividend, the only one received before his death, was for £10 on 21 Feb. 1752.

68. *Journals of the House of Commons,* 25: 785, 808-9, 838, 842 for details of passage in the Commons. Act 22, Geo. II c. 49.

69. The annuity was £300 a year; but by dying in 1752 Warren lost £3,000 capital, having since 1747 received only £1,800 in interest. It was his least successful financial endeavour. See Gage Papers, G/Am/2, also Bedford to Anson, 23 Aug. 1747, Anson Papers, Addit. MSS, 15955, fol. 149, BM.

70. Dickson, *The Financial Revolution in England,* pp. 295, 297, 331 (Clinton's holdings were only in the 4 per cents of 1748).

71. Consols 3% 1757, Ledger, 1752-1759, fol. 4920, BERO.

72. To Sir Horace Mann, 4 Mar. 1749, W.S. Lewis, ed., *Horace Walpole's Correspondence,* 20: 33.

73. To William Johnson, 13 Sept. 1747, Sullivan, ed., *William Johnson Papers,* 1: 117.

74. 11 Aug. 1750, Warren
papers 37, NYHS.

Chapter 12

1. Charles Wilson, *England's
Apprenticeship 1603-1763* (London,
1965), p. 246. Arthur Marwick
refers to the economic historian as
one "who has deliberately decided
to study in great depth one part
of history." *The Nature of History*
(London, 1970), p. 114.

2. J. De Courcey Ireland,
"Admiral of the Fleet The Hon.
John Forbes," *The Irish Sword*,
No. 22, 6 (1963): 13-15.

3. In 1750 and 1751; see Gage
Papers, G/Am/2, G/Am/5, and
G/Am/97. The capital involved
came to £1,000, partly won at the
gaming table.

4. J.P. Kenyon, ed., *Halifax:
Complete Works* (London, 1969),
p. 207.

5. P.J. Marshall, "The Personal
Fortune of Warren Hastings," *The
Economic History Review*, 2nd series,
17 (1964): 284-300.

6. Aspinal–Oglander, *Admiral's
Wife*, pp. 145, 247-48. Captain
George (later Lord) Rodney was
in the same financial league as
Boscawen; and he converted his
prize earnings by 1750 "into
farms and copy-holdings in
Hampshire," where he built
himself a house. Spinney, *Rodney,*

Bibliography

Only those sources actually mentioned in the footnotes have been included.

Manuscript Sources

ENGLAND

Bank of England Record Office, Roehampton
Bank of England Register, 1744-59
South Sea Annuity Ledgers, 1728-44
Annuities 3% 1745, Subscription Ledger, 1745-60
Annuities 4% 1748, Subscription Ledger
Navy 4% Annuities 1749, Subscription Ledger, 1749-53
Annuities 3% 1750, Subscription Ledger, 1750-53
Reduced Annuities 3% Ledger, 1771-79
Consols 3% 1757 Ledger 1752-59 and 1764-69
Consolidated 3% Bank Annuities, Register

British Museum, London
Anson Papers, Addit. MSS. 15955, 15957
Norris Papers, Addit. MSS. 28130
Halifax Papers, Egerton MSS. 929, fol. 168-72
William Povey Papers, Stowe MSS. 845, fol. 56
Egmont Papers, Addit. MSS. 47097/8
Maps 136.s.11 (14): Westbury Estate
Forfeited Irish Estates Addit. MSS. 41159

Guildhall Library, London
Sun Fire Office MSS., Dividend Book, 1744-89, MS. 12020/3-4
Policy Book, MS. 11936/101
Share Transfer Book, 1746-89, MS. 12023/5-6
Extraordinary Dividend Book, 1745-73, MS. 12022/1-2

India Office Records, London
Main Stock Ledgers, 1738-43, L/AG/14/5/8
Stock Ledger 3% Annuities, 1750-56, L/AG/14/5/253
Stock Ledger 3% Annuities, 1756-62, L/AG/14/5/258
Stock Ledger 3% Annuities, 1762-71, L/AG/14/5/261
Stock Ledger 3% Annuities, 1771-78, L/AG/14/5/264
Stock Ledger, 3½% Annuities, 1750-56, L/AG/14/5/330
Transfer Books, 3½% Annuities, 1750-52, L/AG/14/5/336
Allotment Certificates for 3% and 3½% Annuities, 1750-52, L/AG/14/5/354

National Maritime Museum, Greenwich
Lieutenants' Logs, Adm. /L/S/404.

Public Record Office, London
Admirals' Despatches, Channel Fleet (Warren), Adm. 1/88
Admirals' Despatches, Jamaica (Vernon), Adm. 1/233
Unemployed Officers, Adm. 1/578
Captains' Letters (Jefferies and Warren), Adm. 1/1983,
    Adm. 1/2650-2656
Letters from Colonial Governors (Shirley), Adm. 1/3817
Letters from Doctors' Commons (prize papers), Adm. 1/3878
Orders and Instructions (to Warren), Adm. 2/52, 54, 58, 69
Secretaries' Letters (to Warren), Adm. 2/458, 484, 490, 492, 529, 691
Admiralty Board Minutes, Adm. 3/57, 60
Admiralty Board, Letters Patent, Adm. 4/25-26
Commission and Warrant Books, Adm. 6/12
Half Pay Ledgers, Adm. 25/21-23
Ships' Pay Books, Adm. 33/277, 289, 307, 328, 393, 409
Lieutenants' Passing Certificates, Adm. 107/3
Colonial Office, North America (Louisbourg, 1745-46), CO 5/44
Colonial Office, North America (New York), CO 5/1061

Sussex Archaeological Society, Lewes
Gage Papers, American, G/AM/1-338
Gage Papers, Hampshire, G/Ha/1-117
Gage Papers, Ireland, G/Ir/1-2
Gage Papers, Additional 1, GA
Gage Papers, Additional 2, Gage Additional

SCOTLAND

National Library of Scotland, Edinburgh
Hay family papers in the Yester Collection, MS. 7111

IRELAND

Genealogical Office, Dublin
Abstract of Wills, Irwin MS. vol. 437 (Michael Warren)

Public Record Office, Dublin
Wills Prerogative, 1726-28 (Catherine Warren)

Register of Deeds, Dublin
Deed Books

UNITED STATES OF AMERICA

Baker Library, Harvard University, Graduate School of Business, Boston
Peter Faneuil Letterbook, 1737-39
Thomas Hancock Papers
John Hancock Papers

Boston Public Library
Chamberlain Collection of Hancock MSS.

William L. Clements Library, Ann Arbor
Peter Warren Papers, 4 vols.
George Clinton Papers, I-IV

Department of State, Albany
Deed Books, XIV, XIX

Henry E. Huntingdon Library, San Marino
Henry Pelham Papers, HM 9707

Library of Congress, Washington, D.C.
Vernon–Wager Papers, MS. 46018-9

Massachusetts Historical Society, Boston
Belknap Papers 61C
Hancock Papers
Belcher Letter Book
F.L. Gay Collection
Norcross Autograph Collection in the Greenough Collection

Massachusetts State Archives, Boston
Massachusetts Archives, I, XIII, XX

Museum of the City of New York
DeLancey Papers
DeWitt Clinton Papers

New-York Historical Society, New York City
Warren Papers and Deeds
DeLancey Papers and Deeds
DePeyster Papers and Deeds
Watts Papers
Robert Watts Papers
John E. Stillwell Collection
John Tabor Kempe Papers

New York Public Library
Horace Lyman Weeks MSS. (manuscript division)
Stokes Cat. No. 1773 B-77(print division)

Sleepy Hollow Restorations, Tarrytown, N.Y.
Pierre Van Cortlandt Papers, V 1644, V 1689, V 2301

South Carolina State Archives, Columbia
Colonial Plat Books, I, III
Land Papers, I-II
Quit Rent Ledgers, 1735-42

CANADA

Public Archives of Canada, Ottawa
Daniel Claus Papers, XIV

Printed Sources

PRIMARY

Abingdon, Willoughby Bertie, Earl of. *Thoughts on the Letter of Edmund Burke, Esq., to the Sheriffs of Bristol, on the Affairs of America.* Oxford, 1777. Reprinted in *English Defenders of American Freedoms 1774-1778: Six Pamphlets Attacking British Policy,* compiled by Paul H. Smith. Washington: Library of Congress, 1972, pp. [193]-[203].

Aspinall-Oglander, Cecil. *Admiral's Wife Being the Life and Letters of the Hon. Mrs. Edward Boscawen from 1719-1761.* London: Longmans, Green, 1940.

The Boston Gazette, 1738.

Carswell, John and Dralle, Lewis Arnold, eds. *The Political Journal of George Bubb Dodington.* Oxford: Clarendon Press, 1965.

[Castaigne, John and Shergold, Richard], eds. *The Course of the Exchange and Other Things.* London, 1741-58.

Cobbett, William and Hansard, T. C., eds. *The Parliamentary History of England from the Earliest Period to the Year 1803,* vol. 14. London, 1813.

Connecticut. *The Public Records of the Colony of Connecticut 1726 to 1735.* Edited by Charles J. Hoadley. Hartford, 1873.

Considerations on the Bill for the Better Government of the Navy: By a Sea Officer. London, 1749.

Dalton, Rev. John. *A Sermon preached at the Parish-Church of St. Anne Westminster, on Thursday, April the 25th, 1751, before the Governors of the Middlesex-Hospital, for Sick and Lame, and for Lying-in Married Women.* London, 1751.

Davis, Andrew McFarland, ed. *Colonial Currency Reprints 1682-1751.* 4 vols. Reprint edition. New York: Burt Franklin, 1965.

Day, Richard E., ed. *Calendar of the Sir William Johnson Manuscripts in the New York State Library.* Albany: New York State Library, 1909.

DeForest, Louis Effingham, ed. *Louisbourg Journals 1745.* New York: Society of Colonial Wars in the State of New York, 1932.

Delaware. *Laws of the State of Delaware from the Fourteenth Day of October, One Thousand Seven Hundred, to the Eighteenth Day of August, One Thousand Seven Hundred and Ninety-Seven.* 2 vols. Newcastle, 1797.

The Dublin Gazette, 1752.

The Dublin Journal, 1752.

Erskine, David, ed. *Augustus Hervey's Journal being the Intimate Account of the Life of a Captain in the Royal Navy Ashore and Afloat, 1746-1759.* London: William Kimber, 1953.

The Gentlemen's Magazine and Historical Chronicler. (London) 1744, 1747, 1752.

Georgia. *Acts passed by the General Assembly, 1755-1774, now first printed.* Edited by George Wymberley-Jones de Renne. Wormsloe, 1881.

Goebel, Julius, ed. *The Law Practice of Alexander Hamilton.* 2 vols. New York: Columbia University Press, 1964-69.

Great Britain. *His Majesty's Royal Charter, granted on the Eleventh Day of October, 1750, in the Twenty-Fourth Year of the Reign of King George the Second, for incorporating the Society of the Free British Fishery, with Power to make Bylaws, & c. for the Improvement of the British White-Herring Fisheries, and better Regulation of the Trade thereof.* London, 1750.

Great Britain, House of Commons. *The Bill for Amending, Explaining, and Reducing into One Act of Parliament, the Laws relating to the Government of His Majesty's Ships, Vessels, and Forces by Sea.* London, 1749.

Great Britain, House of Commons. *The Irish Pound 1797-1826, A Reprint of the Report of the Committee of 1804 of the British House of Commons on the Condition of the Irish Currency, with selections from the Minutes of Evidence presented to the Committee.* Edited by Frank Whitson Fetter. London: Allen and Unwin, 1955.

Great Britain, House of Commons. *Journals of the House of Commons,* vols. 25, 26 [1745-54]. London, 1803.

Great Britain. *The Statutes at Large, from Magna Carta to the End of the Last Parliament, 1761.* 8 vols. London, 1768-69.

[Hervey, Augustus]. *A Detection of the Considerations of the Navy Bill.* London, 1749.

Ireland. *19th Report of the Deputy Keeper of the Public Records of Ireland, 29th April, 1887,* C-5185. Dublin, 1887.

Ireland. *Statutes at Large passed in the Parliament held in Ireland from the third year of Edward the second A.D. 1310, to the first year of George the third, A.D. 1761, inclusive,* 8 vols. Dublin, 1765.

Kalm, Pehr. *Travels in North America, Containing Its Natural History, and A circumstantial Account of its Plantations and Agriculture in general with the Civil, Ecclesiastical and Commercial State of the Country, The manners of the inhabitants and several curious and important remarks on various Subjects.* 2 vols. Translated form the Swedish by John Reinhold Forster. Warrington, 1770.

Kimball, Gertrude Selwyn, ed. *The Correspondence of the Colonial Governors of Rhode Island 1723-1775.* 2 vols. Boston, 1902-3.

Labaree, Leonard W., and Bell, Whitfield J., eds. *The Papers of Benjamin Franklin,* vol. 1. New Haven: Yale University Press, 1959.

A Letter from a Friend in the Country to a Friend at Will's Coffee-House; In Relation to Three Additional Articles of War. London, 1749.

Lewis, W.S., ed. *Horace Walpole's Correspondence,* vol. 20, *Horace Walpole's Correspondence with Sir Horace Mann,* vol. 4. New Haven: Yale University Press, 1960.

Maryland. *Acts of the Assembly Passed in the Province of Maryland from 1692 to 1715.* London, 1723.

Massachusetts. *The Acts and Resolves, Public and Private, of the Province of Massachusetts Bay,* vol. 1. Boston, 1869.

Massachusetts Historical Society. *Collections,* 6th series, vol. 5. Boston, 1892.

Mortimer, Thomas. *Every Man His Own Broker: or, A Guide to Exchange-Alley, in which The Nature of the several Funds, vulgarly called the Stocks, is clearly explained; and the Mystery and Iniquity of Stock-Jobbing laid before the Public in a New and Impartial Light.* 2nd edition. London, 1761.

New Jersey. *Acts of the General Assembly of the Province of New-Jersey, from . . . 1702, to . . . 1776 . . . .* Edited by Samuel Allinson. Burlington, 1776.

Newman, Aubrey N., ed. "Leicester House Politics, 1750-60, from the Papers of John, Second Earl of Egmont." *Camden Miscellany,* vol. 23. *Camden Fourth Series,* vol. 7. London: Royal Historical Society, 1969.

New York. *Calendar of New York Colonial Manuscripts, indorsed Land Papers in the Office of the Secretary of State of New York.* Albany, 1864.

New York. *The Colonial Laws of New York from the Year 1664 to the Revolution.* 5 vols. Albany, 1894-1896.

New York City. *Minutes of the Common Council of the City of New York, 1675-1776.* 8 vols. New York, 1905.

New York City. *Minutes of the Common Council of the City of New York, 1784-1831.* vol. 9 [1820-1821]. New York, 1917.

New York, Dutchess County. *Eighteenth Century Records of the Portion of Dutchess County, New York, that was included in Rombout Precinct and the Original Town of Fishkill.* Edited by Helen Wilkinson Reynolds. Dutchess County Historical Society, *Collections,* vol. 6. Poughkeepsie, N.Y., 1938.

New-York Historical Society. *Abstract of Wills on File in the Surrogate's Office, City of New York,* vols. 3-4 (1730-53). New-York Historical Society, Collections for the years 1894 and 1895. New York, 1895-96.

New-York Historical Society, *The Letter Book of John Watts, Merchant and Councillor of New York, January 2, 1762–December 22, 1765.* New-York Historical Society Collections for the year 1928. New York, 1928.

New-York Historical Society, *The Letters and Papers of Cadwallader Colden.* 9 vols. New-York Historical Society Collections, for the years 1917-1923, 1934-1935. New York, 1918-23, 1937.

New-York Historical Society, *Papers of the Lloyd Family of the Manor of Queens Village, Lloyd's Neck, Long Island, New York,* vol. I. New-York Historical Society Collections for the year 1927. New York, 1928.

The New York Mercury, 1752-53.

The New York Weekly Post Boy, 1752-53.

North Carolina. *The State Records of North Carolina.* Edited by Walter Clarke. 26 vols. Goldsboro, N.C., 1904, vol. 23 [Laws: 1715-1776].

Objections to the Thirty-Fourth Article of the Navy Bill. London, 1749.

O'Callaghan, E. B., ed. *The Documentary History of the State of New York.* 4 vols. Albany, 1849-51.

O'Callaghan, E.B., and Broadhead, John Romeyn, eds. *Documents relative to the colonial history of the State of New York; procured in Holland, England and France.* 15 vols. Albany, 1855-87.

Pennsylvania. *The Statutes at Large of Pennsylvania from 1682 to 1801.* Edited by James T. Mitchell and Henry Flanders. vols. 2 and 3. Harrisburg, 1896.

The Remarkable Case of Peter Hasenclever. London, 1773.

Remarks on a Pamphlet, Called, Considerations on the Bill for the better Government of the Navy In which Remarks it will appear, That the Thirty-Third and Thirty-Fourth Articles designed in the Bill, will no way tend to the Honour and Security of this Kingdom, but may greatly prejudice his Majesty's Sea-Service. By a Sea-Officer. London, 1749.

Rhode Island. *Acts and Laws of the English Colony of Rhode-Island and Providence-Plantations in New England in America: Made and Passed since the Revision of June, 1767.* Newport, 1772.

Simington, Robert C., ed. *The Civil Survey A.D. 1654-1656.* Vol. 5, *County Meath with returns of Tithes for the Meath Baronies.* Dublin: Irish Manuscripts Commission, 1940.

Simms, J.G., ed. "Irish Jacobite Lists from Trinity College Dublin MS.N.1.3." *Anelecta Hibernica,* no. 22. Dublin, 1960.

South Carolina. *The St. Augustine Expedition of 1740: A Report of the South Carolina General Assembly.* Reprinted from the Colonial Records of South Carolina with an introduction by John Tate Lanning. Columbia, S.C.: University of South Carolina Press, 1954.

South Carolina. *The Statutes at Large of South Carolina.* Edited by Thomas Cooper. Vol. 3. Charleston, 1838.

Sullivan, James, Flick, Alexander C., and Hamilton, Milton W., eds. *The Papers of Sir William Johnson.* 14 vols. Albany: University of the State of New York, 1921-65.

Virginia. *The Statutes at Large, being A Collection of all the Laws of Virginia From the First Session of the Legislature in the Year 1619.* Edited by William Waller Hening. Vols. 4 and 6. Richmond, 1819.

Walpole, Horace. *Memoirs of the Reign of King George the Second.* 3 vols. London, 1847.

Webber, Mabel L. "Peter Manigault's letters." *South Carolina Historical and Genealogical Magazine,* 32 (1931): 270-80.

[West, Captain Temple]. *An Examination and Refutation of a late pamphlet intitled, Considerations on the Navy Bill . . . by a Real Sea Officer.* London, 1749.

SECONDARY

Aldridge, D. D. "Admiral Sir John Norris, 1670 (or 1671)-1749: His Birth and Early Service, His Marriage and His Death." *The Mariner's Mirror,* 51 (1965): 173-83.

Alexander, Edward Porter. *A Revolutionary Conservative, James Duane of New York.* New York: Columbia University Press, 1938.

Ashton, T. S., *Economic Fluctuations in England 1700-1800.* Oxford: Clarendon Press, 1959.

Ashton, T. S. *An Economic History of England: The 18th Century.* Reprint edition with corrections. London: Methuen, 1961.

Aylmer, Sir Fenton J. *The Aylmers of Ireland.* London: Mitchell, Hughes and Clarke, 1931.

Baugh, Daniel A. *British Naval Administration in the Age of Walpole.* Princeton: Princeton University Press, 1965.

Baldwin, Benjamin Redford. "The Debts owed by Americans to British Creditors 1763-1802." Ph.D. dissertation, Indiana University, 1932.

Bemis, Samuel Flagg. *Jay's Treaty. A Study in Commerce and Diplomacy.* Revised edition. New Haven: Yale University Press, 1965.

Bezanson, Anne; Gray, Robert D; and Hussey, Miriam. *Prices in Colonial Pennsylvania.* Philadelphia: University of Pennsylvania Press, 1935.

Billington, Ray Allen and Hedges, James Blaine. *Westward Expansion, a history of the American frontier.* New York: Macmillan, 1949.

Bining, Arthur Cecil. *British Regulation of the Colonial Iron Industry.* Philadelphia: University of Pennsylvania Press, 1933.

Bond, Beverley Waugh. *The Quit Rent System in the American Colonies.* New Haven: Yale University Press, 1919.

Bonomi, Patricia U. *A Factious People. Politics and Society in Colonial New York.* New York: Columbia University Press, 1971.

Buell, Augustus C. *Sir William Johnson.* New York: Appleton, 1903.

Buffinton, Arthur H. "The Canada Expedition of 1746. Its Relation to British Politics," *American Historical Review,* 45 (1940): 552-80.

Burr, David H. *An Atlas of the State of New York.* New York, 1829.

Campbell, Sybil. "Usury and Annuities of the Eighteenth Century." *The Law Quarterly Review,* 44 (1928): 473-91.

Canedy, Charles Roscoe, III. "An Entrepreneurial History of the New York Frontier 1739-1776." Ph.D. dissertation, Case Western Reserve University, 1967.

Capen, Louise L. "A History of Bills of Credit during the Colonial Period with a Detailed Investigation of the Issues of New York Currency." Ph.D. dissertation, New York University, 1925.

Chambers, J. D. and Mingay, G. E. *The Agricultural Revolution, 1750-1880.* London: Batsford, 1966.

Chapin, Howard Millar. *Rhode Island Privateers in King George's War 1739-1748.* Providence: Rhode Island Historical Society, 1926.

Cheves, Langdon. "Izard of South Carolina." *South Carolina Historical and Genealogical Magazine,* 2 (1901) : 205-40.

Clay, Christopher. "Marriage, Inheritance, and the Rise of Large Estates in England, 1660-1815." *The Economic History Review,* 2nd series, 21 (1968) : 503-18.

Cogan, Rev. Anthony. *The Diocese of Meath Ancient and Modern.* 3 vols. Dublin, 1862-70.

[Cokayne, George Edward and Gibbs, Vicary, eds.]. *Complete Peerage of England, Scotland, Ireland, Great Britain, and the United Kingdom.* 12 vols. London: The St. Catherine Press, 1910-59.

Cole, Arthur Harrison. *Wholesale Commodity Prices in the United States, 1700-1861.* Cambridge, Mass.: Harvard University Press, 1938.

Connell, K. H. *The Population of Ireland, 1750-1845.* Oxford: Clarendon Press, 1950.

Crouse, Maurice Alfred. "The Manigault Family of South Carolina 1685-1783." Ph.D. dissertation, Northwestern University, 1964.

Cullen, L. M. *Anglo-Irish Trade 1660-1800.* Manchester: Manchester University Press, 1968.

Cullen, L.M. "The exchange business of the Irish banks in the eighteenth century." *Economica,* new series 25 (1958): 326-38.

Cullen, L.M. "Problems in the interpretation and revision of eighteenth-century Irish economic history." *Royal Historical Society Transactions,* 5th series, 17 (1967) : 1-22.

Cundall, Frank. *The Governors of Jamaica in the First Half of the Eigtheenth Century.* London: The West India Committee, 1937.

Curtin, Philip D. *The Atlantic Slave Trade: A Census.* Madison: University of Wisconsin Press, 1969.

Davis, Andrew McFarland. *Currency and Banking in the Province of the Massachusetts Bay.* 2 vols. Reprint edition. New York: Augustus M. Kelley, 1970.

Delaney, Edmund T. *New York's Turtle Bay Old and New.* Barre, Massachusetts, 1965.

Dickson, P.G.M. *The Financial Revolution in England. A study in the development of public credit 1688-1756.* London: Macmillan, 1967.

Dickson, P.G.M. *The Sun Insurance Office 1710-1960. The History of Two and a Half centuries of British Insurance.* London: Oxford University Press, 1960.

Dix, Morgan. *A History of the Parish of Trinity Church in the City of New York.* Vol. 1. New York, 1898.

Donnan, Elizabeth. "The Slave Trade into South Carolina before Revolution." *American Historical Review,* 33 (1928): 804-28.

Drake, Francis Samuel. *The town of Roxbury, its memorable persons and places, its history and antiquities, with numerous illustrations of its old landmarks and noted personages.* Boston: Municipal Printing Office, 1905.

Driver, Abraham and William. *General View of the Agriculture of the County of Hants, with Observations on the Means of its Improvement.* London, 1794.

Dunkak, Harry M. "John Morin Scott and Whig Politics in New York City (1762-1769)." Ph.D. dissertation, St. John's University, 1968.

East, Robert A. *Business Enterprise in the American Revolution.* New York: Columbia University Press, 1938.

Ellis, David Maldwyn. *Landlords and Farmers in the Hudson-Mohawk Region 1790-1850.* Ithaca, N.Y.: Cornell University Press, 1946.

Ernst, Joseph A., "The Robinson Scandal Redivivus; Money, Debts, and Politics in Revolutionary Virginia," *Virginia Magazine of History and Biography,* 7 (1969): 146-73.

Evans, Emory G. "Planter Indebtedness and the Coming of the Revolution in Virginia." *The William and Mary Quarterly,* 3rd series, 19 (1962): 511-33.

Fairchild, Byron. *Messrs. William Pepperrell; Merchants at Piscataqua.* Ithaca, N.Y.: Cornell University Press, 1954.

Flexner, James Thomas. *Mohawk Baronet, Sir William Johnson of New York.* New York: Harper and Row, 1959.

Foote, Henry Wilder. *Annals of King's Chapel from the Puritan Age of New England to the present day.* 3 vols. Boston, 1896-1900.

Foulke, Roy A. *The Sinews of American Commerce.* New York: Dunn and Bradstreet, 1941.

Fox, Edith M. *Land Speculation in the Mohawk Country.* Ithaca, New York: Cornell University Press, 1946.

Fox, Edith M. "William Johnson's Early Career as a Frontier Landlord and Trader." M.A. essay, Cornell University, 1945.

Francis, John Wakefield. *Old New York; or, Reminiscences of the past Sixty Years.* New York, 1895.

Freiberg, Malcolm. "William Bollan: Agent for Massachusetts." *More Books,* 23 (1948): 43-54, 90-100, 135-46, 168-82, 212-20.

Frégault, Guy. "L'expédition de duc d'Anville." *Revue d'histoire de l'amérique française,* 2 (1948): 27-52.

Fritz, Paul S. "Jacobitism and the English Government 1717-31." Ph.D. thesis, University of Cambridge, 1967.

Gerlach, Don R. *Philip Schuyler and the American Revolution in New York, 1733-1777.* Lincoln, Nebraska: University of Nebraska Press, 1964.

Gilboy, Elizabeth Waterman. *Wages in Eighteenth Century England.* Reprint edition. New York: Random House, 1969.

Greene, Evarts B. and Harrington, Virginia D. *American Population before the Federal Census of 1790.* New York: Columbia University Press, 1932.

Griffis, William Eliot. *Sir William Johnson and the Six Nations.* New York, 1891.

Groulx, Lionel. *Roland-Michel Barrin, Marquis de La Galissonière 1693-1756.* Toronto: University of Toronto Press, 1971.

Habakkuk, H. J. "The English Land Market in the Eighteenth Century." In *Britain and the Netherlands.* Edited by J. S. Bromley and E. H. Kossman. London: Chatto and Windus, 1960, pp. 154-73.

Habakkuk, H. J. "English Landownership, 1680-1740." *The Economic History Review,* 1st series, 10 (1940): 2-17.

Habakkuk, H. J. "The Long-Term Rate of Interest and the Price of Land in the Seventeenth Century." *The Economic History Review,* 2nd series, 5 (1952): 26-45.

Habakkuk, H. J. "Marriage Settlements in the Eighteenth Century." *Royal Historical Society Transactions,* 4th series, 32 (1950): 15-30.

Hamilton, Milton W. "Augustus C. Buell, Fraudulent Historian." *Pennsylvania Magazine of History and Biography,* 34 (1956): 478-92.

Hansbrow, Rev. G. *An Improved Topographical and Historical Hibernian Gazetteer.* Dublin, 1835.

Harrington, Virginia D. *The New York Merchant on the Eve of the Revolution.* New York: Columbia University Press, 1935.

Healy, John. *History of the Diocese of Meath.* 2 vols. Dublin: Association for Promoting Christian Knowledge, 1908.

Hedrick, Ulysses Prentiss. *A History of Agriculture in the State of New York.* New York: New York State Agricultural Society, 1933.

Hemphill, John M., II. "Virginia and the English Commercial System, 1689-1733. Studies in the Development and Fluctuations of a Colonial Economy under Imperial Control." Ph.D. dissertation, Princeton University, 1964.

Hickcox, John H. *A History of the Bills of Credit or Paper Money issued by New York From 1709 to 1789: with a Description of the Bills, and Catalogue of the Various Issues.* Albany, 1866.

Higgins, Ruth Loving. *Expansion in New York, With Especial Reference to the Eighteenth Century.* Columbus, Ohio: Ohio State University Press, 1931.

Higgins, W. Robert. "The South Carolina Negro Duty Law." M.A. thesis, University of South Carolina, 1967.

Hill, William Henry. *Old Fort Edward before 1800; an account of historic ground now occupied by the village of Fort Edward.* Fort Edward, N.Y., privately printed, 1929.

Holliday, John. *The Life of William Late Earl of Mansfield.* London, 1797.

Homer, Sidney. *A History of Interest Rates.* New Brunswick, N.J.: Rutgers University Press, 1963.

Hurst, John and Collins, Frances. *West Meon, Hampshire.* Petersfield, Hampshire, privately printed, 1972.

Hussey, Christopher. *English Gardens and Landscapes 1700-1750.* London: Country Life, 1967.

Ireland, J. DeCourcey. "Admiral of the Fleet the Hon. John Forbes." *The Irish Sword,* no. 22 (1963): 13-15.

Jenkins, Stephen. *The Greatest Street in the World; The Story of Broadway, Old and New, from Bowling Green to Albany.* New York: Putnam, 1911.

Johnson, Allen; Malone, Dumas; Schuyler, Robert Livingston; James, Edward T., eds. *Dictionary of American Biography,* 22 vols. New York, 1927-58.

Jones, Alice Hanson. "Wealth Estimates for the New England Colonies about 1770." *Journal of Economic History,* 32 (1972): 98-127.

Jones, Alice Hanson. "Wealth Estimates for the American Middle Colonies, 1774" *Economic Development and Cultural Change,* 18, no. 4, Part 2 (1970): 1-172.

Jones, E. L. "Eighteenth-Century Changes in Hampshire Chalkland Farming." *The Agricultural History Review,* 8 (1960): 5-19.

Jones, Thomas. *History of New York during the Revolutionary War.* Edited by Edward Floyd DeLancey. 2 vols. New York, 1879.

Katz, Stanley Nider. *Newcastle's New York Anglo-American Politics, 1732-1753.* Cambridge, Massachusetts: Harvard University Press, 1968.

Kim, Sung Bok. "The Manor of Cortlandt and Its Tenants 1697-1783." Ph.D. dissertation, Michigan State University, 1966.

Kim, Sung Bok. "A New Look at the Great Landlords of Eighteenth-Century New York." *The William and Mary Quarterly,* 3rd. series, 27 (1970): 581-614.

Land, Aubrey C. "Economic Behaviour in a Planting Society: The Eighteenth-Century Chesapeake." *The Journal of Southern History,* 33 (1967): 469-85.

Large, David. "The Wealth of the Greater Irish Landowners, 1750-1815." *Irish Historical Studies,* 15, no. 57 (1966): 21-47.

Lodge, John. *The Peerage of Ireland: or, A Genealogical History of the Present Nobility of that Kingdom.* 8 vols. Dublin, 1789.

Lynd, Staughton. *Anti-Federalism in Dutchess County New York; a study of democracy and class conflict in the Revolutionary era.* Chicago: Loyola University Press, 1962.

McCallum, James Dow. *Eleazar Wheelock; Founder of Dartmouth College.* Hanover, N.H.: Dartmouth College Press, 1939.

McCusker, John J. "Sources of Investment Capital in the Colonial Philadelphia Shipping Industry." *Journal of Economic History,* 32 (1972): 146-57.

Mackay, Ruddock, F. *Admiral Hawke.* Oxford: Clarendon Press, 1965.

McManus, Edgar J. *The History of Negro Slavery in New York.* Syracuse, N.Y.: Syracuse University Press, 1966.

Mark, Irving. *Agrarian Conflicts in Colonial New York, 1711-1775.* New York: Columbia University Press, 1940.

Marshall, P.J. "The Personal Fortune of Warren Hastings." *The Economic History Review*. 2nd series, 17 (1964): 284-300.

Mason, George Champlain. *Reminiscences of Newport*. Newport, Rhode Island, 1884.

Meriwether, Robert Lee. *The Expansion of South Carolina 1729-1765*. Kingsport, Tenn.: Southern Publishers, 1940.

Mingay, G.E. *English Landed Society in the Eighteenth Century*. London: Routledge & Kegan Paul, 1963.

Mingay, G. E. "The Land Tax Assessments and the Small Landowner." *The Economic History Review*, 2nd series, 14 (1964): 381-88.

Naish, M. C. "The agricultural landscape of the Hampshire chalklands, 1700-1804." M.A. thesis, University of London, 1961.

Namier, Sir Lewis and Brooke, John. *Charles Townsend*. London, 1964.

Namier, Sir Lewis and Brooke, John, eds. *The History of Parliament. The House of Commons 1754-1790*. 3 vols. London: H.M.S.O., 1964.

Norton, Mary Beth. *The British-Americans: The Loyalist Exiles in England, 1774-1789*. Boston: Little, Brown, 1972.

Oliver, Vere Langford. *The History of the Island of Antigua*. 3 vols. London, 1894-99.

Owen, David. *English Philanthropy 1660-1960*. Cambridge, Mass.: Harvard University Press, 1965.

Page, William, ed. *The Victoria History of the Counties of England: Hampshire and the Isle of Wight*. 6 vols. Westminster: Constable, 1900-14.

Pares, Richard. "A London West India Merchant House 1740-69." In *Essays Presented to Sir Lewis Namier*. Edited by Richard Pares and A. J. P. Taylor. London: Macmillan, 1956, pp. 75-107.

Pares, Richard. *Yankees and Creoles. The trade between North America and the West Indies before the American Revolution*. London: Longmans, Green, 1956.

Parsons, Usher. *The Life of Sir William Pepperrell, Bart*. Boston, 1855.

Pearse, John B. *Concise History of the Iron Manufacture of the American Colonies up to the Revolution and of Pennsylvania until the Present Time*. Reprint edition New York: Augustus M. Kelley, 1970.

Phillips, Hugh. *Mid-Georgian London: A Topographical and Social Survey of Central and Western London about 1750*. London: Collins, 1964.

Potter, Elisha R. *Memoire concerning the French Settlements and French Settlers in the Colony of Rhode Island*. Providence, 1879.

Potter, J. "The Growth of Population in America, 1700-1860." In
    Population and History. Edited by D. V. Glass and D. E. C. Eversley.
    London: Aldine, 1965, pp. 631-63.

Pound, Arthur and Day, Richard E. *Johnson of the Mohawks, a Biography of Sir
    William Johnson, Irish Immigrant, Mohawk War Chief, American Soldier,
    Empire Builder.* New York: Macmillan, 1930.

Pressnell, L. S. *Country Banking in the Industrial Revolution.* Oxford:
    Clarendon Press, 1956.

Pressnell, L. S. "The Rate of Interest in the Eighteenth Century." In
    Studies in the Industrial Revolution. Edited by L. S. Pressnell. London:
    Athalone Press, 1960, pp. 178-214.

Preston, Howard W. "Godfrey Malbone's Connecticut Investment." Rhode
    Island Historical Society *Collections,* 16 (1923): 115-20.

Price, Jacob M. "Capital and Credit in the Chesapeake Tobacco Trade,
    1750-1775." In *Of Mother Country and Plantations: Proceedings of the
    Twenty-Seventh Conference in Early American History.* Edited by Virginia
    Bever Platt and David Curtis Skaggs. Bowling Green, Ohio: Bowling
    Green State University Press, 1971, pp. 7-36.

Price, Jacob M. "The Economic Growth of the Chesapeake and the
    European Market, 1697-1775." *Journal of Economic History,* 24 (1964):
    496-517.

Price, Jacob M. "The Rise of Glasgow in the Chesapeake Tobacco Trade."
    William and Mary Quarterly. 3rd. series, 11 (1954): 179-200.

Recum, Franz V. *The Families of Warren and Johnson of Warrenstown, County
    Meath.* New York, privately printed, 1950.

Richmond, Sir Herbert W. *The Navy in the War of 1739-1748.* 3 vols.
    Cambridge: at the University Press, 1920.

Rosenblatt, Samuel M. "The Significance of Credit in the Tobacco
    Consignement Trade; A Study of John Norton & Sons, 1768-1775."
    William and Mary Quarterly, 3rd. series, 19 (1962): 383-99.

Sachs, William S. "The Business Outlook in the Northern Colonies,
    1750-1775." Ph.D. dissertation, Columbia University, 1957.

Sachs, William S. "Interurban Correspondents and the Development of a
    National Economy Before the Revolution: New York as a Case Study."
    New York History, 36 (1955): 320-35.

Sachs, William S. and Hoogenboom, Ari. *The Enterprising Colonials: Society on
    the Eve of the Revolution.* Chicago: Argonaut, 1965.

Sakolski, Aaron Morton. *Land Tenure and Land Taxation in America.* New
    York: R. Schalkenbach Foundation, 1957.

Schumpeter, Elizabeth B. "English Prices and Public Finances, 1660-1822." *Review of Economic Statistics,* 20 (1938): 21-37.

Schutz, John A. *William Shirley, King's Governor of Massachusetts.* Chapel Hill, N.C.: University of North Carolina Press, 1961.

Schuyler, George W. *Colonial New York, Philip Schuyler and His Family.* 2 vols. New York, 1885.

Schwab, John Christian. "History of the New York Property Tax." *Publications of the American Economic Association,* 5, 1890, pp. 373-466.

Sedgwick, Romney, ed. *The History of Parliament. The House of Commons 1715-1754.* 2 vols. London: H.M.S.O., 1970.

Sellers, Leila. *Charleston Business on the Eve of the American Revolution.* Chapel Hill, N.C.: University of North Carolina Press, 1934.

Seymour, Flora Warren. *Lords of the Valley, Sir William Johnson and his Mohawk Brothers.* New York: Longmans, Green, 1930.

Sheridan, Richard B. "The British Credit Crisis of 1772 and the American Colonies." *Journal of Economic History,* 20 (1960): 161-86.

Sibley, John Langdon, and Shipton, Clifford Kenyon. *Harvard Graduates: Biographical Sketches of those who attended Harvard College.* 14 vols. Cambridge, Mass.: Harvard University Press, 1873-1968.

Simms, J. G. "The Civil Survey, 1654-56." *Irish Historical Studies,* 9 (1955): 253-63.

Simms, J. G. *Jacobite Ireland, 1685-1691.* London: Routledge and Kegan Paul, 1969.

Simms, J. G. "Land Owned by Catholics in Ireland in 1688." *Irish Historical Studies,* 7 (1951): 180-90.

Simms, J. G. *The Treaty of Limerick.* Dundalk: Dundalgon Press, 1961.

Simms, J. G. *The Williamite Confiscation in Ireland, 1690-1703.* London: Faber and Faber, 1956.

Sirmans, M. Eugene. *Colonial South Carolina: A Political History 1663-1763.* Chapel Hill, N.C.: University of North Carolina Press, 1966.

Spencer, Charles Worthen. "The Land System of Colonial New York." *New York State Historical Society Proceedings,* 16 (1917): 151-62.

Spencer, Charles Worthen. "Sectional Aspects of New York Provincial Politics. *Political Science Quarterly,* 30 (September 1915): 397-424.

Spinney, David. *Rodney.* London: Allen and Unwin, 1969.

Stackpole, Rev. Everett S. *History of Durham, Maine with Genealogical Notes.* Lewiston, Maine, 1899.

Stoker, Herman M. "Wholesale Prices at New York City, 1720 to 1800." Part II of *Wholesale Prices for 213 Years, 1720 to 1932.* By George Frederick Warren and F. A. Pearson. Cornell University, Agricultural Experiment Station Memoir 142. Ithaca, N.Y., 1932, pp. 201-22.

Stokes, Issaac Newton Phelps. The *Iconography of Manhattan Island, 1498-1909.* 6 vols. New York: R. H. Dodd, 1915-28.

Stone, William I. *The Life and Times of Sir William Johnson, Bart.* 2 vols. Albany, 1865.

Story, D. A. *The Delanceys; A Romance of a Great Family with Notes on those Allied Families Who Remained Loyal to the British Crown during the Revolutionary War.* [London]: Nelson, 1931.

Supple, Barry. *The Royal Exchange Assurance. A History of British Insurance 1720-1970.* Cambridge: at the University Press, 1970.

Sutherland, Dame Lucy S. "Samson Gideon: Eighteenth Century Jewish Financier." *Jewish Historical Society of England Transactions,* 17 (1951-52): 79-90.

Sutherland, Dame Lucy S. "Samson Gideon and the Reduction of Interest, 1749-50." *The Economic History Review,* 1st series, 16 (1946): 15-29.

Sutherland, Dame Lucy S. *A London Merchant 1695-1774.* Reprint edition. London: Frank Cass, 1962.

Sutherland, Stella Helen. *Population Distribution in Colonial America.* New York: Columbia University Press, 1936.

Tate, W. E. "Field Systems and Enclosures in Hampshire." *Hampshire Field Club and Archaeological Society Papers and Proceedings,* 16 (1947): 257-79.

Thompson, Edgar K. "George Anson in the Province of South Carolina." *The Mariner's Mirror,* 53 (1967): 279-80.

Thompson, F. M. L. *English Landed Society in the Nineteenth Century.* London: Routledge and Kegan Paul, 1963.

Tolman, Ruel Pardee. *The Life and Works of Edward Greene Malbone 1777-1807.* New York: New-York Historical Society, 1958.

Trow-Smith, Robert. *A History of British Livestock Husbandry 1700-1900.* London: Routledge and Kegan Paul, 1959.

Upton, L. S. F. *The Loyal Whig William Smith of New York and Quebec.* Toronto: University of Toronto Press, 1969.

Vancouver, Charles. *General View of the Agriculture of Hampshire including the Isle of Wight drawn up for the consideration of the Board of Agriculture and Internal Development.* London, 1813.

Varga, Nicholas. "Robert Charles: New York Agent, 1748-1770." *The William and Mary Quarterly,* 3rd series, 18 (1961): 211-35.

Wakefield, E. *An Account of Ireland, Statistical and Political.* 2 vols. London, 1812.

Wall, Maureen. "The rise of a Catholic middle class in eighteenth-century Ireland." *Irish Historical Studies,* no. 42, 11 (1958): 91-115.

Ward, W. R. *The English Land Tax in the Eighteenth Century.* London: Oxford University Press, 1953.

Warren, Rev. Thomas. *A History and Genealogy of the Warren Family in Normandy, Great Britain and Ireland, France, Holland, Tuscany, United States of America, etc. (A.D. 912-1902).* London, 1902.

Weedon, William B. *Economic and Social History of New England, 1620-1789.* 2 vols. Boston, 1890.

White, Philip L. *The Beekmans of New York in Politics and Commerce, 1647-1877.* New York: New-York Historical Society, 1956.

Wilkinson, Rev. John. "The Farming of Hampshire." *The Journal of the Royal Agricultural Society of England,* 22 (1861): 239-371.

Wilson, Charles. *Anglo-Dutch Commerce and Finance in the Eighteenth Century.* Cambridge: at the University Press, 1941.

Wilson, Charles. *England's Apprenticeship 1603-1763.* London: Longmans, Green, 1965.

Wright, J. "South Carolina's First Paper Money." *Sound Currency,* 5 (1898): 34-45.

Yoshpe, Harry B. "The DeLancy Estate: Did the Revolution Democratize Landholding in New York?" *New York History,* 17, (1936): 167-79.

Yoshpe, Harry B. *The Disposition of Loyalist Estates in the Southern District of the State of New York.* New York: Columbia University Press, 1939.

Zeichner, Oscar. "The Loyalist Problem in New York after the Revolution." *New York History,* 21 (1940): 282-302.

Correction

Index entries for pages 208–64 are incorrect. The material will be found four pages earlier   e.g., *for* Abburrow, Mary, 259 n. 37 *read* Abburrow, Mary, 255 n. 37.

Index

Abburrow, Mary, 259 n. 37
Abercrombie, Gen. James, 50
Abingdon, Montagu, fifth Earl of, 116
Abingdon, Willoughby, fourth Earl of 32, 46, 64, 88, 89, 91, 104, 136, 140, 143, 158, 172, 173, 202; marriage, 25, 261 n. 36; pamphlet, 65–66
Admiralty, Board of, 6, 11, 12, 15, 22, 23, 162, 171
Admiralty, High Court of, 17
Africa, 8, 9
Aix–la–Chapelle, Peace of (1748), 14, 77
Albany, 69, 70, 71, 73, 81, 87, 107
Albany County, 87
Allen, James, 241 n. 2
Ambrose, Capt. John, R. N., 164, 166, 198; biographical note, 257 n. 10
America, colonial, 3, 5, 31, 96, 102, 110, 144, 160, 164, 198, 199, 200, 202
American Iron Company, 41, 95
American War of Independence, 4, 47, 48, 49, 52–53, 54, 56, 57, 63, 65, 68, 103, 104, 115, 118, 124, 199
Amherst, Gen. Jeffrey, 50
Annapolis Royal, N. S., 16
Anson, Adm. George, 11, 22, 119, 145, 158, 159, 194, 200, 213 n. 2, 247 n. 47; agent for Warren, 122, 124, 125; creditor with Warren, 164; investments, 194; and Navy Bill, 23; and Western Squadron, 14, 17, 20, 145, 186
Antigua, 12, 13, 17, 31, 124, 166, 175, 198, 246 n. 14; English harbour, 17, *See also* Leeward Islands

Apthorp, Charles, 109, 110, 112, 113, 114, 115, 244 n. 44
Armstrong, George, 169, 170, 175
Army debentures, 178
Arnold, Capt. Thomas, R. N., 122
Aylmer, Sir Christopher, first Bart. of Balrath, 8
Aylmer, Elizabeth, 8
Aylmer, Sir Gerald, Bart., 134, 165, 167, 257 n. 10
Aylmer, Henry, 198
Aylmer, Rev. John, 227 n. 154
Aylmer, Adm. Matthew, Baron of Balrath, 8, 197
Aylmer, Patrick, 134
Aylmer, Williamza, 249 n. 27
Ayrault, Daniel, Jr., 112, 243 n. 28

Bagley, Capt. Jonathan, 111, 112; biographical note, 242 n. 18
Bagley, Capt. Timothy, 99
Baker, Richard, 148, 254 n. 21
Baker, Samuel, 18, 19, 162, 179, 180, 181, 183, 188, 191, 260 n. 11, 261 n. 28
Baker, Sir William, 18, 19, 162, 179, 180, 181, 182, 183, 188, 191, 243 n. 33, 260 n. 11, 261 n. 28
Ballydowde, county Dublin, 133, 137, 140; plan of, 248 n. 19
Baltic, 8
Bank of England: funds government loan of 1744, 182; of 1745, 182–85, 190, 193; of 1748, 185, 190; of 1750 "million loan," 185–86, 190; consolidated funds "consols," 185, 186, 190, 193; suspends specie payments, 138; stock of, 259 n. 2
Barbados, 12, 18, 168
Barbarie, John, 38, 100
Barclay, Rev. Henry, 75
Bard, Dr. John, 211
Barony of Deece, 130, 137
Barony of Ratooth, 137
Bastide, John Henry, 241 n. 2

DATE DUE

30 505 JOSTEN'S			